WORLD RELIGIONS

AND CULTS

Counterfeits *of* Christianity

VOLUME 1

General Editors

BODIE HODGE &
ROGER PATTERSON

First printing: August 2015
Fourth printing: September 2017

ISBN: 978-0-89051-903-5
ISBN: 978-1-61458-460-5 (digital)
Library of Congress Number: 2015910670

Cover by Left Coast Design, Portland, Oregon

Image credits:
Flickr: 224; Shutterstock: 8, 37, 46, 63, 96, 124, 130, 131, 154, 164, 167, 229, 290, 332; Wikimedia Commons: 12, 43, 71, 73, 76, 79, 81, 114, 121, 142, 181, 192, 193, 206, 216, 234, 235, 236, 257, 266, 284, 285, 291, 296, 299, 302, 304, 308, 338, 347, 353, 359, 368, 384, 392, 397; Wikipedia: 372

Please consider requesting a copy of this volume be purchased by your local library system.

Printed in the United States of America

Please visit our website for other great titles: www.masterbooks.com

For information regarding author interviews, please contact the publicity department at (870) 438-5288.

Master Books®
A Division of New Leaf Publishing Group
www.masterbooks.com

Acknowledgments

Our appreciation to the following for their contributions to this book: Dr. Terry Mortenson, Dr. Corey Abney, Steve Fazekas, Ken Ham, Roger Patterson, Bodie Hodge, Troy Lacey, Frost Smith, Pastor David Chakranarayan, Lori Jaworski, Linda Moore, Pastor Gary Vaterlaus, Dr. Georgia Purdom, David Wright, Pastor Brian Edwards, Dr. Tom Triggs, Brandie Lucas, Michael Houdman (and the Got Questions team), Dr. Royce Short, Steve Golden, and Mark Vowels (PhD candidate).

Contents

Preface

Bodie Hodge

Why is there a need for another book on world religions? The answer is simple. While there are many great resources that dive into various religions, I wanted to have a book series that did not shy away from origins accounts. Also, I had a desire to have a book series that offers a critique from a presuppositional apologetics perspective. Like other resources, we still wanted to explain the differences between various religions as to why they believe and practice certain things. I also wanted a book series that did not ignore the many secular religions, with their sects and cults, like secular humanism, atheism, and agnosticism. This book series is unique in those respects.

I hope this book series will be a welcome addition as a supplement for study when trying to understand world religions and why they fall short of God's standard. This book and those that will follow dive into various popular world religions, lesser-known religions, and also cults and philosophical systems.

"What is the difference?" you might ask. Sometimes it is quite nebulous. A cult is a religion, after all, and so is based in a philosophical system! They all subscribe to a worldview and govern how people live their lives, as well as attempting to explain the origins of life and what happens after death. They tend to have codes to live by, and many hold to a system of works to achieve some ultimate goal.

Typically, a *world religion* is a belief system that attempts to explain some aspect of reality and often how the physical and spiritual world operates; and yet it is independent of another world religion (though they often have different sects, cults, or denominations). But for all practical purposes, this is usually how a world religion is defined.

For example, Buddhism, secular humanism, and biblical Christianity are entirely different religions that do not share a common historical foundation. Each of these religions has variations within its constituents —

Buddhist statue in Japan

Buddhism has Mahayana and Theravada forms, biblical Christianity has Lutheran, Baptist, Presbyterian, etc., and secular humanism has atheism, agnosticism, and the like.

A *cult* is typically defined as a religious offshoot of a major world religion that no longer holds to the core tenets of that world religion. They would no longer be seen as orthodox by the majority of that religion's practitioners and are often seen as distant from them. For example, there are several cults of Christianity where there has been such a great deviation on core doctrines that they would no longer be considered orthodox. Usually this is due to one person's teachings that initially led people away from those core tenets.

Let's use Christianity as an example. There are cults like Mormonism and Jehovah's Witnesses (JWs), and some even include Islam as a cult of Christianity. Each affirms that the Bible is true, *to a certain degree*, but due to charismatic leaders like Joseph Smith (Mormons), Charles Taze Russell (JWs), or Muhammad (Islam/Muslims), their basic teachings have moved

The Book of Mormon

far away from the Bible's core doctrines. In each of these variations, the Bible has been demoted (or reinterpreted) in light of the new leader's views on the subject. These self-proclaimed prophets have produced "new revelations" such as *The Book of Mormon* (Mormonism), *Studies in the Scriptures* (JWs), and the Koran (Muslims).

Instead of one God that is three persons (Father, Son, and Holy Spirit; making Christ God and Creator) as the Bible teaches, Mormonism says there are three gods (and many more, too) and you too can become a god within this universe. Jehovah's Witnesses and Muslims deny the three persons of the Godhead and say Jesus is a creature. So you can see how (on this one foundational point) their core tenets are radically different from biblical Christianity.

Many people overlook *philosophical systems* as religious, but they should be considered religions that frame the worldview of those who hold to the philosophy. This is why stoicism, Epicureanism, relativism, empiricism, hedonism, and naturalism are discussed in this series. These religious philosophical systems are all around us, but rarely do we treat them as such.

Naturally, we cannot examine every world religion, cult, sect, or system, so we have selected quite a few from different genres, which we will critique. At this stage, we are intending to cover over 50 religious views for this book series.

I hope that through these books, many will be equipped to not only understand the errors within these religious views, but also point the followers to the only hope of salvation — Jesus Christ. Jesus said,

> And I, if I am lifted up from the earth, will draw all peoples to Myself (John 12:32; NKJV).

> Most assuredly, I say to you, he who believes in Me has everlasting life (John 6:47; NKJV).

Introduction

God vs. Man — World Religions and Cults

Ken Ham and Bodie Hodge

Introduction to the Series

There are two religions in the world — God's and "not God's." Or another way of putting it: *God's Word* and *Man's Word*. Really, other than Christianity, there is only one other religion that comes in many forms — a religion built on man's fallible ideas. In fact, this battle between two religions began in Genesis 3 with the temptation. Really, Eve was tempted to doubt and not believe God's Word, and instead trust in her own word *(man's word)* when the tempter stated:

> "Indeed, has God said, 'You shall not eat from any tree of the garden'?" (Genesis 3:1).[1]

I hope you understand this basic concept, as it is very important. So important that it must be stated again to get us started: there are two religions in the world — God's and "not God's."

God only has one religion, and it is His true religion by virtue of it coming from a God who is the truth (John 14:6). All other religions do not come from God; so by default, where do they come from? They come from

---

1. Scripture in this chapter is from the New American Standard Bible.

Charles Darwin, circa 1874

man. All other forms of religion outside of God's religion are a religion of man (Psalm 118:8; Isaiah 2:22).

God created man (Genesis 1:27), yet in today's modern secularized culture, man is trying to elevate himself to be above God to say that man created God! Charles Darwin popularized this in modern form in his book *The Descent of Man* in the 1871. He said:

> The same high mental faculties which first led man to believe in unseen spiritual agencies, then in fetishism, polytheism, and ultimately in monotheism, would infallibly lead him, as long as his reasoning powers remained poorly developed, to various strange superstitions and customs.[2]

But this is nothing new. Man's opinions have been used since the beginning when Adam and Eve elevated their own thoughts to be greater than God's Word and ate the forbidden fruit. This sin against a holy and perfect God demanded punishment, and the punishment for sin was death (Genesis 2:17). So man was thrust into a sin-cursed world where sin and death reigned and the need for a Savior was necessary to conquer sin and death (Genesis 3:15).

All false religions are based on man's opinions as they inadvertently, or sometimes intentionally, elevate man's autonomous[3] reason to be greater than God and the 66 books of His Word. It is true that Satan and demonic spirits could have their involvement, but either way a religion would still require the involvement of men and can rightly be called a *religion of man.*

---

2. Darwin, Charles, *The Descent of Man and Selection in Relation to Sex*, chapter III ("Mental Powers of Man and the Lower Animals"), 1871, as printed in the *Great Books of the Western World*, Vol. 49, Robert Hutchins, ed. (Chicago, IL: 1952), p. 303.

3. Autonomous reason is reason apart from God or "leaving God out of it" rather than taking every thought captive to the obedience of Christ.

Humanism, the religion of man in its broadest form, would encompass all religions that oppose God and His Word. When a religion elevates a book, books, or extra teachings to be Scripture, then they are taking man's opinions and elevating them to supersede or be equal to God's Word. When a religion deletes a book or books or otherwise subtracts teachings from Scripture, then they are taking man's opinions and elevating them to supersede or be equal to God's Word. Dr. Werner Gitt writes,

> We consider the phenomenon of the multitude of religions from the perspective of man's creative nature. Where man finds a gap, he invents something. He creates something. He fills the "hole" with either intellectual or material matter. Most people trust in inventions to solve problems. . . . But even religions are man-made inventions . . . born out of human creativity to fill gaps where knowledge of the Creator and His character are missing.[4]

In other words, some take man's ideas and use that to delete parts of God's Word, some completely reject all of God's Word as the truth, and others take man's ideas and elevate them to be equal or, in most cases, above God and His Word.

That is why it is so distressing to find (from research conducted by America's Research Group for Answers in Genesis in 2014) that of those aged 20–29 who currently attend church regularly, 20 percent believe there are other books (other than the Bible) that are inspired by God, and an additional 10 percent that don't know if there are.[5]

Man's religion, that is humanism in its broadest sense, is opposed to the truth of God's Word at its most fundamental level. Yet many religions that elevate man's ideas to that ultimate level often teach that they *are* in accord with God and His Word in one way or another; but we must be discerning and compare these beliefs to the 66 books of God's Word. Only by standing on the authority of God's Word, the 66 books of the Bible, will we be able to ascertain when man's ideas and religious philosophies are being elevated to be greater than God's revealed religion.

---

4. Werner Gitt, *What about the Other Religions?* translated by Royal Truman, (Bielefeld, Germany: Christliche Literatur-Verbreitung e.V., 1995), p. 12.
5. Britt Beemer, "Answers in Genesis Survey & Market Research Findings," Volume I & II (America's Research Group, Summerville, South Carolina), September 2014.

Forms of Man's Religion

There are a lot of forms of humanism (man's religions). But in a generic form, any time man's ideas are put on par with God's Word or elevated above God's Word, then that would encompass humanistic elements — the religion of man. Some religions honor man's ideas to such a degree that they completely reject God's Word. Some pay lip service to God's Word, but then change it to conform to their man-made religious system (by rewriting it, reinterpreting it, or otherwise attacking the Bible).

Some religions mimic God's Word but do not respect God's Word as coming from God. Only those who stand on God's Word as the absolute authority — inerrant, infallible, inspired, and sufficient in every way — will be in a position to see God's true religion from God's perspective. God will never be wrong in what He records in His Word, but man can and will be wrong as he seeks to stand in God's place.

Fallible mankind can never measure up to a perfect and infallible God and His Word. So all religions that have an element of man's ideas that have been elevated to be equal or to supersede God's Word are false. Sometimes these elements of human autonomy are deceptively clever, but one must discern if it comes from God or from man by comparing it to what God says in His Word. False religions may have elements of truth, but they have borrowed that truth from God and His Word, whether they realize it or not.

Even people who claim they are not religious are humanistic and base their religion on man's ideas — thus they are religious. Atheists claim they don't have a religion. However, they are religious, as they hold a worldview that is based on certain beliefs. Their religion is one of faith with the prominent tenet of naturalism — they believe the whole universe, including life, arose by natural processes. This belief is based on a faith — a blind faith, but a faith nonetheless. This is because they have already allowed their own human beliefs to sit in authority over God's Word and rejected it by suppression in their hearts (Romans 1:18–20). They are indeed religious, and do not let them deceive you into believing they are not.

When Bill Nye debated with Ken Ham in February 2014, he claimed the universe came into being by natural processes. He rejected that he has a religion (while inconsistently claiming to be agnostic and humanistic), but he cannot escape the fact he does have a religion — a faith that natural processes involving properties inherent in matter, produced the universe, including earth and all the life that inhabits it. Former radical Muslim turned Christian apologist Daniel Shayesteh confirms this when he writes,

> Willingly or unwillingly, every person in the world is affected by their beliefs. . . . Religious values are present everywhere we go; they are present in the lives of everybody with whom we have contact.[6]

There are two religions in the world — God's and "not God's." Man's religion ("not God's") is manifested in many ways that are being elevated to a position of being equal to or greater than God and His Word. But man's religions are purely based on man's arbitrary opinion that carries no weight when compared to the ultimate authority on the subject of religion — the triune God. Thus, they are refuted! Let God be true and every man a liar as we dive into the subject of world religions, cults, and philosophical systems, all of which are religious worldviews.

Preliminary Comments

Grouping of religions

There are several ways to group man's religions:

1. Polytheistic, monotheistic, pantheistic, and atheistic
2. Personal god(s), impersonal god(s), or no god(s)
3. Based on various alleged holy books
4. Spiritual, dualistic, or materialistic
5. Counterfeits of Christianity, mystical religions, and moralistic
6. Objective religion and subjective religion
7. Etc.

Although any of these classifications work, we've opted to select the breakdown that is similar to what philosopher and pastor Dr. Greg Bahnsen did when lumping religions into a philosophical framework. Our breakdown encompasses:

- Counterfeits of Christianity
- Mystical religions
- Moralistic religions
- Materialistic religions

6. Daniel Shayesteh, *Christ Above All* (Sydney, Australia: Talesh Books, 2010), p. 4.

We include a chapter that encompasses how religions can be broken down by the listing in #4 above (spiritual, dualistic, and materialistic) that will appear in a later volume but have opted to place materialistic religions as their own category within the framework of the listing in #5 (counterfeits of Christianity, mystical religions, moralistic; now including materialistic).

With this arrangement, and due to the nature of certain religious views, we sometimes had to make a judgment call on where to place them. In some cases, a religion has variations where some practitioners are materialistic where other forms are theistic (Satanism or Buddhism). In several cases, a religion could have been placed into more than one category, so we ask forgiveness if you feel a religion should have been placed under a different heading.

Due to the nature of our historical review of biblical Christianity (Protestantism or reformer-based Christianity brought on by the Reformation) and introductory material, we've opted to place Roman Catholicism and Orthodoxy prior to the counterfeits of Christianity section, even though some argue they could have been placed *under* this subheading (e.g., for those who hold to views like Mary being co-redemptrix [i.e., co-redeemer]). Again, it was a judgment call. But we do want people to read our thought-provoking and kind, yet bold, assessments of these deviations from biblical Christianity.

Refutations of Religions

There are several ways to refute false religions. The first and simplest is to point out where these religions are being *arbitrary* by appealing to fallible man as a being superior to God (arbitrariness). In many cases, their very foundation is simply arbitrary. Thus, they are refuted as logically untenable (proven false). Keep in mind that the opinion of man, whether Joseph Smith, Muhammad, Buddha, etc., regardless of who they are, carries no weight when an argument is arbitrary.

One might ask about the Bible's authors: are they arbitrary too? If an opinion came from Peter or Moses, it would carry no weight of its own accord. The fact that those books carry absolute weight in a debate is not due to their persons, but instead it is due to the weight of their co-author, the Holy Spirit, who is God, and not arbitrary in any way. Remember, all Scripture is "God breathed" (2 Timothy 3:16–17; 2 Peter 1:20–21).

Other forms of refutation can be done using *inconsistencies,* including logical fallacies. Pointing out where these religions are inconsistent with the truth of God's Word or inconsistent within their own religion can accomplish this type of refutation. For example, in an atheistic worldview, which is a materialistic religion by its very nature, immaterial things like logic, truth, reason, morality, and knowledge cannot exist. Hence, atheism is inconsistent within its own story when they try to use logic or say truth exists — they are refuted by their own self-contradictory inconsistencies.

Another way to refute a world religion or cult is to show where such has to borrow from God's Word to make sense of things like knowledge, clothing, reality, a week, and so on (this is called *preconditions of intelligibility* in philosophy). In other words, their own religion cannot make sense of their actions or beliefs, so we can point that out and show where they have actually borrowed from a biblical doctrine as a foundation for their own religion. It would be like asking what must be true for something to be possible. Allow us to explain this concept with a couple of examples.

First, let's say there is someone with a secular humanistic worldview. They believe that we are just evolved animals that came from the slime billions of years ago and that there is no God who sets what is right and wrong. And yet, these same people wear clothes. What must be true for people to believe it is right to wear clothes? Not the secular worldview, which should teach the opposite, as people are just animals. But instead, a biblical worldview where clothing came as a result of sin and shame in Genesis 3 gives a foundational reason for wearing clothing. The secularist is borrowing from the biblical worldview based on the Bible to make sense of clothing, and they don't even realize it.

Another example could be when an atheist says they hold to a particular "holiday." A holiday is a holy day and is predicated on God, who is holy, to make a day "holy." In the atheistic religion, there is no God and there is no holiness because there is no objective standard of right and wrong. So a holy day or holiday is actually meaningless in their religious worldview. But their actions betray their religion, demonstrating that they are actually borrowing from the Bible, whether the atheist realizes it or not.

So one way to refute a false religion is to show where their religion doesn't make sense of things and show where they must borrow from God and His Word to make sense of things. The presence for morality is another area where this lack of a foundation is evident and can be used to demonstrate how various worldviews borrow from the Bible while denying God is the standard of truth.

Another way to refute a false religion is to show where their religion leads (i.e., when it goes to *absurdity*). Many fail to realize that the religion they claim to adhere to when applied to other things becomes absurd. For example, in the atheistic religion there is no purpose, and many atheists are happy to promote this idea. But they fail to realize that by promoting the idea that there is no purpose, they are revealing that they *do* believe purpose exists!

Or when a follower of New Age mysticism says that whatever is true for you is true for you, but not for them, then they live in a way that presumes that everyone would agree that 2+2=4! When one points out where their religion leads, it shows the absurdity of their religious position and philosophy. They expect their banker to function in a way that is consistent with their understanding of truth, but then want truth to be relative in other areas — a fundamental absurdity.

To recap, some of the best ways to refute a false religion is by exposing:

- Arbitrariness
- Inconsistencies (with the Bible or within their own religion)
- Where they borrow ideas that are actually predicated on the Bible being true but not their own religion
- When their religion leads to absurdities

Because the Bible is true, we have a basis for using these tools to refute false worldviews. God is not arbitrary, being the ultimate authority (Isaiah 40:28; Romans 1:20). God cannot deny Himself, and His character is perfectly consistent (2 Timothy 2:13). This is why contradictions cannot exist within His Word or His nature, and why the law of noncontradiction does exist.

Building on this, we can use this law of logic to reveal people's inconsistencies and absurdities. God's Word is the basis for doctrine, and other religions often borrow from God and His Word (who is the source of all knowledge; e.g., Psalm 147:5; Colossians 2:3). In the character of the God who created this universe, the Christian has a logical foundation to stand on as he argues against false religious philosophies and claims, pointing others to repentance and faith in Jesus Christ as Creator and Savior.

Focus: Origins and Foundational Beliefs

There are many world religions books, articles, websites, courses, and so on. Why one more? The answer is our focus. We wanted a world religions series that viewed religions for what they are — either God's or man's. Furthermore, we wanted to emphasize the area of origins (cosmological and biological), which is an ideal place to spot man's arbitrary opinions and inconsistencies in a religion.

To get to the root of it, a false religion must borrow from God's Word for origins, or they must make up an arbitrary worldview to try to assemble a foundation for their religion. But a religion stands or falls on its foundation — its view of origins. So, unlike many other resources, many of which contain excellent information, we wanted to focus on origins and expose false thinking in their worldviews.

Diverse Authors — Yes, Indeed!

Authors for the respective chapters are from various theological walks. In fact, you will no doubt detect varied styles among the authors. We intend this to reduce monotony while reading. As you look through the author list, you might be wondering how this was possible. In fact, looking back on it, we too tried to figure out how we obtained such a diverse group of brilliant scholars, apologists, professors, pastors, Christian leaders, and a state congressman to work together on such a project! But it makes sense.

Yes, these authors would disagree with each other on a host of topics within their denominational or theological views like Calvinism vs. Arminianism, various eschatological positions, modes of baptism, covenant theology versus dispensational theology, and the like. These are indeed important issues, and we want to encourage everyone to know what they believe on these subjects and to do so *biblically*. Even though our authors try to avoid these denominational doctrine debates in a publication like this, there may be times where an author skirts along this line and may slightly cross into denominational issues unintentionally. For this, we ask forgiveness as well.

Denominational doctrines (secondary doctrines) are discussions that Christians have, by and large, while they are standing on the authority of the Bible. Though we save these doctrinal debates for other venues with each other to develop iron-sharpening-iron skills, we stand together when defending primary doctrines like the authority of the Bible against all other religions. Yes, there may be exceptions on particular arguments, however, when it comes to the issue of world religions and man's ideas being used to attack the authority of the Word of God, these Christians stand together to defend the authority of the Bible from the very first verse. And for this we praise the Lord and may He receive the glory.

Purpose of This Book Series: The Gospel of Jesus Christ and the Authority of His Word

The reason for this book series is first and foremost the promotion of the gospel of Jesus Christ. Jesus Christ and His Word, the 66 books of the Bible, have come under attack in this day and age. And with the multitude of religions that emanate from man, many get caught up in the popular notion that biblical Christianity is just one of many from which to choose.

However, biblical Christianity is not one of the many man-made religions to pick from a list like one would pick their favorite side dish from a menu. Instead, God's true religion revealed by Him in the Bible is the truth, and all other religions are deviants based on man's false ideas that have been elevated to challenge God's Word as the truth. So the second reason for this series is to challenge the false idea that there are many individual, compartmentalized religions.

There are only two — God's and man's — as we have already explained. When people realize that there are two religions, the true one and the false one (with many variations within these false religions), it becomes easier to see the so-called multitudes of religions for what they are. They are merely variants of the false ideas of man trying to take your attention away from the true religion — God's. Biblical Christianity that teaches the triune God is the Creator of all things and that Jesus Christ is the only Savior for all of humanity is the only true religion. There are not many paths that lead to God, but Jesus alone is the door (John 10:7–19, 14:6–7).

We pray this book series will open your eyes to the false aspects of man's religions and reveal where man's ideas have been used to supersede God's Word. In doing so, our hope is that you, the reader, will be able to see the truth of God's Word through the Holy Spirit by opening you up to see the gospel found only in the work of God through Jesus Christ our Lord and His work on the Cross for our sin. Let us share the good news that has brought us salvation with all those who are following man-made religions to the praise of the glory of God's grace.

And Jesus came up and spoke to them, saying, "All authority has been given to Me in heaven and on earth. Go therefore and make disciples of all the nations, baptizing them in the name of the Father and the Son and the Holy Spirit, teaching them to observe all that I have commanded you; and lo, I am with you always, even to the end of the age" (Matthew 28:18–20).

Chapter 1

Defending the Faith: Approaching World Religions

Dr. Kenneth Gentry

Biblical Christianity is a philosophy of life (worldview) surrounded by many opposing philosophies (worldviews). In this book we are promoting biblical Christianity over competing worldviews.

God calls upon Christians to "sanctify the Lord God in your hearts, and always be ready to give a defense [Gk., *apologia*] to everyone who asks you a reason for the hope that is in you, with meekness and fear" (1 Peter 3:15; NKJV). As we obey Him, we must defend the faith in such a way that it "sanctifies the Lord" in our hearts. This requires that we defend the faith from a position of faith. Simply put, the way that we argue for the faith must be compatible with the faith for which we argue.

In defending the faith we are engaging in what is called "apologetics." The English word "apologetics" is a compound of two Greek words *apo* ("from") and *logos* ("word"). Basically, an apologetic is a word from someone in his or her defense. It was originally a judicial term used in a court setting whereby someone defended himself from accusations.

The verb form of the word (*apologeomai*) occurs ten times in the New Testament (Luke 12:11, 21:14; Acts 19:33, 24:10, 25:8, 26:1, 26:2, 26:24; Romans 2:15; 2 Corinthians 12:19). The noun (*apologia*) appears eight times (Acts 22:1, 25:16; 1 Corinthians 9:3; 2 Corinthians 7:11; Philemon 1:7,

1:16; 2 Timothy 4:16; 1 Peter 3:15). Several of these appearances involve an actual court defense (e.g., Luke 12:11, 21:14; Acts 19:33, 24:10, 25:8, 25:16; etc.).

Gradually, apologetics evolved over time to become a branch of Christian theology that engages in a reasoned defense of the Christian faith. It sets forth the rational basis upon which the faith rests, and through that it challenges all forms of non-biblical truth claims. It challenges unbelieving thought with the confidence of "come, let us reason together" (Isaiah 1:18).

Unfortunately, too many defenses of the Christian faith today cede the method of approach to the unbeliever by arguing on his terms. This generally ends up "proving" at best only the *possibility* that *a god* exists — not the *certainty* that the *God of Scripture* exists. But we should argue from a "presuppositional" perspective that builds on the sure foundation of that which we believe. That is, we must believe that God's Word is the absolute authority in all areas of life and thought. This method of apologetics is called "presuppositionalism."

But what is presuppositionalism? And how does it effectively challenge all forms of unbelieving (non-biblical) thought? Answering these questions is the task of this chapter. To understand the presuppositional apologetic method, we must begin by considering the role of presuppositions in thought.

The Role of Presuppositions in Thought

As we begin to engage presuppositionalism, we must understand the following.

The Uniformity of Nature and Thought

We exist in what is known as a "*uni*verse." The word "universe" is composed of two Latin parts: "uni" (from *unus,* meaning "one," as in "unit") and "verse" (from *vertere,* meaning "turn"). It speaks of all created things as collective whole. This word indicates that we live in a *single* unified and orderly system that is composed of many diverse parts. These parts function coordinately together as a whole, singular, rational system.

We do not live in a "*multi*verse." A multiverse state of affairs would be a disunified, totally fragmented, and random assortment of disconnected and unconnectable facts. These unconnectable facts would be meaninglessly scattered about in chaotic disarray and ultimate disorder.

The concept of a *"universe"* is vitally important to science, for the very possibility of scientific investigation is totally dependent upon the fact of a *"uni*verse" — an orderly, rational coherent, unified system. If reality were haphazard and disorderly, there would be no basic scientific and mathematical laws that govern and control all the various physical phenomena of reality. And if this were so, there could be no unity at all in either reality itself, in experience, or in thought.

In such a multiverse, each and every single fact would necessarily stand alone, utterly disconnected from other facts, not forming a system as a whole. Consequently, nothing could be organized and related in the mind because no fact would be related to any other fact. Thus, science, logic, and experience are absolutely dependent upon uniformity as a principle of the natural world.

Uniformity and Faith

But now the question arises: how do we know assuredly that the universe is in fact uniform? Has man investigated every single aspect of the universe from each one of its smallest atomic particles to the farthest corners of its galaxies — and all that exists in between — so that he can speak authoritatively? Does man have totally exhaustive knowledge about every particle of matter, every movement in space, and every moment of time? How does man know uniformity governs the world and the universe?

Furthermore, how can we know that uniformity will continue tomorrow so that we can conjecture about future events? And since man claims to have an experience of external things, how do we know our experience is accurate and actually conforms to reality as it is? That is, how do we know that our senses are basically accurate and our memory is essentially reliable?

Such questions are not commonly asked, even though they are vitally important. The point of these questions is to demonstrate an important truth: we must realize that any and every attempt to prove uniformity in nature necessarily requires *circular reasoning*. To prove uniformity one must assume or presuppose uniformity.

If I set out to argue the uniformity of the universe because I can predict cause and effect, am I not presupposing the uniformity and validity of my experience? How can I be sure that my experience of cause and effect is an accurate reflection of what really happens? Furthermore, am I not presupposing the trustworthy, uniform coherence of my own rationality — a rationality that requires uniformity?

The issue boils down to this: since man cannot know everything he must *assume* or *presuppose* uniformity and then think and act on this very basic assumption. Consequently, the principle of uniformity is not a scientific law but an act of faith that undergirds scientific law. Thus, adherence to the principle of uniformity — though basic to science — is an intrinsically religious commitment.

Presuppositions in Thought

Scientists follow a basic pattern in discovering true scientific laws. First, they observe a particular phenomenon. Then on the basis of their observations they construct a working hypothesis. Next, they perform experiments implementing this hypothesis. This is followed in turn by attempting to verify the experiments performed. Then a verified hypothesis is accepted as a theory. Finally, a well-established theory is recognized as a scientific law that governs in a given set of circumstances.

Thus, the basic pattern of scientific activity is:

1. observation
2. hypothesis
3. experimentation
4. verification
5. theory
6. law

Christians agree wholeheartedly with the validity of this scientific methodology. We accept the notion of a uniform universe that allows for such, for "in the beginning God created the heavens and the earth" (Genesis. 1:1; NASB).

Physicist Thomas Kuhn, in his epochal 1962 work titled *The Structure of Scientific Revolutions,* notes that scientists *must* work from certain preconceived ideas, certain presupposed concepts about things in order to begin formulating their theories and performing their experiments.[1]

That presuppositions are always silently at work is evident in that when dealing with a particular problem, scientists select only a few basic facts to

1. Thomas Kuhn, *The Structure of Scientific Revolutions* (Chicago, IL: University of Chicago Press, 1962).

consider while rejecting or overlooking numerous others. They perform certain types of experiments while neglecting others. And *they do this in keeping with their presuppositions.* One of the most basic presuppositions held by scientists is the one we are considering: the universe is in fact one orderly, logical, coherent, predictable system. Were this not assumed, then science could not even get off the ground.

But, as a matter of fact, there are *numerous* presuppositions that *all* rational people hold that play a vital role in all human thought and behavior. The various presuppositions we hold govern the way we think and act, all the way down to how we select and employ specific facts from the countless number presented to us each moment. Basic presuppositions are the foundation blocks upon which we build our understanding of the world about us. Presuppositions are the very basis for what is known as our "world-and-life" view (or "worldview").

A worldview is the very framework through which we understand the world and our relation to it. Everyone has a particular way of looking at the world that serves to organize ideas about the world in his mind. This worldview must be founded on basic presupposed ideas that we hold to be truth. We begin with certain presuppositions and build from there in our learning, communicating, behaving, planning, and so forth. Because of this, we must recognize the impossibility of neutrality.

The Impossibility of Neutrality

Everyone holds to presuppositions. No one operates — or even *can* operate — in a vacuum. We simply do not think or behave "out of the blue." It is impossible to think and live as if we were aliens having just arrived to this world from a radically different universe, totally devoid of all knowledge of this world, absolutely objective and utterly impartial to ideas about truth. People behave in terms of a basic worldview that implements their conceptions regarding truth.

Consequently, neutrality in thought is impossible. Each person — the philosopher and scientist alike — has his own bias. This bias has predetermined the *facts* on the basis of his presuppositions. Yet almost invariably, scientists claim to be presenting neutral, unbiased, impartial, and objective facts in their research. But man is not and cannot be truly objective and impartial. *All thinking must begin somewhere!*

All thinking must have some fundamental, logically-primitive starting point or presupposition. At the very least, we must presuppose the reality of the external world, the rationality of mental activity, the compatibility between external reality and the mind, and the uniformity of nature, that is, the law of cause and effect. As noted previously, a certain *faith* is necessary in the selection and organization of the several facts chosen from the innumerable set of facts flowing toward us in every moment of experience.

Clearly, *presuppositions are necessarily self-authenticating or self-evidencing.* Facts are inseparable from their interpretation. Facts *cannot* stand alone. They must be understood in terms of some broad, unified whole or system. They must be organized in our rational minds in terms of their general relationships to other facts and principles.

This leads us then to our most basic questions: Which system of thought can give meaning to the facts of the universe? Which worldview can provide an adequate foundation for reality? Why is the world in which we live conducive to rational thought and behavior? What is the basis for an orderly universe?

Worldviews in Collision

When we contrast Christian thought with non-Christian thought we must realize that we are *not* contrasting two series of isolated facts. We are not comparing two systems of truth that share a basically similar outlook and that have only occasional differences between them at specific turns. *We are contrasting two whole, complete, and antithetical systems of thought.*

Each particular item of evidence presented in support of the one system will be evaluated by the other system in terms of the latter's own entire implicit *system* with all of its basic assumptions. Each fact or piece of data presented either to the Christian or the non-Christian will be weighed, categorized, organized, and judged as to its possibility and significance in terms of the all-pervasive worldview held.

Consequently, it is essential that we see the debate between the Christian and the non-Christian as between two complete worldviews — between two ultimate commitments and presuppositions that are contrary to one another. Two complete philosophies of reality are in collision. Appealing to various *scientific evidences* will be arbitrated *in terms of* the two mutually exclusive and diametrically opposed, presupposed truths held by the systems.

Thus, the debate between the Christian and the non-Christian *must eventually work its way down to the question of one's ultimate authority.* Every series of argument must end somewhere; one's conclusions could never be demonstrated if they were dependent upon an infinite series of arguments and justifications. So all debates must terminate at *some* point — at some premise held as unquestionable. This is one's foundational starting point, one's ultimate authority or *presupposition.*

The question that surfaces at this point is this: which system of truth provides the foundational preconditions essential for observation, reason, experience, and meaningful discourse? Thus, which *faith* system should be chosen: the Christian or the non-Christian?

The Christian System and Presuppositions

What is the Christian's starting point? What is his most basic presupposition upon which he builds his entire worldview? Where do we begin our argument?

Christian thought holds as its most basic, fundamental, all-pervasive, and necessary starting point or presupposition, the being of God who has revealed Himself in Scripture. Thus, our presupposition is God and His Word. The Scripture, being His own infallible Word (2 Timothy 3:16), reveals to us the nature of the God in whom we trust.

God is self-sufficient, needing absolutely nothing outside of Himself (Exodus 3:14; John 5:26). All else in the universe is utterly dependent upon Him (Colossians 1:17; Hebrews 1:3). God is the all-powerful Creator of the entire universe (Genesis 1:1; Exodus 20:11; Nehemiah 9:6). God is personal, thus giving meaning to the vast universe (Acts 17:28). And God has clearly and authoritatively revealed Himself in Scripture (2 Peter 1:20–21), so we may build upon His Word as truth (Psalm 119:160; John 17:17).

The entire Christian system of thought is founded solidly upon this God — the all-ordering God of Scripture (Psalm 33:9; Isaiah 46:10). We presuppose God for what He is. If God exists and demands our belief in Scripture, we cannot challenge or test Him in any area (Deuteronomy 6:16; Matthew 4:7). We recognize the independence of God and the utter dependence of man and the universe.

Because of this, we do not have to exhaustively know everything in order to be sure of anything. God knows all things and has revealed to us in

His Word the truth of uniformity (Genesis 8:22; Colossians 1:17; Hebrews 1:3) and all other truths we need in order to reason and to function in His world.

The Non-Christian System and Presuppositions

Against this presupposed system, what does the non-Christian presuppose as ultimate truth? What does the secularist have to offer as its ultimate authority?

The non-Christian must ultimately explain the universe *not* on the basis of the all-organizing, self-sufficient, all-wise, personal God as his starting point. In rejecting God and His Word, the default position for all other worldviews must be established on the ideas of man to one degree or another. Perhaps one of the most popular worldviews of man today is secularism, also known as humanism. It holds that reality is ultimately rooted in the nebulous, chaotic, and impersonal world. Due to its widespread and influential presence in our culture, this popular religious view will be compared and contrasted to the Christian worldview in the remainder of this chapter.

The secularist asserts that the universe was produced by a combination of impersonal chance plus an enormous span of time. Thus, in this worldview the ultimate starting point and the all-conditioning environment of the universe is time plus chance.

Because the unbeliever's worldview is based upon time plus chance, *rational* science is rooted in the *irrationality* of chance. The scientist cannot speak of design or purpose in the universe because there is no Designer or purpose. There can be no goal or purpose in a random system.

On this view, secular science *must* by the very nature of its non-Christian commitment assume facts to be bits of irrationalism strewn about awaiting rationalization by man. Thus, modern secular science is schizophrenic. On the one hand, everything has its source in random, ungoverned chance. On the other hand, evolution assumes all is not random, but uniform. It holds that all is ungoverned, yet, nevertheless, is moving in an upward direction from disorder to order, from simplicity to complexity.

In this regard, Christian apologist Dr. Cornelius Van Til has noted: "On his own assumption his own rationality is a product of chance. . . . The rationality and purpose that he may be searching for are still bound by products of chance."[2] To prove a rational universe by chance, man must believe the rational is the product of, and is dependent upon, the irrational.

Not only is all of reality founded on chance, but this leaves man to be the final criterion of truth. Man — sinful, fallible, finite man — becomes ultimate in the non-Christian system.

Presuppositions Make a Difference

Now let us consider four important areas of philosophy that govern our outlook.

Reality

When asked to give the basis and starting point for the orderly universe and all external reality, the Christian points to the self-contained, ever-present, all-powerful, all-wise, infinitely rational God of Scripture.

When the non-Christian secularist is asked to give the basis and starting point for the orderly universe and external reality, he points literally to . . . *nothing.* All has risen from nothing by the irrational mechanism of chance.

When asked if something can miraculously pop into being from nothing in an instant, the non-Christian vigorously responds in the negative. Instant miracles are out of the question. But when asked if something can come out of nothing *if given several billion years,* the non-Christian confidently responds in the affirmative. As Dr. Van Til has noted, the non-Christian overlooks the fact that if one zero equals zero, then a billion zeros can equal only zero.

Thus, the Christian has a *more than adequate reason* for the universe, whereas the non-Christian has *no reason whatsoever.*

Knowledge

The Christian establishes his theory of knowledge on the all-ordering, all-knowing God of Scripture. God has instantaneous, true, and exhaustive knowledge of everything, and He has revealed to man in the Bible comprehensive principles that are clear and give a sure foundation for knowledge. Such a foundation ensures that what man does know (although he cannot know all things), he can know truly. Knowledge does work because man's mind as created by God is receptive to external reality and is given validity by

---

2. Cornelius Van Til, *The Defense of the Faith* (Philipsburg, NJ: P & R Publishing, 1972), p. 102.

God Himself. We are, after all, made in the image of the logical, all-knowing God of truth (Genesis 1:26–27, 9:6)!

On the other hand, the non-Christian must establish his theory of knowledge on the same foundation upon which he establishes reality: nebulous chaos and irrational chance. If followed consistently, the non-Christian theory of knowledge would utterly destroy all knowledge, causing it to drown in the turbulent ocean of irrationalism. *There is no reason for reason in the non-Christian system.* The concepts of probability, possibility, order, rationality, and so forth, are impossible in a chance and purposeless system.

Thus, the Christian has a sure foundation for knowledge, whereas the non-Christian has none.

Morality

When we consider the issue of moral law, the standard for judging right and wrong, again the question must be settled in terms of one's foundational system.

For the Christian, morality is founded upon the all-good, all-knowing, everywhere present, all-powerful, personal, and eternal God of Scripture. His will, which is rooted in His being and nature, is man's standard of right. Since God is all good (Psalm 119:137; Mark 10:18) and all-knowing (Psalm 139; Proverbs 15:3), moral principles revealed in Scripture are always *relevant* to our situation. Since God is eternal (Psalm 90:2, 102:12), His moral commands are always *binding* upon men.

For the non-Christian there is no sure base for ethics. Since reality is founded on nothing and knowledge is rooted in irrationalism, morality can be nothing other than pure, impersonal irrelevance. In such a system as presupposed by non-Christian thought, there are no — *indeed, there can be no* — ultimate, abiding moral principles. Everything is caught up in the impersonal flux of a random universe. Random change is ultimate in such a system. And because of this, ethics is reduced to pure relativism. Non-Christian thought can offer no justification for any moral behavior whatsoever.

Purpose

To the question of whether or not there is *any* significance and meaning to the universe and to life, the Christian confidently responds in the affirmative. There is meaning in the world because it was purposely and purposefully created by and for the personal, loving, all-ordering, eternal God of Scripture (Nehemiah 9:6; Psalm 33:6–9).

In our system of thought, man came about as the direct and purposeful creation of the loving God who has revealed Himself in the Bible (Genesis 2:7). Furthermore, man was assigned a specific and far-reaching duty by God on the very day he was created (Genesis 1:26–29). Man and *his task* must be understood *in terms* of the eternal God and His plan, rather than in terms of himself and an environment of chance and change.

Non-Christian secularist thought destroys the meaning and significance of man by positing that he is nothing more than a chance fluke, an accidental collection of molecules arising out of the slime and primordial ooze. Man is a frail speck of dust caught up in a gigantic, impersonal, multi-billion-year-old universe. That, and nothing more.

The famous 20th-century atheist Bertrand Russell put it well when he wrote:

> The world is purposeless, void of meaning. Man is the outcome of accidental collocations of atoms; all the devotion, all the inspiration, all the noonday brightness of human genius are destined to extinction in the vast death of the solar system. Only on the firm foundation of unyielding despair can the soul's habitation be safely built. From evolution no ultimately optimistic philosophy can be validly inferred.[3]

Conclusion

To the question concerning which system is the most adequate for explaining external reality, the possibility of knowledge, a relevant and binding ethic, and the significance of man, the answer should be obvious: only the worldview presupposing the truth claims of the Bible is sufficient for the task.

Actually, the defense of Christianity is simple: we argue *the impossibility of the contrary*. Ironically, those who assault the Christian system must actually *assume* the Christian system to do so. That is, they must assume a rational world for which only Christianity can account. In fact, atheism assumes theism. If the God of Scripture did not exist, there would be no man in any real world to argue — there would be no possibility of rationality by which an argument could be forged, and there would be no purpose in debate!

---

3. Bertrand Russell, *Mysticism and Logic* (New York: Doubleday, 1917), p. 45–46.

Charles Darwin stated this problem in his personal letter to W. Graham on July 3, 1881:

> But then with me the horrid doubt always arises whether the convictions of man's mind, which has always been developed from the mind of the lower animals, are of any value or at all trustworthy. Would any one trust in the convictions of a monkey's mind, if there are any convictions in such a mind?[4]

Paul spoke powerfully when he declared in Romans 3:4, "Let God be true but every man a liar" (KJV).

The God of Scripture, the Father of our Lord Jesus Christ, is the ultimate and necessary foundation for a rational, coherent worldview. Every other system is built upon a lie — the fallible ideas of sinful and rebellious man. The Christian system begins with: "In the beginning God. . . ." And from that foundational reality, all the rest of a rational worldview falls into place.

---

4. Francis Darwin, ed., *The Life and Letters of Charles Darwin* (New York: Basic, 1959), 1:285.

Chapter 2

What Is Biblical Christianity, and Why Is It Different?

Dr. Joel R. Beeke and Pastor Paul M. Smalley

On April 18, 1521, Martin Luther stood before Charles V in Worms, Germany, a lowly monk before the emperor who ruled Spain, the Netherlands, Germany, and much of Italy. With the emperor stood powerful officials of the church and state who demanded that Luther renounce his teachings, saying they contradicted the traditions of men. Luther answered, "My conscience is captive to the Word of God. I cannot and I will not recant anything, for to go against conscience is neither right nor safe. God help me. Amen."[1] With those words, Luther provoked the wrath of the imperial court, which proceeded to condemn him as a heretic and a devil. Yet with these words Luther also fanned into flame a reformation and revival of biblical Christianity across Europe.

Christians have always been people of the Word. Jesus Christ said, "If ye continue in my word, then are ye my disciples indeed; and ye shall know the truth, and the truth shall make you free" (John 8:31–32).[2]

The term *Christian* means disciple of Christ (Acts 11:26). It refers to one who has submitted to Christ as Master, follows His teachings, and imitates His life no matter what the cost (Matthew 10:24–25, 16:24). The Word of

---

1. Roland H. Bainton, *Here I Stand: A Life of Martin Luther* (New York: Abingdon Press, 1950), p. 185.
2. All Scripture quotations in this chapter will use the King James Version of the Bible.

Christ is central to a Christian's life. By the Word, God gives faith (Romans 10:17), and by the Word, He makes His people holy (John 17:17). Today, that Word exists in the form of the ancient writings of the Bible, or Holy Scriptures, which were "given by inspiration of God" (2 Timothy 3:16).

Christianity is an ancient religion, as old as the promises of God. Its roots reach back thousands of years to the very first man and woman, whose faith grasped hold of God's first promise of salvation (Genesis 3:15, 3:20). Over the centuries, God revealed more of His Word to Noah, Abraham, Moses, David, Isaiah, and many others. Under God's direction, Moses began writing the Word of God down, and prophets who followed him added to these writings. These writings were preserved and brought together into what we call the Old Testament. The climax of God's plan was the arrival of God's Son, Jesus Christ, upon earth (Galatians 4:4). Through His Apostles and prophets, the Lord Jesus gave the final revelation of God and His will, with God testifying to the trustworthiness of His Word by signs and wonders (Ephesians 2:20, 3:5; Hebrews 1:1–2, 2:3–4). As a result, we have the New Testament, with four Gospels about Christ's life and teachings, and the Epistles, which were letters written to various churches and believers. The Apostles and their coworkers testified to Christ's death and Resurrection, and planted churches from Jerusalem westward to Rome and eastward to India.

The early Church in the pagan Roman Empire was often despised and at times suffered violent persecution. Yet the Church continued to expand into Europe, Africa, and Asia, bringing the message of the Bible to people who worshiped many gods and spirits and followed various philosophies. After the Emperor Constantine became favorable to Christians (A.D. 313), they experienced increasing freedom. At the same time, false teachings pressed believers to consider more carefully what the Bible says. They expressed their beliefs in the form of creeds. Over the first few centuries, basic Christian beliefs were summarized in the Apostles' Creed (though not written by the Apostles themselves). Also, Christian leaders met to work out statements of what they believed about God and Jesus Christ at the Council of Nicea (325), the Council of Constantinople (381), and the Council of Chalcedon (451).

Over the centuries, man-made traditions, rituals, and spurious forms of devotion crept into the Church. The bishop of the Church of Rome (the pope) gradually rose in authority and came to rule Christians of many nations as if he were a spiritual emperor. The Church increased in power, erecting massive cathedrals in Europe. Islam arose in the seventh century, and Muslims conquered the Middle East, North Africa, Spain, and Portugal, putting ever-increasing pressure on the Church. The Greek- and Aramaic-speaking Christians of the eastern Mediterranean drifted away from Latin-speaking Christians in the west, officially splitting with Rome in 1054. This resulted in a lasting divide between the Eastern Orthodox Churches and the Roman Catholic Church.

The Cathedral at Cologne

In the 16th century, the Reformation launched various churches in Europe and Britain, most notably the Lutherans, the Reformed, and the Anabaptists, as many people sought to return to the biblical Christianity of the early Church. They expressed their understanding of the Bible in confessional statements such as the Augsburg Confession (1530), the Heidelberg Catechism (1563), and the Westminster Confession of Faith (1646). Sadly, since the 19th century many Reformation churches have fallen prey to the influences of modern unbelief and no longer adhere to the teachings of their own creeds and confessions.

This is barely a sketch of Christianity. Rather than attempting to explore the subject of church history in more detail, this chapter will focus on what biblical Christianity teaches. While each church has its own confession and catechism, what follows is a summary of commonly held beliefs in the Reformation churches, organized in answer to seven key questions. In answering these questions, this chapter will cover more than 50 distinct points of doctrine. That may seem like a lot, but they are just a fraction of the truths taught in a typical Reformation confession of faith. Here, then, is a basic introduction to the teachings of biblical Christianity.

Question 1: Who Is God, and How Is He Active in the World?

The first words of the Apostles' Creed are, "I believe in God." Yet we can no more understand the depths of God than a three-year-old child can understand how a computer controls electronic ignition and fuel injection to make a car engine run. God is a Spirit (John 4:24); He does not have a body so we cannot see Him (Colossians 1:15). God is infinite; He is beyond any limitation, measurement, or understanding (Job 11:7). "His greatness is unsearchable" (Psalm 145:3). Martin Luther (1483–1546) said, "God hides himself" and yet wills to be "revealed" (see Isaiah 45:15, 45:19).[3]

We cannot completely understand God, but He has made it possible to know Him. We should not boast about being intelligent, powerful, or rich, for the only thing worth boasting about is knowing God (Jeremiah 9:23–24). God is beautiful (Psalm 27:4). Eternal life consists in knowing God (John 17:3). Therefore, we need to know God. Who then is God?

1. *God is one God and three persons.* Christians do not believe in three gods, nor do they believe in one person who acts in three different ways at different times. They believe in the Trinity: one God who has always existed in three distinct persons. We find the three persons at Christ's baptism (Matthew 3:16–17), and they are named in the baptism of Christians. As Matthew 28:19 commands, we baptize "in the name of the Father, and of the Son, and of the Holy Ghost." Each of the three persons possesses all the attributes of deity. In Deuteronomy 6:4, Israel was told, "Hear, O Israel: The LORD our God is one LORD." The Son is Lord and God (John 1:1, 20:28), one with the Father (John 10:30). The Spirit is Lord and God (Acts 5:3–4; 2 Corinthians 3:17). The Athanasian Creed (late fifth century) explains:

> Such as the Father is, such is the Son, and such is the Holy Spirit. . . . The Father eternal, the Son eternal, and the Holy Spirit eternal. And yet they are not three eternals, but one eternal. . . . The Father is almighty, the Son almighty, and the Holy Spirit almighty. And yet they are not three almighties, but one almighty. So the Father is God, the Son is God, and the Holy Spirit is God. And yet they are not three Gods, but one God.[4]

The Trinity is very mysterious and yet also beautiful. It includes three persons so close to each other that they share one essence, one wisdom, one power, and one love. That is the beauty of God.

---

3. Martin Luther, *The Bondage of the Will,* ed. and trans. Philip S. Watson, in *Luther's Works* (Philadelphia: Fortress Press, 1972) 33:139.
4. Athanasian Creed, in *Doctrinal Standards, Liturgy, and Church Order,* ed. Joel R. Beeke (Grand Rapids, MI: Reformation Heritage Books, 2003), p. 3.

2. *God is love and righteousness.* Though God is one, there are many ways of describing His beauty. If you hold a prism in the sunshine, one beam of light produces a lovely rainbow of many colors. Similarly, God is one, yet when He reveals Himself in His Word, we see His glory in many beautiful attributes. "God is love," says John 4:8. Exodus 34:6 says, "The Lord God, [is] merciful and gracious, longsuffering [patient], and abundant in goodness and truth." God is also righteous. As Deuteronomy 32:4 says, "He is the Rock, his work is perfect: for all his ways are judgment [justice]: a God of truth and without iniquity, just and right is he." God loves what is right and hates what is wrong (Psalm 11:5–7, 33:5). You can trust this God.

God is perfect in every way, and He alone deserves our worship. It is our highest duty to love Him with all that we are, for to know and worship such a great God is the deepest delight of man (Psalm 27:4, 63:3, 84:1–2, 84:10). Augustine (354–430), a pastor and theologian in North Africa, said, "Thou hast made us for Thyself, and our heart is restless until it rests in Thee."[5] Augustine knew this by experience, for prior to his conversion he spent many years seeking happiness in sex, in his work as a teacher, and by studying various human philosophies. When he turned from sin to trust in Jesus Christ, he prayed, "What things I feared to lose, now were a joy to cast away. . . . Thou didst cast them out and enter in to supplant them with a pleasure more sweet, brighter than light . . . more sublime than all honor."[6]

3. *God is Lord.* He is the great King. In His presence the angels cover their faces and cry, "Holy, holy, holy is the Lord of hosts" (Isaiah 6:3). He is very different from us. God has no beginning and no end (Psalm 90:2). He does not need us for anything (Acts 17:25). He is in every place at all times (Psalm 139:7–8; Jeremiah 23:24). He never changes in who He is or what He has planned (Numbers 23:19; Malachi 3:6). He knows everything (Psalm 33:13–15; John 16:30), even what we will do in the future, for He planned everything before we were born (Psalm 139:16; Isaiah 46:8–11). He is wise in all that He does (Psalm 104:24). He is all powerful (Daniel 2:20–21), doing whatever He desires to do (Psalm 115:3) and whatever He wills to do (Jeremiah 32:17).

---

5. Saint Augustine, *Confessions*, trans. and ed. Henry Chadwick (Oxford: Oxford University Press, 1991), 3 [1.1].
6. Augustine, *Confessions*, 155 [9.1]. We thank Ray Lanning for translations from Augustine's Latin in this paragraph.

4. *God created all things visible and invisible.* The first sentence of the Bible is, "In the beginning God created the heaven and the earth" (Genesis 1:1). In six days, the Lord made everything that exists (Genesis 1:1–31). Irenaeus said around A.D. 180 that the church received from the Apostles the belief that God is the "Maker of heaven, and earth, and the sea, and all things that are in them."[7] The universe has not always been here, nor was it shaped by accident. God is Lord not only of spiritual things but also of the physical world. Everything that we can see or that scientists can measure was made by God, so He is Lord of all (Acts 17:24). God also made what we cannot see, such as the invisible spirits of the angels (Colossians 1:16). God made everything very good, for He is good (Genesis 1:31). The things that He made show His glory (Psalm 19:1; Romans 1:20). Creation is the work of the Father, the Son, and the Holy Spirit, for these three are one God (Genesis 1:2; Job 33:4; John 1:1–3; Hebrews 1:2). We should thank Him every day, for every good gift is from Him (James 1:17).

5. *God provides for and controls all things.* God did not leave His world after creating it, but continues to uphold it by His power (Hebrews 1:3). He works through natural processes such as the falling of rain to keep plants, animals, and people alive (Psalm 104:10–15). God rules over all His creation (Psalm 103:19, 135:6). He gives life and takes life away. He makes one person rich and another person poor (1 Samuel 2:6–7). He controls the great kings of the world for His secret purposes (Proverbs 21:1; Isaiah 10:5, 10:15).

In His wisdom, God made a plan for His world. The Bible calls God's plan His "decree" (Psalm 2:7; Daniel 4:24), for it is the purpose and decision of the sovereign King. William Perkins (1558–1602) wrote of God's "eternal and unchangeable decree, whereby he has ordained all things either past, present, or to come, for his own glory."[8] That is a great comfort, for even bad things have a purpose in God's plan. Joseph's brothers sold him into slavery, so that he spent 13 years in bondage in a foreign country, but later he told the brothers that what they had intended for evil, God had planned for good (Genesis 50:20). If God had no plan, the world would be chaos. Imagine a construction site without a plan. The excavators do not know where to dig.

---

7. Irenaeus, *Against Heresies*, 10.1, in *Ante-Nicene Fathers* (New York: Charles Scribner's Sons, 1913), 1:330.

8. William Perkins, *An Exposition of the Symbole or Creed of the Apostles, According to the Tenour of the Scriptures, and the Consent of Orthodox Fathers of the Church* (London: John Legatt, 1595), p. 53.

The masons do not know where to construct walls. Everyone is arguing. You ask the supervisor to see the blueprints for the building. What if he says, "We don't have any plans. We are just putting the building together however it seems best, and we'll see what it turns out to be"? No self-respecting construction company would be so foolish! God is not like that either. When He created the world, He already had a definite plan for what He intended to do, and He is working all things according to His wise decree for His glory (Romans 11:33–36; Ephesians 1:4, 1:6, 1:11–12).

Question 2: Who Are We, and Where Do We Come From?

People have long marveled over God's purposes for mankind. Given how small we are compared to the vast reaches of outer space, we might expect God to pay no heed to us. David looked up at the stars and wondered, "What is man, that thou art mindful of him?" (Psalm 8:4). Abraham humbly considered himself to be only "dust and ashes" before the Lord (Genesis 18:27). However, David confessed, "thou . . . hast crowned him with glory and honour. Thou madest him to have dominion over the works of thy hands" (Psalm 8:5–6). What are we humans that we can be both dust and ashes and the crown of God's creation?

6. *God created the first man out of the earth.* God created man on the sixth day of creation (Genesis 1:26, 1:31). Genesis 2:7 says, "And the LORD God formed man of the dust of the ground, and breathed into his nostrils the breath of life; and man became a living soul." The first man did not evolve from a lower life form but was formed by God "of the earth" (1 Corinthians 15:47). God's creation of the first man from the dust is an important doctrine of the Christian faith. It is explicitly affirmed in the Belgic Confession (1561) and the Westminster Larger Catechism (1647).[9] The Lord took some flesh and bone from that man's side and made the first woman, who became his wife and the mother of all mankind (Genesis 2:21–24, 3:20). The Bible does not treat Adam and Eve as mythology but as real people (1 Chronicles 1:1; Luke 3:38), whom God made "from the beginning of the creation," as the Lord Jesus Christ said (Mark 10:6). Our humble origins from the dust remind us that we owe our life and breath — all that we are and all that we have — to God.

---

9. Belgic Confession, art. 14., in *Doctrinal Standards*, ed. Beeke, p. 11; Westminster Larger Catechism, Q. 17, in *Reformed Confessions of the Sixteenth and Seventeenth Centuries in English Translation, Volume 4, 1600–1695*, ed. James T. Dennison, Jr. (Grand Rapids, MI: Reformation Heritage Books, 2014), 4:302.

7. *God created man in His image for His glory.* God made man, male and female, "in the image of God" (Genesis 1:27). God designed man to visibly represent His glory, much as children are living images of their father (Genesis 5:3). Man was created to be a child of God (Luke 3:38; Acts 17:29). That means humans are far more valuable than animals (Genesis 9:3, 9:6), just as Christ taught us (Matthew 6:26, 10:31, 12:12). We are not just physical bodies but also souls (Matthew 10:28). When God created man, God commissioned him to rule over and care for all other creatures of the earth (Genesis 1:26, 1:28). The image of the Creator includes the ability to do such things as agriculture, architecture, the arts, and manufacturing (Genesis 4:17, 4:20–22). Yet man was to rule as God's obedient servant. God entered into a covenant of obedience with man so that if he continued to obey, he would continue in life; but if he disobeyed God's Law, he would surely die (Genesis 2:9, 2:15–17, 3:22). The essence of being created in God's image is to be endowed with spiritual knowledge, righteousness, and holiness (Colossians 3:10; Ephesians 4:24). The Westminster Shorter Catechism (1647) says that the chief end of man is "to glorify God, and to enjoy him forever."[10] It is a noble thing to be a human being, for each one of us has a high calling and a glorious privilege.

8. *Man fell into sin and misery.* Although God made mankind righteous, we have turned away from Him to our own ways (Ecclesiastes 7:29; Isaiah 53:6). When tempted by Satan, a fallen angel who had rebelled against God, the first man and woman broke God's Law (Genesis 3:1–6). Consequently, sin, death, and damnation afflicted the whole human race, for the first man was the representative of us all (Romans 5:12, 5:16–17). Sin turned us against God and against each other in hatred, fear, and shame (Genesis 3:7–12). Every thought of our hearts became evil; no one is righteous or seeks God (Genesis 6:5; Psalm 14:1–3). The entire human race became spiritually dead under the rule of Satan. By nature, we are driven by the lusts of our bodies and minds and thus deserve the righteous anger of God (Ephesians 2:1–3). We are no longer the children of God, but children of the devil, whom we follow in his lies and hatred (John 8:42–44; 1 John 3:10).

God made man as a beautiful temple in which He would dwell and reign as King. But that was defiled and became a ruin filled with filth and garbage,

---

10. Westminster Shorter Catechism (Q. 1), in Dennison, *Reformed Confessions of the Sixteenth and Seventeenth Centuries in English Translation, Volume 4, 1600–1695*, p. 353.

and haunted by demons. When you view the ruins of God's image in man, you still sense how beautiful he once was, but you also see how tragically broken and empty of God's glory mankind has become (Romans 3:23). We should be deeply humbled by knowing that God gave us so much, yet we have fallen so far from Him.

Question 3: What Is the Bible, and How Is It Different from Other Books?

Immediately after the Fall of man, God revealed His promise of salvation (Genesis 3:15). Just as God created the world by speaking a word of command, so He began a new creation in the fallen world by His Word of promise. Humanity's hope rests upon the Word of God.

9. *God has spoken, and the Bible is His Word.* One of the most common phrases of the Bible is, "Thus saith the LORD." God spoke to and through His prophets in various ways (Hebrews 1:1). The words of the prophets are the words of God (Jeremiah 1:9, 36:6, 3:10–11). The Bible does not merely contain the Word of God, or just provide a way to experience the Word of God. Christ said the Bible *is* the Word of God, and it cannot be broken (John 10:35; see Matthew 5:17–18). Calling this Word "the Holy Scriptures," which means "the sacred writings," the Apostle Paul said, "All scripture is given by inspiration of God, and is profitable for doctrine, for reproof, for correction, for instruction in righteousness" (2 Timothy 3:16). Literally, "given by inspiration of God" means *God-breathed,* meaning that the Bible came straight from God's mouth. The Holy Spirit moved men to write exactly what God wanted them to say (2 Peter 1:20–21). Thus, whenever we read or hear the Bible, we should respond with humble reverence to God, for He is speaking (Isaiah 66:2).

10. *The Bible consists of the 66 books of the Old and New Testaments.* The Lord has given His Word since the beginning of time. He directed His prophet Moses to write down God's words (Exodus 17:14, 24:4, 34:27; Deuteronomy 31:9). The first five books of the Bible were thus called the the *Torah,* meaning "Law" or "Instruction"

Papyrus P52 from the Gospel of John by papyrologist Bernard Grenfell, 1920, as preserved at the John Rylands Library

The Uniqueness of the Bible

Here is the spring where waters flow,
to quench our heat of sin:
Here is the tree where truth does grow,
to lead our lives therein:
Here is the judge that stints the strife,
when men's devices fail:
Here is the bread that feeds the life,
that death cannot assail.
The tidings of salvation dear,
come to our ears from hence:
The fortress of our faith is here,
and shield of our defense.
Then be not like the hog that has
a pearl at his desire,
And takes more pleasure in the trough
and wallowing in the mire.
Read not this book in any case,
but with a single eye:
Read not but first desire God's grace,
to understand thereby.
Pray still in faith with this respect,
to fructify [produce fruit] therein,
That knowledge may bring this effect,
to mortify [put to death] thy sin.
Then happy thou in all thy life,
what so to thee befalls,
Yea, double happy shalt thou be,
when God by death thee calls.
— Preface to the Geneva Bible (1599)

(Joshua 8:31; Mark 12:26; Luke 24:44). After Moses died, God continued to add to the Scriptures through the works of other writers. In time, the Hebrew Bible contained three parts: the Law, the Prophets, and the Writings (including the Psalms). Christ affirmed all of these as the Word of God (Luke 24:44), and they now comprise the 39 books of the Old Testament. Through Apostles and prophets sent by Christ, the 27 books of the New Testament were added to the Holy Scriptures (2 Peter 3:16; compare 1 Timothy 5:18 with Luke 10:7). Though men have tried to add other books to the Bible, the 66 books of the Old and New Testaments are the only divinely inspired books in the world. Other writings may be helpful, but they are only human and fallible at best, and false and misleading at worst.

11. *The Bible is true in all that it teaches.* God cannot lie (Titus 1:2; Hebrews 6:18), and His knowledge is unlimited (Psalm 147:5). All Scripture is "given by inspiration of God" (2 Timothy 3:16). Therefore, we can trust that everything the Bible says is true and without error, whether it is Genesis or a genealogy or Paul's Epistle to the Romans. God will not let one of His words fall to the ground (1 Samuel 3:19; 2 Kings 10:10). Proverbs 30:5–6 says, "Every word

of God is pure: he is a shield unto them that put their trust in him. Add thou not unto his words, lest he reprove thee, and thou be found a liar."

We should trust the Bible because it is God's Word. On one occasion, the horse of Napoleon, emperor of France, began to race off wildly in the midst of a parade. A low-ranking junior officer suddenly stepped forward, seized the animal's bridle, and forced it to stop so that Napoleon could mount his steed. Once on the horse, Napoleon said, "Well done, *captain*." The soldier did not question this unexpected promotion, but asked, "In what regiment, sire?" The commander-in-chief answered, "In my own."[11] The soldier's response showed that he believed he was promoted because he had the word of the emperor. We might have difficulty believing the promises of God's Word, especially when God promises so much grace to poor, believing sinners. But we honor Him by believing His Word, for it is the word of the greatest Emperor, even the King of kings.

12. *The Bible is our supreme authority.* We should receive the Scriptures not as the word of mere men, though God used men to write them, but as the Word of God (1 Thessalonians 2:13). We must submit to what God has said: "For the LORD giveth wisdom: out of his mouth cometh knowledge and understanding" (Proverbs 2:6). Sometimes the Bible seems to contradict the teachings of the wise men of this world regarding history, science, human nature, salvation, and church growth. It is possible that, at times, we are misunderstanding what the Bible says. But whenever God's Word contradicts man's ideas, God must be right.

13. *Scripture alone is the divine rule of faith and obedience.* Some people seek spiritual wisdom by mystical experiences and contact with spirits, but apart from the Bible we have no spiritual light (Isaiah 8:19–20). Other people would add to the Bible the traditions of men to decide how to worship and serve God, but Christ warned, "Howbeit in vain do they worship me, teaching for doctrines the commandments of men. For laying aside the commandment of God, ye hold the tradition of men" (Mark 7:7–8). The only foundation for what we are to believe about God is the Word of God (Proverbs 22:17–19; Romans 10:17). The Scriptures are sufficient to teach us God's will, to rebuke us for our sins, to correct us unto repentance, and to train us in doing what is right (2 Timothy 3:17). Man-made acts

---

11. William H. Ireland, *The Life of Napoleon Bonaparte,* 4 vols. (London: John Cumberland, 1828), 1:123.

of devotion are not what God desires; He seeks obedience to His Word (1 Samuel 15:22). We should read the Bible with the intent to do God's will, whatever it may be.

14. *The basic message of the Bible is clear.* The Bible itself declares that some parts of it are hard to understand, although this does not excuse people who twist the Bible into false teachings (2 Peter 3:15–16). However, the Bible as a whole is not an obscure book that only experts can understand. Psalm 119:105 says, "Thy word is a lamp unto my feet, and a light unto my path." The fun-

Earthenware oil lamp

damental teachings of the Bible about salvation and righteous living are plain enough for anyone who studies it with an open mind to understand.

15. *All of the Scriptures center upon Jesus Christ.* The Lord Jesus said that the Scriptures "testify of me" (John 5:39). The entire Old Testament points ahead to Christ, His sufferings, His Resurrection from the dead, and the preaching of the gospel of Christ to all nations (Luke 24:44–47). The Apostles preached Christ (1 Corinthians 2:2; 2 Corinthians 4:5), and the New Testament revolves around Jesus Christ, His work, and the implications for those who believe in Him. Thomas Adams (1583–1652) said Christ is the sum and center of the whole Bible, for He is the pattern of our joy, the fountain of life, and the foundation of all happiness.[12] The Holy Scriptures are precious because they are able to make us "wise unto salvation through faith which is in Christ Jesus," even if you are a child (2 Timothy 3:15). Therefore, we should read Scripture to know Jesus Christ, so that we might trust Him and have eternal life (John 20:31).

Question 4: Who Is Jesus Christ, and What Did He Accomplish?

The Bible teaches that God exists in three persons: the Father, the Son, and the Holy Spirit (2 Corinthians 13:14). The Son of God is Himself "the mighty God" (Isaiah 9:6), which means that He is the Lord and Jehovah (Isaiah 10:20–21). He already existed in the beginning of creation (John

---

12. Thomas Adams, *Meditations upon Some Part of the Creed, in The Works of Thomas Adams* (1861–1866 repr., Eureka, CA: Tanski Publications, 1998), 3:224.

1:1) and shares in all of the Father's works (John 5:19). The gospel reveals all three persons of the Trinity (Galatians 4:4–6), but it centers upon the person and work of the Son. John 3:16 says, "For God so loved the world, that he gave his only begotten Son, that whosoever believeth in him should not perish, but have everlasting life." God shows the greatness and glory of His love supremely in His Son (Romans 5:8; 1 John 4:9–10). Why is this so?

16. *Christ is the only Mediator of the covenant of grace between God and sinners.* The Apostle Paul wrote that there is "one mediator between God and men, the man Christ Jesus" (1 Timothy 2:5). A mediator is a middle-man, or broker, between two parties hostile to each other — someone who can put a hand on each and bring them back together (Job 9:33). Our sins have made us enemies of God, but "God was in Christ, reconciling the world unto himself," and "we were reconciled to God by the death of his Son" (2 Corinthians 5:19; Romans 5:10). Only Christ can bring sinners to God. Jesus said, "I am the way, the truth, and the life: no man cometh unto the Father, but by me" (John 14:6).

Christ is the mediator of the covenant of grace. Throughout the Bible, God made "covenants of promise" with nations and individuals (Ephesians 2:12). Robert Rollock (c. 1555–1598) observed that "God speaks nothing to man without the covenant."[13] The covenant of grace is God's solemn promise of faithful love to sinners, through faith in the gospel. Jesus as mediator brings sinners into a covenant relationship with God so that He is their God and they are His people (Hebrews 8:6, 8:10). In a sense, Christ *is* the covenant, for all its promises are fulfilled in Him (Isaiah 42:6; 2 Corinthians 1:18–20). The covenant can be compared to a spiritual marriage between the Lord and His people (Isaiah 54:5, 54:10; Hosea 2:18–23).

17. *Christ is the Savior of a people given to Him by God.* His very name means Savior, for the angel said, "thou shalt call his name JESUS: for he shall save his people from their sins" (Matthew 1:21). Jesus knew that God had given Him particular people to rescue from sin and to give them eternal life (John 6:37, 6:39, 10:29, 17:2, 17:6, 17:9). Christ called those people "my sheep" for He was their Shepherd and laid down His life for them, even before they had heard His Word and believed in Him (John 10:16, 10:27–29). The Bible calls this God's "election" (Romans 9:11, 11:5), for

---

13. Robert Rollock, *A Treatise of God's Effectual Calling,* in *The Works of Robert Rollock,* ed. William M. Gunn (repr., Grand Rapids, MI: Reformation Heritage Books, 2008), 1:33.

God made a selection before time began of whom He would save (Ephesians 1:4). The Holy Spirit works powerfully in God's chosen ones so that they believe in Christ and follow in His holy ways (1 Thessalonians 1:4–6; 2 Thessalonians 2:13–14). Election is the friend of sinners because unless God first chooses us, we would never choose Him. Election teaches us that the gospel is a love story in which the Father chose a bride for His Son — His Church — to whom His Son came in love. Various denominations may vary slightly on the detailed understanding of election, like many doctrines.

18. *Christ serves as the prophet, priest, and King of His people.* Though some people think that "Christ" is the last name of Jesus, it is actually a title. Literally meaning "anointed," the title tells us that the Lord Jesus is the person sent by God to be the mediator. As the Heidelberg Catechism (1563) explains, Jesus is called Christ "because He is ordained of God the Father, and anointed with the Holy Ghost" to be our chief prophet to teach us God's way of salvation (Deuteronomy 18:18; Acts 3:22), our only High Priest to atone for our sins (Psalm 110:4; Hebrews 7:21), and our eternal King to rule us and defend us (Psalm 2:6; Luke 1:33).[14] We need a prophet because of our ignorance and spiritual darkness, a priest because of our sins that deserve punishment under God's justice, and a King to defend us from the assaults of Satan and the world, and to preserve us in the enjoyment of salvation in the face of our continuing weakness through sin.

19. *The Old Testament points to Christ through promises, appearances, and types.* The first promise of the Bible looked ahead to Christ by referring to "the seed of the woman" who would suffer and yet conquer the devil (Genesis 3:15). The prophets also wrote about the coming Savior (for example, Numbers 24:17; Psalms 2, 22, 45, 110; Isaiah 9:6, 52:13–53:12; Ezekiel 34:23; Micah 5:2). The Son of God was at work throughout the Old Testament, sometimes appearing as the Angel of the Lord (Genesis 16:7–14, 22:11–19; Exodus 3:1–6). God designed particular persons such as Adam, events such as the Passover, and institutions such as the temple and its sacrifices as types that were imperfect yet true pictures of Christ and His work (John 2:19–21; Romans 5:14; 1 Corinthians 5:7). So even the Old Testament believers put their trust in Christ (John 8:56).

20. *God's Son became a man, born of a virgin.* When it was time for God to fulfill His plan, He sent His Son into the world as a human being, a baby

---

14. Heidelberg Catechism (LD 12, Q. 31), in *Doctrinal Standards*, ed. Beeke, p. 40.

Christ's Obedience and God's Law

Active Obedience	Passive Obedience
He voluntarily obeyed God's commands	He voluntarily suffered God's wrath
He satisfied the Law's precepts	He satisfied the Law's penalties
He merits glory and immortality	He saves from condemnation

born of a woman (Galatians 4:4). The eternal Son of God became flesh (John 1:14), taking upon Himself a truly human nature like ours in every way except sin (Hebrews 2:14, 2:17, 4:15). This is called the *Incarnation.* Mary of Nazareth, a young Jewish woman who had not had sexual relations with any man, conceived the child by the power of the Holy Spirit, so that her child was holy and the Son of God (Luke 1:31–35). Jesus grew tired and slept, and yet the stormy wind and sea obeyed His commands (Matthew 8:23–27). The Council of Chalcedon (451) concluded from Scripture that Jesus Christ is "truly God and truly man," having "two natures" with "the property of each nature being preserved," and yet "one Person," not "two persons, but one and the same Son."[15] Therefore, the Savior as God-man (Colossians 2:9) is uniquely equipped to bring sinful human beings to God. No other religion can offer such a mediator as Christianity.

21. *Jesus preached the Word to Israel and confirmed it with miracles.* After living and working as an ordinary carpenter for many years, Jesus began His public ministry in Galilee and Judea at about age 30 (Luke 3:21–23). He went out in the power of the Spirit, preaching the gospel, healing the sick, and casting out demons (Matthew 4:23–24; Luke 4:14–44). His miracles, or works of supernatural power, testified that God was with Him (Acts 2:22, 10:38). He called men to repent and believe the gospel, and to lead a life of self denial, cross-bearing, and obedience to His commands (Matthew 16:24).

22. *Christ lived a perfect life of obedience and died for sinners.* God's Son came as the Servant to do His Father's will (Psalm 40:7–8; Isaiah 42:1; John 6:38, 17:4; Galatians 1:4). The essence of His saving work is His voluntary obedience to God (John 10:18; Philippians 2:8; Hebrews 10:7). Though Christ is the Lord and lawgiver (Mark 2:28), He came as a man "under the

---

15. The Symbol of Chalcedon, in *The Creeds of Christendom*, ed. Philip Schaff, rev. David S. Schaff (1931; repr., Grand Rapids, MI: Baker, 1983), 2:62.

law" (Galatians 4:4). He lived and died as the surety who paid the debt of sinful men to God (Hebrews 7:22).

Christ's obedience consists of two aspects, answering to the two sides of the Law. His active obedience is His flawless keeping of the Law's commands. He could claim that "the Father hath not left me alone; for I do always those things that please him" (John 8:29). Thus, He represents His people as a man of perfect righteousness in God's sight (Isaiah 53:11; Hebrews 7:26; 1 John 2:1). His passive obedience is His voluntary suffering of the Law's penalties against lawbreakers, the curse of God (Galatians 3:10, 3:13). Thus, Jesus represents His people as the One who has completely satisfied God's justice for the sins of His people and propitiated or appeased God's wrath (Romans 3:25; 1 John 2:2).

Christ finished this work of bringing everlasting righteousness when He died on the Cross (John 19:30). As prophet, His death glorified God and commended God's love to us (John 13:31; Romans 5:8). As priest, He offered Himself once for all as the only sacrifice that atones for sin (Hebrews 10:12). As King, He conquered sin and Satan at the Cross (Colossians 2:15).

Many people think that they can atone for their own sins against God by feeling sorry and doing good works. To such people, Anselm of Canterbury (c. 1033–1109) said, "You have not yet considered what a heavy weight sin is."[16] It would be better for the universe to be destroyed than to commit the least sin, for sin is rebellion against the will of the Creator. If sinners could be saved by works of the Law, then Christ died for nothing (Galatians 2:21). The fact that God sent His Son to die for sinners shows that the price to atone for sin must be so great that we could never save ourselves.

23. *Christ rose from the dead as the living Savior.* Christ submitted to the powers of death for a time, but the decree and promises of God made it impossible for death to hold Him (Acts 3:24). On the third day, Christ rose bodily from the dead, leaving behind an empty tomb (Matthew 28:1–10). He appeared many times to individuals and to various groups of people, proving that He was not a ghost but the resurrected Son of man (Luke 24:36–43; Acts 1:3; 1 Corinthians 15:4–8). He will never die again, for He has conquered death for His people (Romans 6:9; Revelation 1:18). His resurrected life is the life of His people. He said, "Because I live, ye shall live also" (John 14:19).

---

16. Anselm of Canterbury, *Why God Became Man*, 1.21, in *A Scholastic Miscellany: Anselm to Ockham*, ed. and trans. Eugene R. Fairweather, Library of Christian Classics (Philadelphia, PA: Westminster, 1956), p. 138.

24. *The Lord Jesus ascended into heaven and sat down at God's right hand.* After visiting with His disciples for 40 days, the risen Lord was received up into the glory of heaven (Acts 1:3, 1:9–11). He sat down at the right hand of God in total triumph and absolute glory (Psalm 110:1; Ephesians 1:20–22; Hebrews 8:1). On the basis of the merit of His finished work, He intercedes as a living priest for His people so they will be saved to the end (Romans 8:33–35; Hebrews 7:25). He also continues to act as the living prophet and King of His people (John 10:16; Acts 11:20–21), working in them through the Word by the Holy Spirit (2 Corinthians 3:3, 13:3–4), whose ministry He obtains by His priestly intercession (John 14:16).

25. *Christ poured out the Holy Spirit on His Church at Pentecost.* Shortly after the Lord Jesus went up to heaven, He gave the Holy Spirit in great power to His gathered church in Jerusalem at the Feast of Pentecost, just as He had promised (Acts 1:4–5, 1:8, 2:1–4). The Spirit has been at work among God's people since the beginning (Psalm 143:10; Isaiah 63:10–11, 63:14; Haggai 2:5); however, Christ received the Holy Spirit as God's reward for faithful service, when He was lifted up to God's right hand and poured out His fullness on His Church (Acts 2:32–36). The Holy Spirit now does greater works than ever before to save sinners as the Spirit of the risen Lord Jesus Christ.

When we consider the love of the Father in sending His Son, and the love of the Son in coming to do His Father's will, we should be overwhelmed at the goodness of God. Jesus Christ is worthy of all our trust, all our love, all our obedience, and all our suffering. Samuel Rutherford (1600–1661) was banished from his church for faithfully preaching the Word of Christ. Yet as he prepared to leave his beloved home and congregation, he wrote, "My chains are gilded with gold." How could he say that? No matter what he lost, he had Christ. Rutherford wrote, "No pen, no words, no skill can express to you the loveliness of my only, only Lord Jesus."[17] Is Jesus Christ lovely to you? Is He like treasure hidden in a field that you are willing to let go of everything to gain? If the Holy Spirit opens your eyes to see the glory of Jesus Christ in the gospel, you will never be the same.

Question 5: What Is Christ Doing Now by the Holy Spirit?

The Gospels record what "Jesus began both to do and teach," but His activity did not cease when He went to heaven (Acts 1:1). As the mediator of the

---

17. Samuel Rutherford, Letter to Alexander Gordon of Earlston, Sept. 5, 1636, in *The Letters of Samuel Rutherford*, ed. Andrew Bonar (1891; repr., Edinburgh: Banner of Truth, 2006), p. 143. We have slightly modernized his words.

new covenant, Christ is working now to fulfill God's promises (Hebrews 8:6, 8:10–12). Christ did not leave His disciples alone but sent them "another Comforter," that is, "the Spirit of truth." With the coming down of the Holy Spirit from heaven to dwell in and among the disciples, Christ Himself has come to them and lives in them (John 14:16–23). What then is the Lord Jesus doing through the Spirit?

26. *The Spirit convicts sinners of their sin.* Christ said that He would send the Spirit to convict the world of sin (John 16:8). The fulfillment of this promise began when the Spirit filled the Apostles with power to preach the Word at Pentecost. Those who listened were pierced in their hearts as if by a spiritual arrow (Psalm 45:5) and cried out, "What shall we do?" (Acts 2:37). Ever since then, the Spirit has been convicting sinners so that they sense the weight of their sins against God and cry out, "What must I do to be saved?" (Acts 16:30).

27. *The Spirit causes sinners to be born again by grace alone.* Conviction of sin is not salvation from sin, for you can feel guilt and fear and yet put off turning to God (Acts 24:25). Sinners are dead in their sins; only God can make them alive by His grace (Ephesians 2:4–5). God does not do this in response to any good thing in us. Rather, as a gift of sheer mercy to foolish slaves of sin, He pours upon needy sinners the Holy Spirit through Jesus Christ. The Bible calls this work of the Spirit a "washing" because it takes away the guilt of our sins, a "regeneration" because it is a new creation or beginning of life, and a "renewing" because it gives a person a new heart and a new life (Titus 3:3–7; see Ezekiel 36:25–27; 1 Corinthians 6:9–11; 2 Corinthians 5:17; Ephesians 2:10). Believers are said to be "born again" as the Holy Spirit engenders a new life in the soul — a life of faith, repentance, love, and obedience (John 3:1–8; 1 John 2:29, 3:9, 4:7, 5:1, 5:4, 5:18).

28. *The Lord Jesus gives sinners faith and repentance.* The gospel of Christ calls all sinners to repentance and faith (Mark 1:15; Acts 17:30, 20:21). Through the Word, the Holy Spirit offers Christ, and promises "that whosoever believeth in him should not perish, but have everlasting life" (John 3:16). By nature, men resist the Holy Spirit (Acts 7:51). The Word is a light that exposes their evil deeds, and so they hate the light, love the darkness, and do not come to Christ in faith (John 3:19–20, 6:44). When God regenerates a sinner by the Spirit, Christ draws that sinner to Himself by the power of His saving death (John 12:32–33). Christ was lifted up to

God's right hand to give repentance to sinners (Acts 5:30–31). Faith and repentance are gifts of Christ. Thus we read in Acts 11:20–21, "And some of them were men of Cyprus and Cyrene, which, when they were come to Antioch, spake unto the Grecians, preaching the LORD Jesus. And the hand of the Lord was with them: and a great number believed, and turned unto the Lord." Only Jesus can open our hearts and our eyes (Acts 16:14, 26:18).

We need the Holy Spirit to show us our sins and also to show us the Savior. When Hector Macphail (1716–1774), a minister in the Scottish Highlands, was traveling to some church meetings, he stopped for the night at a household along the way. There he met a kitchen maid who knew little of the Christian faith. He told the girl that when he returned he would give her a scarf if she would pray this simple prayer every morning and evening, "Lord, show me myself." A couple of weeks later he came back, and discovered that she was in great distress over her sins. She told the minister, "He has shown me myself, and oh, what an awful sight it is!" The kind minister then explained the good news of Christ's saving work, and taught her another simple prayer, "Lord, show me Thyself." Many years later, he was delighted to meet her again, now a grown woman and mother of children. She told him that in the first prayer she came to feel her need of the Savior, and in the second she came to see the Savior that she needed.[18] Sometimes even pastors need to learn this lesson. Macphail was once a minister who preached mere morality and good behavior. However, the Lord used his wife's spiritual hunger to deeply convict him of his sins, and he became a godly believer and preacher of Christ for the rest of his life.[19] Whether adults or children, we all need the Spirit to open our eyes to our horrible sinfulness and to the beauties and perfection of the Savior.

29. *God unites people to Christ by the Spirit.* When God saves sinners, the Holy Spirit dwells in them as His temple and lives within him; as a result, they become one with Jesus Christ (1 Corinthians 6:17, 6:19). The same Spirit who lives in Christ also lives in Christians. God joins them to Christ in a living relationship, just as the members of the body are joined to the head (1 Corinthians 12:12; Ephesians 4:15–16). Jesus promised His disciples that the Holy Spirit would "abide with you forever" (John 14:16), and so Christ is always with them, too (Matthew 28:20).

---

18. "The Highland Servant-Girl," in *The Church* (July 1, 1866), 187.
19. F.R. Webber, *A History of Preaching in Britain and America* (Milwaukee, WI: Northwestern Publishing House, 1955), 2:226–28.

> Man, accordingly, has no works in which to glory before God; and hence, stripped of all help from works, he is justified by faith alone. But we define justification as follows: the sinner, received into communion [oneness and fellowship] with Christ, is reconciled to God by his grace, while, cleansed by Christ's blood, he obtains forgiveness of sins, and clothed with Christ's righteousness as if it were his own, he stands confident before the heavenly judgment seat.
>
> — John Calvin, *Institutes*, 3.17.8

30. *God justifies sinners by faith in Christ alone.* God is a righteous Judge, and He demands that mankind be righteous in His sight. Yet fallen mankind has no righteousness in itself (Romans 3:10). When God joins believers to Jesus Christ by faith, He becomes their righteousness (1 Corinthians 1:30). God credits them with "the righteousness of God" because they are in Christ, and Christ took upon Himself the penalty of their sins (2 Corinthians 5:21). God the Judge "justifies" or declares them righteous, not because of their own righteousness or works of obedience, but only because of their faith in Christ and because of His works of obedience (Galatians 2:16; Philippians 3:9). John Calvin (1509–1564), a French Reformer who served in Geneva, said that justification by faith alone is the hinge of true religion and the sum of godliness.[20] In justification, the sinner finds himself standing before the Lord as Satan accuses him of his sins. But by faith in Christ, the Lord takes away the filthy garments of our guilt and clothes us with the beauty of Christ's obedience (Zechariah 3:1–5). That is good news for sinners!

31. *The Holy Spirit makes people holy so that they do works of love.* Joined to the Lord Jesus, believers also find that Christ is their sanctification (1 Corinthians 1:30). The Spirit of Christ now dwells in them as the Spirit of life and freedom (Romans 8:2, 8:9). He changes their basic mindset to one of submission to God's Word, and leads them to increasingly put sin to death and live as obedient children of God (Romans 6:17, 8:5–9, 8:13–15). Their souls become a battleground where the Spirit moves them to fight against the sinful desires that once delighted them (Galatians 5:16–17). The Spirit produces love, joy, peace, patience, gentleness, goodness, faithfulness, meekness, and

---

20. John Calvin, *Institutes of the Christian Religion*, ed. John T. McNeill, trans. Ford Lewis Battles, The Library of Christian Classics, XX, XXI (Philadelphia: Westminster Press, 1960), 3.11.1; 3.15.7.

Double Grace in Christ

Justification	Sanctification
For all in Christ	For all in Christ
By faith Alone	Faith and works
Change in legal status	Change in nature and character
Immediate and complete at conversion	Beginning at conversion but growing through life
Invisible	Visible in fruits
Right to heaven	Fitness for heaven
Necessary	Necessary

self-control in believers so that by the power of Christ's Cross they increasingly obey God's Law (Galatians 5:22–24). While Christians never stop sinning in this life (1 John 1:8–9), they have begun a work of cooperation with the God who works in them to sanctify them (Philippians 2:12–13).

We must never separate justification and sanctification, though they are distinct blessings. As Calvin explained, God lovingly gives Christ to us to be grasped and received by faith, so that when we are united to Christ, we receive a *double grace*. First, by justification God does not condemn us as a Judge but accepts us as a Father. Second, by sanctification we change and grow in holiness and purity of life.[21] Anyone who is not being sanctified in daily life has not been justified, and those who have been justified will be made holy.

32. *The Spirit gives believers assurance by enabling them to trust fully in God's promises of salvation in Christ and by testifying that they are God's children.* The promise of God to all who receive Christ by faith is that they are the children of God (John 1:12; Galatians 3:26). Yet how can someone know if he has saving faith in Christ? God does not will that His children live in uncertainty and fear of punishment, but that they enjoy assurance of their salvation. John said, "These things have I written unto you that believe on the name of the Son of God; that ye may *know* that ye have eternal life, and that ye may believe on the name of the Son of God" (1 John 5:13, emphasis added). As John explains elsewhere in that letter, the signs of having eternal life are Christ's love in our hearts and Spirit-prompted obedience to God's

---

21. Calvin, *Institutes*, 3.11.1.

commandments (1 John 2:3, 4:12–13). By growing in the grace of God, we become sure that God has chosen and called us to Himself (2 Peter 1:5–10). The Holy Spirit witnesses to us that we are children of God by granting us to experience the marks and fruits of grace (such as the Beatitudes in Matthew 5:3–12 and the fruits of the Spirit in Galatians 5:22–23), and by moving us to live as children of God, even in hard times (Romans 8:13–17).

33. *The Spirit of Christ moves God's children to pray to their Father.* Prayer is as essential to the life of a Christian as breathing. The Holy Spirit works in God's children as "the Spirit of adoption," causing them to pray to God as their Father (Romans 8:15). Even when believers do not know what to pray, the Spirit intercedes for them, expressing the groaning of their hearts (Romans 8:26). Real spiritual prayer is far more difficult than many people think; the grace of God is necessary for even the least spark of prayer. John Bunyan (1628–1688) confessed that when he went to pray, he found his heart so reluctant to go to God that he must first ask God "that he would take my heart, and set it on himself in Christ, and when it is there, that he would keep it there," and help him to pray by the Spirit despite his weakness.[22]

The Spirit teaches us to pray by the Scriptures. While the entire Bible is a help in prayer, the Lord Jesus gave us special instructions on how to pray in Matthew 6:9–13. This prayer teaches us to come to God with faith in His love and majesty, to pray primarily for His honor and reign among people, to pray for all our needs, especially our need for justification and sanctification, and to praise Him for His glory.

34. *Christ empowers His people by the Spirit to serve Him to the glory of God alone.* Christ sends His people into the world to make disciples of

> **The Lord's Prayer**
> After this manner therefore pray ye:
> Our Father which art in heaven,
> Hallowed be thy name.
> Thy kingdom come,
> Thy will be done in earth,
> as it is in heaven.
> Give us this day our daily bread.
> And forgive us our debts,
> as we forgive our debtors.
> And lead us not into temptation,
> but deliver us from evil:
> For thine is the kingdom, and the
> power, and the glory, for ever.
> Amen (Matthew 6:9–13).

22. John Bunyan, *The Doctrine of the Law and Grace Unfolded and I Will Pray with the Spirit*, ed. Richard L. Greaves (Oxford: Clarendon Press, 1976), p. 256–57. See also *The Works of John Bunyan*, ed. George Offor (1854; repr., Edinburgh: Banner of Truth, 1991), 1:631.

all nations, and promises that He will always be with them as the Lord of all (Matthew 28:18–20). Christ imparts His gifts to each Christian so that every believer can help to fill the world with God's Kingdom (Ephesians 4:7–10). The Holy Spirit distributes these "spiritual gifts" to every member of Christ's Church to serve as God has willed (1 Corinthians 12:7, 12:11). God's grace comes in various ways to different people, some more gifted to speak and others to serve, but the purpose of all gifts and ministry is the same: ". . . that God in all things may be glorified through Jesus Christ, to whom be praise and dominion for ever and ever. Amen" (1 Peter 4:11). The Reformers used a Latin phrase to capture this idea: *soli Deo gloria* ("glory to God alone")! No one in the Church should be lifted up to receive glory for himself, for we are only servants who exist to glorify God.

Question 6: What Is the Church of Jesus Christ?

God's purposes revolve around the people of Jesus Christ (Ephesians 3:10–11). They are His true Church — not the building and not only the pastors and other leaders, but all the people of God. Through the Church, God will glorify Himself in Jesus Christ forever (Ephesians 3:21). Jesus Christ loves the Church (Ephesians 5:25). The gospel does not call us to follow Christ all alone but to stand in unity with the Church (Philippians 1:27). What then is the Church?

35. *The Church is the body of all who are united to Christ.* The word *Church* means an assembly called together "that belongs to the Lord." The Church is people who are called by the gospel into holy fellowship with God's Son, Jesus Christ, and with each other (1 Corinthians 1:2, 1:9). The same Greek word was used of the assembly of Israel in the old covenant (1 Chronicles 13:2; Acts 7:38) for "the congregation of the LORD" (Deuteronomy 23:1–3, 23:8; 1 Chronicles 28:8). The true Church consists of all those who are redeemed by Christ's death (Ephesians 5:25). It is the body of the Lord Jesus Christ (Ephesians 1:22, 5:23; Colossians 1:18, 1:24), joined to Him as closely as His own flesh and bones (Ephesians 5:29–30). The Church is Christ's creation and possession, for He said, "I will build my church" (Matthew 16:18). Joined with the One who sits at God's right hand, the Church is a heavenly people even while some of its members are still pilgrims on earth (Hebrews 12:22–24; see Ephesians 2:7; Philippians 3:20).

36. *The Church is one body with many diverse members.* The Apostle Paul wrote, "For as the body is one, and hath many members, and all the members

of that one body, being many, are one body: so also is Christ. For by one Spirit are we all baptized into one body, whether we be Jews or Gentiles, whether we be bond [slave] or free; and have been all made to drink into one Spirit" (1 Corinthians 12:12–13). Racial, cultural, and social differences cannot break the bond of oneness created by the Holy Spirit in Christ. Like the eye, hand, and foot of a human body, the members of Christ's Church have different strengths and weaknesses; every member is needed, needs the others, and should serve each other (1 Corinthians 12:14–26).

37. *The Church is organized into local congregations where Christians are members.* The vast majority of the uses of the word for *church* in the New Testament refer to particular churches gathered in specific locations (e.g., Acts 9:31, 15:41; Romans 16:1). Each Christian is a part of the life of the body (Ephesians 4:16; Colossians 2:19). Christians are not only members of Christ, but are also members of one another (Romans 12:4–5). Each church should have a clear sense of the value of membership as it receives new members (Acts 2:41, 2:47) and removes others when they refuse to walk in obedience to God despite repeated attempts by fellow Christians to lovingly call them to repent of sin (Matthew 18:15–17).

38. *Christ has given pastors to edify and equip His Church.* The risen and ascended Lord Jesus gives spiritual shepherds to build up His people (Acts 20:28; Ephesians 4:11–12). He calls them to devote themselves to prayer, the ministry of the Word, watching over the souls of their people, and living in holiness as an example to others (Acts 6:4; 1 Timothy 3:1–7, 3:14–15, 4:11–16; 2 Timothy 3:8–4:5; Titus 1:5–9). They are accountable to Christ to shepherd each member of the flock of God entrusted to them (Hebrews 13:17; 1 Peter 5:2). Each believer should be a member of a local church so that he is under the pastoral care of elders and overseers who can direct and comfort him (1 Corinthians 16:15–16; James 5:14).

39. *God commands His Church to keep His moral Law.* The moral Law of God obligates all mankind to obedience (Romans 3:19–20). God has placed His Law in the form of conscience in every man to commend right and condemn wrong (Romans 2:14–15). However, the Lord gave a special revelation of His Law to His people Israel after redeeming them from slavery in Egypt. He summarized its moral principles in the Ten Command-ments, which the Lord spoke directly to Israel and wrote down on stone tablets, which were stored in the ark in the Most Holy Place (Deuteronomy

> **Summary of the Ten Commandments**
> (1) Thou shalt have no other gods before me.
> (2) Thou shalt not make unto thee any graven image.
> (3) Thou shalt not take the name of the LORD thy God in vain.
> (4) Remember the sabbath day, to keep it holy.
> (5) Honor thy father and thy mother.
> (6) Thou shalt not kill [murder].
> (7) Thou shalt not commit adultery.
> (8) Thou shalt not steal.
> (9) Thou shalt not bear false witness against thy neighbor.
> (10) Thou shalt not covet . . . any thing that is thy neighbor's.

10:1–5). The Scriptures record these laws twice, which is also a sign of their great importance (Exodus 20:3–17; Deuteronomy 5:6–21). The commandments are stated in brief in the sidebar.

God does not give His Laws to keep people from real happiness, but for their good (Deuteronomy 10:13). If a three-year-old girl sees her father's blood-pressure medicine, she might think it is candy. Her father's command that she not eat the medicine is not an act of hatred but of great love. If she tries to eat it anyway and her father stops her, she might cry, pout, and think he is mean. However, she is being foolish and should trust her father. In the same way, we should trust that God's Laws are good for us, even if it seems at times that He is holding us back from enjoying something sweet and pleasant. Obedience to God enriches life.

Though Christ released His people from the ceremonies of the Old Testament, the Ten Commandments continue to direct their lives (1 Corinthians 7:19). Jesus Christ said that He did not come to abolish God's Laws, but to fulfill them. He taught that these commandments require not only outward action but obedience in the heart. Thus, the commandment against murder also prohibits sinful anger and hatred, and the commandment against adultery also prohibits sexual lust (Matthew 5:17–28). The Law shows us how much we all need a Savior, for even people with outwardly moral lives are full of sinful thoughts and desires. It also points us beyond mere good behavior to a life of obedience that springs from goodness in the heart.

40. *God summarizes His moral Law in love for God and man.* When asked what the greatest commandment is, Christ did not select any of the Ten

Commandments but instead summarized them all in two commandments: "Thou shalt love the Lord thy God with all thy heart, and with all thy soul, and with all thy mind. This is the first and great commandment. And the second is like unto it, Thou shalt love thy neighbour as thyself. On these two commandments hang all the law and the prophets" (Matthew 22:37–40). In the great commandment (Deuteronomy 6:5), Christ summarized the first four of the Ten Commandments, and in the greatest commandment the last six (Leviticus 19:18).

The Law and the gospel belong to each other. The Law shows us how sinful we are, so that we run to the gospel for salvation. The gospel shows us how loving God is so that we love Him in return and seek to obey His commandments. How can anyone not love God when his eyes are opened to see the love that sent God's Son to die for sinners? Bernard of Clairvaux (1090–1153) asked, "What is the result of contemplating such great mercy and mercy so undeserved, such generous and proven love, such unlooked-for condescension, such persistent gentleness, such astonishing sweetness?" He said that the result is that the church "runs eagerly" after God, "yet even when she has fallen wholly in love she thinks that she loves too little because she is loved so much. And she is right. What can repay so great a love and such a lover?"[23] Ultimately, Christians learn to love God for His own sake, "not because he meets your needs," as Bernard said, but rejoicing that you and all things exist *for Him*, and therefore finding no greater delight than to know His will is being done in your life.[24]

41. *God calls the Church to submit to civil authorities.* Though Christ is the only King of His people, His kingdom is not of this world. It is not a political kingdom but a spiritual kingdom created and preserved by the teaching of the truth (John 18:36–37). God has instituted human authorities ("magistrates") to rule in the political sphere, granting them the right to use force to punish evil-doers. God commands Christians to submit to the authorities as appointed by God, giving them appropriate honor and obedience (Romans 13:1–7; John 19:11). However, if the civil government or any human authority commands us to act against God's will, then we must say with the Apostles, "We ought to obey God rather than men" (Acts 5:29).

---

23. Bernard of Clairvaux, *On Loving God*, 4.13, in *Bernard of Clairvaux: Selected Works*, trans. G.R. Evans, The Classics of Western Spirituality (New York: Paulist Press, 1987), p. 184.
24. Ibid., p. 194–96.

42. *Christ blesses the Church with Christian freedom.* The Apostle Paul summarized the gospel in the word *liberty* because "Christ hath made us free" (Galatians 5:1) and "where the Spirit of the Lord is, there is liberty" (2 Corinthians 3:17). The essence of Christian liberty is "the glorious liberty of the children of God" (Romans 8:21). In the coming age, this will mean freedom from all sin and misery so that believers will behold the glory of Christ as God's beloved children (Romans 8:17–18; Revelation 21:3–7). In this present age, this means that Christ has released believers from the curse of God's Law, its rigorous demands for perfection in order to please God, the enslaving power of sin, the ceremonies of the old covenant, the tyranny of human expectations, and shame upon their consciences (John 8:31–36; Romans 6:17–18, 8:1–2; 1 Corinthians 7:22, 9:19, 10:25–31; 2 Corinthians 3:17–18; Galatians 5:1–2). It is not freedom to live however we please (2 Peter 2:19), but the liberty to serve God, for His commands are "the law of liberty" (Galatians 5:13; James 1:25; 1 Peter 2:16). In Christ, God overlooks the imperfection of our works and is genuinely pleased with our obedience (2 Corinthians 5:9, 5:19; Philippians 4:18), welcoming us to come freely into His presence (Ephesians 2:18, 3:12).

43. *God calls the Church to public worship.* Christ promises His special presence to the Church when it gathers in His name (Matthew 18:20, 28:18–20). Christians should also worship privately, for every Christian is a temple of the Holy Spirit (1 Corinthians 6:19). Believers should meditate on the Word and pray and sing privately and with their families every day (Psalm 1:2; James 5:13). They should talk with their children at home about the Word (Deuteronomy 6:6–7). However, the Bible's primary emphasis is on the temple of the Church (1 Corinthians 3:16; Ephesians 2:21–22). Christians worship God not as isolated individuals but as living stones fitted together into a holy temple in which His people declare His praises (1 Peter 2:5, 2:9). Christians who are filled with the Word and Spirit show this by building one another up through the teaching, preaching, and singing of the Church (Ephesians 5:18–20; Colossians 3:16). God has set aside one day a week for rest and worship, which since the time of Christ's Resurrection has been the first day of the week — the Lord's Day (Revelation 1:10). People who claim to be Christians but do not regularly participate in public worship, unless physically unable, are missing out on God's special presence, breaking the command of God, and discouraging His Church (Hebrews 10:22–25).

The Church is crucial to our spiritual growth, for we need each other. Wilhelmus à Brakel (1635–1711), a Dutch minister, wrote, "How refreshing it is for God's children, being hated by the world, to have communion with each other, to make their needs known to each other, and in love and familiarity may enjoy each other's fellowship!"[25] We isolate ourselves to our own harm.

A pastor once visited a Christian who had not attended his church's worship services for some weeks. The man sat down with his pastor by a fireplace, waiting to be rebuked for not coming to church. Instead, the pastor sat silent, looking into the fire. After a while, he took a pair of metal tongs from beside the fireplace and removed a coal from the center of the fire, placing it by itself on the stones of the hearth. The pastor and Christian watched as the glowing coal died out. Then the man looked at the pastor with pain in his eyes, and said, "I understand. I will be in church next Sunday."

44. *God marks the Church with baptism as a sign of its union with Christ.* God's people under the old covenant were required to keep a complex system of rituals for worship. Christ fulfilled the rigorous demands of the old covenant so that these ceremonies no longer bind believers (Colossians 2:16–17). Instead, Christ instituted a simple form of worship with only two visible signs. The first is baptism with water in the name of the Father, the Son, and the Holy Spirit (Matthew 28:19). Baptism does not save us, however. Paul wrote, "For Christ sent me not to baptize, but to preach the gospel," for "the preaching of the cross" is "the power of God" for salvation (1 Corinthians 1:17–18). Baptism is a sign of union with Christ (Galatians 3:27), especially in His death and Resurrection (Colossians 2:12). Reflecting upon one's baptism with faith in the gospel is a means of growth in grace, as the Apostle Paul shows when he appeals to the baptism of Christians to remind them that they have died and risen with Christ and therefore cannot live in sin (Romans 6:1–4).

45. *God provides the Church with the Lord's Supper as a sign of its communion with Christ.* The second sign is the sacred eating of the bread and drinking of the cup as instituted by Christ with His disciples on the night on which He was betrayed. Through the Lord's Supper, the Church remembers and proclaims Christ's death until He comes again (1 Corinthians 11:23–26). It is a sign of the new covenant between God and Christians, ratified by

---

25. Wilhelmus à Brakel, *The Christian's Reasonable Service*, trans. Bartel Elshout, ed. Joel R. Beeke (Grand Rapids, MI: Reformation Heritage Books, 1993), 2:100.

Christ's broken body and shed blood (Luke 22:20). Like baptism, the Lord's Supper is no guarantee of salvation (1 Corinthians 10:1–5), but it can be a means of fellowship with Christ (1 Corinthians 10:16). Eating a meal is a visible representation of receiving spiritual nourishment and love from the Savior

Bread and cup for the Lord's Supper

by the exercise of faith in His Word (see John 6:35; Revelation 3:19–20).

46. *Christ commissioned the Church to preach the gospel to all nations.* After rising from the dead, the Lord Jesus explained to His disciples that the Scriptures foretold His death and Resurrection, and the preaching of repentance and forgiveness of sins in His name to all nations (Luke 24:44–46). The Lord entrusted this mission to the Church (John 20:21). He said to the Apostles, "All power is given unto me in heaven and in earth. Go ye therefore, and teach all nations, baptizing them in the name of the Father, and of the Son, and of the Holy Ghost [Spirit]: Teaching them to observe all things whatsoever I have commanded you: and, lo, I am with you always, even unto the end of the world. Amen" (Matthew 28:18–20). The mission of the Church continues today and will continue until the gospel is preached in every nation despite persecution, false teachers, and spiritual coldness (Matthew 24:9–14). The Lamb has purchased people of every nation, ethnic group, and language, and He will bring them into His kingdom (Revelation 5:9, 7:9, 7:14).

Trusting such promises, the Church should expect great things from God and attempt great things for God, as William Carey (1761–1834) said a year before leaving England to spend the rest of his life as a missionary in India.[26] The basic stance of biblical Christianity is optimism, not based on pride in mankind, but on confidence in the Lord who has promised to spread His Kingdom throughout the world by the gospel, and who will one day bring His Kingdom in open glory to the earth.

---

26. "Narrative of the First Establishment of This Society," *Periodical Accounts Relative to a Society Formed among the Particular Baptists for Propagating the Gospel among the Heathen,* no. 1, in *Periodical Accounts Relative to the Baptist Missionary Society, Volume 1* (Clipstone: J.W. Morris, 1800), p. 3, downloaded from "Expect Great Things; Attempt Great Things," http://www.wmcarey.edu/carey/expect/ (accessed Nov. 3, 2014).

Question 7: How Will Christ Bring His Kingdom to Earth in Glory?

The Christian life can be summarized in the words *faith, love,* and *hope* (1 Corinthians 13:13; 1 Thessalonians 1:3, 5:8). Faith looks back to the finished work of Christ and relies upon Him for salvation. Love responds to Christ's work by adoration of God and faithful service to other human beings. Hope looks forward to the future, when God's promises will come to full fruition (Romans 8:24–25). Biblical Christianity is a future-oriented religion that looks beyond this life to another world. It teaches that when the bodies of men die, the spirits of wicked men go to a place of conscious, fiery punishment, but the spirits of the righteous enter into Christ's presence in heavenly glory to rest from their labors (Luke 16:19–26, 23:43). However, the future hope of Christianity goes far beyond life after death; it looks primarily to everlasting communion with Christ, to the appearing of God's glory and Kingdom and the beginning of a new age.

47. *Jesus Christ will come again in visible glory.* The "blessed hope" of Christians is "the glorious appearing" of their God and Savior Jesus Christ in the Second Coming (Titus 2:13). Christ said, "For the Son of man shall come in the glory of his Father with his angels; and then he shall reward every man according to his works" (Matthew 16:27). He will come with a glory that is visible to all nations (Matthew 24:30, 26:64), returning bodily from the skies just as He ascended physically to heaven (Acts 1:9–11). Presently, believers on earth yearn to know their Bridegroom better. They long to see the One whom they love, but on the day of the Lord, their Bridegroom will return to their great joy (Matthew 9:15, 25:1–10; Revelation 19:7–9).

48. *Christ will raise from the dead everyone who has ever lived.* By the sheer power of His word of command, Christ will resurrect all deceased human beings, both the righteous and the wicked (John 5:28–29; Acts 24:15). The wicked will rise to experience everlasting shame, but Christ's people will shine with radiant beauty, sharing in the glory of their Lord (Daniel 12:2–3; Colossians 3:1–4). Christians who are still alive when Christ raises the dead will not die but be suddenly changed to share in His glory and immortality (1 Corinthians 15:51–53; 1 Thessalonians 4:13–18).

49. *The Son of God will judge everyone according to his works.* When Christ returns, He will come as the glorious King to sit in judgment on behalf of His Father, so that all men will honor the Son as they honor the

Father (Matthew 25:31; John 5:22–23). All living, intelligent beings will bow before Jesus Christ and acknowledge that He is Lord (Philippians 2:10–11). Using His divine knowledge of every heart and every act, Christ will judge everyone, great or small, rich or poor, according to his works (Romans 2:6–11, 2:16; Revelation 2:23). The Apostle Paul wrote, "For we must all appear before the judgment seat of Christ; that every one may receive the things done in his body, according to that he hath done, whether it be good or bad" (2 Corinthians 5:10).

50. *Christ will damn the wicked to forever suffer God's anger in hell.* The Lord Jesus will say to sinners, "Depart from me, ye cursed, into everlasting fire, prepared for the devil and his angels" (Matthew 25:41). Regardless of what outwardly religious acts or even miracles they may have done, their lifestyle of sin and failure to repent, put their faith in Christ, and obey God's commands will show that Christ never knew them in a saving relationship (Matthew 7:21–23). Condemned by the mouth of God incarnate, "these shall go away into everlasting punishment" (Matthew 25:46). This is hell, which Jesus repeatedly described as a place of "weeping and gnashing of teeth" (Matthew 8:12, 22:13, 24:51, 25:30; Luke 13:28). Christ once died as the Lamb (Revelation 5:6), but now the wicked will face the wrath of that Lamb (Revelation 6:17). Thomas Manton (1620–1677) said, "The majesty of Christ is the cause of their torments; and his look and face will be terror enough to sinners" (see 2 Thessalonians 1:9).[27] Their pain will never end (Revelation 14:10–11).

51. *Christ will bless the righteous with the enjoyment of God's love forever.* To the righteous, whose lives are characterized by love and compassion for other believers in their sufferings, Jesus Christ will say, "Come, ye blessed of my Father, inherit the kingdom prepared for you from the foundation of the world" (Matthew 25:34). Manton wrote, "To the wicked he saith, 'Depart,' but to the saints, 'Come.' . . . Come, draw near to me."[28] The essence of all that Christians have desired, and the glory of heaven, is to be near to the Lord forever (1 Thessalonians 4:17–18).

In the judgment of the righteous, their works will be assessed. They are not saved by their works, but their good works show that God has saved them and changed their nature through Jesus Christ (Matthew 12:33;

---

27. Thomas Manton, *Several Sermons upon the Twenty-Fifth Chapter of St. Matthew,* in *The Complete Works of Thomas Manton* (London: James Nisbet, 1872), 10:24.
28. Ibid., 10:49.

Ephesians 2:8–10). Though their acts of obedience deserve nothing (Luke 17:10), Christ will graciously reward even the smallest acts they have done for Him in obedience to His Word (Matthew 10:42). He will be like a master rewarding his servants for their work after a long absence, saying, "Well done, good and faithful servant; thou hast been faithful over a few things, I will make thee ruler over many things: enter thou into the joy of thy lord" (Matthew 25:23).

For all eternity, the triune God will glorify Himself by pouring out the riches of His grace and kindness upon His people through Jesus Christ (Ephesians 2:7). They will live with God in the new heavens and new earth where there is no sin or sadness (Revelation 21:1–3). They will look into the face of the Lord who died for them, and His glory will surround them and fill them (Revelation 22:4–5). The hope of believers is that "when he shall appear, we shall be like him; for we shall see him as he is" (1 John 3:2). Then Christians will truly know what it means to glorify God and enjoy Him forever.

The eternity of heaven shows us that God's love for His people is boundless. Someone might fear that he requires so much grace, love, and patience from God that it will all be used up and God will cast him away. But that will never be true of any who believe in Christ alone for salvation.

Charles Spurgeon (1834–1892) was coming home at the end of a weary day feeling depressed, when he remembered the promise, "My grace is sufficient for thee" (2 Corinthians 12:9). It struck him so forcefully that it made him laugh because it was absurd to think that God could run out of grace. He imagined a little fish being afraid that he might drink the River Thames dry, and the great river saying in response, "Drink away, little fish, my stream is sufficient for thee."[29] When Christ says, "If any man thirst, let him come unto me, and drink," He is not promising trickles of grace but "rivers of living water" (John 7:38).

Conclusion: The Simplicity and the Depth of Biblical Christianity

The study of biblical Christianity reveals a beautiful tapestry of many truths woven together. We have put our face close to the tapestry and traced over 50 threads of truth that run through it. However, when we step back from the tapestry, a single picture appears: *God gives eternal life to sinners through*

---

29. William Williams, *Personal Reminiscences of Charles Haddon Spurgeon* (London: Religious Tract Society, 1895), p. 19.

Jesus Christ. Thus, Christianity is both simple and deep. As Gregory the Great (540–604) said, "Scripture is like a river, broad and deep, shallow enough here for the lamb to go wading, but deep enough there for the elephant to swim."[30] Children, like little lambs, can understand enough of the Bible to trust Jesus Christ and follow Him as His disciples. Yet strong and mature Christians, who may be called elephants of the faith, still find truths in the Bible that are beyond their comprehension. Since God is God, we would expect to never completely understand Him. The great question is not whether you fully understand the Lord, but whether you know and trust Him.

This chapter has sought to summarize biblical Christianity by answering seven questions, which may be stated as the following.

1. Who is God, and how is He active in the world? God is one God existing eternally in the three persons of the Trinity. In His essence, God is the Lord, a being of infinite love and righteousness. He created all things visible and invisible. He provides for and controls all things.

2. Who are we, and where do we come from? God created the first man out of the earth. God made mankind, male and female, in His image for His glory, but we fell into sin and misery when the first man, Adam, disobeyed God's commandment. Yet God gave Adam and Eve a promise of grace, the first of many promises contained in the Bible.

3. What is the Bible, and how is it different from other books? The Bible, which consists of the 66 books of the Old and New Testament, is the written Word of God. Since God is God and cannot lie, the Bible is true in all that it teaches, and it functions as our supreme authority. It teaches all the essentials, what we must believe about God, and what God requires from us as His creatures. The basic message of the Bible is clear, and the central message that runs throughout the book is Jesus Christ.

4. Who is Jesus Christ, and what did He accomplish? Christ is the only mediator of the covenant of grace between God and the people given to Him by God. In particular, Christ serves as the prophet, priest, and King of His people. The Old Testament points to Christ through promises, appearances, and types. The New Testament tells us how God's Son was born of a virgin, grew to an adult man, preached to Israel, and worked miracles. He lived a perfect life of obedience and died for sinners to satisfy God's justice.

---

30. Gregory the Great, *Moralia or Commentary on the Book of Job*, Epistle, sec. 4, http://faculty.georgetown.edu/jod/texts/moralia1.html (accessed November 3, 2014).

Christ rose from the dead as the living Savior. He ascended into heaven, sat down at God's right hand, and poured out the Holy Spirit at Pentecost.

5. What is Christ doing now by the Holy Spirit? He convicts sinners of their sin, and causes people to be born again into a new life of faith and repentance. God unites people to Christ by the Spirit, and justifies sinners by faith in Christ alone. The Holy Spirit also makes people holy so that they do works of love. The Spirit gives believers the privileges of the children of God, including an assurance of God's fatherly acceptance, a heart to pray to the Father, and the power to serve Him so that He is glorified in the Church.

6. What is the Church of Jesus Christ? The Church is a people united to Christ. It is one body with many diverse members. It is organized into local churches in which Christians are members under the rule and care of Christ's appointed pastors. God commands His Church to keep His moral Law, which Christ summarized as love for God and man, and to submit to the authority and laws of civil government. However, in obeying God the Church is blessed by Christ with true spiritual freedom as children of their Father. God calls the Church to public worship, to baptism as a sign of union with Christ, and to partake of the Lord's Supper as a sign of oneness with Christ. Christ commissioned the Church to preach the gospel to all nations, calling sinners to come to Christ and become part of His Kingdom.

7. How will Christ bring His Kingdom to earth in glory? Jesus Christ will come again to earth in visible majesty and power. He will raise the dead, and judge all of us according to our works as signs of what we truly are. Christ will damn the wicked to suffer in hell forever, but He will bless the righteous to enjoy God's love forever.

There is, however, a final question that must be asked. *Are you a Christian?* Biblical Christianity is not just a set of ideas; it is an experience and a way of life. As William Ames (1576–1633) wrote, the major point of Christian teaching is "living to God." Christians do so "when they live in accord with the will of God, to the glory of God, and with God working in them."[31] Do you know the God of the Bible personally? Have you come to see, sense, and feel the evil of your sins against Him? Do you believe the Bible, submitting to it as the Word of God? Have you put your trust in

---

31. William Ames, *The Marrow of Theology,* trans. John D. Eusden (Grand Rapids, MI: Baker, 1968), 1.1.1, 6.

Christ alone to save you from God's wrath and your sins? Have you received Him as your prophet, priest, and King? Do you love and participate in the Church as a member of a local congregation that believes in the biblical faith? When Jesus Christ returns, will that be the happiest day of your life? Is Christ your Lord, your life, your righteousness, your love, and your hope? If this is not the case with you, then the Bible warns that you are in extreme danger. Today might be the day you meet your Maker, either through death or at Christ's return. Do not let it end without calling upon the name of the Lord Jesus Christ to save you.

If you would like to learn more about biblical Christianity, let me offer a few recommendations. First, read the Bible. There is no substitute for reading and thinking about the Word of God. Second, pray continually that God would show you both yourself and Himself, so that you would repent of sin and believe in Christ alone for salvation. Third, find a good church that believes, preaches, and practices the kind of biblical Christianity this chapter has described; be there every time it meets for worship and prayer, and make its members your best friends. Fourth, do not just read and hear the Word of God — *do* it. Put it into practice. Finally, read good books about Christian teachings, godliness, and the lives of exemplary Christians. God has blessed us with a rich heritage of good literature; we should make use of it. A disciple of Christ is always a learner.

Summary of Biblical Christianity Beliefs

Doctrine	*Biblical Christianity Teaching*
God	God is triune, existing in three persons of the Godhead — Father, Son, and Holy Spirit; God is eternal and transcendent; the Son took on flesh to dwell on earth
Authority/ Revelation	God and His revelation of Himself in the 66 books of the Bible
Man	Man is created in the image of God; mankind is fallen as a result of Adam's sin; man is unable to do good and please God on his own
Sin	Any thought or action that is contrary to the will of God as revealed in the Bible

Salvation	Salvation is possible through the substitutionary atonement of Jesus on the Cross and His Resurrection; individuals receive salvation by repentance and faith in Jesus' work on their behalf; works have no merit for salvation; salvation is a free gift received by God's grace alone; eternal punishment in hell awaits those who die in their sins, while eternal joyful existence with God awaits those who receive salvation
Creation	The universe and all that is in it was created out of nothing in six, 24-hour days about 6,000 years ago; all living things were created according to their kinds in supernatural acts of God; mankind was specially created by God in supernatural acts

Chapter 3

A Brief Introduction of Christianity

Bodie Hodge

From the Apostolic Age to the Present

Christianity exploded in the first century and rightly so. Many were eye-witnesses of the risen Savior prior to His ascension into heaven to sit on the right hand of the throne of God. Massive numbers of Jews believed (3,000 in one day, no less) and became the saved remnant; then Gentiles (non-Jews) began repenting and pouring into ranks of the saved through the blood of Jesus Christ.

During these early years, it was not easy to be a Christian and follow Christ. Christians were undergoing persecution from the Jews, from people practicing local religions, and from those in the Roman government. Paul was beaten, flogged, left for dead, and arrested. The New Testament outlines much of this persecution.

Nero, the Roman emperor, was extremely cruel to Christians beginning about A.D. 64 until his suicide about three

Nero is one of the most well-known persecutors of the early Christian Church.

and half years later. It was under Nero that Church fathers recorded Paul's beheading and Peter's crucifixion upside-down (around A.D. 68). During Nero's reign, the Jews and Romans went to war, and by A.D. 73, Judea was utterly devastated. During the war, Jerusalem was destroyed and the Temple sacrifice had come to an end. Persecution from the Jews was significantly reduced, but others continued persecuting Christians. And in the mid-90s the Roman Emperor Domitian began attacking Christians.

For a couple of centuries, Christianity continued to explode, even in the face of persecution. Then the first Christian-influenced Roman emperor emerged. His name was Constantine. This obviously eased tensions and the harshness that Christians endured. By the power of the Holy Spirit, the gospel had moved slowly but surely from a few people near Jerusalem to the entire Roman Empire. Constantine moved the center of power from Rome to Constantinople. After his death, the Empire split into two: an eastern and western empire, and so the Roman Empire officially went into the pages of history. The western empire declined steadily with the sack of Rome in A.D. 410 and finally ceased about A.D. 476, according to most historians.

The eastern empire (Byzantine Empire) continued until the fourth Crusade in the 12th century. But even with some minor recoveries, the empire finally went into the pages of history in 1453 when the Ottoman Turks finally took Constantinople for good.

The Church had grown progressively, especially in Europe, the Middle East, and North Africa, but Muhammad began conquering much of Arabia and beyond in the early 600s. Muslims then controlled and stopped the growth of the Church by execution and compulsion by the sword for their new unitarian-based religion (i.e., the non-Trinitarian view of one God that they call Allah; Christ is not seen as God, but a prophet).

Christianity, though still growing in quiet circles in the Muslim world, has been forced into silence or persecution since those days. Even in our day, it is not uncommon to hear of Christians put to death in the name of Allah in Muslim lands on a regular basis.

The first major church split occurred in 5th century A.D. when the Oriental Orthodox churches (Coptic, Ethiopian, Eritrean, Syriac, Indian Orthodox, and Armenian Apostolic) split from the rest of the Church over and definitions at the Council of Chalcedon in A.D. 451. Another significant split in the Church called the Great Schism happened about A.D. 1054. It split the Church into the Eastern Churches led by Patriarch Michael Cerularius and the Western Church of Rome led by Pope Leo IX. There had been growing tension of numerous issues between the churches of the east and west as early as the 5th century. This culminated in the split.[1]

Fast forward, and we find that some within the Western Church were fed up with the direction that the Church was heading. It continued to move away from the Scriptures with indulgences (paying for dead loved ones to be freed from purgatory) and many other unbiblical doctrines and stances (e.g., image worship and praying to saints) that the popes of the Roman Catholic Church were imposing. These types of precursors finally led to the Reformation, generally acknowledged as beginning with Martin Luther, whose initial intention was to reform the Roman Church and get the leadership back to the authority of the Word of God. Luther's reform of the Roman Church failed, and Luther was commanded to recant of his "heresies."

Martin Luther
(Retouched restoration art by Lucas)

But Luther remained faithful to his testimony of standing on the Word of God as the supreme authority while standing before Roman Church authorities. This was the popular event that detonated the Protestant Reformation as people began going back to the Bible for their theology, ultimately leading to the Protestant denominations that we have today (from Anglican, Lutheran, Reformed, and Anabaptist to Presbyterian, Baptist, Mennonite, Methodist, Amish, Evangelical Free, Assemblies of God, Wesleyan, Christian and Missionary Alliance, Nazarenes, to independent churches, Christian churches, community churches, Calvary Chapels, and many more). While these denominations vary in particular doctrinal positions and styles of worship, all claim to look to the Bible rather than popes and tradition as the standard of truth.

---

1. The final nail in the coffin was over the *filioque* clause; for more on this see "What is the filioque clause/filioque controversy?" GotQuestions.org, http://www.gotquestions.org/filioque-clause-controversy.html.

Rome then reacted with the Counter-Reformation to reclaim those who left the grip of Rome. They formed the Jesuit order and began the Inquisition, among other tactics. Though not the main point of the meeting, the Council of Trent of the Roman Catholic church elevated the apocryphal books to a full canon status to support many of the doctrines disputed by the Protestant reformers (hence why Catholics and Protestants have two different listings of authoritative books in the Old Testament).[2]

Without going into the extensive distinctions of denominational doctrinal breakdowns, this is where we are today. The Church, by and large, is still evangelizing. It is reaching vast parts of the world and is still growing — as God wills until Christ returns.

The key to a healthy church, whether in its global or local expressions, is the authority of God and His Word in all areas — whether science, theology, history, logic, morality, education, and so on. Every deviation from the truth of God's Word has the mind and hand of man trying to supersede God's Word. The Church is not immune to these corrupting influences. We can and have all fallen short, and this brief review of Church history should simply remind us of this: we must humble ourselves to the truth of God's Word from the very first to the very last verse. God will never be wrong. We can be wrong, but God will never be wrong.

---

2. Protestants also enjoy the apocryphal books, but do not see them as inspired by God but valuable for history like Josephus (a Jewish historian in the first century) and other ancient books. Most Catholics such as Jerome (who translated the Bible from Greek and Hebrew into Latin about A.D. 400) up until the Council of Trent viewed the apocrypha as *second canon* or *deuterocanon* (useful but not Scripture).

Chapter 4

How Is Roman Catholicism Different?

Dr. Terry Mortenson

Since becoming a Christian in 1972, I have lived in four different countries and have shared the gospel and taught the Scriptures in 23 countries, many of them dominated by Roman Catholicism. While I have met numerous devout Roman Catholics who believe many of the things that I also believe, I have found that almost none of them had a good understanding of the gospel or a confident assurance of their salvation. From talking to many others, I learned that my interactions with Catholics are not unique, but commonplace. Why is that? That's what we want to explore in this chapter.

Today there are about 1.3 billion Roman Catholics in the world. The largest number of Catholics is in Brazil (128 million, which is 63 percent of Brazil), Mexico (98 million, 81 percent), the Philippines (81 million, 80 percent), the United States (76 million, 24 percent), and Italy (50 million, 81 percent). The top ten countries are these five followed by France, Congo, Columbia, Spain, and Poland, which together account for just under half of all Catholics.[1]

Compared to other major religions, as of 2013, Christianity has about 2.2 billion adherents (a little over half of them Roman Catholic), Islam about 1.8 billion, atheism/agnosticism about 1.1 billion, Hinduism about

---

1. http://en.wikipedia.org/wiki/Catholic_Church_by_country: statistics from 2010 put the number at 1.228 billion in the various independent countries of the world and about five million more people in several dependent territories.

Saint Peter's square from the St. Peter's Basilica's dome in Vatican City

1 billion, and Buddhism about 376 million (numbers tend to slightly vary depending on the source).

The Roman Catholic Church is the only religion that has its own political territory as an independent state (Vatican City, a walled enclave of 110 acres within the city of Rome) with its own coinage (though it uses euros), its own central bank, and diplomatic relations with other countries.[2]

The Roman Catholic Church claims to be the only church on earth that has Jesus Christ as its founder, and the pope is its earthly head. Within the church there are two dominant *rites* or *forms of liturgy*: the Western, Roman or Latin rite (practiced by the vast majority of Catholics) and the Eastern rite (found mainly in Romania, Ukraine, and India).[3] All other professing

2. http://en.wikipedia.org/wiki/Vatican_City.
3. Though the liturgies are different, there is complete unity on doctrine and submission to the pope.

Christians (Eastern Orthodox, liberal Protestants, evangelicals, etc.) are considered "separated brethren" whom the church wants to draw back into itself, where it claims the true gospel is preserved and taught.

Given the Roman Catholic Church's claims and its size, we need to carefully compare its doctrines and practices to what is taught in the Scriptures and the gospel revealed therein.

Structure of the Roman Catholic Church

The Roman Catholic Church is led by the pope, who is considered to be the supreme representative of Jesus Christ on earth. He serves for life or until he resigns. His headquarters are at the Vatican in Rome. Under the pope is the College of Cardinals, which is responsible to elect the pope and assists the pope in the governing of the church.

A cardinal is usually an ordained bishop or archbishop. Next down the chain of leadership are the archbishops, who are responsible for Catholic churches in a very large area, such as Boston, Chicago, or New York City. Under the archbishops are the bishops, who each head up a diocese and supervise all the church's teaching and activities in the various parishes of the diocese to ensure faithfulness to the doctrines of the church. Each parish is led by a priest, who gathers the faithful Catholics for worship, instruction, and service.

Besides these main positions of leadership, there are many other administrative positions serving along with these clerical leaders, as well as hundreds of religious orders of nuns, monks, and missionaries carrying out the work of the Roman Catholic Church. One of the most well-known and influential orders is the Society of Jesus, whose members are called Jesuits. They control most Catholic educational institutions of higher learning and were a dominant force in the bloody Counter-Reformation response to the early Protestants.

History of the Roman Catholic Church

Church history is a vast subject, and we have space only for the briefest sketch related to the development of the Roman Catholic Church.[4] The church claims that its history goes all the way back to the Apostle Peter. Catholics believe and teach that Jesus ordained Peter as the head of the

---

4. For an in-depth layman's treatment of church history, including the historical developments of Roman Catholicism, Eastern Orthodoxy, and Protestantism, see Earle E. Cairns, *Christianity Through the Centuries* (Grand Rapids, MI: Zondervan, 1996, 3rd ed.), and Bruce Shelley, *Church History in Plain Language* (Nashville, TN: Thomas Nelson, 2013, 4th ed.)

worldwide Church. Since they believe that Peter became the first bishop of the church in Rome, all his successors in that church (eventually called popes) also are the head of the true worldwide church. We will come back to these claims later.

The modern Roman Catholic Church is very different from the early Church in organization, doctrine, and practices. Changes took place gradually over many centuries. According to the New Testament, Jesus Christ is the cornerstone and the Apostles and prophets were the foundation (Ephesians 2:19–20). The Apostles taught that there were two offices in the Church: elders (also called bishops and pastors) and deacons.

The first three centuries of Christian history were a time of persecution, (sometimes extreme) throughout the entire Roman Empire. In addition to persecution, the Church had to deal with false teaching and heresy within. By the middle of the 2nd century, some church leaders were talking of the "catholic" (meaning universal) Church (but this did not mean Roman Catholic Church) and the role of bishop began to be distinct from and superior in authority to elders or pastors (also called priests). Soon bishops in key cities (Jerusalem, Antioch, Alexandria, and Rome, and in the fourth century, Constantinople) rose to preeminence. The Roman bishop was especially important because Rome was the capital of the empire, the city where the Apostles Paul and Peter were martyred, and the Church there was one of the largest and wealthiest. By A.D. 300, the doctrine of apostolic succession of bishops, each of whom had monarchial rule over a congregation, was a reality, and the bishop of Rome came to be seen at the "first among equals" of the bishops.

Also during this time a separation between clergy and laity developed, with the bishop being regarded as a dispenser of grace, and some began to view the Lord's Supper (communion) as a sacrifice to God. Whereas in the New Testament baptism was administered to a person after he believed, in the 2nd and 3rd centuries some bishops began to practice infant baptism as an initiation into the Christian faith.

Church and State Together

Things changed significantly in 313 when after almost three centuries of persecution against Christians the Roman emperor Constantine fully legalized Christianity. He restored confiscated property to the Church, made Sunday a day of worship and rest, and transformed Byzantium (modern-day Istanbul) by renaming it Constantinople and making it his eastern capital. He also ordered the building of the Church of the Holy Sepulchre near the supposed tomb of Jesus in Jerusalem, which soon became the holiest place in Christendom. Although Constantine was not baptized until 337 on his deathbed, and it is questionable if Constantine was ever truly saved, he called for and presided over the

The First Council of Nicea, wall painting at the church of Stavropoleos, Bucharest, Romania

Council of Nicaea (325) to solve the Arian doctrinal controversy about the deity and humanity of Christ. By 381, under Emperor Theodosius I, Christianity became the state religion of the empire. So began a long, increasingly spiritual and moral corruption of the church as first the state ruled the church and later the church, through the popes, controlled the state.

In the 4th through 6th centuries, monasticism[5] and asceticism[6] arose as people reacted against the growing worldliness of the institutional church. In addition to the Council of Nicaea, other emperors convened four other ecumenical (universal) councils of bishops to iron out doctrinal problems. These strengthened the office of the bishop and the power of the Roman bishop grew. Some historians consider Leo I as the first Roman Catholic pope because as he took the episcopal throne in Rome in 440, he began to assert his supremacy over all other bishops, a claim that was soon affirmed by the Roman emperor, but not by all the other bishops. Although he did not claim the title "pope,"[7] he certainly established the doctrinal basis of the papacy.

---

5. This is a system or way of life in which a person withdraws from society to live alone or in a residence (monastery) with other monks for religious reasons to try escape the corruption in the world.

6. An ascetic (monk or hermit) is someone who for religious reasons lives with rigorous self-denial and self-discipline without the usual pleasures and comforts of life.

7. The word "pope" comes from the Latin *papa* meaning father. "The term 'pope' itself is not crucial in the emergence of the doctrine of papal primacy. The title 'papa' originally expressed the fatherly care of any and every bishop of his flock. It only began to be reserved for the bishop of Rome in the sixth century, long after the claim of primacy." Shelley, *Church History in Plain Language*, p. 133.

During these centuries many pagans came into the church through mass conversions (i.e., a tribal prince or territorial leader "converts" and then forces everyone under his leadership to "convert"). To help such converts feel comfortable in the church, priests and bishops introduced the use of images into the liturgy and the veneration of angels, saints (martyrs from earlier centuries), relics, pictures, and statues.

More "holy days," including Christmas, were officially added to the church calendar. In addition to the sacraments of baptism (especially of infants) and the Lord's Supper (also called the Eucharist or Mass) the prominent theologian Augustine and other church leaders added new sacraments:[8] marriage, penance,[9] confirmation[10] and extreme unction.[11] Augustine also helped to develop the doctrine of purgatory (a spiritual state of final purification after death and before entering heaven). The veneration of Mary, the mother of Jesus, developed rapidly during this time. Belief in her perpetual virginity (introduced into churches in the middle of the second century) and in her sinlessness placed her at the head of the list of "saints,"[12] and festivals in her honor sprang up. People began to believe that she had intercessory powers to influence Jesus on behalf of believers. Veneration of other saints included the selling of relics from their bodies.

During the 7th through 8th centuries, the Eastern church dealt with the threat of Islam while the Western church sought to evangelize the Teutonic hordes of northern and western Europe. Gregory I ("the Great") became bishop of Rome in 590. He never accepted the title of "universal pope," but he exercised all the power and prerogatives of later popes, significantly

---

8. In the Catholic Church, a sacrament is a visible rite that imparts grace to the recipient who properly receives it. *Catechism of the Catholic Church* (Citta del Vaticano: Libreria Editrice Vaticana, 1997, second edition), #1131. Hereafter referred to as CCC, this document was approved and promulgated by Pope John Paul II. I will always cite the paragraph numbers (rather than page numbers) of the CCC, which is also available online.

9. Acts of fasting, prayer, and almsgiving are signs of a conversion of the heart toward God and serve as a means of forgiveness. CCC, #1431 and 1434.

10. Combined with baptism and the Eucharist, confirmation is part of Christian initiation more perfectly binding the person to the Catholic Church. CCC, #1285.

11. This is when the priest anoints with oil a person who is very sick or near death. CCC, #1499 and 1512.

12. While the Catholic Church uses the word "saint" to refer to all believers (as does the New Testament), in this instance and many others in Catholic literature (and through this chapter) the word refers to a special person whom the pope has canonized as a "saint" because of his or her "life of heroic virtue" or faithfulness to God through martyrdom (CCC, #828). But the New Testament never uses the word with this specialized meaning.

increased the wealth of the bishopric of Rome, and made the church a formidable power in politics. While he believed in the verbal inspiration of Scripture, he regarded church tradition as an equal authority, upheld the idea of purgatory, and considered each performance of the Eucharist to be a sacrifice of Christ's body and blood.

Pope Leo III crowns Charlemagne

In 800, Pope Leo III crowned the king of the Franks, Charlemagne, as emperor of the revived Roman Empire. The pope ruled the spiritual realm, and the emperor ruled the temporal realm, constituting together (so they thought) the kingdom of God on earth. But when Charlemagne died in 814 his Frankish empire quickly disintegrated, and for the next 250 years there was a power struggle between the popes and the Frankish rulers. Many of the more than 40 popes between 800 and 1054 were corrupt; in 1045, three popes claimed supreme authority at the same time!

Other developments at this time included the initial teaching that by divine miracle the bread and wine of the Eucharist was actually transformed into the body and blood of Christ (though without changing appearance). This further strengthened the power of the local priest and the pope and paved the way for the official doctrine of transubstantiation in 1215 and the final definition of it by the Council of Trent in 1545. In the 10th and 11th centuries reforms were made to deal with the wealth and corruption of the monasteries.

The Zenith of the Papacy

The Great Schism of 1054 occurred when the pope of Rome and the patriarch of Constantinople excommunicated each other because of disagreement about the use of unleavened bread in the Eucharist. This permanently divided the Roman Catholic Church (hereafter referred to simply as Catholic Church) from the Eastern Orthodox, and the mutual excommunications were not removed until 1965. After the schism and until 1305 the papacy attained its zenith of temporal and spiritual power over all of life in the Roman Empire.

In 1059, under Pope Nicholas II, the election of the pope was taken out of the hands of the Roman populace and given to the College of Cardinals, a group of priests and bishops in and near Rome that had begun in the 4th century.

From the beginning of his enthronement in 1073, Pope Gregory VII enforced the celibacy of the priesthood, and in his *Dictatus Papae* (1075) he declared the absolute supremacy of the papacy and that the Catholic Church has never erred and would never err.

According to church tradition, the rosary (a repetitious prayer with beads) became a part of the Catholic veneration of Mary after an "apparition of Mary" in 1214, and it has been promoted and modified by many popes from the 16th century to the present.[13]

Seven or eight major crusades and many minor ones occurred in the years between about 1095 and 1290. These were intended to resist the advance of Islam in Europe and retake control of the Holy Land. The popes offered crusading armies earthly riches and eternal blessings for killing Muslims, heretics, and anyone who rejected the supremacy of the pope.

Two important religious orders were formed in the 13th century. The pope approved the Franciscans in 1209 and the Dominicans in 1216. The Franciscans lived by alms and were committed missionaries for the church whereas the Dominicans produced scholars for the church.

The Catholic theologian Aquinas (1225–1274) presented arguments that cemented the doctrine of the perpetual virginity of Mary for her whole life, which added to the veneration she was already receiving as the "Mother of God."

The years 1305–1377 witnessed the "Babylonian Captivity" of the papacy, as French popes ruled not from Rome but Avignon, France. In 1378, the non-French objected, leading to the "Great Schism" of the papacy (not to be confused with the Great Schism of 1054), which lasted until 1415. For most of that time there were two popes, one ruling from Rome and the other from Avignon, each with his own College of Cardinals. The last six years the church suffered (as it had in 1045) under three simultaneous popes contesting the claims of each other! Finally, one resigned and the Council of Constance deposed the other two. After taking power from the College of Cardinals the Council elected a new pope.

---

13. http://en.wikipedia.org/wiki/Rosary, accessed February 27, 2015.

Attempts at Reformation

As we have noted, from time to time attempts were made to reform (return to the teachings of the Bible) the Catholic Church, though with limited success. John Wycliffe (1330–1384) made another attempt. An English priest, he translated the Bible into English so that the common man could know the truth and see the errors in the church. He died of disease but the Catholic authorities later exhumed his body and burned him as a heretic in 1428. The Czech priest Jan Hus adopted the ideas of Wycliffe and was burned at the stake in 1415 for his efforts at reform. But these men were preparing the ground for a German Augustinian monk named Martin Luther. In 1517, he nailed his Ninety-Five Theses on the door of the church in Wittenburg, Germany, exposing many doctrinal and practical errors in the Catholic Church.

One of those practices was the selling of indulgences — paying money to the church to obtain forgiveness for oneself and to free one from the temporal penalty of sin. Declared a dogma by Pope Clement VI in 1343, it was extended in 1476 by Pope Sixtus IV so that a person could pay to shorten a loved one's time in purgatory. Luther and others condemned this and other doctrines and practices that perverted the gospel and undermined the authority of Scripture. But the Catholic Church firmly rejected his efforts, triggering the Protestant Reformation, which led eventually to the development of Lutheran, Reformed, and Anglican state churches and various Anabaptist free churches mainly in northern and western Europe. Viewing Protestants as heretics, the Catholic Church fought this movement through the Counter-Reformation.

Throughout the 16th century its popes sought to make financial and spiritual reforms and new religious orders were founded which contributed to missionary expansion to Africa, Southeast Asia, Latin America, and Quebec led by the Jesuits, Franciscans, and Dominicans.

Pope Paul III authorized the Order of the Jesuits in 1540 to raise up well-educated preachers to convert the heathen and reconvert the Protestants. He also set up the Roman Inquisition in 1542, which, following practices of the Medieval Inquisition in the 1200s and the Spanish Inquisition in the 1400s, used confiscation of property and imprisonment as punishment for becoming Protestant.

The inquisitions were first instituted by Pope Innocent III (1198–1216), who used his crusading armies to torture and kill thousands of Albigensians and Waldensians (godly Christians that the church condemned as heretics) in southern France and northern Italy. Over the next 600 years, 75 popes ordered, devised, or approved some of the world's most brutal and horrific methods of torture and murder to try to force Jews, Muslims, and Bible-believing Christians to abandon their faith and trust in the "Holy Mother Church." Tens of millions of people (some historians estimate 50 million) suffered and died under these wicked and completely unbiblical inquisitions as the popes sought to establish their absolute rule over the church and society.[14]

In 1559, Pope Paul IV issued the Index of Prohibited Books, which forbid Catholics (on threat of damnation) from reading Protestant literature. The list was kept up to date until 1966 when Pope Paul VI abolished it.

A few years earlier, Pope Paul III had called the Council of Trent (1545–1563) to respond to the Protestant teaching. The Council affirmed that the Apocrypha[15] and church tradition are equal in authority with the Bible. It also affirmed the doctrine of transubstantiation as well as the doctrine of purgatory that the Council of Florence (1439–1445) had elevated to official dogma. It anathematized (condemned to hell) anyone who held to the biblical teaching of justification by faith alone, in Christ alone, through grace alone, as proclaimed by Protestant reformers. Still in force today,[16] those anathemas clearly condemn truly Bible-believing evangelicals.

After the Council of Trent, the structure and doctrines of the Catholic Church remained essentially as they are today. But a few new doctrines were officially added.

- In 1854, Pope Pius IX made the doctrine of the Immaculate Conception of Mary (that she was born without a sin nature and never sinned her whole life) an official dogma.

14. See the thoroughly documented research of David A. Plaisted, "Estimates of the Number Killed by the Papacy in the Middle Ages and Later," http://www.cs.unc.edu/~plaisted/estimates.html. This documentary film features, among others, a former Roman Catholic priest and a Roman Catholic layman who have done much research on the Inquisitions: https://www.youtube.com/watch?v=Rx8PdvOELvY&list=PLE1CB721E3CA65D76&index=94&feature=plpp_video. It describes and pictures a number of the torture techniques devised by the popes and also documents and quotes from Roman Catholic historians and official Catholic teaching.

15. Jewish writings between the last book of the Old Testament and the time of Jesus.

16. Except with respect to the Lutheran World Federation: http://www.vatican.va/roman_curia/pontifical_councils/chrstuni/documents/rc_pc_chrstuni_doc_31101999_cath-luth-joint-declaration_en.html. See point 2, paragraph 13, on "The Doctrine of Justification as Ecumenical Problem." However, theologically conservative Lutherans would not accept this Lutheran-Catholic joint declaration.

- Pope Pius IX also convened the First Vatican Council (1869–1870) and persuaded the gathered bishops to declare the doctrine of papal infallibility (i.e., the pope speaks without error when he speaks *ex cathedra* on faith and morals).

- Since Pope Pius IX, many popes have called Mary "Mediatrix," because, it is claimed, she intercedes for all believers and is the principal dispenser of grace. Pope Pius X (1903–1914) and other later popes have declared in papal documents that Mary is "Co-Redemptrix," referring to her indirect and unequal role with Christ in the redemption process.

- In 1950, Pope Pius XII declared the dogma of the Assumption of Mary (that she did not die and suffer decay but was miraculously taken body and soul to heaven).

The conflict between Roman Catholics and Protestants became very bloody during the Thirty Years' War (1618–48). Millions died from the conflicts, disease, and famine, and it took decades for devastated towns and villages to be rebuilt. But it did bring an end to religious persecution in Europe (except for the late 20th-century Catholic-Protestant conflicts in Northern Ireland), and the modern European system of states emerged from this conflict.

For the next 150 years, monarchs endeavored to limit papal power in their countries. From the end of the 18th century up to World War I, the Catholic Church lost many of its physical possessions and much of its political influence. Since then, the church has had increasing difficulties due to the spread of communism, liberal theology, and the havoc created by World War II. But it has pursued ecumenical relationships with the Eastern Orthodox and Protestants and has been significantly influenced by the charismatic movement.

The Second Vatican Council (1962–1965) created no new dogmas. But it was more open toward Protestants, calling them "separated brethren" rather than heretics and schismatics. It encouraged Bible reading (with interpretation directed by the Magisterium, the teaching authority of the bishops, cardinals, and popes) and partnerships with Protestants in Bible translation efforts and in social issues (such as abortion). It permitted the Mass to be conducted in the mother tongue of the worshipers (rather than only in Latin). It increased attempts for ecumenical unity with the Eastern Orthodox and Protestant churches, though without any compromise on official Catholic doctrine. It also opened the door to Roman Catholic dialogue with representatives of non-Christian religions.

It is clear from this survey of history that the doctrines, organization, and practices of the Catholic Church have been developing slowly since early in the post-apostolic age. The claim that the Roman Catholic Church goes back to the Apostles is simply not true. Some of its doctrines and practices do, but many others do not, and many of those are of very recent origin in the last few hundred years. As we shall see, they also seriously contradict the teaching of Scripture. It should also be noted that according to the teaching of the New Testament and the experience of the churches in the first few decades (as evidenced in the Book of Acts and the Epistles) it does not take centuries or even decades for false teaching and false practices to gain considerable influence among Christians.

But Roman Catholicism and Eastern Orthodoxy were not the only expressions of Christianity during the centuries leading up to the Protestant Reformation. There were local bodies of believers in North Africa, the Middle East, Europe, and elsewhere who sought to hold fast to the Word of God and sound doctrine and the true gospel of salvation through faith in Jesus Christ alone, and they opposed the growing corruption of the Catholic and Orthodox churches. Much of what we know about them, however, comes from the Catholics and Orthodox who condemned and persecuted them as "heretics." Therefore, they were not in a position to develop scholarship after the church became wedded to the state at the time of Constantine.[17]

One result of the efforts by the Catholic Church after Vatican II to seek ecumenical unity with non-Catholics was the "Evangelicals and Catholics Together" document signed or endorsed in 1994 by a number of prominent evangelical leaders and scholars and their Roman Catholic counterparts.[18] In sufficiently vague language to obtain agreement, this unofficial and non-binding document avoided serious doctrinal differences. Many evangelicals, including this author, believe that has contributed to a decline in doctrinal discernment among evangelicals. Before discussing some of the

17. Two excellent works, still available, that discuss these believers are Leonard Verduin, *The Reformers and Their Stepchildren* (Grand Rapids, MI: Eerdmans, 1964) and E.H. Broadbent, *The Pilgrim Church* (1931, republished by Resurrected Books in 2014).

18. Many evangelicals, including this author, were and are very concerned about this agreement between evangelicals and Catholics, for reasons discussed at http://www.gty.org/resources/Sermons/GTY54.

more important differences, we should note some of the important agreements between evangelicals and Catholics.

Roman Catholic Doctrines and Practices That Are Consistent with Scripture

There are many important doctrines and practices in the Catholic Church that are right in line with Scripture, and on these evangelicals can agree with Roman Catholics. These include:

1. Roman Catholicism is monotheistic: there is only one God who created the world. And the Church is Trinitarian. It teaches that God exists as three co-equal, co-eternal, and distinct persons: Father, Son (Jesus Christ), and Holy Spirit, each of which is fully God, and yet there is only one God.

2. The church affirms that the whole Bible is the inspired Word of God. The Bible teaches "without error that truth which God, for the sake of our salvation, wished to see confided to the Sacred Scriptures."[19] But the Roman Catholic Bible contains more books than the Bible used by Jews and Protestants, as explained later.

3. The church holds to the full deity and full humanity of Jesus Christ, His virgin birth and sinless life, and that He performed miracles, died for our sins, rose bodily from the dead, ascended to heaven, and will come again to judge the living and the dead.

4. It teaches that men and women are made in the image of God but are sinful and in need of salvation. Those who do not repent of their rebellion and respond to Christ's mercy and grace in this life will suffer eternally in hell, separated from God.

5. It teaches that marriage is sacred and instituted by God and is defined as one man united to one woman. It officially declares that homosexual acts are of "grave depravity" and "intrinsically disordered" and "under no circumstances can they be approved."[20] (However, Pope Francis seems to be warming up

---

19. CCC, #107.
20. Ibid., #2357.

to homosexuals as he gave VIP seats to members of an LGBT group from America at his October 15, 2014, speech at the Vatican.[21])

6. The Church has been strongly pro-life and therefore anti-abortion in both public declarations and actions, and historically this was so before many evangelicals began to express their concern about the holocaust of abortion.

Doctrines and Practices That Are Contrary to Scripture

While the Catholic Church holds to many beliefs and practices that are consistent with Scripture, it is critical to understand many other very important teachings and practices of the church that are incompatible with the Word of God. Here are just a few.

The Supreme Authority in the Church

The New Testament Apostles established only two offices in the local churches: elders and deacons. A comparison of the relevant passages[22] shows that the terms "elder" (or presbyter, from the Greek word *presbuteros*), "pastor" (or shepherd), and "overseer" (or bishop, from the Greek word *episkopos*) all refer to the same position of leadership. The Apostles gave no instructions for higher levels of leadership over multiple churches or over all churches in a large city or over the whole world. The New Testament indicates that the 1st-century local churches were to be independent congregations under the Lordship of Christ and the authority of the Word of God.

In contrast, as we have seen in the historical developments of the spread of Christianity in Western Europe, some bishops began to claim authority over more than one congregation, then over a city, and then over the worldwide church, and along the way cardinals, archbishops, and patriarchs were added to provide leadership under the absolute monarchy of the papacy.

The Catholic Church claims that the pope is infallible when he speaks *ex cathedra* ("from the chair of Peter"); when he speaks as the supreme teacher of the church he is incapable of teaching any false doctrine. Likewise, the bishops do not and cannot err when they teach religious and moral doctrines. This Magisterium (consisting of the pope and the bishops) is endowed

---

21. http://www.christianpost.com/news/vatican-gives-vip-seats-to-gay-positive-lgbt-catholic-group-at-pope-francis-speech-reportedly-first-gesture-of-its-kind-134384/.
22. 1 Timothy 3; Titus 1–2; 1 Peter 5; Acts 6 and 20:28–32.

"with the charism of infallibility in matters of faith and morals."[23] And, it is claimed, God has given this Magisterium the task of providing the correct interpretation of the Scriptures for the rest of the church.[24]

How does the Magisterium accomplish this task of interpreting Scripture without error? First, it includes in the Catholic version of the Scriptures the apocryphal books,[25] which are not accepted as the Word of God by either the Jews or Protestants.[26] But in those books, the popes and bishops find justification for some Roman Catholic doctrines, such as praying for the dead. Second, the Catholic Church equates unwritten "Tradition" with written Scripture. She "does not derive her certainty about all revealed truths from the holy Scriptures alone. Both Scripture and Tradition must be accepted and honored with equal sentiments of devotion and reverence."[27] This is because "Sacred Tradition and Sacred Scripture make up a single sacred deposit of the Word of God."[28] In Roman Catholic doctrine, "Tradition" (capital 'T') is the Church's "doctrine, life, and worship."[29] It is "a current of life and truth coming from God through Christ and through the Apostles to the last of the faithful who repeats his creed and learns his catechism."[30] And "Sacred Scripture is written principally in the Church's heart rather than in documents and records, for the Church carries in her Tradition the living memorial of God's Word."[31]

So the Catholic Church leadership relies heavily on man-made ideas and practices accumulated over the centuries as the basis for their interpretation of the Word of God.

The pope also claims his supreme authority by asserting that he inherited it from Peter who, according to official Catholic doctrine, was the bishop of Rome and the first pope over the worldwide church. "The Roman Pontiff, by reason of his office as Vicar [i.e., earthly representative] of Christ, and as

23. CCC, #890–891.
24. Ibid., #85.
25. Ibid., #120.
26. For reasons why the apocryphal books are rejected as Scripture, see https://answersin-genesis.org/OnlineBible/help/helpeng/source/html/apocryphainfo.htm and https://an-swersingenesis.org/bible-questions/is-the-bible-enough/.
27. CCC, #82.
28. Ibid., #97
29. Ibid., #78.
30. *The Catholic Encyclopedia*, quoted in James G. McCarthy, *The Gospel According to Rome: Comparing Catholic Tradition and the Word of God* (Eugene, OR: Harvest House, 1995), p. 291.
31. CCC, #113.

pastor of the entire Church has full, supreme, and universal power over the whole Church, a power which he can always exercise unhindered."[32]

But nowhere does the New Testament make either of those papal claims (infallibility and authority), nor does it teach the infallible authority of the bishops or describe any kind of magisterium. In fact, the Bible never says that Peter was in Rome (though we know from church history that he was martyred there), which is strange if he was the head of the church in Rome. And if he was the bishop of Rome, it is equally strange that when Paul wrote his letter to the church in Rome in about A.D. 57, he greeted many believers by name (Romans 16), but does not mention Peter. How could Paul overlook greeting the bishop, especially since his letter was giving very authoritative teaching to the Church there? Furthermore, Paul says that the Christian Church was built on the foundation of the Apostles (plural) and prophets, with Jesus Christ as the cornerstone (Ephesians 2:19–20).

It is also significant that in Peter's two letters written to all Christians in Asia Minor (modern-day Turkey) he describes himself as an Apostle and bondservant of Jesus Christ (1 Peter 1:1; 2 Peter 1:1), not as bishop of Rome. In Peter's first letter he humbly exhorts elders of the various churches as "a fellow elder," not as a supreme elder in authority over them and says they should not "lord over" the Christians that they shepherd in their flocks under the authority of the Chief Shepherd, Jesus Christ (1 Peter 5:1–4). In 2 Peter 3:2, he admonishes his readers to follow the commandments of Jesus and "your apostles" (plural), not his writings as uniquely authoritative.

It is true that Peter gave the "birthday sermon" of the Church to Jews in Jerusalem on the day of Pentecost (Acts 2). But it was the Apostles (plural: Acts 6) who led the Church there in the earlier years and there is no biblical evidence that Peter was the supreme leader of the Apostles then or any other time. Peter did lead the first Gentiles to faith in Christ in Caesarea (Acts 10), but when questioned about this by the Apostles a few days later in Jerusalem, Peter did not have supreme authority (Acts 11:1–18). When Philip led the first Samaritans to Christ, the Apostles in Jerusalem did not send Peter alone, but Peter and John together to confirm that the Samaritans were full members of the Church (Acts 8:5–17).

When Paul and Barnabas reported to the Church in Antioch about the many Gentiles coming to Christ, a dispute arose with other Jewish Christians

---

32. Ibid., #882.

who contended that Gentiles needed to be circumcised. The Church then sent Paul and Barnabas to the Apostles and elders (note: both are plural words, Acts 15:2, 15:4) in Jerusalem to resolve this matter. Peter was there and spoke, but so did Barnabas, Paul, and James. If anyone had supreme authority there, it was James, for it was after he spoke that "the apostles and elders with the whole church" decided to send Paul and Barnabas back to Antioch with instructions about Gentile believers (Acts 15:13–22). Peter had no unique authority in this situation.

Three years after Paul's conversion he went to Jerusalem and met Peter and James, the Lord's half-brother (Galatians 1:18–19). Then after 14 more years of ministry among the Gentiles, Paul went to Jerusalem again with Barnabas and Titus to explain to the Church there about their ministry among the Gentiles (Galatians 2:1–9). Paul says that God had committed him to take the gospel to the Gentiles, just as God had committed Peter to take the gospel to Jews, and Paul saw his apostolic authority as equal to Peter's. Paul names James, Peter, and John (in that order, again suggesting that James was the leader of the Church in Jerusalem) as ones who "seemed to be pillars" in the Church (Galatians 2:9). Those three together gave Paul and Barnabas the right hand of fellowship, signifying their equal authority in the churches, but with James, Peter, and John focusing on evangelism to the Jews and Paul and Barnabas going to the Gentiles.

But some time later Paul found Peter at the church in Antioch and had to confront and rebuke Peter in front of the other Christians for his hypocrisy, caving into peer pressure from Jewish Christians, and by his behavior undermining the truth of the gospel (Galatians 2:11–14). This is hardly consistent with the idea that Peter was the head of the whole Church. Peter obviously responded positively to this humbling rebuke, evidenced by his affirming statement that Paul's writings were Scripture (2 Peter 3:16).

There is no basis in Scripture for the papal claims of infallibility and supreme authority over the worldwide Church. The claims come from a long series of men grabbing more and more power, starting with Leo I in A.D. 440, and as we noted, it has led to a massive amount of political, moral, and theological corruption through the centuries.

Because the Catholic Church denies the supreme authority of Scripture, through its popes and bishops, it has been able to proclaim numerous doctrines that are contrary to Scripture. Clearly, this is a case of faith in man's word over faith in God's Word.

But the Apostles made it perfectly clear in the New Testament that the primacy belongs to Jesus Christ alone and is not shared with any man. "And he is the head of the body, the church: who is the beginning, the firstborn from the dead; that in all things he might have the preeminence" (Colossians 1:18).

The Bible is also clear that the "traditions" spoken of by the Apostles must be the same as the teaching in their New Testament writings, not contradictory to it or adding to or taking away from the doctrines in those books (2 Thessalonians 2:15, 3:6; 1 Corinthians 11:2). Because of the dangers of false prophets, false teachers, and false gospels (Matthew 24:4; Galatians 1:6–9; 2 Peter 2:1–3), Scripture repeatedly proclaims its supreme authority. Believers are not to turn to the right or the left from God's Word (Joshua 1:6–8) but walk in the ancient paths of the biblical prophets (Jeremiah 6:16–19; Isaiah 8:20). Jewish and Christian fathers were expected to know the Scriptures and teach them to their children (Deuteronomy 6:1–9; Ephesians 6:4).

Jesus taught His followers (not just church leaders) to treat the Word of God as their necessary daily food (Matthew 4:4), and that Scripture was the means by which God would produce holy maturity in their lives (John 17:17). His followers were to reject any man-made traditions that contradicted Scripture (Mark 7:6–13) and to test every truth claim against Scripture (Acts 17:11) because demonic spirits would seek to lead believers astray (1 John 4:1). Paul also warned that men would arise in the Church speaking perverse things to draw Christians away from the truth. So he urged people to follow the Word of God (Acts 20:28–32). This repeated insistence on the supreme authority of God's Word is a reflection of the fact that He has magnified His Word above His name (Psalm 138:2).

On the Question of Origins

Up until about 1800, the almost universal belief among those who identified themselves as Christians (whether Protestant, Catholic, or Eastern Orthodox) was that God created in six literal days about 6,000 years ago and destroyed the earth with a global Flood at the time of Noah. But with the development of the idea of millions of years by deistic and atheistic geologists and other scientists in the late 18th and early 19th centuries, most of the professing Christians abandoned that long-held belief. [33]

Today, most Roman Catholic clergy and laity would appear to be theistic evolutionists, although like most Protestants and Eastern Orthodox believers, Roman Catholics are very ignorant of the biblical and scientific evidence against microbe-to-microbiologist evolution and millions of years. This is not surprising given the Church's lack of commitment to the supreme authority of Scripture and its vague teaching on these matters in its official *Catechism of the Catholic Church* and in various pronouncements by popes and others.

Teilhard de Chardin (1881–1955), who was a Jesuit priest, philosopher, and paleontologist, took part in the discovery of the supposed ape-man "Peking Man" and likely was involved in the "Piltdown Man" hoax in 1912. He said,

> [Evolution] is a general postulate to which all theories, all hypotheses, all systems must henceforward bow and which they must satisfy in order to be thinkable and true. Evolution is a light which illuminates all facts, a trajectory which all lines of thought must follow.[34]

Many of de Chardin's writings were censored by the Catholic Church during his lifetime, primarily because of his views on original sin. "However, in July 2009, Vatican spokesman Fr. Federico Lombardi said, 'By now, no one would dream of saying that [de Chardin] is a heterodox author who shouldn't be studied.' "[35] Pope Benedict XVI has also praised him for his work.[36]

In a 1996 speech to the Pontifical Academy of Sciences, the Belgian Catholic priest and astronomer Georges Lamaître (1894–1966) was the first to propose the big-bang theory for the origin of the universe from a "cosmic egg."[37]

In 1996, in a speech to the Pontifical Academy of Sciences, Pope John Paul II commented about the 1950 encyclical by Pope Pius XII called

---

33. See chapters 1–3 in Terry Mortenson and Thane H. Ury, eds., *Coming to Grips with Genesis: Biblical Authority and the Age of the Earth* (Green Forest, AR: Master Books, 2008).

34. Cited in Francisco Ayala, "Nothing in Biology Makes Sense Except in the Light of Evolution: Theodosius Dobzhansky, 1900–1975," *Journal of Heredity*, (V. 68, No. 3, 1977), p. 3.

35. http://en.wikipedia.org/wiki/Pierre_Teilhard_de_Chardin, accessed February 27, 2015.

36. http://teilhard.com/2013/05/21/orthodoxy-of-teilhard-de-chardin-part-i/, accessed February 27, 2015.

37. http://en.wikipedia.org/wiki/Georges_Lemaître, accessed March 30, 2015.

Humani Generis:

> In his encyclical *Humani Generis* (1950), my predecessor Pius XII has already affirmed that there is no conflict between evolution and the doctrine of the faith regarding man and his vocation, provided that we do not lose sight of certain fixed points. . . . Today, more than a half-century after the appearance of that encyclical, some new findings lead us toward the recognition of evolution as more than a hypothesis.[38] In fact it is remarkable that this theory has had progressively greater influence on the spirit of researchers, following a series of discoveries in different scholarly disciplines. The convergence in the results of these independent studies — which was neither planned nor sought — constitutes in itself a significant argument in favor of the theory.[39]

But both of these documents indicate that these two popes and the Catholic Church are not necessarily opposed to evolution as long as Catholics still affirm that Adam and Eve were the first two humans and their souls were created and they fell in sin. The evolution of Adam's body from a pre-existing form of life is not categorically ruled out. Both of these popes' documents are filled with very vague language about the "fruitfulness of frank dialogue between the Church and science" and are completely devoid of reference to specific Scriptures relevant to the issue. Many observers have interpreted Pope John Paul II's statements to mean that he accepted biological evolution but only questioned the "mechanism of evolution." In other words, science has established that evolution is a fact, but scientists are not in agreement

---

38. The Roman Catholic "Eternal Word Television Network" had a footnote to John Paul's remark here stating, "The English edition at first translated the French original as: 'Today, more than a half-century after the appearance of that encyclical, some new findings lead us toward the recognition of more than one hypothesis within the theory of evolution.' The L'Osservatore Romano English Edition subsequently amended the text to that given in the body of the message above, citing the translation of the other language editions as its reason. It should be noted that a hypothesis is the preliminary stage of the scientific method and the pope's statement suggests nothing more than that science has progressed beyond that stage. This is certainly true with respect to cosmological evolution (the physical universe), whose science both Pius XII and John Paul II have praised, but not true in biology, about which the popes have generally issued cautions (as [in Pope John Paul's 1996 lecture] and *Humani Generis*)."

39. Pope John Paul II, "Message to the Pontifical Academy of Sciences: on Evolution," October 22, 1996, http://www.ewtn.com/library/papaldoc/jp961022.htm, accessed March 30, 2015.

about how it happened. So the popes have denied atheistic evolution but not theistic (God-guided) evolution.

More recently, Pope Francis has also affirmed theistic evolution with similar vague and pompous language. In his address to the Pontifical Academy of Sciences in 2014 for the dedication of a sculpture of Pope Benedict XVI, Francis said,

> When we read the account of Creation in Genesis we risk imagining that God was a magician, complete with an all powerful magic wand. But that was not so. He created beings and he let them develop according to the internal laws with which He endowed each one, that they might develop, and reach their fullness. . . . And thus Creation has been progressing for centuries and centuries, millennia and millennia, until becoming as we know it today, precisely because God is not a demiurge or a magician, but the Creator who gives life to all beings. . . . The Big Bang theory, which is proposed today as the origin of the world, does not contradict the intervention of a divine creator but depends on it. Evolution in nature does not conflict with the notion of Creation, because evolution presupposes the creation of beings who evolve. As for man, however, there is a change and a novelty. When, on the sixth day in the account of Genesis, comes the moment of the creation of man, God gives the human being another autonomy, an autonomy different from that of nature, which is freedom.[40]

Given the church's lack of commitment to the supreme authority of Scripture, the ambiguity of these papal pronouncements for over six decades, and the lack of any clear teaching in the official *Catechism* about evolution, the length of the creation days in Genesis 1, and the age of the creation,[41] it is no surprise that a great many Roman Catholics have a very shallow understanding of the issues and see no problem with accepting the evolution of the cosmos (from the big bang) and of living creatures, even possibly Adam's body, under the guiding hand of God.

---

40. Pope Francis, "Address of His Holiness Pope Francis on the Occasion of the Inauguration of the Bust in Honour of Pope Benedict XVI," October 27, 2014, https://w2.vatican.va/content/francesco/en/speeches/2014/october/documents/papa-francesco_20141027_plenaria-accademia-scienze.html, accessed March 30, 2015

41. See CCC, #282–289 and 337–342.

There are, however, some Roman Catholics who reject biological evolution and apparently hold to young-earth creation. The Kolbe Center for the Study of Creation, based in Virginia, was founded in 2000.[42] The Daylight Origins Society is a small Catholic group active in the UK.[43] But the influence of these groups in the Catholic Church appears to be very minimal.

The Catholic View of the Virgin Mary

Another area of very erroneous teaching in the Catholic Church relates to Mary, the earthly mother of Jesus.

Immaculate Conception

In 1954, Pope Pius IX first proclaimed as an official dogma the doctrine of the Immaculate Conception, which teaches that "The most Blessed Virgin Mary was, from the first moment of her conception, by a singular grace and privilege of almighty God and by virtue of the merits of Jesus Christ, Savior of the human race, preserved immune from all stain of original sin."[44] And so "by the grace of God Mary remained free of every personal sin her whole life long."[45]

This novel doctrine has no basis in Scripture. The Bible clearly teaches (through quoting her own words) that Mary was not sinless, but in need of the saving grace of Jesus Christ, just like all other humans. Mary said when she was pregnant with Jesus, "My soul exalts the Lord, and my spirit has rejoiced in God my Savior" (Luke 1:46–47; NASB).

Perpetual Virginity of Mary

The Catholic Church rightly teaches that Mary was a virgin when she conceived Jesus by the power of the Holy Spirit, but it goes on to claim that Mary remained a virgin all her life,

Statue of the Virgin Mary

42. http://kolbecenter.org/.
43. http://www.daylightorigins.com/.
44. CCC, #491.
45. Ibid, #493.

something that has no biblical support. In the church's liturgy they call her *Aeiparthenos*, the "ever virgin."[46] Furthermore, the Church affirms that,

> Jesus is Mary's only son, but her spiritual motherhood extends to all men whom indeed he came to save: "The Son whom she brought forth is he whom God placed as the first-born among many brethren, that is, the faithful in whose generation and formation she co-operates with a mother's love."[47]

Evangelicals and most other Protestants object to this doctrine because Scripture teaches that Joseph and Mary had four sons (James, Joses [Joseph], Judas [Jude], and Simon) and at least two daughters after Jesus was born (Matthew 13:55–56; Mark 6:3: cf. Mark 3:31–35; 1 Corinthians 9:5; Galatians 1:19). Aware of these verses, the Catholic Church responds,

> The Church has always understood these passages as not referring to other children of the Virgin Mary. In fact James and Joseph, "brothers of Jesus," are the sons of another Mary, a disciple of Christ, whom St. Matthew significantly calls "the other Mary."[48] They are close relations of Jesus, according to an Old Testament expression.[49]

But this reply fails for a number of reasons. First, while there are several women named Mary and more than one James and Simon named in the New Testament, the context in each case enables us to determine which individual is in view in each passage. Second, if the named brothers and sisters were cousins, why didn't Mark use the Greek word for cousin (*anepsios*), which Paul used in Colossians 4:10? Or for a more distant relative or kinsman Mark could have used *sungenis*, as Luke did to describe the relationship of Elizabeth to Mary (Luke 1:36). Instead, Mark used the normal Greek words for brother and sister. Third, the context of Mark 6:3 indicates that Jesus was in His hometown (Mark 6:1) and He refers to "his own relatives" in contrast to "his own household" (Mark 6:4). Fourth, in Mark 3:31–35, a crowd had gathered around Jesus and told Him, "Your mother and your brothers are outside looking for you." If "your brothers" were the sons of

---

46. Ibid, #499.
47. Ibid, #501.
48. Ibid., #500, footnote 158 says: "Matt. 13:55, 28:1; cf. Matt 27:56."
49. Ibid., #500.

some other Mary, then "your mother" would be referring to some other woman too, which is an impossible interpretation in this context. Fifth, Matthew 1:25 says that after the angel appeared to Joseph, he took Mary as his wife and kept her a virgin "until" she gave birth to Jesus, which strongly implies that they did have sexual relations after Jesus was born and thereby would have had children by her. Finally, Matthew 13:53–57 confirms this understanding because along with his mother, brothers, and sisters, the townspeople refer to Joseph, the supposed father of Jesus. It makes no sense for those people to mention his father and mother and then refer to more distant relatives.[50]

The Assumption of Mary

On November 1, 1950, Pope Pius XII proclaimed as official dogma that Mary did not die as all other humans have and will. Rather, God took both her body and soul to heaven supernaturally. The pope wrote,

> By the authority of our Lord Jesus Christ, of the Blessed Apostles Peter and Paul, and by our own authority, we pronounce, declare, and define it to be a divinely revealed dogma: that the Immaculate Mother of God, the ever Virgin Mary, having completed the course of her earthly life, was assumed body and soul into heavenly glory.[51]

The pope further dogmatically proclaimed,

> It is forbidden to any man to change this, our declaration, pronouncement, and definition or, by rash attempt, to oppose and counter it. If any man should presume to make such an attempt, let him know that he will incur the wrath of Almighty God and of the Blessed Apostles Peter and Paul.[52]

But there is no biblical support for this teaching, as the few New Testament verses that the pope footnoted demonstrate. Jesus never taught this and both Peter and Paul would certainly oppose this doctrine as false. Neither was this

---

50. For more on this topic, see Bodie Hodge, "Is the Perpetual Virginity of Mary a Biblical View?" in Ken Ham and Bodie Hodge, eds., *How do we know the Bible is True?* Volume 1 (Green Forest, AR: Master Books, 2011), p. 219–226.

51. Pope Pius XII, "Munificentissimus Deus," 1 Nov. 1950, point 44, https://www.ewtn.com/library/PAPALDOC/P12MUNIF.HTM, accessed March 30, 2015.

52. Ibid, point 47.

teaching in the "Apostles' Creed" or the Nicene Creed (which the Catholic Church highly regards), nor was it in the decisions of the 20 ecumenical councils recognized by the Catholic Church. So the only real authority for this is "our own," that is, the pope's and bishops' self-proclaimed authority.[53]

Titles and Roles of Mary

Given all the doctrines that have accumulated to the honor of Mary, it is not surprising that she has been given many titles. She is called the "Mother of the Church" who "by her charity joined in bringing about the birth of believers in the Church."[54] She is also called the "Queen over all things,"[55] "Mother of Mercy, the All-Holy One,"[56] and "the Mother of God." None of these titles have any basis in Scripture. Jesus Christ is the King (Luke 19:38; Revelation 19:11–16), but Mary is not His queen. The Bride of Christ is the Church (Ephesians 5:25–32), the assembly of individuals being gathered from every tribe, tongue, people, and nation — individuals who have personally repented of their sins and trusted in Christ alone for salvation (Revelation 5:6–9).

Mary is also said to be "a mother to us in the order of grace." She is the "Mother of God, to whose protection the faithful fly in all their dangers and needs."[57] The Catholic Church adds,

> Taken up to heaven she did not lay aside this saving office but by her manifold intercession continues to bring us the gifts of eternal salvation. . . . Therefore the Blessed Virgin is invoked in the Church under the titles of Advocate, Helper, Benefactress, and Mediatrix.[58]

But the Bible teaches that there is only one Mediator between God and people: the Lord Jesus Christ (1 Timothy 2:5). He alone is our advocate before our holy Judge, for He alone by His death was a propitiation for our sins, taking the wrath of God for us (1 John 2:2; Hebrews 2:17). There is no other name in all of heaven and earth by which we can and must be saved

---

53. For an enlightening discussion of how this doctrine was shoehorned into the category of infallible dogma, see James G. McCarthy, *The Gospel According to Rome* (Eugene, OR: Harvest House, 1995), p. 293–300.
54. CCC, #963.
55. Ibid., #966
56. Ibid., #2677.
57. Ibid., #971.
58. Ibid., #968–969.

(Acts 4:12). Jesus promised us another helper after He left the earth, but it was not Mary. It was the Holy Spirit (John 14:16–17, 16:7–15). Mary does not bring believers the gifts of eternal salvation. Jesus is the only source of eternal salvation (Hebrews 5:9). He is the only one to whom we should flee in our time of danger and temptation (Hebrews 2:18, 4:14–16). The Roman Catholic exaltation of Mary robs Jesus Christ of the honor and glory and trust and obedience that He alone deserves.

Veneration of Mary

The Roman Catholic *Catechism* says, "The Church's devotion to the Blessed Virgin is intrinsic to Christian Worship."[59] Catholics are instructed to venerate Mary above all people and angels. The church technically distinguishes between worship (reserved for God alone) and veneration (for Mary and "the saints"), but in practice it is hard to see the difference. The most common way that Catholics venerate Mary is by praying the rosary as they finger their way along a string of beads.[60] The church considers the rosary "the epitome of the whole Gospel."[61] The rosary involves the repetition of a prayer to Mary 50 times, punctuated after every ten with the Lord's Prayer. The repeated prayer to Mary is, "Hail Mary, full of grace, the Lord is with thee. Blessed are thou among women and blessed is the fruit of thy womb, Jesus. Holy Mary, Mother of God, pray for us sinners now and at the hour of our death. Amen."[62]

There is no biblical basis for venerating Mary or praying to her for help and intercession with her Son, Jesus. In fact, Mary is not even mentioned in the New Testament after Acts 1:14–15, where her name is in the middle of a list of some of the 120 disciples who after Jesus' ascension to heaven were waiting in Jerusalem for the coming of the Holy Spirit on the Day of Pentecost. Jesus once had a perfect opportunity

59. Ibid., #971.
60. With 1.3 billion Catholics in the world, the manufacture and sale of rosary beads in great variety is obviously big business: http://www.rosarymart.com/ is one of many places to buy one of the multitude of designs.
61. Ibid.
62. CCC, #2676–2677.

to teach His disciples to venerate and pray to Mary, but He did quite the opposite. Luke records,

> While Jesus was saying these things, one of the women in the crowd raised her voice and said to Him, "Blessed is the womb that bore You and the breasts at which You nursed." But He said, "On the contrary, blessed are those who hear the word of God and observe it." (Luke 11:27–28; NASB)

Christians are instructed to pray to the Father in Jesus' name (John 14:13–14, 15:16, 16:23–26). We are never told in Scripture to pray to Jesus in Mary's name or pray to Mary that she might intercede for us with Christ. The believer needs no mediator between himself and the Savior, and Jesus is the only mediator between the believer and God (1 Timothy 2:5–6). Jesus also taught that we should never use vain repetition as we pray (Matthew 6:7).

Apparitions of Mary

In addition to this Roman Catholic teaching, the many supposed appearances of Mary have increased devotion to Mary. The first appearance or apparition of Mary was to Pope John XXII (1316–1334). Another appeared in Guadalupe, Mexico, in 1531. But since 1830 there has been a growing worldwide movement of Roman Catholic devotion to Mary, fueled by the blessing and promotion of the popes. The apparitions have occurred in many countries, most notably in Europe. Some of the most well-known ones are Lourdes, France (1858), Fatima, Portugal (1917), and Medjugorje, Bosnia-Herzegovina (1981). In the latter case, the apparitions have been almost daily since 1981 and

> over 40 million people of all faiths, from all over the world, have visited Medjugorje and have left spiritually strengthened and renewed. Countless unbelievers and physically or mentally afflicted, have been converted and healed. You owe it to yourself and your loved ones, to investigate with an open mind and heart the events, which are occurring in Medjugorje. I invite you to explore the over 4000 pages of information contained on this Web Site, and decide for yourself whether you will answer Our Lady's call to prayer, and conversion.[63]

---

63. http://www.medjugorje.org, accessed February 27, 2015.

"People of all faiths" have been spiritually strengthened and renewed and unbelievers have been converted? A Muslim or Hindu or Buddhist or animist cannot be strengthened and renewed in his faith and also converted to Christ. Therefore the "conversion" referred to here must be a conversion to venerating Mary and mixing that veneration with the person's non-Christian religion. "Mary's" message on February 2, 2015, in Medjugorje was this:

> Dear children! I am here, I am among you. I am looking at you, am smiling at you and I love you in the way that only a mother can. Through the Holy Spirit who comes through my purity, I see your hearts and I offer them to my Son. Already for a long time I have been asking of you to be my apostles, to pray for those who have not come to know God's love. I am asking for prayer said out of love, prayer which carries out works and sacrifices. Do not waste time thinking about whether you are worthy to be my apostles. The Heavenly Father will judge everyone; and you, love Him and listen to Him. I know that all of this confuses you, even my very stay among you, but accept it with joy and pray that you may comprehend that you are worthy to work for Heaven. My love is upon you. Pray that my love may win in all hearts, because that is the love which forgives, gives and never stops. Thank you.[64]

These clearly are the words of a deceiving demon, not the words of Mary, the earthly mother of Jesus. According to the Bible, Mary, the mother of Jesus, was not pure. She herself admitted she was a sinner in need of a savior. The claim that the Holy Spirit comes through Mary and her purity is completely contrary to Scripture. Furthermore, Mary had no apostles. The apostles in the Bible were messengers of Jesus Christ sent into the world to glorify Him and proclaim His gospel (Mark 3:13–19; Acts 1:15–26; Ephesians 1:1; 2 Timothy 1:1; 1 Peter 1:1). Scripture never encourages Christians to mindlessly accept all messages that claim to come from God, but rather to test everything against Scripture (Acts 17:11; 1 John 4:1). Also, no Christian is worthy to work for heaven. Finally, it is not Mary's love that forgives, gives, and never stops. It is God's love through Jesus Christ alone that accomplishes those things.

---

64. Ibid.

We must conclude that these "apparitions of Mary" are not manifestations of her presence, but rather are demonic deceptions.[65] The Apostle Paul warned the 1st-century Christians about "false apostles, deceitful workers, disguising themselves as apostles of Christ. No wonder, for even Satan disguises himself as an angel of light" (2 Corinthians 11:13–14; NASB). He also warned about "deceitful spirits and doctrines of demons" (1 Timothy 4:1; NASB) who would bring people "another gospel" that is deceptively close to but significantly different from the gospel of Jesus Christ (Galatians 1:6–9). But that is exactly what these apparitions are doing as they reinforce devotion to "Mary," the Catholic doctrines about her and about salvation, and the authority of the pope, which keeps Catholics from the true faith in Jesus Christ for salvation revealed in Scripture.

Conclusion Regarding the Virgin Mary

Mary indeed was blessed to be the human mother of the incarnate Son of God. And for Christians, she certainly is a model of faith and submission to the will of God (when the angel announced that she would be the mother of our Lord, although later in the gospels she was not always an outstanding example of faith). But as James McCarthy succinctly states, "The Mary of Roman Catholicism is not the Mary of the Bible. Scripture says nothing of a woman conceived without sin, perfectly sinless, ever virgin, and assumed into heaven."[66] She is not the co-redeemer or the queen of heaven or the mother of the Church.

The Roman Catholic Mary never existed, but is the product of centuries of man-made traditions confirmed by demonic deception ("miracles" and "apparitions") that hinder millions of Roman Catholics and followers of other religions from coming to know the only one who can save them from sin and the holy judgment of God to come, that is, the Lord Jesus Christ. Mary plays no role in a person's salvation or sanctification. The gospel is all about Jesus.

The Catholic View of Salvation

Given the Catholic Church's erroneous views about Scripture and tradition, the authority of popes and bishops and the person and work of Mary,

---

65. Because of the claims of supernatural phenomena associated with the apparitions and the way they are attracting followers of other religions, it seems extremely unlikely to me that any of these apparitions are merely the result of humans deceiving themselves.

66. James G. McCarthy, *The Gospel According to Rome: Comparing Catholic Tradition and the Word of God* (Eugene, OR: Harvest House, 1995), p. 198.

it is no surprise that the Roman Catholic Church's teaching about salvation is a complicated mixture of truth and error that badly distorts the gospel and the process of sanctification in the life of a true follower of Jesus Christ.[67]

According to the Church, salvation from the coming judgment of God is a life-long process, not an event. It starts with baptism but then includes the repeated use of the sacraments and the person's cooperation with grace and then after death almost certainly some time in purgatory.

Baptism

The Catholic Church teaches, "Holy Baptism is the basis of the whole Christian life, the gateway to life in the Spirit, and the door which gives access to the other sacraments."[68] Except for adult converts to Roman Catholicism, Catholics are baptized as infants very shortly after birth. The Church teaches that baptism causes the new birth (making the person a child of God), frees the person from the power of darkness, and provides forgiveness of "all personal sins as well as all punishment for sin." It makes the person a temple of the Holy Spirit, a part of the priesthood of Christ, and incorporates him into the church. It gives the person the grace of initial "justification," enabling him to believe in God, giving him the power to live and enabling him to grow in moral virtues.[69]

In addition to baptism, the other six sacraments that also impart grace to the Catholic believer are the Eucharist, penance, confirmation (by a priest usually of a child at about age 12 after finishing a preparatory course on doctrine), the marriage ceremony, holy orders (ordination of men to the priesthood), and extreme unction (anointing of those who are seriously ill or nearing death).

Purgatory

Formulated by the Councils of Florence (1439) and Trent (1563), this doctrine says that when the Catholic faithful dies in an imperfect state, he must "undergo purification, so as to achieve the holiness necessary to enter the joy of heaven." To help those in purgatory, the Roman Catholic Church

---

67. For a fuller discussion than can be given here, readers are encouraged to get McCarthy's *The Gospel According to Rome*, which provides an excellent biblical refutation of Catholic teaching.
68. CCC, #1213.
69. Ibid., #1250, 1263–1270.

encourages prayer for the dead, almsgiving, indulgences, and penance on their behalf. But there is no actual biblical support for this doctrine.[70]

Penance and Indulgences

Penance is what the Catholic believer does "as means of obtaining forgiveness of sins." It begins with confession to a Catholic priest, but also is expressed primarily through fasting, prayer, and almsgiving. Additional means include efforts at reconciliation with one's neighbor, tears of repentance, prayers for the saints, acts of charity, reading Scripture, and praying parts of the liturgy.[71] But "taking up one's cross each day and following Jesus is the surest way of penance."[72]

Closely linked to the effects of penance is the doctrine and practice of indulgences.

> An indulgence is a remission before God of the temporal punishment due to sins whose guilt has already been forgiven, which the faithful Christian who is duly disposed gains under certain prescribed conditions through the action of the Church which, as the minister of redemption, dispenses and applies with authority the treasury of the satisfactions of Christ and the saints. An indulgence is partial or plenary according as it removes either part or all of the temporal punishment due to sin. The faithful can gain indulgences for themselves or apply them to the dead.[73]

By obtaining spiritual goods from the "Church's treasury," the repentant Catholic can "be more promptly and efficaciously purified of the punishments for sin." That treasury is "the infinite value which Christ's merits have before God." But it also "includes as well the prayers and good works of the Blessed Virgin Mary" which "are truly immense, unfathomable, and even pristine in their value before God," as well as the prayers and good works of

---

70. Ibid., #1030–1032.The only two Bible verses that the Catechism cites (besides one verse from the Apocrypha, which Protestants do not accept as Scripture) in support of this doctrine are taken out of context and twisted. First Corinthians 3:15 does not say that a person's sins will be burned away in purgatory so that they can enter heaven. Rather it teaches, in context, that the *quality* of the believer's works will be tested by fire on the day of judgment. First Peter 1:7 speaks of fiery trials in this life that test the believer's faith, not to a fiery purging of sins in the afterlife.
71. CCC, #1434–1437, 1456.
72. Ibid., #1435.
73. Ibid., #1471.

all the saints. This "treasury of the merits of Christ and the saints" obtains for the repentant Catholic the remission of the temporal punishments due for his sins.[74] But one can only wonder why the prayers and good works of Mary and the saints must or can be added to the "infinite value" of the merits of Christ.

But again, there is no basis in Scripture for indulgences or the merits of Mary or "saints" (those considered very holy Catholics, to whom the pope has assigned sainthood) that can remit temporal punishment for sin.

Eucharist (Mass, Holy Communion, Lord's Supper)

The night before His crucifixion Jesus instituted the "Lord's Supper" as an ordinance whereby Christians are to remember His saving work on the Cross and in the Resurrection on their behalf until He returns (Matthew 26:17–30; 1 Corinthians 11:17–34). The Catholic Church calls this the Eucharist or the Mass.

Whereas Protestants view it as a memorial, the Catholic Church says it a memorial *and* "the unbloody reenactment of the sacrifice of Calvary" which "perpetuates the sacrifice of the Cross by offering to God the same Victim that was immolated on Calvary . . . and applies the fruits of Christ's death upon the Cross to individual human souls."[75] When the priest consecrates the bread and the wine, the elements do not change in appearance but are transubstantiated into the literal body and blood of Jesus. As the Council of Trent says, the sacrifice of the Mass "is identical with the Sacrifice of the Cross" and is "propitiatory . . . atoning for our sins, and the sins of the living and of the dead in Christ."[76] The Church also teaches, "The sacrifice of the Mass is the most effective form of supplication which we humans can offer to the Eternal Father."[77] Catholics are told and believe that,

> When the priest bends low over the bread and wine and pronounces those tremendous words, the most momentous ever framed by human lips, "This is My body . . . this is My blood," the

---

74. Ibid., #1476–1477.
75. John A. O'Brien, *The Faith of Millions* (Huntington, IN: Our Sunday Visitor, 1974), p. 304. Written by a Catholic priest, this book has been endorsed by three prominent archbishops and translated into many languages to instruct Catholics and non-Catholics in the teachings of Roman Catholicism.
76. Ibid., p. 307.
77. Ibid., p. 308.

heaven of heavens opens, and the King and Ruler of the universe, Jesus Christ, comes down upon our altar, to be lifted up as a sacrificial Victim for the sins of the world.[78]

But Jesus Christ does not come down on thousands of earthly Catholic altars around the world every week at the beckoning of a priest. Scripture repeatedly teaches that ever since His ascension to heaven 40 days after His Resurrection, He has been seated at the right hand of God, constantly interceding before the Father for all true believers in Jesus Christ (Romans 8:34; Colossians 3:1; Hebrews 1:3–4, 8:1, 12: 1 Peter 3:22; 1 John 2:2).

In the consecration of the bread and the wine the priest prays,

> Receive, O holy Father, almighty, eternal God, this immaculate victim which I, Thy unworthy servant offer to Thee, my living and true God, for my innumerable sins, offenses and negligences, for all here present, and for all the faithful living and dead, that it may avail me and them to everlasting life.[79]

But the Bible teaches no such things regarding the meaning and results of the Lord's Supper or the consecration and prayer of the priest. On the contrary, referring to Jesus' death on the Cross, Hebrews 10:12–18 (NKJV) teaches,

> But this Man, after He had offered one sacrifice for sins forever, sat down at the right hand of God, from that time waiting till His enemies are made His footstool. For by one offering He has perfected forever those who are being sanctified. . . . Now where there is remission of these, *there is* no longer an offering for sin.

It is the death of Jesus on the Cross, not the memorial of that death, that provides the forgiveness of sins for the repentant, believing sinner. There is no bloodless sacrifice for sin (Hebrews 9:22).

The Catholic doctrine of transubstantiation is based on a literal interpretation of Jesus' words "This is my body" and "This is my blood" in the accounts of the Last Supper in Matthew 26; Mark 14; and Luke 22. But

---

78. Ibid., p. 317.
79. Ibid., p. 308.

these are not literal, just as Jesus' other statements are not: "I am the bread of life" (John 6:48), "I am the light of the world" (John 8:12), "I am the door" (John 10:9), and "I am the true vine" (John 15:1). These are all figurative statements to teach a spiritual truth. The bread and the wine in the Lord's Supper are simply symbolic or representative of the body and blood of Christ given for our salvation once for all on the Cross.[80]

Justification and Sanctification

According to the Catholic teaching, "Justification is not only the remission of sins, but also the sanctification and renewal of the interior man."[81] Volumes have been written on the difference between the Roman Catholic view of justification and the evangelical understanding of the biblical teaching.[82]

The Bible teaches four important truths about justification. First, justification is not gradual but *instantaneous*, at the moment a person trusts in Jesus Christ as Lord and Savior. Second, in justification the sinner is *declared righteous* in the sight of God, not actually made righteous in his experience. We are declared righteous by faith in the substitutionary atoning work of Christ on the Cross and in His Resurrection. Third, justification means that righteousness is *imputed* or reckoned into the spiritual account of the sinner, not infused into his person. And fourth, the sinner is justified *by faith alone in Christ's saving work alone*, not by faith in Christ plus the sinner's good works. We cannot add anything to His work. He took the wrath of God for our sins, so that in Christ we can be righteous in God's sight (2 Corinthians 5:21). We are saved by Christ's finished work at Calvary (John 19:30). According to the Word of God, we must individually repent of our sins and trust in Jesus Christ to be saved, born again, and justified (Ephesians 2:8–9; Romans 10:17; 1 Peter 1:23–24; John 1:12; Romans 3:20–28, 4:25). From that moment, we can be confident that we "have been justified" (Romans 5:1) and we can know (not hope) that we have eternal life (1 John 5:11–13).[83]

80. For a refutation of the Catholic view of the Mass, see McCarthy's *The Gospel According to Rome*, p. 133–144.

81. CCC, #1989.

82. Because of the vital importance of this doctrine, I encourage readers to consider James McCarthy's *The Gospel According to Rome* and John MacArthur's *Reckless Faith: When the Church Loses Its Will to Discern* (Westchester, IL: Crossway Books, 1994).

83. For biblical amplification of these points see, http://www.gty.org/resources/distinctives/ DD09/roman-catholicism?Term=Catholic%20evangelical%20justification, which is a summary of the analysis in MacArthur's *Reckless Faith*.

That the Catholic Church denies this view of justification is clear from the response of the Council of Trent (1545–1563) to the Protestant Reformation. Its Canon 9 on justification (still in force) states:

> If any one saith, that by faith alone the impious is justified; in such wise as to mean, that nothing else is required to co-operate in order to the obtaining the grace of Justification, and that it is not in any way necessary, that he be prepared and disposed by the movement of his own will; let him be anathema.[84]

But once we are justified, born again, saved, redeemed, and reconciled to God, which happens the moment we repent of our sins and trust in Christ as Savior and Lord, we then begin the life-long process of sanctification. Biblically speaking, sanctification means becoming increasingly holy in our experience in the sight of men just as we already are in our judicial standing in the sight of God. Jesus said that believers are sanctified by the Word of God (John 17:17). As we trust and obey His Word (learned through personal study and fellowship in a Bible-teaching local church) and yield moment-by-moment to the Holy Spirit (who takes up residence in our hearts the moment we are saved), we grow in Christ-likeness in our thoughts, attitudes, and behavior (2 Peter 1:3–4; Galatians 5:16–23). We walk in the good works that God prepared for us to do (Ephesians 2:10).

The Bible clearly teaches that a repentant, believing sinner *has been saved* (justification), *is being saved* (sanctification), and *will be saved* completely and eternally in heaven (glorification). To confuse or equate these is to distort the gospel of Jesus Christ.

The Catholic Church terribly confuses these teachings of Scripture by mixing biblical truth with man-made dogmas accumulated over the centuries. It turns justification into a process that begins at baptism (*not* when a person repents and trusts in Christ) and doesn't end until the completion of purgatory. Through unbiblical doctrines and rituals it also introduces all kinds of error regarding the process of sanctification. The result is another gospel, a different gospel than the one revealed in Scripture, something Paul

---

84. Anathema means excommunication from the Catholic Church, which, it is claimed, is the only place where salvation is found. Therefore the anathema is a condemnation to hell, unless the person embraces the Catholic teaching on salvation and comes into (or back into) the Catholic Church.

sternly warned against (Galatians 1:6–9, 2:20–21). It is a gospel of faith plus works, which subtly subverts the totally sufficient, glorious, saving work of Jesus Christ and distorts the Word of God.

Conclusion

The Roman Catholic Church's horrendous persecution of true Christians, its brutal military crusades against the Muslim, Jews, and anyone else who would not submit to the pope, the unbiblical structure of its hierarchy and the political, moral, and spiritual corruptions of the papacy, the centuries of widespread homosexual and heterosexual immorality by the clergy (which is still occurring today),[85] its rejection of the supreme authority of Scripture by equating man-made tradition with Scripture, and its gospel-subverting doctrines about Mary, baptismal regeneration, the sacrifice of the mass, sainthood, justification, and sanctification lead us to only one conclusion. The Catholic Church is not the true church of Jesus Christ but is a false church that enslaves hundreds of millions of people in a false gospel that is a serious distortion of biblical Christianity.

I have no doubt that there are Roman Catholics who have a true saving faith in Jesus Christ. I have known some of them and prayed and studied the Scriptures with them. But in my experience of sharing my faith with many Catholics and serving as a missionary for almost 20 years in Eastern and Western European countries where Roman Catholicism is prominent or dominant, the true believers I have met who are still in the Catholic Church almost invariably were led to a proper understanding of the gospel either directly or indirectly by an evangelical Christian.

Sadly, most Roman Catholics are still lost in their sin, trusting in their baptism, good works, attendance at confession and Mass, and prayers to Mary and the saints. They need to hear a clear presentation of the biblical gospel and then be encouraged to trust in Jesus Christ alone for salvation, come out of the Catholic Church, and become involved in a Bible-teaching, gospel-preaching local church that gives all the honor and glory to Jesus Christ.

---

85. The sexual immorality of a staggering number of priests and bishops in recent decades and the concerted efforts by bishops, cardinals, and the popes to cover-up the scandals is documented in this 84-minute documentary: http://www.pbs.org/wgbh/pages/frontline/secrets-of-the-vatican/, accessed March 11, 2015.

Summary of Roman Catholic Beliefs

Doctrine	Roman Catholic Teaching
God	Trinitarian Godhead consistent with Bible. Jesus is an insufficient Savior.
Authority/ Revelation	The Bible is viewed as a revelation from God, but heavy emphasis is placed on tradition and teaching of the line of popes holding apostolic authority. Apocryphal books are considered part of the canon
Man	A sinful being who cooperates with God in the process of salvation.
Sin	Transgression of God's will consistent with the Bible, but divided into categories of mortal and venial. Must be confessed to a priest as a mediator between man and Jesus.
Salvation	A cooperation of man with God through sacraments. Sacraments are ministered through apostolic succession to members of the only true church. Jesus' atonement is insufficient to pay for sins. Purgatory following death is necessary for purification from sin. Merit of saints can be applied to others for payment for sin.
Creation	Originally believed in a literal, six-day creation, but influence of evolutionary views is now common. Several popes have made pronouncements that all forms of evolution are compatible with the Bible as long as Adam and Eve are preserved.

Chapter 5

How Is Eastern Orthodoxy Different?

Dr. D. Trent Hyatt

One sunny day in the late 1990s I was walking with friends near the center of Kiev, Ukraine, when I heard some chanting. I looked around and saw a small demonstration taking place. There were, perhaps, about 100 people marching in the street carrying a few placards. The man carrying the placard at the head of the marchers was dressed in the distinctive clothing of an Orthodox priest.[1] On his placard was the claim that the Orthodox Church was the "one, holy, catholic, and apostolic" church. Now, I was raised a Protestant and had personally placed my faith in Christ as a result of an evangelistic message given by a Protestant on the campus of the University of California at Berkeley while I was a student there. So, upon hearing the claim of the demonstrators, I immediately sensed a challenge in their claim. How could they claim something so exclusive?

Eastern Orthodoxy is indeed present in most parts of the world today, but is to a great many in the West little known and even less understood. In fact, the Orthodox Churches found in most countries of the West are immigrant churches, that is, churches started by immigrants from the countries of Eastern Europe (Greek, Russian, Armenian, Romanian, Ukrainian, Serbian, etc.). These churches may recruit new members through conversion of Protestants or Roman Catholics, but the majority of their flocks

---

1. When capitalized, "Orthodox" refers to the Eastern Orthodox Church in its various forms rather than an assent to orthodox biblical doctrine.

Eastern Orthodox Christians participate in a procession in Novosibirsk

are descended from these ethnic groups. Of course, marriage to a member of an Orthodox Church is one of the more common ways for people outside of the traditional ethnic communities to become Orthodox. This was humorously depicted in the wildly popular film *My Big Fat Greek Wedding*. However, since the 1980s a small but growing number of evangelicals have become Orthodox. Some of these have become part of the various national Orthodox churches, such as the Greek Orthodox or Russian Orthodox Churches, but most seem to have become part of the Evangelical Orthodox Church, which became associated with the Antiochian Orthodox Christian Archdiocese of North America. Some have also become part of the Orthodox Church in America, which began as a result of Russian Orthodox missionaries to Alaska in 1794.

How many people belong to the Orthodox Church in all its various expressions? The best estimates put the number between 200 and 300 million worldwide, depending on the way "members" is defined. In any case, the size of the Orthodox community would make it third behind the

Roman Catholics and the Protestants in the Christian tradition. Among those who are active members in Orthodox Churches there are many who are sincere and devout in their Christian faith. This essay, though written from the perspective of an evangelical Protestant, is not intended to simply discredit the faith of all Orthodox believers. Yet, in the spirit of 1 Thessalonians 5:21, I want to "examine everything carefully" and "hold fast to that which is good."[2]

Other than their exclusive claims to being the one true church, to which I will return later, what are the distinctive views of the Eastern Orthodox? I will attempt to survey their most important beliefs and practices by examining the following questions.

1. What is the highest authority in their tradition?

2. What is their view of creation?

3. What is their view of Christ?

4. What is their teaching on how one is saved, and what role do the "sacraments" play in their teaching on salvation?

5. How do they worship (including what an Orthodox Church service looks like)?

6. What is the justification for seeing orthodoxy as the one true church?

Authority

The Orthodox, like Protestants and Catholics, regard the Bible as the inspired Word of God. But like the Catholics, the Orthodox Bible contains a few books not found in the Hebrew Scriptures, that is, books called the Apocrypha (Maccabees, Judith, Tobit, etc.) and written between the close of the Old Testament and the writing of the New Testament.

The inclusion in the canon of Scripture of some books not regarded as canonical by Jesus and the Apostles (based on their lack of reference to them) is not an unimportant matter.[3] However, even more important and resulting in more serious consequences is the place of tradition in connection with the Scriptures.

---

2. All Scripture quotations in this chapter are from the New American Standard Bible.
3. Jesus also affirmed the three divisions of the Old Testament in Luke 24:44 being "the Law, the Prophets, and the writings (Psalms)," which excluded the apocryphal writings.

The Orthodox view of tradition is more complex than the Roman Catholic view. In the Catholic view, Scripture and tradition are both authorities. In other words, tradition exists alongside of Scripture as another authority. In the Orthodox view, the Scriptures are *a part* of tradition. According to their theologians, it is a mistake to pit Scripture *against* tradition. They are both part of one great tradition. They affirm that Scripture may be the highest tradition, but it is still tradition. But Scripture is not, in their view, the highest and final authority for faith and practice in the way Protestants since the Reformation have seen it and confessed it to be. Scripture, as part of the great tradition, must be interpreted *authoritatively*. Though the Orthodox do not have a *Magisterium*[4] comparable to the Roman Catholic Church, they do, practically speaking, have something functionally similar.

For the Orthodox, the church's tradition is the *authoritative interpretation* of the Scriptures. This means, practically, that no believer has the right to interpret Scripture on his or her own, so to speak. The proper way to read Scripture according to the Orthodox is with the writings of the church fathers[5] alongside the Bible, guiding us in our understanding of what the Bible says. Of course, in practice, there may be very few Orthodox who literally read their Bibles with the writings of the church fathers open beside them. But what they do seems (to this outside observer) to be: (1) they read the church fathers a good deal more than the Scriptures and then (2) when they do read Scripture, they come up with their understanding of what the Scriptures are supposed to mean from the church fathers and thus find in the Bible what they have already become convinced of by reading the church fathers. No doubt, this may facilitate a quicker and correct understanding of some parts of the Bible. However, the possibility that one or

---

4. The "magisterium" is defined as the official teaching authority of the church. This authority is "uniquely vested in the Pope and the bishops in communion with him. Further, the Scriptures and Tradition make up a single sacred deposit of the Word of God, which is entrusted to the Church," and the magisterium is not independent of this, since "all that it proposes for belief as being divinely revealed is derived from this single deposit of faith." Definitions found in the Catechism of the Catholic Church. This source can also be accessed on Wikipedia.

5. The "church fathers" refers to the theologians, bishops, or scholars from the first few centuries of the history of Christianity, whose writings played a significant role in shaping the church's doctrine and practice in the following centuries. These are also referred to as the patristics from the Latin form of "father." A few examples: Tertullian, Augustine, Basil the Great, John Chrysostom, Jerome, Ambrose, etc.

more of the church fathers has misunderstood or misinterpreted Scripture does not seem to come into play. When the church fathers and the church's tradition as a whole are used as a *means* of understanding Scripture, rather than using Scripture to correct and guide the church's beliefs and practices, the result is often seen in putting the church's tradition as an authority *over* or *above* the Scripture.

The implications of this approach to authority are clear. Paul's words to Timothy, his faithful disciple, in 2 Timothy 3:16–17 tell us that "All Scripture is inspired by God and is profitable for teaching, for reproof, for correction, for training in righteousness; so that the man of God may be adequate, equipped for every good work." This teaching, reproving, correcting, and training work of the Scripture in the lives of believers is at least partially shackled by the Orthodox approach to authority since the Scriptures can't do that *directly!* Any teaching or reproof that isn't grounded in the church's tradition must be set aside — disqualified.

A good example of how this works can be imagined, if this had been applied to the "discoveries" made by Martin Luther and the other Protestant reformers of the 16th century. Luther found peace for his tortured conscience when he discovered that he could be justified by faith alone (apart from works) and that God credited Christ's righteousness to him when he trusted in Christ and His work on the Cross for him. He *did not* find this understanding in the Roman Catholic Church's tradition. He found it in the Bible, particularly in Romans. If the Orthodox principle of reading the Bible only with the help of the church fathers and the church's tradition had been applied, Luther would have had no message. *Sola fides, sola gratia, sola scriptura, solus Christus, soli Deo gloria,*[6] the slogans of the Reformation, would have never corrected the practices and beliefs of the church. Though partial or basic understandings of these truths can be found here and there in some of the church fathers, no clear championing of them is to be found in the church's tradition.[7] Does that mean that the principles expressed in the slogans are wrong? According to the Orthodox understanding of authority, this would certainly be the case. But what about the fact that all of

---

6. The Latin phrases mean: by faith alone, by grace alone, by the Scripture alone, by Christ alone, and to God alone be the glory.
7. This is true of both Western (Roman) and Eastern traditions. Of course, the Reformation was an affair that took place only in the West. Eastern Orthodoxy has never had a Reformation-type movement and insists that it does not need one!

these principles that were of such life-changing significance for Luther and so many others in the Roman Catholic Church of the 16th century are found *explicitly* and *implicitly* in the Bible? If the Bible clearly teaches something, is it not valid, even if it is not found clearly in the church fathers? Luther, Zwingli, Calvin, and the other reformers insisted that the Bible's teaching was *over* the church's teaching, and when the church's teaching did not correspond to the Bible's, then it was the church's teaching that had to be changed, not the Bible's.

The Bible teaches its supreme authority repeatedly. For example, Moses taught the Israelites to trust and obey God's Word and teach it to their children (Deuteronomy 6:1–9). God told Joshua not to turn to the right or the left from following His Word (Joshua 1:6–9). Psalm 1 blessed the person who clings to God's Word, Psalm 19 says it is far superior to any truth we learn from nature, and Psalm 119 magnifies the importance of Scripture, making the believer wiser than his teachers (119:97–104). The prophets continually called the Jews back to the Word of God (e.g., Isaiah 8:20; Jeremiah 6:16–19; Hosea 4:6). Jesus condemned the Jewish religious leaders of His day for undermining the teaching of Scripture by their traditions (Mark 7:6–13). And the Berean Jews were commended for evaluating the truthfulness of Paul's teachings in the light of the Old Testament (Acts 17:11). Scripture is the only sure foundation and authority for the Christian.

Creation

Due to their high regard for tradition and belief that what the church fathers taught was permanently valid, the Orthodox Church has not been significantly involved in the debates of the last two centuries over creation and evolution. This is beginning to change as secular and rationalist thinking has come to dominate the sciences in the West. Andrew Louth is a theologian and professor emeritus from Durham University in England. He is at the same time a priest of the Russian Orthodox Church and serves the parish in Durham. Louth reveals the kind of approach likely to be taken with increasing frequency. He asks:

> Do Christians have to believe that Adam and Eve existed, and that they sinned, and that their sin has infected all subsequent human beings? Do we have to believe that there was an

original couple, that *Homo sapiens* emerged from some kind of *Homo erectus* as a single couple, in a particular place. . . . There are . . . Christians who believe this, and indeed not a few of them are Orthodox Christians. I do not, however, think we, as Orthodox, need to commit ourselves to such a position.[8]

Louth goes on to discuss the many characteristics that we humans share with animals. Thus a common origin is seen as quite reasonable. He does, of course, affirm that man possesses reason and is a higher being and in the image of God. Even so, this identity need not be tied to a historical Adam and Eve, according to Louth.

But what about the Fall? For Louth, the fallen state of humanity is an undeniable fact. Yet he is content to argue that man's condition is something that slowly evolved as humanity found "that the pull of more evident pleasure, or a sense of the self expressing itself in aggression towards the other, was too great to resist." What Louth is arguing is clearly a view of sin, but not just sin as we know it, but what he refers to as "ancestral sin" (the term he prefers to "original sin").

Ancestral sin, he thinks, is a consequence of man's ontology. In other words, man's nature is such that sin is a regrettable but unavoidable reality of his being. If, then, sin is more of an ontological problem than a moral or spiritual problem, a historical Adam and Eve and a historical Fall are not really necessary. These two perspectives, that is, our commonalities with the animal world and an obscure beginning for "ancestral sin" in the distant shadowy past, present no problem for Louth and those who agree with him in seeing an evolutionary beginning for life and a process of "millions" (his term) of years rather than a recently created historical pair who sinned by disobeying God's explicit command.

Father Serphim Rose (1934–1982), an American Orthodox monk and scholar, wrote a lengthy book surveying the teachings on Genesis 1–11 of Orthodox theologians and scholars down through the centuries. He documents with lengthy quotes from the "Holy Fathers" of Eastern Orthodoxy that up until the 19th century the Orthodox Church held to a literal six-day creation week about 6,000 years ago and a global catastrophic Flood at the time of Noah. But, he tells us, by the 20th century a very large percentage of

---

8. Andrew Louth, *Introducing Eastern Orthodox Theology* (Downers Grove, IL: InterVarsity Press, 2013), p. 74.

Eastern Orthodox believers had accepted the ideas of evolution and millions of years.[9]

Christ

Eastern Orthodoxy has historically maintained and defended a high view of the deity of Christ. The Orthodox make a great deal out of being "the Church of the seven councils," that is, the seven ecumenical councils of the early Church. The first five of these councils dealt with challenges to the full deity or full humanity of Christ. The first of these councils was held in Nicea and the fourth was held in Chalcedon. These two councils affirmed the biblical doctrine of Christ as being one person with two natures, thus fully divine and fully human. From the side of His divinity, He is the second person of the Trinity and is as fully God as are the Father and the Holy Spirit. From the side of His humanity, He is the virgin-born son of Mary and the heir of David. All these things the Orthodox Church faithfully teach and affirm. Thus, there is no debate between evangelical Protestants and the Orthodox on the deity of Christ or His incarnation. Difficulties emerge, however, when the meaning of the incarnation for redemption is considered. This is best considered in connection with the next question.

Salvation and the Sacraments

"What must I do to be saved?" This was the question the Philippian jailer asked Paul and Silas in Acts 16:30. It remains the critical question for all of mankind. Indeed, if we are given the wrong answers to this question, a catastrophic loss is the prospect we face. Strangely, in contrast to both Protestants and Catholics, the Orthodox do not seem to focus very much on this question. There are, of course, reasons for this.

Like Roman Catholicism, Eastern Orthodoxy places great emphasis on the "sacraments." Like Catholicism, Orthodoxy sees baptism as bringing about the regeneration of the person receiving the sacrament. The Orthodox

---

9. See Terry Mortenson's helpful review of Fr. Rose's book *Genesis, Creation and Early Man* on the Answers in Genesis website, December 1, 2002. For an in-depth biblical and historical defense of young-earth creation see Terry Mortenson and Thane H. Ury, eds., *Coming to Grips with Genesis* (Green Forest, AR: Master Books, 2008). For a layman's treatment see Ken Ham, *Six Days* (Green Forest, AR: Master Books, 2013). Jonathan Sarfati, in *Refuting Compromise* (Green Forest, AR: Master Books, 2011, second ed.) thoroughly, biblically, and scientifically refutes the progressive creationism of Hugh Ross. *The New Answers Book*, Volumes 1-4, edited by Ken Ham (Green Forest, AR: Master Books), answer the 130 most-asked biblical and scientific questions related to origins.

typically baptize infants but, of course, adult converts to Orthodoxy are baptized as well. In contrast to Roman Catholics, the Orthodox baptize by immersion. Immersion is carried out three times in succession, in the name of the Father and the Son and the Holy Spirit.

Unique to the Orthodox is a second sacrament applied immediately following baptism, called "chrismation." Chrismation is performed by the priest on the newly baptized individual by anointing him or her with oil and making the sign of the cross over the various parts of the body (the forehead, eyes, nose, mouth, ears, chest, hands, and feet) of the newly baptized and saying, "The seal of the gift of the Holy Spirit, Amen." According to Orthodox teaching, this sacrament brings about the indwelling of the Holy Spirit in the newly baptized individual. In the Orthodox view then, even if the individual being baptized is an infant, he or she is consequently a full member of the church from that point on. The oil used in the anointing

A gold vessel for chrism

of the person being baptized is called the "chrism." According to Orthodox belief, the chrism may be administered by a priest but the chrism must have first been blessed by a bishop.

The Orthodox do not believe that faith on the part of the person being baptized is necessary in order for these sacraments to be effective. Indeed, Orthodox theologians take great pains to clarify and emphasize that the effectiveness of the sacraments is entirely independent of any faith or particular desires for God or sanctity. To quote a prominent Orthodox theologian: "In no way is the efficacy of the sacrament contingent upon the faith or moral qualifications of either celebrant [i.e., priest or bishop] or recipient."[10] How is such a thing possible? The answer becomes clearer when we read Karmiris' explanation of what happens when the

---

10. John Karmiris, "Concerning the Sacraments," *Eastern Orthodox Theology: A Contemporary Reader*, ed. by Daniel B. Clendenin (Grand Rapids, MI: Baker Books, 1995), p. 22.

sacraments are dispensed: "Baptism and chrismation transmit justifying and regenerating grace."[11] Quite explicitly then, these two sacraments, according to Orthodox teaching, *automatically transmit* God's saving and regenerating grace.

How is it possible that a person can be baptized without any faith or spiritual hunger, by a priest of whom no moral qualifications are required, and yet that baptism be effective without fail? The answer to this question is that the sacrament itself, by virtue of being a genuine sacrament of the Orthodox Church, is certainly effective. In other words, all that is necessary is that the priest or bishop celebrating the sacraments must be a duly ordained minister of the Orthodox Church. The baptisms that take place in the Protestant Church or even the Roman Catholic Church are not regarded as valid baptisms. Why not? Karmiris explains this quite clearly:

> Furthermore, the Orthodox Catholic Church believes that divine grace is not dispensed outside of the true church, and thus the church does not recognize in their fullness sacramental acts which are performed outside of her, except in extraordinary cases.[12]

Thus, it is because of the belief of the Orthodox that the ancient maxim of Cyprian (3rd century) is true, that is, "outside of the church there is no salvation." Since only the Orthodox Church is the true church, then only the ministers of the Orthodox Church are genuinely in the apostolic succession.[13] Thus these ministers play the role of transmitting God's grace when they administer the sacraments.

It is ironic that the Orthodox regard the faith of the one being baptized as inconsequential while they at the same time believe that all baptisms administered by legitimate Orthodox ministers are effective. From the perspective of an outside observer, their faith is great but it is in the wrong thing. The Bible makes the faith of the believer the decisive thing. Notice Paul's response to the question of the Philippian jailor: "Believe in the Lord Jesus, and you will be saved" (Acts 16:31). As a *result* of his faith, the Philippian

---

11. Ibid., 22.
12. Ibid., 23.
13. The concept of apostolic succession is that the authority of the church has been passed on from the apostles in a direct line through the ministers of the church. Roman Catholics and Orthodox generally point to Matthew 16;13–20 as a justification of this belief.

jailor was *then* baptized (Acts 16:33). What a perfect situation for Paul to have clarified the effectiveness of baptism to bring salvation! All he would have had to say was, "Receive baptism from us and you will be saved!" But, of course, he did not say that. He placed the emphasis squarely on the faith of the individual sinner as the essential thing to receive salvation.

Two things must be said to clarify the picture further. It is quite true that Eastern Orthodoxy is a very sacramental tradition. The portal to enter the Orthodox Church is through the sacraments. Great emphasis is placed on these sacraments. There is a deeply rooted belief that the visible acts of the church's priests and bishops signify the invisible works of God. Because of the authority of the church to perform these acts and transmit the grace pertinent to the particular purpose, grace is transmitted to the recipient by virtue of the work of God through the church's ministers. Thus the members are taught that these sacraments are the means of salvation and becoming "deified." (More will be said about "deification" momentarily.) The point I want to make is this: the members of the Orthodox Church naturally assume that they can depend on the sacraments and that they will be effective. Consequently, the great majority of those within the Orthodox Church rely on the sacraments to "get them through," that is, to gain their salvation for them.

The second thing that needs to be said here is to clarify to people outside of the tradition that the salvation believed to have been imparted at one's baptism and chrismation is *not* viewed within Orthodoxy as a permanent possession. In fact, it is viewed merely as a beginning. Whether or not one will end up actually saved depends on a number of other things. Thus, it would be a misrepresentation of Orthodox teaching to leave people with the understanding that all that was needed was to be baptized and chrismated. Though it is true that the Orthodox believe that baptism and chrismation bring regeneration and justification, it is not true that they regard the new member of the church as having a "free pass to heaven," so to speak. The spiritual life in this newly baptized and chrismated individual must be nurtured. This is especially done through participation in "the Eucharist" (i.e., the Lord's Supper). But other matters are important as well. The main thing I wish to make clear at this point is that salvation in Orthodoxy is regarded as a process, indeed a life-long process. The sacraments play a very great role, but other things matter as well.

Salvation and Deification

One of the great points of confusion among outsiders trying to understand Orthodoxy is the concept of "deification" or "*theosis*." Translated, the thought is "becoming god." To most Westerners this concept is totally alien. Paul does, of course, speak of being "conformed to the image of Christ" (Romans 8:29). Is that all the Orthodox mean by *theosis*? No, it is not. In fact, the Orthodox have a major and complex theology built around the idea of deification.

Most frequently quoted by the Orthodox is a statement by Athanasius: "God became man that we might become gods."[14] Athanasius was by no means the only church father to speak of deification in similar terms.[15] Outsiders might be tempted to think that the Orthodox have similar views to the Mormons, believing that humans can become divine, "gods" in an ontological sense. This would be quite mistaken. The Orthodox are quite clear in their Trinitarian belief that the divine essence resides only in the triune God. Man cannot by any means cross over the divide between the divine essence (the one true God) and human nature. But they do indeed mean more than what Protestants mean with their doctrine of sanctification. Where then does the Orthodox doctrine of *theosis* (deification) fit in their doctrine of salvation?

An Orthodox icon depicting Athanasius

If, in fact, the Orthodox thought of deification only in terms of sanctification (i.e., the process of becoming more and more like Christ through faith and obedience and the work of the Holy Spirit), there wouldn't be a real problem with their doctrine other than the natural confusion that arises from the use of the term. But a careful survey of the writings of Orthodox

14. *Concerning the Incarnation of the Word*, De Inc 54.3; http://www.antiochian.org/content/theosis-partaking-divine-nature.

15. The concept is addressed by Basil the Great, Gregory Nazianzus, and Irenaeus among others!

theologians leads one to the conclusion that *theosis* is much more important than that. Indeed, it becomes clear that the Orthodox think of *theosis* as the process of salvation. In other words, one is *saved* by becoming "deified."

The basic perspective of the Orthodox on *theosis* is that it is a life-long process of becoming more and more holy, more and more like God, or as they often express it, more and more "a god." This transformation can also be spoken of as "union with God" or "sharing the divine nature."[16] The ultimate goal is not even reachable in this life. However, significant progress toward it can and must be made. How is progress toward *theosis* made? First of all, through active participation in the sacraments. According to one theologian,

> The road toward our theosis, our union with God, can be formulated in the following short statement: divine grace and human freedom . . . We *are* able to walk that road. We will be accompanied and strengthened by divine grace. The holy mysteries (sacraments) are what transmit this grace of the All-Holy Spirit. His sanctifying and deifying energy is actualized in the holy services of the church, especially in holy baptism, repentance, and the divine Eucharist.[17]

Two things emerge from this claim: *theosis* requires both divine grace and human action and the critical role played by the sacraments. The interaction of divine grace and human action is referred to often by Orthodox theologians and is called *synergy*. Of course, in the sacraments, according to the Orthodox view, grace is transmitted from God to man. However, in synergy, man must bring his part. Man's part is essential to the success of the venture.

The prominent and highly regarded Orthodox theologian Vladimir Lossky refers to what the Orthodox Church calls the "synergy of divine grace and human freedom." On this point Lossky quotes St. Macarius of Egypt as saying: *"The will of man is an essential condition, for without it God does nothing"*[18] (my emphasis). This logically would mean that man is a participant in his own salvation. This is indeed what the Orthodox Church

---

16. Frequent reference is made to 2 Peter 1:4 where Peter uses the metaphor of "sharing in the divine nature" to refer to process of sanctification.
17. Christoforos Stavropoulos, "Partakers of Divine Nature" from Clendenin, *Eastern Orthodox Theology: A Contemporary Reader*, p.192.
18. Vladimir Lossky, *The Mystical Theology of the Eastern Church* (Crestwood, NY: St. Vladimir's Seminary Press, 1976), p. 199.

teaches. Lossky goes on to quote a 19th-century Russian ascetic writer to this effect: " 'the Holy Ghost, acting within us, accomplishes with us our salvation,' but he says at the same time that 'being assisted by grace, *man accomplishes the work of his salvation*' "[19] (my emphasis).

When one surveys the vast literature from Orthodox asceticism (as practiced by the countless monks in Orthodox monasteries), one finds this viewpoint that man participates in his own salvation in many places. *Theosis* is a synergistic process in which *the believer pursues the goal of union with God by means of* (my emphasis) denial of the flesh and pursuit of holiness. We are told that this involves struggle and striving: "Fastings, vigils, prayers, alms, and other good works which are done in the name of Christ are means which help us reach that goal which always remains the same: the reception of the Holy Spirit and the making him our own, that is theosis."[20]

Human effort, then, is an essential part of *theosis*; it is the *means* of pursuing union with God. Since *theosis* is accomplished by the synergy of God's grace and man's effort, then salvation depends not on God's grace alone — it is not a gift, but is a reward for man's effort. The seriousness of the Orthodox pursuit of holiness, at least on the part of many of the monks, is indeed impressive.

But is this explanation of how one is saved reconcilable with Ephesians 2:8–9? "For by grace you have been saved through faith, and that not of yourselves, it is the gift of God; not as a result of works, so that no one may boast." In fact, Paul's central thrust in the Book of Romans is to establish that "apart from the Law the righteousness of God has been manifested . . . even the righteousness of God through faith in Jesus Christ for all those who believe . . . being justified as a gift by His grace through the redemption which is in Christ Jesus" (Romans 3:21–24).

Romans and Galatians both speak eloquently of justification by faith and of the substitutionary atonement accomplished by Jesus Christ's completed work on the Cross. Strangely, these themes are scarcely, if ever, addressed by Orthodox theologians. When questioned about this deficit, the reply is that there are many metaphors for salvation in the Bible and that the Orthodox preference is to think in terms of union with God rather than in the legal terms so favored in the West. Is it not rather an error of perception to think

19. Ibid. p. 199.
20. Ibid. p. 190, Stavropoulos, "Partakers of Divine Nature."

in terms of preferences when discussing the great biblical theme of salvation? What does the Scripture itself emphasize? Is not the Book of Romans the longest and most systematic treatment of the doctrine of salvation in the New Testament? How can we ignore its clear teaching on grace, faith, the substitutionary atonement, and justification, and hope to have a truly biblical understanding of God's plan of salvation?

Salvation and the Atonement

A final point on the Orthodox teaching on salvation should be added before leaving this topic. There is comparatively little focus in Orthodoxy on the atonement or the Cross but a significantly greater focus on the doctrine of the Incarnation and the Resurrection. Protestants and Catholics are accustomed to thinking of the Incarnation as part of the process ending in the death of Christ on the Cross for our sins. Of course, the doctrine of Incarnation is a rich vein that bears many treasures for Christian theology, not the least of which is an affirmation by God of the inherent goodness of the material creation.[21] But in Scripture, the Incarnation of Jesus is seen first and foremost as a revelation of God to man of His goodness and character (Hebrews 1:1–3) to redeem man by means of the atonement. This is seen with great clarity in Jesus' own statement of the purpose of His coming: "to give His life a ransom for many" (e.g., Matthew 20:28; Mark 10:45). It comes as a surprise, then, to find the Orthodox perspective on the incarnation, which is captured well in this statement from Bulgakov:

> For God so loved the world that He spared not His Son to save and deify it. The Incarnation, first decreed to ransom fallen humanity and reconcile it with God, is understood by Orthodoxy as, above all, the deification of man, as the communication of the divine life to him. To fallen man the Incarnation became the supreme way for his reconciliation with God, the way of redemption. This produces the concept of salvation as deification.[22]

---

21. The creation is fallen and cursed because of sin (Genesis 3:14–19) and will be one day set free from its corruption (Romans 8:19–23; Revelation 21:3–5, 22:3), but it is not inherently evil. In fact, at the end of each day of creation, we are told that God saw what He had made and it was good, on the sixth day following the creation of man, "very good." Thus a doctrine of the goodness of the material world as created by God is explicitly present in the creation account in the Bible.

22. Sergius Bulgakov, *The Orthodox Church* (Crestwood, NY: St. Vladimir's Seminary Press, 1988), p. 108.

The incarnation is then said to be the effective "deification" of man. This deification is, according to Bulgakov, the Orthodox view of salvation. From a biblical point of view, it seems strange to gloss over the atonement and attribute to the Incarnation things never declared in Scripture and then end up calling it salvation.

Within the doctrine of redemption as set forth by Orthodoxy, there is also the surprising role attributed to the Resurrection. The Orthodox theologian and priest Andrew Louth makes the following assertions about the Resurrection and redemption:

> Orthodox theology . . . considers the question of Adam's sin and its consequences from the perspective of the resurrection of Christ. The icon, called 'The Resurrection' . . . is a depiction of Christ destroying the gates of hell and bringing out from hell . . . Adam and Eve, as the first of a crowd of people . . . who are being brought out of hell by Christ's victory over death in the resurrection. . . . Adam is commemorated as he is now: one whose penitence made it possible for him to be redeemed from hell by Christ at his resurrection.[23]

This is a remarkable presentation of the Fall and redemption! Though the reality of the Fall and the redemption are affirmed, notice that the Fall is the departure from the path of deification, and that redemption is accomplished *by the Resurrection*. And man's inclusion in the redemption is on the basis of his "*penitence*"! What is missing here? Absolutely no mention is made of the atonement or the Cross. No mention is made of the payment for sin or satisfying the wrath of God. For the Orthodox, Christ's victory over death and *not the Cross or atonement* is what saves from sin, death, and hell.

But Scripture is clear. Peter tells us, "He Himself bore our sins in His body on the cross, so that we might die to sin and live to righteousness; for by His wounds you were healed" (1 Peter 2:24). Luke 24:45–47 records Jesus' charge to His disciples before He ascended to Heaven:

> Then He opened their minds to understand the Scriptures, and He said to them, "Thus it is written, that the Christ would suffer and rise again from the dead the third day, and that

---

23. Louth, *Introducing Eastern Orthodox Theology*, p. 70.

repentance for forgiveness of sins would be proclaimed in His name to all the nations, beginning from Jerusalem."

In Romans 3:23–26, Paul instructs us:

> For all have sinned and fall short of the glory of God, being justified as a gift by His grace through the redemption which is in Christ Jesus; whom God displayed publicly as a propitiation in His blood through faith. This was to demonstrate His righteousness, because in the forbearance of God He passed over the sins previously committed; for the demonstration, I say, of His righteousness at the present time, so that He would be just and the justifier of the one who has faith in Jesus.

And in 1 Corinthians 15:3–4 he says, "For I delivered to you as of first importance what I also received, that Christ died for our sins according to the Scriptures, and that He was buried, and that He was raised on the third day according to the Scriptures." And in 2 Corinthians 5:21 we read, "He [God] made Him (Christ) who knew no sin to be sin on our behalf, so that we might become the righteousness of God in Him."

We cannot bypass the Cross. It is at the heart of the gospel, as Paul makes clear:

> I have been crucified with Christ; and it is no longer I who live, but Christ lives in me; and the life which I now live in the flesh I live by faith in the Son of God, who loved me and gave Himself up for me. I do not nullify the grace of God, for if righteousness comes through the Law, then Christ died needlessly (Galatians 2:20–21).

> But may it never be that I would boast, except in the cross of our Lord Jesus Christ, through which the world has been crucified to me, and I to the world (Galatians 6:14).

Worship

Christians from the West tend to be confused or even shocked when they first attend an Orthodox service. In Eastern Europe and Russia, Orthodox Churches generally do not have seating. (However, Greek Orthodox Churches in America do tend to have pews.) The inside of an Orthodox

Cathedral of Christ the Saviour in Moscow, Russia

Church is typically richly adorned with icons. The word "icon" is simply the Greek word for "image." At the front of the sanctuary is a wall of icons with a door (or doors) in it. This wall is called an "iconostasis" ("icon stand"). It plays an important part in Orthodox worship. The icons on the iconostasis only display the most important icons adorning a particular church. There are often many, many more icons distributed throughout the church. Westerners from the Catholic tradition, or who are familiar with Catholic Churches, are accustomed to religious art being featured prominently in the church. However, in an Orthodox Church, one is immediately struck with the number of pictures and the obvious importance they play in Orthodox worship. Why are icons so important to the Orthodox?

Worship and Icons in Orthodoxy

The place of icons in Orthodox worship is the result of a centuries-long development and some bloody battles. In the year 726, the Byzantine Emperor Leo III decreed that icons should *not* be used in Orthodox worship. This was immediately resisted, indeed violently resisted, and the famous "iconoclastic controversy" was underway. During the next 117 years, the Byzantine Orthodox Church and society were torn by this controversy. By and large, it was the state, the emperors, their families, the patriarchs, and the bishops who attempted to remove icons from the churches and to ban them from use during church services. The monks and many of the laity were vehemently opposed to the attempts of the iconoclasts to suppress the use of icons in the church.

Finally, in 753, Emperor Constantine V called a council of the church in Constantinople, which issued a condemnation of using icons in the church's

Ancient Orthodox icons

worship. This did not stop the controversy, however. There continued to be strong resistance to the prohibition against the use of icons in the church, and there was further persecution from the state against those who insisted on continuing to use icons in worship.

When the emperor died and his wife (Irene), a secret advocate for using icons, became empress, she called another council. This council, held in 787 in Constantinople, reversed all of the decisions of the 753 council and affirmed the correctness of the use of icons in worship. This second council to deal with the use of icons is recognized as the Seventh Ecumenical Council. Even this council did not end the conflict over icons. Not until 843 did the last iconoclastic emperor die. His wife had another synod called to confirm the decrees of the Seventh Council. This victory for the advocates of icon usage is celebrated every year as the Feast of Orthodoxy.

This bitter controversy and its final resolution in favor of those advocating the use of icons in worship has left a deep impression on Eastern

Orthodoxy. The love for and religious use of icons is a distinguishing mark of Orthodoxy. This raises the question: what justification is given for this practice? There is, after all, no mention of using icons in the New Testament. Not only that, there is the second commandment (Exodus 20:4) against making idols to worship and serve as well as the prohibition in Deuteronomy 4:23–27 against making any "graven images."

Those advocating the use of icons countered with the argument that the Apostles affirmed the use of icons even though they did not say anything about them in their surviving writings. We can, they claim, know this through oral tradition. This is, of course, a claim that can neither be proved nor disproved.

But the most important argument brought in support of the validity of icons was that the Incarnation made them acceptable. Since God chose to take on flesh when Christ was born, He made Himself visible. He took on a physical body, that is, made up of matter (Romans 8:3). Thus, the rejection of icons was arbitrarily said to be the denial of a genuine incarnation.[24] To believe that God became man meant that man could represent Him with material elements. The fact that God was able to incarnate Himself, to become man, is clearly a miracle of which only He is capable. It is a great leap to get from the historical Incarnation of God in Jesus to say that that means people are, therefore, competent to create holy images to be venerated in worship.

In fairness, it must also be said that the Seventh Council declared that it is wrong to *worship* icons but that it was acceptable to *venerate* (strong form of the word "to honor") them because they represented holy personages: Jesus, Mary,[25] and the saints. In venerating an icon of the Apostle Paul, for example, one is said to be recognizing and honoring his holiness, which he

---

24. This argument was set forth by the greatly admired (by the Eastern Church) church father from Syria, John of Damascus.

25. Orthodoxy has a very exalted view of Mary. "The Orthodox church venerates the Virgin Mary as 'more honorable than the cherubim and beyond compare more glorious than the seraphim,' as superior to all created beings. The church sees in her the Mother of God, who without being a substitute for the one Mediator, intercedes before her Son for all humanity. We ceaselessly pray to her to intercede for us. Love and veneration of the Virgin is the soul of Orthodox piety, its heart, that which warms and animates its entire body. A faith in Christ which does not include his virgin birth and the veneration of his mother is another faith, another Christianity from that of the Orthodox Church." Sergius Bulgakov, "The Virgin and the Saints in Orthodoxy" in *Eastern Orthodox Theology: A Contemporary Reader,* ed. by Daniel B. Clendenin (Grand Rapids, MI: Baker Books, 1995), p. 66.

achieved during his life. This is even said to result in making the venerator more holy. All of this became standard justification for the use of icons and remains so today.

Is it possible to use icons and not violate the second commandment? Is it possible to venerate icons and not slip over the line into worshiping them? Even the highly respected and prominent Orthodox theologian Alexander Schmemann admitted that the line dividing veneration and worship is a fine line that is easy to cross over. In his own words: the line "dividing the Chalcedoninan essence of icons from real idol-worship is [an] exceedingly fine line."[26] But, even if the worshipers are sufficiently schooled in theology and philosophy to stay on the right side of this fine line, is it an appropriate thing to do in a religious service of a faith that is "word-" and not image-based?

It is the *gospel* that is the power of God for salvation. Christ is said, in John 1, to be the *Word* which became flesh. All of this and much more in the rest of the New Testament emphasizes God's *speaking*. It seems at the least that the great emphasis on icons works counter to this biblical emphasis on the Word of God, what God says to us, and to which we must respond. Thus, with as much good will as we can muster, we still have to say that the particular form of icon veneration now practiced (bowing before, kissing) is rather far removed from speaking and hearing the Word of God, which is precisely what we all need much more than focusing on the image of a "saint."

The Importance of Icons in Orthodox Worship

Perhaps one of the most unfortunate consequences of the tragic iconoclastic controversy was that it actually ended up elevating icons in importance. Before it began, it was entirely possible to be an Orthodox believer and participate in Orthodox worship without venerating icons. Icon veneration, or worship in many cases, was widespread, but it was not a dogmatically defined practice and was not integrated into Orthodox liturgy.

After the Seventh Ecumenical Council of 787, veneration of icons was made an integral part of Orthodox worship and the meaning of icons was dogmatically defined by the council's decrees. This results in a role for icons within the Orthodox Church that is clearly far beyond anything that can be

---

26. Alexander Schmemann, *The Historical Road of Eastern Orthodoxy* (Crestwood, NY: St. Vladimir's Seminary Press, 1992), p. 203.

justified by Scripture. Though linking the making of icons with an affirmation of the Incarnation makes sense to many, just as many see the argument as far from compelling.

And, if that argument is not compelling and not based on any explicit Scripture, why should icon veneration have such an important place in the life of the church? Further, the prohibition against the making of "idols" or "graven images" from Exodus and Deuteronomy, though a part of the law, should still be taken as representing God's revealed will. We did have a supernatural intervention in Peter's life when the Lord wanted to make it clear that eating certain meats prohibited by the law was no longer prohibited (Mark 7:19; Acts 10:9–16). We have no such revelation regarding the making of graven images. It certainly does seem quite unjustified to claim that those of us who reject the use of icons in Christian worship deny the Incarnation.

When I was a very young child (two years old), my father was deployed to China at the end of World War II. I spent a whole year alone with my very young mother. She, of course, missed my dad terribly and wanted me not to forget him. She had a photograph of him by her bed, which I also shared with her that year. Every day she would hold the photo up to me and tell me to "give Daddy a kiss." I, of course, complied.

One day, however, he returned from China to his wife and son. I was initially a bit frightened of this man who had come in and taken my place in bed next to my mother. Wanting to help me get over my reservation about my dad, my mother told me to give my dad a kiss. I ran into the bedroom, got his picture and kissed it! I had become devoted to the image, but didn't know the person the image portrayed. Of course, I was quite limited in understanding images and representation, but until I was able to truly get to know my dad, could it be said that I loved *him*? Probably not. I may have loved the image because it made my mother happy, but I had to get to know him in order to grow in a relationship of love and trust.

It would, in my judgment, be an error to think that the great devotion to icons demonstrated by many Orthodox believers really betokens a great love for the one represented in the icon. And, even if it does indicate a great love for the one portrayed in the icon, is it fitting to develop such devotion to John Chrysostom or Basil the Great or even Mary? Should not our devotion be directed toward our Lord and Savior rather than His servants? That is the message the angel in Revelation gave to John when he prostrated himself at the angel's feet (Revelation 22:8–9). The angel's words make it abundantly clear that worship should *not* be given to fellow servants but only to God.

The Pattern of Orthodox Worship

A brief word about the conduct of Orthodox services should be added to this topic. The priest(s) perform the rituals of the Eucharistic service behind the iconostasis, out of sight of the worshipers. The liturgy is sung or chanted and is quite consistent. In other words, the worshipers who attend regularly know the liturgy and know how to enter into the process. The participation of the worshipers is seen in their responding at appropriate points in the liturgy and in much bowing, kneeling, and kissing of the icons. Some worshipers will stay through an entire service, but many will come in at some later point and many will leave before the service is over. In fact, there are at least two services that take place each Sunday, the first being "Matins," which lasts about an hour. The Eucharistic service lasts another hour and a half. Thus, many come and partake of whatever portion of the service they wish to be present for and participate in. As strange as it seems to Westerners, it is not considered inappropriate for people to come late or leave early during a service. There is a sense that entering into the liturgy when one arrives and praying and kissing the icons is enough. The liturgy is, after all, for God. Of course, participation in the Eucharist requires that one stay until the priest comes out from behind the iconostasis and distributes the bread and wine. This is the high point of the service. A sermon, generally called a "homily," is typically short and not many seem to wait to hear it. The important thing in the service is the liturgy and the Eucharist. Preaching does not tend to be valued very highly.

Curious to many, it is precisely this liturgy and the artwork (i.e., the icons) that have attracted many Westerners to Orthodoxy. There is, in the eyes of many, something worshipful about the solemn atmosphere and the ancient liturgy that gives a sense of connection with the past. However, the question that begs for attention is whether or not the exposition of the Scriptures should not play a central role in Christian worship. Paul's exhortation to Timothy in his last epistle before martyrdom was "Be diligent to present yourself approved to God as a workman who does not need to be ashamed, accurately handling the *word of truth*" (2 Timothy 2:15). Further, he tells him that it is *the Scriptures* that are "profitable for teaching, for reproof, for correction, for training in righteousness" (2 Timothy 3:16) and that he should "preach *the word*" (2 Timothy 4:2, emphasis added). Liturgy, per se, is certainly not a bad thing. The Greek word from which it comes simply means "service of worship." It was used of the pagan worship of the gods, but it is also used in the New Testament to refer to Christian worship. Thus, it is not the use of liturgy as such that I find questionable but rather the very limited place the exposition of the Scriptures have in Orthodox worship. Hearing Scripture read and expounded are clearly primary concerns of Paul in his pastoral letters. This should tell us something very important.

The Claim to Be the One True Church

As was pointed out at the beginning of this chapter, the Eastern Orthodox have a very exalted view of their church. Of course, the same could be said of Roman Catholics. In fact, from the fourth century until Vatican II (1962–1965), the claims made by Roman Catholics were just as great as those made by the Orthodox. However, with Vatican II it began to be possible for Catholics to see Protestants as "separated *brethren*" (my emphasis). This was a great advance over just seeing Protestants as heretics. From a Protestant perspective, it is possible to think in terms of different "denominations." Each denomination may be more or less close to what one sees as "fully biblical." The differences that Baptists have with Presbyterians need not lead to rejecting one another as "heretics." In fact, they may engage in various activities cooperatively to get the gospel out to an unbelieving world. From an Orthodox perspective, this notion of different *legitimate* denominations, different churches that have a valid justification for thinking of themselves as the people of the body of Christ, is not possible. In their view, there can only be one true church and they are quite confident that they are it! Why?

The reason is actually quite simple. The claim to be the one true church is connected to their claim to be "apostolic." By "apostolic," the Orthodox do not just mean that they believe and teach the message and doctrines of the Apostles. They do claim that — *and more*. What they are ultimately claiming is that their bishops and priests are the actual heirs of the Apostles, the "*successors*" of the Apostles. In other words, the claim is based on what theologians call "apostolic succession." The way this is claimed to have worked is simple. The Apostles appointed their successors before they died. These successors ordained priests and bishops in their years of ministry and, then, when they died, the ones they had appointed in turn appointed their successors. That means, they say, that there is an unbroken succession of appointees that goes right back to the Apostles, who started the succession. The implication for the Orthodox is also that anyone *not* in that succession is not regarded as a legitimate minister of the true Church, the one founded by Jesus and the Apostles. Even at this point in history, the Orthodox believe that all of their bishops stand in a direct line of succession, an unbroken chain, going all the way back to the Apostles and thus have been ordained to lead the true Church and to appoint (i.e., ordain) future ministers for that Church.

If we stop and reflect for a moment on the logic employed in this justification for the claim to be the one true Church, it should become obvious that there is a logical fallacy involved. Just for the sake of illustration, let us say John ordains Bill, who in turn ordains Jim, who ordains Carl. Now let's say that Jim begins to be influenced by a number of his friends and begins to add things to his teaching that did not come out of the Bible. Let's say further that in his teaching he also leaves out a few of the important points from the Bible. When Jim then appoints and ordains Carl to be his successor, he makes sure that Carl shares his values and viewpoints. As the process continues, we may find that by the time we get to Andy a few centuries later, he is teaching many things that the Apostles didn't teach and not teaching a number of things that they did teach. Is he in the "succession" beginning with the Apostles? Perhaps so, but this would be in a relational sense. But if he is not a *theological* successor in terms of holding to *the teaching of the Apostles*, how important is it that he has a formal link back to the Apostles? Can we doubt that the message, the teaching of the Apostles, is far more important, indeed decisively important, for the role of leading and serving the Church of Jesus Christ? We see exactly this kind of problem in the Gospels. Jesus pointed out that the scribes and Pharisees had seated themselves in the chair of Moses (being Jews, they had a relational link to him) but that their example should *not* be followed (Matthew 23:2ff) because their traditions undermined the truth of the Scriptures (Mark 7:6–13).

As the 16th-century reformers pointed out in their conflicts with the Roman Catholic Church of the time, where the gospel is truly proclaimed and the ordinances (baptism and the Lord's supper) are administered, there is the Church. Of course, they made it very clear that the Bible was the final authority for all things in the faith and practice of the Church, but they decisively rejected the notion of apostolic succession based on formal descent from the Apostles. It was the message and teaching of the Apostles, which is *found in the written Scriptures,* that give us the message and teaching that the Church must proclaim. Where Christ and His atoning death on the Cross and His Resurrection make up the central content of a community's faith, and the written Word of God *found in the Bible* is the final authority for faith and practice, the Church is present, whatever denomination or tradition it belongs to. This is a far more important measure of the true Church than the formal descent referred to as "apostolic succession."

A Concluding Question

One last question might trouble some. Is it possible for a born-again believer to be a practicing member of the Orthodox Church? Of course it is as long as they repent and believe on the Lord Jesus Christ and His death, burial, and Resurrection! As Jesus told Nicodemus, the Spirit blows where He wills (John 3:8). There are without doubt born-again believers in all kinds of places and churches. What is not possible is to claim that *all* in any particular church or denomination are saved just because they are members of that church or denomination. This certainly applies to the Orthodox Church, but it also applies to Protestant churches. Salvation and membership in the Body of Christ, the Church universal, is dependent on a personal relationship with the Christ of Scripture that comes about by personal repentance and faith in Him, not through belonging to any particular local church, denomination, or tradition. The Lord knows those who are His (2 Timothy 2:19)!

Many years of missionary work in Eastern Europe and Russia have led me to conclude that the gospel is not often proclaimed in the Orthodox Church. Church services are ritualistic exercises that focus on the icons and the sacraments. It is all too easy to trust in those sacraments to save one and on the icons to sanctify one rather than in the finished work of Christ on the Cross in our behalf. Though we cannot judge what is in the heart of another, we can certainly assume that most people in the Orthodox Church need to hear and respond to the good news of Jesus Christ and need to turn to Him for forgiveness of sins and to trust in *His* work on the Cross for their salvation. This is, indeed, the message that all people need to hear.

Summary of Eastern Orthodox Beliefs

Doctrine	Eastern Orthodox
God	Trinitarian Godhead consistent with Bible
Authority/ Revelation	The Bible is considered a part of tradition, thought the highest and most important tradition. The apocrypha is also considered part of Scripture, though on a lower level; tradition, particularly in the Church Fathers, gives the authoritative way to interpret Scripture.
Man	A fallen creature, yet not without the ability to cooperate with God in the process of deification (becoming "god," i.e., reaching salvation)
Sin	Transgression of God's will; sin is not seen as the powerful force controlling and enslaving people's will (cf. Romans 7; Ephesians 2:1–10).
Salvation	A cooperation of man with God; most important in this process is participation in the sacraments; the sacraments must be received from duly ordained ministers (priests and bishops) of the Orthodox Church who stand in the line of apostolic succession; beyond the sacraments, the individual believer must strive to become increasingly "holy"; the doctrine of the Atonement (the substitutionary death of Christ on the Cross for our sins) is not emphasized, but rather the Incarnation and Resurrection are the focus.
Creation	Originally believed in a literal, six-day creation, but influence of evolutionary views is increasing.

Chapter 6

Counterfeits of Christianity: The Overview

Bodie Hodge and Roger Patterson

In the grand scheme of religion in the world today, Christianity dominates and is currently the fastest-growing religion, particularly in conversions.[1] Recent numbers indicate 31.5 to 33 percent of the world's population are Christians and are evenly distributed around the world.[2] Most religions outside of Christianity dominate in *localized* regions of the world. The religion with the second most adherents is Islam (known as Muslims or Muhammadans) with about 23.2 percent.[3]

But note something profound: Over 50 percent of the world's religions are tied to the claim that the Bible is true. Obviously, the Bible claims its words are true many times, and this is consistent by virtue that it is from God who *is* the truth (John 14:6). But what many fail to realize is that Muhammad, founder of Islam, *also* affirmed that the Bible was true in the

1. Fastest Growing Religion, Fastestgrowingreligion.com, 2009, http://fastestgrowingreligion.com/numbers.html; see also: Brother Andrew, "The Myth about Islam Being the Fastest Growing Religion," Encyclopedia of Islamic Myths, Islam Review, http://www.islamreview.com/articles/mythaboutislam.shtml, accessed March 12, 2015.
2. Ibid.; Pew Research Center, "The Global Religious Landscape," Washington D.C., December 18, 2012, http://www.pewforum.org/2012/12/18/global-religious-landscape-exec/.
3. Ibid.

Koran (e.g., Surah, [chapter] 2:40–42, 126,136, 285; 3:3, 71, 93; 4:47, 136; 5:47–51, 69, 71–72; 6:91; 10:37, 94; 21:7; 29:45–46; 35:31; 46:11).

Take note that Jews affirm the Old Testament to be true (about 77 percent of the Bible); Mormons agree that the Bible is true (insofar as it is properly translated); Jehovah's Witnesses affirm the Bible is true (as they have translated it); and so it is the case with many variations and cults of Christianity. Of course, many groups say they see the Bible as the standard, but in practice they hold to authorities above the Bible. But in practice, only pure Christianity really views the Bible as being absolutely true.

Richard Dawkins at the 34th American Atheists Conference in Minneapolis, 2008

Furthermore, just because someone assumes the name Christian, does that mean they really believe in the Jesus Christ of the Bible and have repented of their sin and received Christ as Lord and Savior? Do they really believe the Bible is the sole authority in their lives? Or do they merely accept the name "Christian" without believing in Christ or His Word, as a "cultural Christian." A leading atheist, Dr. Richard Dawkins, will openly call himself a "cultural Christian."[4] Of course, he is an atheist and that is his religion, not Christianity by any means, but he sings carols at Christmas because he lives in a land (England) that was dominated by Christianity and Christian thought and a remnant of that still exists in cultural practices.

As we dive into this book series, we are not arguing for "a god" or merely a monotheistic view of God. Instead, we are arguing for the triune God of the Bible (Father, Son, and Holy Spirit) and no other. It is Christ above all others. So this includes arguing against those who may profess to be Christians but deny the Christ of the Bible, or, for that matter, claim to believe the Bible as the authority but then elevate other authorities higher than God's Word.

---

4. Dawkins, Richard on BBC's "Have Your Say," BBC News, December 10, 2007, http://news.bbc.co.uk/2/hi/uk_politics/7136682.stm.

This is a biblical authority issue where man's ideas have been elevated to be greater than what God has declared. It should be the other way around — our ideas need to be judged based on God's Word. The Bible is the standard that judges all other truth claims because it is the only written revelation from God to man. The arguments in this book will be made on the presupposition that the Christian God is the only God and that He has revealed Himself to us in the 66 books of the Bible.[5]

As biblical Christians, we are not arguing that we stand side by side with Jews, Muslims, Jehovah's Witnesses, Baha'i, or Mormons (and so on), saying that *together* we are arguing for theism in general. By no means! We argue for the God of the Bible alone, even against these religious views that *borrow* similarities from the God of the Bible, but deviate from the Bible. These are known as counterfeits of Christianity and we will focus on a few of these in this overview chapter from a big picture so you can better understand how counterfeits distort the truth about God. Each of the chapters in this volume will examine these counterfeits of Christianity in more detail.

Enter Man

As discussed in the introduction of this book, man's ideas often get elevated to be greater than God and His Word. Man's opinions begin to dilute or replace God's Word rather than serving as a sure foundation. And Christians are not immune! This disease or infection of thinking we are greater than God has even caused many Christians to adopt false beliefs by elevating man's ideas to be greater than God's Word.

This is clearly the case with religions like Islam, Judaism, Mormonism, Jehovah's Witnesses, and so on. Sadly, it is even the case within Christianity, and so it is a lesson for all of us. Furthermore, this is also the case with religions that have many similarities to Christianity but still deviate from the truth like Zoroastrianism, Deism, Gnosticism, and the like. This brings us to the issue of defining counterfeits of Christianity in more detail.

---

5. Since this volume focuses on the religious views that predominantly acknowledge the existence of God, our aim is to demonstrate that all other religions apart from biblical Christianity are false when compared to the Bible as God has revealed Himself to us. Discussions of the existence of God will be discussed elsewhere. For more information, see: "What Is the Best Argument for the Existence of God?" Jason Lisle, *New Answers Book 3*, Ken Ham, ed. (Green Forest, AR: Master Books, 2009), p. 263–270, https://answersin-genesis.org/is-god-real/what-is-the-best-argument-for-the-existence-of-god.

When it comes to paper money, a counterfeit is something pawned off or pretended to be the real thing, but isn't. It is not an authentic bill, but one that imitates the real bill, which has real value. Sometimes the bill is obviously faked but in other cases it can seem very convincing to deceive someone into believing that it is the real bill. There is a broad range of counterfeits! But what we know about a counterfeit bill is that it is ultimately without any value and fake.

In contrast to biblical Christianity (as defined by the 66 books of God's Word), a counterfeit of Christianity is any worldview that deviates from truths revealed in these 66 books by taking man's ideas to supersede God's Word by addition, deletion, unbiblical reinterpretation, syncretism with another religion, and so on; and yet, still has many elements of the Bible incorporated into its religious thinking and practices, whether they acknowledge it or not.

Now let's just put it right out there since this is what you are probably thinking: "But none of us get it exactly right except God, so how can *we* be expected to get it exactly right?" This is where the grace of God is extended, but each Christian is to strive to be as biblical as possible in all things (2 Timothy 2:15–16). It is a *process* whereby we are being made perfect, but that will not be brought to finality until we see the new heavens and new earth in consummate form where we will be in perfection with God for all eternity. But the greater point is that God gets it right, and the first step is realizing we can trust what He has revealed to us.

From a Christian worldview, we expect that there will be counterfeit religions very similar to a biblical worldview, and others that are heavily mutilated since this is exactly what Satan does. He cannot create but can only deceive by counterfeits (2 Corinthians 11:12–15). And so when we turn on our "radar," we can usually spot these variations. From a big picture, when cults and religions deviate from Christianity, they usually do it in a number of areas but none more often than the nature and work of Christ.

Arbitrariness: Looking at Counterfeits of Christianity

Let's start with two similar, but different, popular unitarian (God is not triune) counterfeits: Islam and Judaism. Both Muhammadism (Islam) and Judaism have much similarity to Christianity but have significant deviations. They both agree with Christians that there is only one God, and both have great respect for *much* of the Bible. But both of these groups deviate into a unitarian variant of God. Islam does so by adding to the Bible, making it subject to the alleged new revelation of Islam's Koran (Qur'an) and Hadith. Judaism does so by denying parts of God's Word as authoritative (the New Testament) while elevating man's traditions (Talmud) to the level of Scripture.

Note that in both cases, the 66 books of the Word of God were affected because man's ideas were elevated to be greater than God's Word. In the case of Islam, they held Muhammad's words to be higher than God's Word. With Judaism, Jews rejected Christ, elevating their own ideas to supersede the Word of God in the New Testament by denying its authority.

Jehovah's Witnesses, another unitarian counterfeit of Christianity, do something very similar. The founder of Jehovah's Witnesses, Charles Taze Russell, also claimed he was a prophet of God and introduced his writings as Scripture with his *Studies in the Scriptures* book series and set up what became the Watch Tower Bible and Tract Society whose publications (*Watchtower* and *Awake!* magazines) are seen as Scripture to the adherents of that cult. They produced a translation of the Bible in 1961 where many verses were changed to conform to their unitarian theology (New World Translation, NWT).

Now let us turn to the popular polytheistic (multiple-god) counterfeit of Mormonism (The Church of Jesus Christ of Latter-day Saints). They hold the Bible in high esteem, but, like Muslims and others, elevate a man's ideas to be greater than God's Word. Enter Joseph Smith Jr., who wrote several books that are seen by Mormons as being of greater authority than the Bible (*The Book of Mormon, Doctrine and Covenants*, and *The Pearl of Great Price*). Smith went so far as to rewrite the Bible, changing over 4,000 verses to conform to his new theology (Joseph Smith Translation, JST). The current Mormon organization still retains in its leadership people who claim to speak as prophets of God and thus sit in judgment over any previous revelation, including the Bible.

Note that in each case above, the ideas of man are used to overrule the Word of God. This makes their positions and their claims arbitrary, because man is not in a position to judge God and His revealed Word. God can speak for God, but man cannot without the help of God. In the case of the Bible, men were moved by God (the Holy Spirit) to write the inspired text (1 Timothy 3:16–17; 2 Peter 1:20–21). In the case of Muhammad, he claimed an angel informed him of this new "word of God" in trance-like revelations and ultimately found the word in his heart. Smith also encountered several angelic beings who he claims gave him special authority to receive revelations and do translations with special seer stones. Russell claimed of his own accord he was a prophet and spoke for God. The Jews, of their own accord, have merely set aside much of the Word of God and denied Jesus as the Messiah. Man cannot arbitrarily speak for God of His own authority and autonomy; only God can speak for God.

In most of these counterfeits, we find that a single person was the cause of deviation — whether Muhammad, Smith, Russell, Zarathustra (for Zoroastrianism), a pope, or another self-proclaimed leader. In some cases, when subsequent generations of followers came to power, such as the case with Jehovah's Witnesses and Mormons, the new leaders began to deviate from what was stated previously with further revelation! The arbitrary nature of these claims to new revelations from God became apparent as conflicting teachings surfaced within each group. If they had really been from God, they would not have contradicted one another.

But note that it is basically one person's views that are seen to supersede the Bible. In contrast, the Bible, which is unique in its authorship by having over 40 different authors with the same consistent message, is definitely a mark of the Holy Spirit's divine authorship.

Misconception: But Each Has Their Book and Their God(s) so It Is Like Preferring Chocolate over Vanilla?

So Muslims have the Koran, Mormons have *The Book of Mormon*, Jehovah's Witnesses have the *Awake!* magazine , the Jews have the Talmud, and the list continues. Christians have the Bible (Old and New Testament), so is the debate simply a matter of *preference*? Actually, this is a misconception.

These competing religious claims are not all equally valid. Not at all. It is not like a buffet, where you pick what you like, while someone else prefers to fill their plate with different foods. Truth is not a matter of opinion. If you pick what is truth based on your personal opinions, then truth is nonexistent since there would be no standard for truth! Thus, when we decide which "god" we feel like serving and what holy book is holy, it is merely arbitrary based on a human authority. Truth must be based on a standard. Only one God is the true God — all others are counterfeits.

When comparing the various religious views, there are some obvious conclusions we can draw. For instance, could it be true that Islam is a counterfeit of Mormonism? No. Mormonism was founded far later than Islam. Neither of their respective religious views hold the teachings of the other to be true — Muslims don't follow *The Book of Mormon*, and vice versa. Most of these counterfeits openly borrow or affirm the Bible, or at least parts of it, to be true whether Gnostics, Muslims, Mormons, Jehovah's Witnesses, Roman Catholic, Jews, Baha'i, and so on. Others borrow from biblical doctrines whether they realize it or not. (Zoroastrianism borrows a single God, creation, a need for salvation, final judgment, etc.) The Bible borrows teachings from none of these other religions, so it is obvious that they are counterfeits arising from the Bible. Biblical Christianity is the standard by which we can judge all other religious views.

Inconsistency

We are required to test these other religious worldviews against the truth of God's Word (1 Thessalonians 5:21; 1 John 4:1). In keeping with this, are they consistent? For example, let's look at two tests of consistency. First, it must be able to account for the existence of a rational universe in a consistent manner.[6] Second, it must contain no internal inconsistencies (e.g., false prophecies, truly contradictory revelations, competing omnipotent beings, etc.). The Bible, being the very standard at hand, obviously meets these two consistencies, so we judge all other truth claims by this same ultimate standard.

These different religions have gods that differ from the God of the Bible. Naturally, this is inconsistent when we consider that many popular cults tend to affirm the Bible is true! Further, their holy books do not agree with one another, so they can't all be from God (who cannot deny Himself). The God of the Bible is not arbitrary, is not inconsistent, and gives us a basis for knowledge. Other religions must borrow from the Bible to make sense of the world around us. In doing so, they inadvertently acknowledge the absolute truthfulness of the Bible.

Let's look at some examples. Mormons, Jehovah's Witnesses, and Muslims all affirm the Bible is true (to some degree), but then they deviate from that stated position. How?

---

6. Only the God of the Bible can consistently and logically account for the universe we live in; see Lisle, *New Answers Book 3*, p. 263–270.

	Bible true?	Are their subsequent Scriptures consistent with the Bible?	Their proposed solution?
Jehovah's Witnesses	Yes, but . . .	No	1. Rewrite the Bible to better fit their theology (NWT). 2. Say that when the Bible disagrees, then it must be corrected in light of their new revelations (*Awake!* or *Watchtower*, etc.)
Muslims	Yes, but . . .	No	1. Christians and Jews changed the text of Scripture since Muhammad's day. 2. Later revelations like the Koran are to be used to correct the errors.
Mormons	Yes, but . . .	No	1. Rewrite the Bible to better fit with their theology (Joseph Smith Translation/JST). 2. Say that when the Bible disagrees, then it must be corrected in light of their new revelations (*The Book of Mormon*, etc.)

Of course, there are large problems with each of these tired responses. Where is the textual support for such changes to the Bible? It simply does not exist. The text of the Bible we have before and after Muhammad is essentially identical. No doctrinal conflicts exist. There are variants (updated words, variant spellings of a word, minor copyist mistakes), but due to the immense witness of the texts (thousands of manuscripts to analyze) we can demonstrate the authenticity of the historical work; the text of the Bible is easily seen.

So there is no basis to say Jews and Christians changed the text of the Bible — let alone teamed up to do it! Furthermore, both Christians and Jews would be irate if they found the other doing such a thing, as the text of the Old Testament is sacred in the eyes of both, while the New Testament is sacred in the eyes of Christians.

Thus too, any alleged translation like that of Jehovah's Witnesses or Mormons must ultimately be judged by the text of the Bible manuscripts, which have not changed. There is no reason for the blatant changes they have sought to put in their translations other than to force the Bible to match their man-made doctrines. For example, there is no textual witness for a prophecy of Joseph Smith in any ancient document at the end of Genesis as Joseph Smith's "translation" of the Bible conveniently adds (Genesis 50:30–36, JST).[7]

On the Koran's own claims, the Bible is true. This puts the Muhammadan scholars in a predicament, since the Koran clearly disagrees with the Bible on many points — the most important being the deity of Christ.

For example, in the Koran, Mary the mother of Jesus was mistaken for Miriam the sister of Moses (Surah 19:27–28 and 66:12).[8] Many sets of mental gymnastics have been offered to get around this conflict, but it is merely an error from the mind of Muhammad (or his scribe or subsequent successor) confusing Mary with Miriam in this oral-based culture at the time of this dictation. Jesus was not crucified according to the Koran, yet the New Testament makes it clear He was. Another intriguing glitch is that the Koran teaches that the Word of God cannot be changed (Surah 6:115), then the Muslim scholars proceed to argue that the Word of God in the Old and New Testaments (e.g., books of Moses, writings [Psalms], and the Gospels) have been changed, yet Muhammad, disagreeing with the later scholars, affirmed them to be true!

Another interesting situation arises when the Koran claims that the nature of Allah is so far beyond us in transcendence, that nothing in changing human experience can be used to describe him. This is the doctrine of *tanzih*. Dr. Greg Bahnsen writes:

> The two worldviews are dissimilar in pivotal ways when one reflects on Islam's unitarianism, fatalism, moral concepts, lack of redemption, etc. Islam can be internally critiqued on its own presuppositions. Take an obvious example. The *Koran* acknowledges the words of Moses, David, and Jesus to be the words of prophets sent by Allah — in which case the *Koran* may be, *on*

---

7. Genesis 50:30–36 from the Joseph Smith Translation, LDS.org, https://www.lds.org/scriptures/jst/jst-gen/50.

8. "Mary, Sister of Aaron & Daughter of Amram," Qur'an Contradictions, Answering Islam, accessed April 7, 2015, http://www.answering-islam.org/Quran/Contra/qbhc06.html.

its own terms, refuted because of its contradictions with earlier revelation (cf. Deuteronomy 13:1–5). Sophisticated theologies offered by Muslim scholars interpret the theology of the *Koran* (cf. 42:11) as teaching the transcendence (*tanzih*) of unchanging Allah in such an extreme fashion that no human language (derived from changing experience) can positively and appropriate describe Allah — in which case the *Koran* rules out what the *Koran* claims to be.[9] (Italics in original)

Also, the Koran says all of Noah's family survived the Flood, then says some of his sons drowned in the Flood (e.g., Surah 11:42–43 and 21:76). Hosts of contradictions with the Bible can be found within the Koran as well as internal contradictions.[10]

But is the Jewish God (from the Judean religion/Judaism) the same as the Christian God? It is also commonly claimed that the Muslims, Jews, and Christians believe in and worship the same God. If that were the case, then Jews and Muslims would pray to Jesus, right? They do not. So it is not the same God. There is a major difference. Jews hold to a unitarian God, whereas Christians hold to a triune God — one God that is three persons (the Father, the Son, and the Holy Spirit).

But like the Jews, Christians completely agree with the Old Testament. So why do they have different views of God? This occurred as Jews continued to deviate from what was clearly stated in the Old Testament Scripture and relied on the traditions of men to supersede what the Scriptures said, denying Jesus as the Messiah. The ideas of man became so elite that they were used to reinterpret the Old Testament into a unitarian God, despite so many clues to the opposite (see appendix 1).

From Genesis to Malachi, it speaks of Jesus, the second person of the Triune God — this is what the New Testament is primarily about. In types, shadows, and direct language, it is difficult to miss Jesus as the Christ (Messiah),[11] who is the Creator who humbled Himself and came to the Jews and

---

9. Greg Bahnsen, "Presuppositional Reasoning with False Faiths," *Penpoint* VII:2, Feb./Mar., 1996, http://www.cmfnow.com/articles/pa208.htm.

10. For more please see: "Contradictions in the Qur'an," http://www.answering-islam.org/Quran/Contra/qbhc06.html.

11. The New Testament writers refer to Jesus in various ways. He came as the Jewish Messiah, which is the Christ in its Greek form. Reference to Jesus, the Messiah, Christ, or various combinations are all referring to Jesus Christ, the Messiah.

took on flesh to become a man (Colossians 2:5–10). Christ is the seed of the woman in Genesis 3:15 (Galatians 3:16); Jesus is the Messiah (Daniel 9:25–26; John 1:41); Christ is the ultimate Passover lamb sacrificed once for all (1 Corinthians 5:7); Christ is the great *I Am* (John 8:58), and the fulfillment of *God with us*/Immanuel (Isaiah 7:14, Matthew 1:21–23); and Christ is the mediator of the new *everlasting* covenant spoken by Jeremiah (Jeremiah 32:40; Matthew 26:28; Hebrew 8:6–13, 13:20).

Even Old Testament language speaks of a non-unitarian God. Some examples are:[12]

	Lord speaking (emphasis added)	Reference
1	"Let Us make man in *Our* image . . ."	Genesis 1:26
2	Then the Lord God said, "Behold, the man has become like one of *Us,* to know good and evil."	Genesis 3:22
3	"Come, let *Us* go down and there confuse their language . . ."	Genesis 11:4
4	Also I heard the voice of the Lord, saying: "Whom shall I send, and who will go for *Us?*"	Isaiah 6:8

The point is that the Jewish religion has deviated to go against the teachings in the Old Testament in denying Jesus as Messiah and a person in the Godhead. As Christians, we want to call our Jewish friends to fully trust the Word of God in both the Old Testament and the New Testament. For our heart is that they too will be saved through Jesus Christ for all eternity.

Christianity — as described in the New Testament — fulfills and is judged by previous revelation — the Old Testament — and is not internally inconsistent (e.g., Deuteronomy 13:1–5; Acts 17:11; etc.). *The Book of Mormon, Watchtower*, Koran, and other religious writings try to go backward. Instead of allowing their books/writings to be judged by previous revelation from God, they claim the prior must be looked at in light of their new revelation, reinterpreting their predecessors or claiming the new supersedes the old. How convenient! But this is the mark of a false teaching — declaring your view as true and then saying all other things must be judged by your new view. Counterfeits simply do not stand up to scrutiny when judged by previous revelation from God.

---

12. All Scripture quotations in this chapter are from the New King James Version of the Bible.

Consider that what Islam tries to do with Christianity (add a later prophet's revelations to supersede what came before), Baha'i does to Islam! The Baha'i religion tries to supersede Muhammad with later prophets who reinterpreted the Koran and Bible and produced their own writings!

In Muhammadism (Islam), the only supposed guarantee of paradise is by dying in a holy war. So if there are no holy wars, then the certainty of salvation really diminishes, so this helps explain the bloody history of Islam. The rest of the non-militant Muslims then have hopes that good works will be enough to save them.

In fact, most counterfeits have this idea that good works will get them to heaven. But good works are expected from a good God who created man in His image. Good works should be a given, not a means of salvation! It is not good works that God looks at to decide if someone is worthy of heaven. Ever since Adam sinned, God looks at each person as sinful, and judgment will come for all sinners (Galatians 3:22). The punishment from an infinitely holy God is, by extension, an infinite punishment. So if 99.999 percent of all you do is good, then it still doesn't matter; that 0.001 percent will still be punished by an infinite God, which means you are not worthy to enter heaven. So what is the hope of heaven since all have sinned?

No created being could take that punishment — only the Lord Jesus Christ, who is God, could do it. The infinite Son of God became a man, lived a sinless life, and took the infinite punishment from the infinite Father, which is the only way the debt to sin can truly be covered. God was the only one in a position to take that punishment on our behalf. And this is what Jesus did on the Cross — He bore the wrath of God for sinners. To acknowledge His perfect sacrifice, the Father raised Him from the dead.

The only means of salvation is grace-based, not works-based, through Jesus Christ, by repenting of your sin and receiving by faith the Jesus Christ of Scripture as Lord of your life — not by dying in a holy war or trying to do "good works." The counterfeits of Christianity all demand righteousness earned by the individual — an impossibility — rather than trusting in the righteousness of Christ offered to all who trust in Him as Savior. When one receives Christ, the righteousness of Christ is transferred to you like a covering (imputed to you) so then you are seen as righteous in God's eyes and able to enter heaven.

Returning to an earlier idea, having later prophets (Joseph Smith, Charles Taze Russell, Muhammad, Ellen White, etc.) after the Bible was written has big problems. Most take a position that denies the Bible in saying sin hasn't been covered and that works are what is required to possibly achieve salvation.

Of course, none of these later prophets ever came back from the dead to prove they were right about the afterlife. Only the Lord Jesus Christ did. But consider other problems of having prophets after the Bible was written:

1. Apostles of Christ were given authority over prophets and, together with the prophets of the Old Testament, are the foundation with Christ as the chief cornerstone (e.g., 1 Corinthians 12:28–29; Ephesians 2:20; 2 Peter 3:2). The implication is that any alleged prophets after the Apostles of Christ are subject to the Apostles' teachings (i.e., the New Testament, which holds authority over any of them). This is consistent with previous revelation being used to judge any alleged new revelation.

2. In the New Testament, Jude 1:3 affirms that the faith was once for all delivered to the saints (Christians) now that Christ fulfilled the Old Testament (e.g., Matthew 5:17; Acts 3:18). So there is no reason for the faith to have to change; it was completed and salvation was made possible once and for all.

3. Some Christians hold to this third point as well: the Old Testament prophesied that prophecy (no more prophets) would cease upon the destruction of the Temple's sanctuary, when it would be burned with fire per Psalm 74:3–9. When the sanctuary is destroyed and the things in it with fire and broken down and all the meeting places (e.g., synagogues in Israel) are destroyed, there will no longer be any prophet in the land. This is confirmed by Daniel 9:24–27 when the vision and prophecy shall cease when the Holy City (that is Jerusalem, per Nehemiah 11:1; Isaiah 52:1) and sanctuary (that is, the Temple; e.g., 1 Kings 6:19) are destroyed, which occurred in the first century.[13] So vision and prophecy (i.e., new prophets)

---

13. Prophets like Jeremiah, Daniel, Ezekiel, and Obadiah still existed when the Babylonians came in and destroyed Solomon's Temple. Also, the items were largely taken out of the Temple by the Babylonians and were later returned and not destroyed (2 Chronicles 36:7; Ezra 5:14; etc.). This is why some Christians hold this Psalm/Daniel passages for what occurred in the first century. But as noted, not all Christians are in agreement here.

should no longer be possible after the New Testament was completed (i.e., in Muhammad's day about 500 years later, or Joseph Smith's day about 1,700 year later).

Borrowing from the Bible

Many religions borrow from the Bible, in particular those that have many similarities to Christianity. Many do this unknowingly while others are open about it.

Consider a big-picture simplistic point for a moment. God has all knowledge (cf. Psalm 147:5; Colossians 2:3). For anyone to have any knowledge whatsoever, it had to be borrowed from God. For example, for any religion to agree to the claim that there is one God, they had to borrow this concept from the one true God.

Have you ever considered that many other things are also borrowed from the God of the Bible? The concepts of good and evil are defined by the all-good God. So when people use terminology like "good" or "bad" or "better" or "worse" or "evil" or "proper" or "improper" and so on, then they are borrowing from the God of the Bible. Morality in and of itself is a Christian outworking from the God of the Bible who defines morality. Apart from a single, absolute standard, there can be no understanding of what is right or wrong, good or bad. The triune God of the Bible is that standard of goodness (Matthew 19:17).

Why do logic and reason and truth exist? They exist because God is the truth (John 14:6) and God is the standard of truth. Logic and reasoning are tools by which infinite truth can be better understood with our finite minds. But just because God makes logic, reason, and truth a possibility does not mean that man can reason. So why can man use logic to reason and know

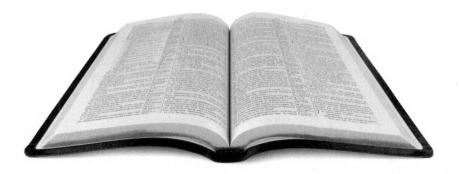

that truth exists? It is simple. The God of the Bible made man in His own image — the image of a logical, reasoning God who is the truth.

In what other religion is man made in the image of God? This idea comes from the Bible, though many borrow this openly. Islam and Mormonism both have creation stories that are similar to the account in the Bible. And when another religion doesn't borrow this openly, then they merely assume it (borrow it unknowingly) from the God of the Bible.

Consider other doctrines that are borrowed from the Bible with biblical references. Here are a few:

Clothing	Genesis 3
Marriage	Genesis 1
Marriage between a man and a woman	Genesis 1
Don't marry close relatives anymore	Leviticus 18
Logic exists and people can understand it	Genesis 1
Why people can often mess up logic	Genesis 3
Lying is wrong	Exodus 20,
Stealing is wrong	Exodus 20, Leviticus 19:11, etc.
Murder is wrong/preserving life	Genesis 4:8-14, Exodus 20, etc.
Knowledge exists	Genesis 2:9, Exodus 31:3, Colossians 2:3, etc.
Immaterial/spiritual exists	Genesis 1:1 (God is not part of creation), 1:2, 6:2, etc.
Why evil exists	Genesis 3

More Christian doctrines that the world must borrow from the Bible (still not exhaustive):

Trust exists

Honesty exists

Science possible (God upholds the universe in a particular uniform way)

Week

Weekend

Why death exists and is bad

Sadness exists

Joy exists

Love exists

Why hate exists

People have value

Safety due to things having value

Laws (why governing necessary)

Righteous judgments

Why disasters happen

Why a remnant of good in the world

Why the need for a Savior

Cleanliness

Why fight disease

Suffering is bad

Origins can be known

Gold/silver, etc., have value

Why eat vegetarian foods and meat

Why sin exists

Why things wear out (e.g., our bodies)

Why thorns and thistles exist

Agriculture/cultivation

Why people name things

Reproduction

Why classify things (class concept)

Work

Surgery possible

Sleep

Medicine

Timekeeping

Care for elderly, sick, orphans, etc.

Why sedimentary rock layers

Genealogies and their importance

Truth exists

Why hair should be kempt

Law of biogenesis

Astronomy, e.g., map and monitor heavens

Origin of languages

Communication possible

Why mutations exist

Miracles

Inheritance

Mercy exists

Grace is possible

Giving

Peace

Forgiveness is possible

Memorials

Mountains, valleys, landscapes

Music possible

Atonement

Existence of angels

Constellations

Animal husbandry

Language style and elements

Authority exists

Desire to do something

Education

Technology (e.g., to counter effects of the Curse)

Dominion

Preservation

Sympathy/Empathy

Honor exists

One race/all related

Holidays

Wearing shoes

History important

Mathematics

Sleep

Spirits/heavenly host exists

Soul

Animals have value

Anger exists

Moderation in certain things

Personal dignity

Morality; right and wrong (good and bad)

Other Smaller Cults with a Leading Human Authority

Cults existed in the first century. For example, Gnostics played off of a leader who led people down a different path. One variant form of Gnosticism in the early stages of the church was by Marcion. He tried to teach that only Paul's writings were Scriptures (neglecting much of the New Testament), but even then, he was selective about that!

Many modern cults usually have one leader (sometimes it can be more than one) who takes them down the wrong road and away from biblical teachings. Though there is no reason to be exhaustive, these examples should help you be able to spot what is occurring. This table outlines a few:

Who	Who was the authority seen to supersede the Bible?
Heaven's Gate	Marshall Applewhite and Bonnie Nettles
People's Temple	Jim Jones
Manson Family Cult	Charles Manson
Branch Davidians (Waco)	David Koresh
Children of God (The Family or Family of Love)	David Berg
Twelve Tribes	Elbert Eugene Spriggs
Christian Science	Mary Baker Eddy
Rastafari	Haile Selassie I

Note that in each case, man is used to supersede God's revealed authority. How sad that the creature would seek to usurp the Creator. Now there is a big point to be made here and it shouldn't go unrecognized. No one is immune from going down the path of a cult, even in what is seen as good biblical denominations. All it takes is one person to lead people down a path opposed to God's Word, claiming to have special revelations or authority that can lead to dangerous areas of compromise and destruction.

All teaching, regardless of its source, should be checked against the Word of God, the 66 books of the Bible. Paul commended the Bereans for doing just that with his teaching that Jesus was the Jewish Messiah (Acts 17:11) — and he was an Apostle of the Lord. So no teacher who really loves the Lord should be upset with having their work checked against Scripture (previous revelation).

With this said, there are some modern denominations moving in the wrong direction. Sometimes it is due to a person leading them there. In other cases, they are not checking certain teachings against the clear teaching in the Bible and gradually move in a false direction.

One great example of that is when people take the secular humanistic view of origins (a naturalistic view as opposed to the biblical view) and try to mix it with their Christianity. Usually, this is done by replacing biblical creation (in six days) with an evolutionary/big bang origins story that comes from the secular humanistic religion. This is not biblical and these types of teachings are leading people down the wrong path. These extra-biblical teachings lead to problems like the presence of death before sin that undermine the gospel of Jesus Christ.[14] We need to call many in various denominations back to God's Word, trusting what God revealed to us about creation as opposed to taking the human-concocted story about origins.

On the opposite end of the spectrum, we have groups that started out in the direction of a cult and have since moved to be more biblical in their outlook. One example comes with some Seventh Day Adventists (SDA). They departed from biblical truth by following Ellen White, who claimed to have visions, and many hailed her as a prophetess. Many within SDA hold to Ellen White's teaching as nearly infallible, so they could easily fit in the chart above. Many people within SDA have moved away from her teachings and tried to go back to the Bible in more modern times. Is this wise? Yes, and we want to encourage this, but the false doctrines must be abandoned for the truth of Scripture alone.

This is the lesson: no matter where you were raised or what circumstances you are in, you can always go back to God's Word to get the truth. The Bible is the Word of God inspired by the Holy Spirit and is the truth. *"All Scripture is given by inspiration of God, and is profitable for doctrine, for reproof, for correction, for instruction in righteousness"* (2 Timothy 3:16).

Conclusion: Christ above All

This first volume of World Religions and Cults dives into religions that seem like they have similarities to Christianity but deviate from the teachings in the Bible in various ways. Some can be considered "Christian" in a very

---

14. Bodie Hodge, "Biblically, Could Death Have Existed Before Sin?" *Answers in Genesis,* accessed March 2, 2010, https://answersingenesis.org/death-before-sin/biblically-could-death-have-existed-before-sin/.

broad and historical sense (as opposed to *biblical* Christianity), but we must be careful not to let that label become a stamp of truth in doctrine and a proper understanding of salvation.

In many of these cases, these religions openly affirm that the Bible is true, while others borrow from the Bible inadvertently. What is the common factor to the Bible's demotion from the position of absolute authority? It is man's fallible opinions that are elevated to be greater than what God has spoken in His Word. In each of these counterfeits, man's ideas are seen as greater than God's ideas. It is back to front.

One way or another, the Bible gets demoted or reinterpreted or completely ignored in light of man's ideas that are being used to throw the Bible's clear teaching out the window! To assume man sits in judgment above God and His Word is arbitrary and fallacious. So the key to not falling into this trap is biblical authority. To know the truth is to follow He who is the truth, and the only way to do that is by following the Bible that God, who is the truth, gave us.

Table of examples of some Bible-based religions that add or take away from the 66 Books of the Bible (included are faulty Christian views of origins where man's ideas have infiltrated) *Not exhaustive*

	Who?	Added to the 66 books of God's Word (man's opinions)?	Subtracted/ Changed from the 66 books of God's Word (man's opinions)
1	Roman Catholicism	Added OT Apocrypha Added papal authority	
2	Orthodox	Added Apocrypha Added authority of patriarchs	
3	Jehovah's Witnesses	Added Charles Taze Russell's writings (e.g., *Studies in the Scriptures*) and *Watchtower* and *Awake!* publications as supreme over the Bible Added Modern governing authorities of JW's	Changed the Bible to mean things other than what it plainly says (New World Translation)

4	Mormons (LDS)	Added Joseph Smith's writings (*The Book of Mormon, The Pearl of Great Price, Doctrines & Covenants*) Added modern prophets	Changed nearly 4,000 verses in the Bible to conform to their theology (Joseph Smith Translation, aka KJV 1833)
5	Islam (Muslims)	Added Muhammad's sayings (Koran and the Hadith) as superior to the Bible	Demoted the Bible as supreme, and Islamic scholars today say it was corrupted even though Muhammad said it was true and to be believed
6	Traditional Seventh Day Adventists*	Added Ellen White's teachings	
7	Theistic Evolution	Added astronomical, geological, and biological evolutionary ideas as supreme above the Bible, so the Bible (special revelation) needs to be reinterpreted in light of these general revelations as interpreted by secularists (i.e., mixing humanistic ideas with the Bible)	The Bible needs to be reinterpreted in light of the secular ideas
8	Progressive Creation	Added astronomical and geological evolutionary ideas as supreme above the Bible, so the Bible (special revelation) needs to be reinterpreted in light of these general revelations as interpreted by secularists (i.e., mixing humanistic ideas with the Bible)	The Bible needs to be reinterpreted in light of the secular ideas

9	Gap Theory	Added astronomical and geological evolutionary ideas as supreme above the Bible, so the Bible (special revelation) needs to be reinterpreted in light of these general revelations as interpreted by secularists (i.e., mixing humanistic ideas with the Bible)	The Bible needs to be reinterpreted in light of the secular ideas
10	Judaism	Adds traditions of the fathers (e.g., Rabbinic Literature like the Talmud, Midrash, etc.)	The 27 books of the New Testament are deleted from God's Word
11	Gnostics (or Marcionism)	Additions of spurious writings like the so-called Gnostic Gospels that some claim to be part of the New Testament or Marcion's claims	Deletion of New Testament texts except most Pauline epistles (they did not accept Paul's letters to Timothy and Titus) and an edited Gospel of Luke
12	Unitarian Universalism	Adds outside sources from other world religions	Demotes biblical teachings that Jesus and the Holy Spirit are the one true God along with the Father (Triune nature of God) Demotes the Bible in favor of false religions
13	Generic Cults	Elevates a leader's teachings to be supreme above the Bible	Because of a leader's authority, the Bible is usually seen as second rate and demoted

14	Deism	Human reason and nature are seen as absolute above God's Word	Demotes the character of God in the Bible Demotes Bible as a source of authority
15	Ba'hai	Added the teachings of Shoghi Effendi with the writings of Bahá'u'lláh, the Báb, and 'Abdu'l-Bahá	Denies the Bible is authoritative but recognizes the Bible as a holy text among others
16	Freemasons	Added Freemasonry teachings (Old Charges)	The Bible, though often revered by some within its ranks, is not the source of ultimate authority and many Masonic teachings contradict the Bible
17	Zoroastrianism	Add the book of Avesta, which includes the ideas of a man named Zarathustra and those following him	Deny the Bible's authority altogether

* Take note that many SDA today do not adhere to the teachings of Ellen White and hold that the Bible is the authority. We encourage this, by the way.

Chapter 7

Islam

Dr. Emir Caner

A Mosque for a Day: The Washington Cathedral Turns Its Prayers to Allah

In 1790, Congress declared Washington, D.C. to be the capital of the United States of America. The first president and namesake of the city, George Washington, diligently began construction plans for the newly formed city in order for it to be the seat of power of the young republic. President Washington appointed a three-person committee, including Frenchman Pierre L'Enfant, to develop the capital and its buildings. One such structure that Washington considered essential to the national welfare was a national cathedral. In 1791, L'Enfant planned a "church intended for national purposes, such as public prayer, thanksgiving, funeral orations, etc., and assigned to the special use of no particular Sect of denomination, but equally open to all."[1]

Unfortunately, due to a myriad of factors, the cathedral did not take shape until more than a century later. In 1907, President Theodore Roosevelt laid the cornerstone, which stated, "The Word became flesh and lived among us" (John 1:14).[2] The English Gothic cathedral, constructed in the shape of a cross and funded with private donations, was erected and given

---

1. Paul Kelsey Williams and Gregory J. Alexander, *Woodley Park* (Charleston, SC: Arcadia Publishing, 2003), p. 113.
2. All Scripture in this chapter is from the New King James Version of the Bible.

the official title "The Cathedral of Saints Peter and Paul."[3] Since its inception, the cathedral has hosted national events such as a national prayer service during the inauguration of Franklin D. Roosevelt and the state funerals of presidents Dwight Eisenhower and Ronald Reagan.

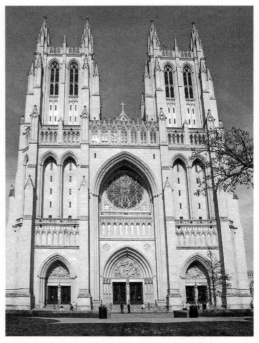

The National Cathedral in Washington, DC

On November 14, 2014, another significant event occurred at the iconic cathedral — the first Muslim Friday prayer service ever held at the historic church. As Pamela Constable reported, "The Arabic call to prayer echoed among the vaulted stone arches and faded away."[4] Prayer rugs were laid out at the northern precept of the cathedral, limited in its iconography, as rows of Muslim men and women prostrated themselves toward Mecca declaring, *Allahu Akbar* ("God is Great"). According to the National Cathedral website, organizers of the event believe "powerful things come out of praying together" and "demonstrates an appreciation of one another's prayer traditions and is a powerful symbolic gesture toward a deeper relationship between the two Abrahamic traditions."[5]

This historic precedent, though, illustrates theological infidelity far more than political correctness. The organizers of the event presuppose that Muslims and Christians worship the same god. How ironic that Muslim

3. Frederick Quinn, *A House of Prayer for All People: A History of the Washington National Cathedral* (Harrisburg, PA: Morehouse Publishing, 2014), p. vii-x.
4. Pamela Constable, "Washington Cathedral's First Muslim Prayer Service Interrupted by Heckler," *Washington Post*, 14 November 2014; at http://www.washingtonpost.com/local/2014/11/14/40c49d06-6c41-11e4-a31c-77759fc1eacc_story.html.
5. Stephanie Samuel, "National Cathedral Hosts Islamic Prayers; Lone Protester Interrupts Service," *Christian Post*, 14 November 2014; at http://www.christianpost.com/news/national-cathedral-hosts-islamic-prayers-lone-protester-interrupts-service-129726/.

rugs were laid out on the cathedral's foundation, which declares the deity of Christ — the Word (John 1:1) becoming flesh (John 1:14). Such a declaration of deity of anyone besides Allah is an unforgiveable sin (*shirk*) in Islam and considered the highest and most heinous sin (Qur'an 4:116).[6] Additionally, in a hope of a better relationship with Muslims, it seems Christian leadership in the cathedral were willing to sacrifice their relationship with the one true God (Isaiah 45:5). Like the nation of Israel under pagan leadership, who worshiped Baal along with Yahweh, so too have many American Christians added idols, including Allah, to their list of gods to worship. But like Elijah, we, too, must ask: "How long will you falter between two opinions? If the Lord is God, follow Him; but if Baal, follow him" (1 Kings 18:21). Any answer other than an exclusive allegiance to the Lord will lead to eternal damnation, not to mention the decline of a nation.

The Five Pillars of Islam: Struggling and Surrendering

> *Ye [Muslims] are the best of Peoples, evolved for mankind. Enjoining what is right, forbidding what is wrong, and believing in Allah.* Qur'an 3:110

With a population surpassing 1.5 billion adherents, Islam[7] is the second largest religion in the world, only surpassed by Christianity. Birthed in the Arabian desert more than 1,400 years ago, Islam, an Arabic word that means "submission to Allah," prides itself as a simple religion that requires its followers to declare exclusive allegiance to Allah and to trust the messengers of Allah, in particular, the final messenger Muhammad (Qur'an 61:6). The creed (*shahada*) of Islam sums up the faith, stating, "There is no god but Allah. Muhammad is the messenger of Allah." All other beliefs are based on this one unchanging statement. In affirming there is only one god, Islam is a monotheistic religion.

This creed — or statement of faith — is required for anyone to convert to Islam. Once someone sincerely repeats this creed three times in Arabic, he or she is considered a Muslim, a follower of the Islamic faith. Such a person is then taught the "five pillars" of Islam, which are as follows:

---

6. The holy book of Islam is commonly spelled as Quran, Qur'an, and Koran. The divisions in the book are similar to the Bible's divisions of chapter and verse, but are called surahs (suras) and ayahs.

7. Islam is the name of the religion, and its practitioners are called Muslims.

1. The Creed (*Shahada*): Acknowledging Muhammad as the prophet of Allah, the believer now submits oneself to the teachings of Islam. The Qur'an, the holy book of Islam, becomes the guiding principle of life and eternity, and Muhammad is now the example by which a Muslim lives (Qur'an 33:21).

2. Prayer (*Salat*): The lifeline of Muslims, prayer is the central practice of Islam. Muslims are obligated to pray five times daily. The prayer ritual includes washing themselves beforehand (*wudu*) and reciting their prayers in Arabic while prostrating themselves before Allah. The Muslim is also required to pray with the Islamic community on Fridays (*jumu'ah*). If a Muslim does not pray regularly, he will forget about Allah and his greatness.

3. Almsgiving (*Zakat*): This pillar demands that Muslims reject individual greed and embrace generosity to others. Therefore, Muslims are commanded to give 2.5 percent of their incomes, excluding debts, to those less fortunate in the community.

4. Fasting (*Sawm*): According to the Qur'an, fasting is prescribed of the Islamic believer in order to learn "self-restraint" (Qur'an 2:183). For one month, from before sunrise to after sunset, the Muslim abstains from food, drink, strenuous activity, and even marital intimacy. In their place, the Muslim should devote himself to such things as reading the Qur'an.

5. Pilgrimage (*Hajj*): The climax of the Muslim experience, followers of Islam who are physically and financially able are required to visit the holiest city of Islam, Mecca (Saudi Arabia). The centerpiece of Mecca is a cube-shaped building called the *Ka'aba*. This structure, which Muslims believe was first established by the Old Testament prophet Abraham as the first house of worship on earth, had become corrupted with hundreds of idols by the time of Muhammad. But Muhammad destroyed all idols and restored the worship of Allah that Abraham had begun. Remember, Muslims face this building to perform their daily prayers from wherever they live in the world. And at least once during their lifetimes, Muslims are

Pilgrims pray at Kaaba, the Holy Mosque in Mecca

required to come, circle this cubed building, and pray. Additional duties include visiting Muhammad's last sermon site, throwing stones at the devil, and sacrificing an animal.

This brief description of the tenets of Islam gives the reader an understanding that Islam is not as simple as it first makes itself out to be. The Qur'an summarizes the pillars in one verse: "Those who believe, *and* do deeds of righteousness, *and* establish regular prayers, *and* give [almsgiving], will have their reward with the Lord" (Qur'an 2:277; italics mine). Notice the "ands" of the verse; that it is required for a Muslim to do all of these things in order to be rewarded, not merely some of the pillars all of the time or all of the pillars some of the time.

As one can easily see, Islam is not only a religion — it is a complete way of life. It engrosses all of life; from the way you dress to how you spend your money; from family life to the afterlife; from women to warfare; from purity to politics; from creation to end times. Muslims accept this lifelong struggle as a strength, not as a weakness of their faith. The faith is both theological and political, and for many Muslims these two cannot be separated. The law of Allah is, at minimum, the law for Muslims if not the accepted law of the land.

What was begun in the sands of modern-day Saudi Arabia has swept across much of the globe. The most populous Muslim nation is not found in the Middle East, near its geographical beginning, but in Indonesia, where more than 200 million Muslims reside. Three countries in South Asia — Pakistan, India, and Bangladesh — hold nearly half a billion Muslims. Indeed, Muslims are a majority in 49 nations of the world.[8] Islam is on the doorstep of the West, with millions of followers in the United States and tens of millions across Europe. The West, much of it known for its aversion to religion during the past century, must wake up from its religious illiteracy and once again begin studying the great religions of the world. If not, the world may just pass it by — or take it over.

The Rise of the Warrior-Prophet: Muhammad (A.D. 570–632)

> *We have truly sent you as a witness, as a bearer of Glad Tidings, and as a Warner: In order that you (O men) may believe in Allah and His Messenger, that you may assist and honour him, and celebrate His praises morning and evening.* Qur'an 48:8–9

In March of A.D. 632, an aged prophet rode on a camel one last time to the plain of Arafat, just outside the holy city of Mecca. A crowd, perhaps one hundred thousand strong, awaited his arrival and, with great expectation, listened intently to the last sermon of Muhammad, their prophet. It seemed he knew his life was fleeting and exclaimed, "O People, lend me an attentive ear, for I do not know whether, after this year, I shall ever be among you again." He then exhorted his followers to remain united in the faith and worship Allah alone for, one day, each person would answer for the deeds they have done.[9] The crowd cheered his farewell address, shouting, "You have fulfilled it, O Messenger of God."[10] Three months later, the prophet was dead. Muhammad had fulfilled his mission and handed the faith to his disciples. As one biographer noted, "Fired with the wild enthusiasm of the new faith,

---

8. Pew Research Center's Forum on Religion and Public Life, "Muslim," at http://www.pewforum.org/2012/12/18/global-religious-landscape-muslim.

9. For the full transcript of Muhammad's Farewell Sermon, see http://legacy.fordham.edu/halsall/source/muhm-sermon.asp.

10. John Glubb, *The Life and Times of Muhammad* (Chelsea, MI: Scarborough House, 1991), p. 21.

his followers poured out of their deserts, bent on conquering the world for God."[11]

Born in Mecca about A.D. 570, the early life of Muhammad was filled with tragedy. His father, Abdullah, died before his birth and his mother, Amina, passed away when Muhammad was just six years old. Muhammad's grandfather, Abd al-Muttalib, became the caregiver for a short while, but he died when Muhammad was only eight years old. Muhammad's uncle, Abu Talib, reared the young man into adulthood. By all accounts, Muhammad lived a normal Arab life; however, he refused to partake in the pagan rituals in his hometown of Mecca.[12]

In time, Muhammad met and married the first love of his life, Khadija, a wealthy merchant widow who had hired Muhammad to lead a caravan to Syria. Although she was 15 years his senior, Khadija bore six children, two boys and four girls. Both boys died in infancy, but the daughters followed the faith of their father, two of whom married future leaders of Islam.

Khadija also played a significant role in the formation of the Islamic faith. When Muhammad was 40 years old, he received his first revelation from Allah. While sitting in a cave in a mountain outside of Mecca, the archangel Gabriel supposedly appeared before the prophet and demanded that Muhammad recite the words of Allah. The encounter was so violent that he believed Gabriel was going to kill him. The prophet returned home, his "heart beating severely," and shared his experience with his wife. Muhammad wondered whether he was delusional or even possessed by an evil spirit. Khadija assured her husband that the revelation from Allah was authentic. Her consolation affirmed the first revelation, which birthed the sacred text of Islam, the Qur'an.[13]

Over the next 23 years in the life of Muhammad, two political events allowed Islam to rise to national prominence in the Arabian Peninsula. First, after Muhammad gained a small but zealous band of followers, the authorities in Muhammad's hometown of Mecca devised a plan to assassinate the emerging leader. Muhammad secretly eluded the assassins, journeyed about

---

11. Ibid., p. 21–22.
12. The earliest and most respected biography of Muhammad was written by Ibn Ishaq. The work, *The Life of Muhammad*, was translated by Alfred Guillaume and published by Oxford University Press (2002).
13. To read more about the encounter, see the collection of Hadith by Sahih al-Bukhari 1.3. The verses given to Muhammad, the very first verses revealed of the Qur'an, are surah 96:1–3.

200 miles to the town of Medina, and then quickly united the city under his political leadership. Muhammad had secured a home base for his religion where he could strategize the expansion and implementation of the Islamic faith.

Second, Muhammad rose as a military leader, a warrior-prophet, sanctioning raids on caravans in order to secure resources for their cause. Muhammad himself fought in dozens of battles over his lifetime and commanded others to do so as well, stating, "Fighting is prescribed upon you, and you dislike it. But it is possible that you dislike a thing which is good for you" (Qur'an 2:216). The prophet viewed war as a religious event, slaying those who "do not believe in Allah or the Last Day" (Qur'an 9:29). He eradicated Jews from Medina and ultimately conquered his hometown, Mecca, with very little resistance. There, Muhammad destroyed hundreds of pagan idols from the Ka'aba and established Islam as the official religion of the Arabian Peninsula. Mecca finally became the focal point of Islam, something it has sustained until this day.

A Trail of Blood: A Very Brief History of Fourteen Centuries of Conquest

And if you are slain or die in the way of Allah, forgiveness and mercy from Allah are far better than all they could amass. Qur'an 3:157

Immediately following Muhammad's death, Abu Bakr, an early convert to Islam, was named the leader (*caliph*) of the Islamic community. Yet some Muslims no longer desired to follow the religion after the prophet's passing and revolted against Islamic authorities. Abu Bakr quickly squelched the civil unrest and secured the entire Arabian Peninsula. The lesson: once a Muslim, you must always remain a Muslim.[14]

Over the next millennium, the world, in particular the Christian realm, witnessed the unprecedented growth of political Islam. As American missionary and scholar Samuel Zwemer explained, "To the follower of Christ, and especially to the student of Christian history, Islam possesses a melancholy interest peculiar to it among the religions of the world. It alone can claim to have met and vanquished Christianity."[15] The conquest of Christian lands by

---

14. Bukhari's Hadith declared, "If a Muslim changes his religion, kill him" (9.57).
15. Samuel M. Zwemer, *Islam: A Challenge to Faith* (New York: Student Volunteer Movement for Foreign Missions, 1907), p. 1.

Muslims was swift and stunning. British historian Bernard Lewis, who taught at Princeton, exclaimed, "For the first thousand years Islam was advancing, Christendom was in retreat and under threat. The new faith conquered the old Christian lands of the Levant and North Africa, and invaded Europe, ruling for a while in Sicily, Spain, Portugal, and even parts of France."[16] Consider the following Christian regions that were conquered by Islamic forces in the years given: Syria (634), Egypt (639), North Africa (700), Spain (711), and Morocco (722). In fact, although not overtaken, even Rome was sacked by Muslims (846). Muslims captured other territory including Persia (642), Afghanistan (670), Turkestan (715), and West Africa (late 900s).

Perhaps the greatest expansion of Islam occurred under the Ottomans, who conquered the city of Constantinople (1453), a city second only to Rome in Christian influence. The Turks would rule much of the civilized world over the next 450 years and challenge Christian supremacy in the very heart of Europe. By the mid-17th century, Turks controlled parts of Europe as far north as the Polish border and as far west as Hungary. In time, the Ottomans faded from political history, replaced by the very ones they attempted to conquer — Europeans.

Beginning in the 18th century, European colonialism halted the onslaught of Islamic expansion and drove back many of the advances made during the first one thousand years of Islamic history. Countries governed by Muslims for centuries, including Egypt, India, and parts of the Arabian Peninsula, were now controlled by British forces. The Dutch ruled Indonesia, the French controlled Morocco and Algeria, and the Italians ruled Libya. The Muslim world was in tatters, and the last Muslim power, the weakened Ottoman Empire, lost its final attempt at regaining any power after its defeat in World War I.

After the war, a new day dawned, a day of Muslim independence from European regimes. Brits and French made one final attempt at establishing rule over the Middle East, but emerging Islamic nationalism halted that effort. Over the course of the 20th century, Muslim-populated countries gained independence and began self-governance. At the same time Islam regained its political power, much of the religion was experiencing a cultural renaissance and theological reformation. Western values waned and Islamic

---

16. Bernard Lewis, "The Roots of Muslim Rage," *The Atlantic Monthly*, vol. 266, no. 3 (September 1990): 47–60.

law as described in the Qur'an and Hadith (*sharia*) came back in vogue. The more literally a Muslim read the Qur'an, the more political his faith became.

Today, many Muslim countries govern under the auspices of Islamic law and regard the holy texts of Islam as their constitution. Freedoms codified in law in the West, like freedom of speech and freedom of religion, are not accepted in Muslim countries. Many Muslim countries enforce criminal laws against proselytizing, and punish those who would criticize Islam in any way.[17] In the harshest of places, leaving the Islamic faith is punishable by death. Some blame the West and its oppression through colonialism for the backwardness and radicalization of these regimes. However, a fairer rendering of history, considering the life of Muhammad and the conquests throughout Islam's history, recognizes that an affirmation of Islamic law has little to do with colonial oppression and far more to do with Muhammad's words and actions. Political Islam, birthed in the seventh century by Muhammad himself, has seen a revival and, it seems, is here to stay for generations to come.

The Two Sources of Authority in Islam: Qur'an and the Example of Muhammad

> *We sent down the (Qur'an) in Truth, and in Truth has it descended: and We sent you but to give Glad Tidings and to warn (sinners). It is a Qur'an which we have divided (into parts from time to time), in order that you might recite it to men at intervals: We have revealed it by stages. Say: "Whether you believe it or not, it is true that those who were given knowledge beforehand, when it is recited to them, fall down on their faces in humble prostration.* Qur'an 17:105–107

The primary source of authority for Muslims is the "Glorious Qur'an" (Qur'an 85:22), the holy book of the faith. This book consists of 114 chapters, 6,616 verses, 77,943 words, and 338,606 letters — each and every part dictated by Allah. The story of the Qur'an comes through the prophet Muhammad, although the sacred text has little to say about him. Instead, the Qur'an affirms itself to be the irreproducible (Qur'an 2:23), incorruptible (Qur'an 15:9), and inspired (Qur'an 42:51) word of Allah recited in Arabic (Qur'an

---

17. For a good example, see Pakistan's blasphemy code (section 295c), which states, "Whoever by words, either spoken, or written, or by visible representation, or by any imputation, innuendo, or insinuation, directly or indirectly, defiles the sacred name of the Holy Prophet . . . shall be punished with death, or imprisonment, and shall also be liable to fine."

12:2). According to the Qur'an, it replaces the corrupted text of the Bible, "revealing to [Jews and Christians] much that you used to hide in the Book, and passing over much [that is now unnecessary]" (Qur'an 5:15). Like Mormonism, the words of Allah came on "a Tablet Preserved!" (Qur'an 85:22). This tablet, of course, does not exist and is only mentioned in this one verse of the Qur'an. As such, many Muslims regard the tablet as metaphorical, meaning Allah promises to preserve the Qur'an from distortion here on earth. Other Muslims believe this verse is literal and that there is a heavenly tablet secured for all of eternity as well.

A critical investigation of the Qur'an, though, contradicts the claims of a tablet preserved. Consider the following troublesome facts:

1. The Qur'an is said to be unchangeable (Qur'an 6:34, 10:64), but Allah removes verses as he pleases (Qur'an 13:39).

2. The Qur'an is regarded as preserved (Qur'an 85:22), yet Allah causes Muhammad to forget some passages (Qur'an 87:6–7).

3. The Qur'an states that it is dictated from Allah (Qur'an 39:1–2) and will be "guarded from corruption" (Qur'an 15:9), yet there were varying copies of the Qur'an during the earliest days of Islam. These differing manuscripts caused the third leader of Islam, Uthman, to choose one copy over another and burn all other irregular manuscripts. Additionally, a Qur'an discovered in Yemen in 1972, perhaps the oldest manuscript in existence, was found to have "small but intriguing aberrations from the standard Koranic text."[18] How can dictation by Allah have any irregularities, however small they may be?

4. Early leaders in Islam admitted they did not have the entire Qur'an. The second leader of Islam, Umar, stated, "Let none of you say, 'I have got the whole of the Qur'an.' How does he know what all of it is? Much of the Qur'an has gone. Let him say instead, 'I have got what has survived.' "[19]

The Qur'an is, as one professor describes it, "the charter of the community. . . . Islamic history has been the effort to pursue and work out the

---

18. Toby Lester, "What is the Koran," *The Atlantic Monthly*, 283:1 (January 1999): 43–56.
19. John Burton, *The Collection of the Qur'an* (Cambridge, MA: Cambridge University Press, 1977), p. 117.

commandments of the Koran in human life."[20] However, if the Qur'an is proven to be riddled with errors then "the whole Islamic struggle of fourteen centuries is effectively meaningless."[21]

But the Qur'an is not the sole and sufficient authority in Islam. The Qur'an itself notes, "Ye have indeed in the Messenger of Allah an excellent exemplar" (Qur'an 33:21). The sayings and practices of Muhammad provide Muslims a detailed example they are obligated to follow. More than two centuries after Muhammad's death, compilations of the prophet's sayings and conduct were collected in written form by Islamic scholars from oral narrations. These compilations, known as *Hadith* or Traditions, are only second to the Qur'an in importance and are regarded by Muslims as the rule of law and faith for the Muslim community. While there are six compilations of these Traditions, two are considered most authentic for Sunni Muslims: Sahih al-Bukhari and Sahih Muslim, named after the two men who collected them. The two editions combined hold more than 16,000 verses attempting to portray the virtuous life and teachings of Muhammad.

The question at hand is whether Muhammad is the noble prophet the Hadith declares him to be. Here is a warrior-prophet who built a faith upon military conquest and demanded allegiance to his cause. The Hadith itself records troublesome facts about the prophet including eradicating enemies who merely spoke against him (Bukhari 5.369), declaring capital punishment upon any Muslim who leaves the faith (Bukhari 9.57–58), and calling for the destruction of the Jewish people (Bukhari 4.177).

Muhammad's personal failures were also grave. Although Muslims are forbidden to marry more than four women (Qur'an 4:3), Muhammad received a special revelation that he could marry as many as he wished due to Allah's favor (Qur'an 33:37, 51). He took full advantage of this blessing. For example, Muhammad was infatuated with a woman named Zaynab. But there was one problem: Zaynab was married to Muhammad's adopted son, Zayd. Eventually the prophet convinced Zaynab to divorce her husband — Muhammad's son — and marry the prophet. Stunning as it sounds, Muhammad married his daughter-in-law. Yet that is not even the most controversial marriage of Muhammad by Christian standards. Such involved a young girl by the name of Aisha. Bukhari's Hadith states that Aisha was

---

20. Stephen Humphreys, in Lester, "What is the Koran?" n.p.
21. Ibid.

six years old when the couple was betrothed and she was nine years old when they sexually consummated the marriage (7.64). Recognizing that the Hadith is considered authentic and authoritative to Muslims, it is difficult to imagine any justification of this action by a biblical standard; much less a desire to consider Muhammad, as many do, as the "excellent exemplar" one should follow. But for the reader, this is why many Muslims marry children of such a young age.

Fundamentals of the Faith #1: Creation in the Qur'an

> Your Lord is God, who in six days created the Heavens and the Earth, and then mounted the throne: He throws the veil of night over the day: it pursues it swiftly: and he created the sun and the moon and the stars, subjected to laws by His behest: Is not all creation and its empire His? Blessed be God the Lord of the Worlds! Qur'an 7:54

The verse above seems to indicate that Muslims and Christians have remarkably similar accounts of creation. The Qur'an affirms the heavens and earth were created in six days (7:54, 50:38), that humans were given responsibility over creation (2:30), and that Eve was tempted by Satan in the Garden (2:36), and that the couple was removed from the Garden due to their transgressions (7:27).

But a more detailed comparison between the two monotheistic faiths illustrates a great chasm on this crucial issue. First, Christians must realize that the Qur'an does not have a detailed account of creation as is found in 80 verses of Genesis 1–3. The reader of the Qur'an, instead, must rely upon a simpler account given in the two main passages, 2:30–39 and 7:11–31, in order to garner an understanding of the Islamic view of creation. Second, while the Bible details clearly the order of creation in six days, thereby ruling out evolutionary models, the Muslim scholars give latitude to evolution due to both the lack of detail in explaining the six days of creation as well as maintaining an allegorical model when stating, "A day in the sight of the Lord is like a thousand years" (Qur'an 22:47). While the Bible has a similar verse to Qur'an 22:47, such an allegorical interpretation cannot be warranted due to the fact that the biblical passage is not dealing with creation but with the Second Coming of Christ (2 Peter 3:8). Finally, the stories of creation differ vastly in their accounts as can be seen in the following chart:

Bible	Qur'an
Precise detail on the six days of creation (Genesis 1)	Little detail on the six days of creation (7:54, 10:3, 11:7)
Jesus is the Creator (John 1:3; Hebrews 1:2)	Jesus is created (3:59)
Eve honored in creation (Genesis 2:18–25)	Eve never mentioned by name (20:117)
Mankind made in the image of God (Genesis 1:26)	Mankind is small part of creation (40:57)
Satan is seen as a cunning serpent (Genesis 3:1)	No mention of Satan as a serpent
Adam became a living being while the "last Adam" (Jesus Christ) gives life (1 Corinthians 15:45)	Adam was the first Muslim and the first prophet of Islam
Adam and Eve were tempted by Satan to eat from the Tree of Knowledge of Good and Evil (Genesis 2:17)*	Adam and Eve were tempted by Satan, who also tempts the rest of humanity (7:23–25)
Adam and Eve's sin recognized the need for a Savior (Genesis 3:15)	Adam and Eve's sin illustrated the need for guidance (30:30)

How important is one's view on creation? In Islam, creation and salvation (guidance) are directly linked. Since mankind is not fallen and death is natural, men and women need not a Savior to redeem them. They need a prophet to guide them. The path to heaven is paved by good works, not grace, by listening to the final prophet Muhammad, not God our Savior (1 Timothy 2:3). Thus, a burdensome struggle is the great virtue of the Muslim (Qur'an 35:18).

Fundamentals of the Faith #2: The Character of God and the Character of Christ

> *He begets not, nor is He begotten; and there is none like unto Him.* Quran 112:3–4

"We respect Jesus!" Such is the claim of Muslims who say they speak reverently of Jesus and His mission on earth. But no one can respect Jesus — Muslim or non-Muslim. Jesus declared Himself God (John 8:58) and the Son

---
* Directly for Eve, indirectly through Eve for Adam.

of God (Matthew 16:16–18) and, as such, each person only has two options regarding Christ: accept His free offer of salvation and bow to worship the King of kings, or reject His offer of salvation and refuse to bend the knee. But no one can state they respect Him; that is an insult to His character and work.

How the Qur'an speaks of Jesus is a complete contradiction to that of the Bible. In the Qur'an, Jesus is the created (3:47) "messenger to the Children of Israel" (3:49) who performed miracles (3:50) in order to declare "It is Allah who is my Lord and your Lord" (3:51). Jesus then rounded up "Allah's helpers" (3:52), the disciples, who bore witness that they were "Muslim" (3:52). In time, Jesus fulfilled His mission of calling Jews to worship Allah and was taken to heaven without experiencing death (3:55). According to the Qur'an, Jesus did not die on a cross but someone replaced Him (4:157–158). The Muslim rejects any notion that Jesus is God or the Son of God (19:88). Allah himself asked Jesus, "'O Jesus, the son of Mary! Did you say unto men, 'Take me and my mother for two gods beside Allah?' He will say: 'Glory to Thee! Never could I say what I had no right [to say]' " (5:116).

As the reader can see, the rejection of the deity of Christ goes hand-in-hand with the rejection of the triune nature of the Lord. Islam rejects the very nature and character of God as revealed in Scripture. Furthermore, any Christian should recognize that Mary is not seen as divine, but rather, it is the Holy Spirit who is God. Instead, the Qur'an reveals a god — Allah — who is transcendent, removed from mankind, and sovereign, arbitrarily choosing to work as he pleases (Qur'an 14:4). Here is a brief comparison between the Islamic god and the God of the Bible:

Yahweh — The God of the Bible	Allah — The god of the Qur'an
For God so loved the world that He gave his only begotten Son (John 3:16)	He begets not nor is he begotten (Qur'an 112:3)
God never changes (James 1:17)	Allah changes as he wills (2:106)
God is knowable (John 17:3)	Allah is ultimately unknowable (6:103)*

---

   * Take note of the devastation of Islam here. If Allah is ultimately unknowable, then how can the Qur'an be what it claims to be: a revelation of an unknowable God? In other words, if the Qur'an is true that Allah is ultimately unknowable, then the nothing about Allah in the Qur'an can be trusted about Allah. That knowledge of Allah could not be accurate.

God is sovereign and intimate (John 14:8–9)	Allah is a dominant master and sovereign (4:78)
God became flesh (John 1:14)	Allah does not become flesh (5:72)
God is one essence (being) in three persons: Father, Son, and Spirit (Matthew 28:19–20)	Allah is one in mathematical terms (5:73)
God's love is unconditional (Romans 5:6–8)	Allah's love is conditional (2:190)
God's Word is truth (John 17:17; see also Titus 1:2 and Hebrews 6:18)	Allah is the greatest deceiver (3:54)
God's Son died on the Cross to atone for the sins of the world (1 John 4:10)*	Allah has no son (2:116)

Nonetheless, according to the Qur'an and Hadith, Jesus is coming back! (Qur'an 43:61). Jesus will one day descend onto a white minaret in the eastern side of Damascus (Muslim 41.7015). Fighting for the cause of Allah, a tradition tells the story of Jesus: "When you see him, recognize him: a man of medium height, reddish hair. . . . He will fight the people for the cause of Islam. He will break the cross, kill swine. . . . Allah will perish all religions except Islam. He will destroy the Antichrist and will live on the earth for forty years and then he will die. The Muslims will pray over him" (Dawud 37.4310). Simply put, Jesus will be the last Muslim warrior that ushers in the end times and witnesses Islamic world domination.

Fundamentals of the Faith #3: Salvation in Islam

And no burdened soul can bear another's burden, and if one heavy laden cries for (help with) his load, naught of it will be lifted. . . . He who grows (in goodness), grows only for himself. Surah 35:18

There is no such thing as redemption or vicarious atonement in Islam. According to the Qur'an, no one is lost (30:30) but all are born "weak" (4:28) and forgetful (20:115). Therefore, human beings are in need of guidance, wisdom that ultimately comes from the Qur'an, which states, "These are Verses of the Wise Book, a Guide and a Mercy to the Doers of Good"

---

* This chart was first published in Emir Caner, "Turning to the Triune God," *Decision* (December 2013): 19. I have modified it slightly.

(31:2–3). The equation for that salvation is three-fold: repentance + faith + works = possible salvation (Qur'an 25:70). Salvation begins with right belief as seen in the Creed, "There is no god but Allah. Muhammad is the messenger of Allah." There are six fundamentals to the faith that are also essential to his salvation: (1) belief in one God alone with no partners, (2) belief in angels, (3) belief in the revelations which came down, most notably, the Qur'an, (4) belief in Allah's prophets from Adam to Muhammad, (5) belief that Allah will judge all men and women, and (6) belief that all men and women will spend eternity in either Paradise or Hell.

But right belief is not enough. Right action must accompany right belief. Regular prayers, charitable giving, fasting, and the pilgrimage all must be done properly or there is little hope of heaven. One must act in accordance with the mandates of the Qur'an and the Hadith and, if not, "Allah loves not transgressors" (Qur'an 2:190). One day, when "the Trumpet is blown" (Qur'an 23:101), each person will give an account of his or her deeds. The Muslim hopes that his "balance (of good deeds) is heavy" (Qur'an 23:102) so that he can enjoy Paradise. For those whose sins are greater than their righteousness, "in Hell will they abide" (Qur'an 23:103).[22]

Salvation seems attainable at first glance. However, there is more to Islamic salvation than just the scale of justice between good and evil. Allah must first want you, for "Allah leads astray those who He pleases" (Qur'an 14:4). Furthermore, the ultimate cause for whatever action you undertake is Allah. The Qur'an states, "If some good befalls them they say, 'This is from Allah'; But if evil, they say, 'This is from you (O Prophet).' Say: All things are from Allah" (4:78). If that is truly the case, one wonders what to make of judgment. It seems the Cause (Allah) is judging the effect (the action). How could that be? Would not Allah be judging himself?[23]

---

22. Note the difference in the Bible. Even one sin is punishable by a Holy God for death (finally resulting in hell) for all eternity. For this is the nature of sin in regards to a perfectly infinite and holy God. Even one sin must be punished by death and that death is an eternal death, which would be infinite in nature due to the infinite nature of God. So no matter how many good deeds are done, the bad ones must still be punished by God according to the Bible. Since no one could take that ever-enduring punishment from God for our sin, only God Himself in the person of Jesus Christ could take that punishment on our behalf. Hence, salvation is by grace, through the work of Jesus Christ alone, not based on good deeds outweighing the bad.

23. Again, note the difference in the Bible. Where good and evil stem from Allah, the God of the Bible has only good stemming from Him. Evil is like a parasite that takes good things and corrupts them (i.e., from Satan who turned to sin or man who also turned to sin in Adam).

Additionally, the Hadith shed light on how many actions can lead to someone's eternal demise. Here is just a partial list:

1. Murdering another Muslim (Bukhari 1.30, 9.204)

   I have heard Allah's Apostle saying, "When two Muslims fight (meet) each other with their swords, both the murderer as well as the murdered will go to the Hell-fire." I said, "O Allah's Apostle! It is all right for the murderer but what about the murdered one?" Allah's Apostle replied, "He surely had the intention to kill his companion."

2. Unintentional Killing (Muslim 32.6338)

   Allah's Messenger (may peace be upon him) said: "None amongst you should point a weapon towards his brother, for he does not know that Satan might cause the weapon (to slip) from his hand and (he may injure anyone) and thus he may fall into Hell-fire."

3. Incorrect Ablution (Ritual Washings) (Bukhari 1.166)

   Perform ablution perfectly and thoroughly for Abul-Qasim (the Prophet) said, "Save your heels from the Hell-fire."

4. Arrogance and Stubbornness (Bukhari 6.440; see also Muslim 40.6835)

   I heard the Prophet saying . . . "And may I inform you of the people of the Hell-fire? They are all those violent, arrogant and stubborn people."

5. Careless Words (Bukhari 8.485)

   The Prophet; said: . . . "A slave (of Allah) may utter a word (carelessly) which displeases Allah without thinking of its gravity and because of that he will be thrown into the Hell-Fire."

6. Cruelty to Animals (Muslim 37.6638)

   Abu Huraira reported Allah's Messenger (may peace be upon him) as saying that a woman was thrown into Hell-fire because of a cat whom she had tied and did not provide it with food. Nor did she set it free to catch insects of the earth until it died inch by inch.

7. Giving in to Temptation (Muslim 40.6778)

   The Paradise is surrounded by hardships and the Hell-fire is surrounded by temptations.

A group of Muslims pray during Ramadan in Sana'a

How difficult is it to obtain Paradise according to Islam? Even infants are not guarded from Hell. In one Tradition, a woman, after her child dies, looks to Muhammad for comfort. She approaches the prophet with the hope that her baby is in Paradise. His response is chilling: "Don't you know that Allah created the Paradise and He created the Hell and He created the dwellers for this (Paradise) and the dwellers for this (Hell)" (Muslim 33.6435). Not even a child could be certain of Paradise.

Moreover, the differences between Heaven and Hell are literally night and day, as one can see below:

Paradise/Heaven	Hell
Gardens of Bliss (Qur'an 56:12)	Boiling springs (Qur'an 88:5)
Couches encrusted with gold and precious stones (Qur'an 56:15)	Tied with chains (Qur'an 14:49)
A feast with the best of food and drink (Qur'an 56:18–20)	Choke on liquid puss (Qur'an 14:16–17)
Sexual companions to meet every need (Qur'an 56:35)	Beaten with rods of iron (Qur'an 22:21)
No more grief; peace and security (Qur'an 43:68–73, 50:31–35)	Fire will consume and burn their faces; ice-cold darkness (Qur'an 14:49–50, 38:57)

In the end, there is absolutely no guarantee of Paradise with the sole exception of dying as a martyr for Allah's cause (Qur'an 9:111).[24] The Muslim must wait and wonder. Will the scales tilt in my favor? Does Allah desire my salvation? Does Allah love me and desire for me to be in Paradise? Is my fate the peace and security of a feast or the cold darkness of boiling springs? One thing is for sure — he cannot be sure.

An Eternal Conversation: Questioning the Claims of Islam and Sharing the Love of Christ

> *If you were in doubt as to what We have revealed to you, then ask those who have been reading the Book from before you: the Truth has indeed come to you from your Lord: So be in no wise of those in doubt.* Qur'an 10:94

Astounding as it may sound, the verse above asserts that Muslims who doubt can seek truth from those "before you," that is, Jews and Christians. Notice the Qur'an maintains the truth was given in the "Book," the sacred texts revealed by God. The Qur'an affirms three specific earlier books were sent from God: "And He sent down the Torah (of Moses) and the Gospel (of Jesus" (3:3), and "to David We gave The Psalms" (4:163). Muslims believe these books are now corrupt, as Jews and Christians "change[ed] the words from their (right) places and forget a good part of the Message that was sent them" (Qur'an 5:13). Regardless, the Qur'an, codified in the seventh century long after the Bible itself was accepted in its present form, contends that truth can be found through conversations with sincere Christian believers "who have been reading the Book." Furthermore, there is no textual support for the claim that the Bible has been corrupted.[25]

Therefore, the *message* of Scripture still stands as the sufficient means in defending the faith and winning a Muslim to Christ. And the *method* for reaching Muslims for the Lord is through conversational evangelism, defined as lovingly confronting an unbeliever with the gospel through sincere questions and honest dialogue. Such was the method of prophets in

---

24. This may be one reason for continual warfare within Islamic circles. If there is no war to die in, then there is no assurance of salvation. So Muslims need war, particularly holy war, not peace, for this possibility to exist.

25. There are variants in the biblical text, but these are not conflicts (such as variant spellings of words or copying mistakes, which are easily identified when looking at multiple texts, and these are expected when copying by hand). But none of these variants change theology or introduce conflicts.

the Old Testament like Elijah (1 Kings 18:21: "How long will you falter between two opinions?"), Jesus Himself in the Gospels (Matthew 16:15: "But who do you say that I am?"), and believers like Phillip in the New Testament (Acts 8:30: "Do you understand what you are reading?"). Having the privilege of speaking to someone on a deeply personal level not only requires the right answer; it demands the right questions.

Islam and Christianity present a clash of worldviews. Islam is a complete repudiation of Christianity, denying the very essentials of the faith including the death, burial, and Resurrection of Jesus our Lord. As such, Islam must be refuted in five key areas:

1. *The Prophet Muhammad.* There is an astonishing audacity for a prophet to come along nearly 600 years after Jesus and claim superiority to everything written beforehand without any historical evidence. Muhammad, an alleged prophet who never foretold future events or performed miracles, disregarded historical claims both inside and outside Scripture and arbitrarily denied the central claim of Christianity — the crucifixion and Resurrection of Christ. The Bible proves its own truthfulness — sources decades after Christ affirmed biblical accounts. Roman historian Tacitus (A.D. 56–117) spoke about the life and death of Christ, and Roman official Pliny the Younger wrote a letter (A.D. 112) detailing how Christians worshiped Christ.[26]

   It should be incumbent upon Islamic scholars not merely to deny Christian claims, but to find evidence from religious history supporting their own arguments. The typical Islamic scholar wishes to portray Muhammad as ignorant. I do not. He was a caravan trader that could have come into contact with many Trinitarian Christians in Damascus or other cities. He could have heard public readings of Scripture in Orthodox churches. One of his concubines was a Coptic Christian. He has more intimate knowledge of the Bible than many are willing to presume. For example, he nearly quotes Psalm 103:12 by heart during his prayers, that he would hope God would

---

26. Joseph M. Holden and Norman Geisler, *The Popular Handbook of Archaeology and the Bible* (Eugene, OR: Harvest House Publishers, 2013), p. 299–300.

remove his sin as far as the east is from the west. So many verses of the Qur'an are exact opposites of Scripture (surah 112:3
v. John 3:16; surah 35:18 v. Matthew 11:28). While there was
obvious heresies within the Arabian peninsula, that does not
excuse Muhammad's supposed ignorance.

Question to Ask a Muslim: What historical proof is there for the Islamic Jesus?

2. *The Qur'an.* As seen in this chapter, the Qur'an asserts that
it is the fourth and final revelation of Allah, even though the
Bible claims the faith was "once for all delivered to the saints"
(Jude 1:3) through the Apostles of Jesus Christ. The earlier
books included the Torah of Moses (Genesis–Deuteronomy),
the Psalms of David, and the Gospels. Supposedly, these three
sacred texts are corrupted and only the Qur'an can be trusted
fully as "a Tablet preserved" (Qur'an 85:22). One can easily
see the problem of such an argument. Why would Allah allow
some of his texts to be corrupted yet preserve his final revelation? As Sovereign, isn't he able to preserve his words from the
beginning? Wouldn't he want his word to be preserved from
the beginning?

*Questions to Ask a Muslim: Do you believe the Torah was inspired by God and
then corrupted? Do you believe the Psalms of David were inspired by God and
then corrupted? Do you believe the gospel was inspired by God and then corrupted? Why would I trust a god to preserve a word the fourth time when he didn't
preserve it the first three times?*

*Another angle to take on the Qur'an is to ask: If the Qur'an is what it claims to
be, that Allah is ultimately unknowable, then how can we trust the Qur'an to be
accurate when it claims to reveal knowledge about Allah?*

3. *The Trinity.* Questions regarding the Trinity often occur when
speaking to a Muslim. In fact, in the author's own experience,
Muslims will ask questions regarding the character of God
more than any other question. Christians oftentimes mishan-
dle the question and say something akin to the following: "I
do not understand the Trinity but I worship the Lord anyway." Such a statement is dangerous as it may affirm to a

Muslim his own worldview — that Christians are ignorant of and in their faith. Instead, the question regarding the character of God comes down to two issues: sovereignty and purpose. God can do anything He pleases, which certainly means He can (and did!) become flesh. The incarnation of Christ demonstrates *why* He became flesh: "but [He] made Himself of no reputation, taking the form of a bondservant, and coming in the likeness of men. And being found in the appearance as a man, He humbled Himself and became obedient to the point of death, even the death of the cross" (Philippians 2:7–8). Jesus came to die for our sins, in our place, that we may obtain eternal life through His sacrifice.

Questions to Ask a Muslim: Can God do whatever He wishes? If so, is it not at least possible that He could become man? Why would He become man?

Also ask about the nature of Allah regarding sin as this relates to the triune nature of God. Ask: Is Allah infinite? If so, then why is his judgment upon sin not infinite? If Allah is infinite, then only Allah would be in a position to take the punishment for sin if he were perfectly holy. Where has Allah taken the punishment for man (which is death) upon himself? How then can Allah claim that salvation exists (to be able to attain paradise) if a means of escaping sin and death have not been dealt with at the ultimate level?

4. *The Crucifixion of Christ.* The Qur'an boldly declares that Jesus Christ never died upon a cross. It states, "But they killed him not, nor crucified him. Only a likeness of that was shown to them" (4:157). Note that Muslims argue that someone replaced Jesus and was a "likeness" of Him. It is key that you understand the biblical passages regarding the crucifixion. The eyewitnesses who watched the Savior's brutal death included Jesus's best friend, John the Beloved, and Jesus' own mother. It seems implausible that the two closest companions of Jesus would not recognize that He had been replaced.

Questions to Ask a Muslim: When was Jesus replaced before the crucifixion? Was it after He was scourged? Did not eyewitnesses see that the stripes were no longer on the back of the surrogate being crucified? How is it possible that Jesus' mother did not recognize Him? Have you read the Gospel accounts that Muhammad repeatedly affirmed were true yet to see what the Christ and His eyewitnesses claimed about the Resurrection, even after His Resurrection?[27]

5. *Salvation by Works.* Along with the affirmation that Allah has no partners, Islam requires the adherent to do works of righteousness in order to obtain Paradise (4:124). The Qur'an also states, "Things that are good remove those that are evil" (11:114). However, in a system of works-based salvation, God can be just or merciful, but He cannot be both. He can be just and punish all sin or He can be merciful (as seen in the verse above) and erase sin without punishment. But only in Jesus Christ, the God-man, can God be both just and merciful. The Lord is just, as He poured His wrath upon His Son to atone for the sins of the world (John 1:29), and He is merciful, as Jesus died in our place, for our sins. God is holy in His judgment yet loving in His mercy.

Questions to Ask a Muslim: If you perform more good works than evil works, can you earn Paradise? If so, what does Allah do with your sins? If he doesn't punish your sins, can he be just? Does Allah overlook sin and its consequences?

The issues above are theological in nature. But one must remember that a Christian's witness must also be personal and practical, speaking to a Muslim's heart as much as one speaks to his head. Here are some practical questions that may help begin a conversation with a Muslim:

1. Are you sure you will go to heaven? (Qur'an 46:9)

2. What has Allah personally said to you during your prayer times?

3. Is there anything in Christianity that if you found were true would cause you to become a follower of Christ?

4. Does Allah still love you when you do wrong? If you do wrong continually (Qur'an 2:190)?

5. Do you ever get tired of trying to earn heaven (Qur'an 35:18 v. Matthew 11:28)?

---

27. Editors, "The Bible as Seen by the Qur'an and the Muslim Traditions," *Answering Islam*, accessed December 29, 2014, http://answering-islam.org/Campbell/s2c1.html.

6. Have you ever read the Bible? Would you read it if I gave you a free copy in your native language?[28]

Muslims are not a different species in need of a unique way of sharing Christ with them. They are — as I once was — like all others, sinners in need of a Savior. Muslims are drawn to the Lord because of His promises — comforting words like, "I will never leave you nor forsake you" (Hebrews 13:5) and "Come to Me, all you who labor and are heavy laden, and I will give you rest" (Matthew 11:28). Like all others, Muslims are looking for an unconditionally loving God (John 3:16) who gives them the secure promise of eternal life (1 John 5:13), a relationship with the Lord that will never end. Our witness is simple: point them to the Lord and show them how Jesus still changes lives. Like two thousand years of Christian witness, believers must recognize that we overcome "by the blood of the Lamb and by the word of their testimony" (Revelation 12:11).

A Final Word: The Meaning of Total Surrender

A faith that's worth living for is a faith that's worth dying for (Romans 12:14–15). The heart of this New Testament message is not one of fame or comfort, but of faith and courage. The life of the disciples echoed this principle well as they gave their lives for their faith. In many parts of the Muslim world, surrendering one's life to Christ means just that — surrender. And, of all Muslim countries that persecute Christians, perhaps none is as unforgiving as Saudi Arabia, where becoming a Christian is punishable by death.[29]

Consider Ali, a young Saudi man who surrendered his life to Christ just a few years ago. Ali had not openly espoused his newfound faith, but the Saudi High Court, nonetheless, sentenced the young Christian to death for treason against Allah (Qur'an 5:33). Ali was to be beheaded. Within a few days of the verdict, Ali was escorted from his prison cell to the site of execution. Awaiting Ali were his wife and three-year-old daughter, forced to watch the execu-

---

28. These are but a few of the questions my students compiled during a graduate class I taught in Thailand. Students would use questions during their witnessing encounters and come back to class to discuss the effectiveness of these questions.

29. Let's just state this for what it is: a form of human sacrifice. This form of human sacrifice of non-Muslims for the cause of Allah has been common through Islamic history and is not restricted to Saudi Arabia but is also often found in Islamic Jihad (holy war). Such killings are seen in Iraq today (with groups like ISIS) and Africa where many Christians in particular are killed for Allah. Be praying for the gospel of Jesus Christ to permeate these lands and save the lost who are hopelessly kept in the darkness of Islam.

tion of their husband and father. The soldiers tied Ali's hands together and stretched Ali's neck out across a wooden block. His wife wept uncontrollably. The last words Ali spoke before the execution were these: "Father, into your hands I commit my spirit." Then he was gone, a martyr for Jesus.[30]

We are not called to be 21st-century Christians by following the culture of the day. We are called to be 1st-century Christians living in the 21st century, following Christ as our 1st-century brethren followed Christ. We are called to surrender. If the Muslim world is going to hear the gospel, it will be through Christians who are willing to sacrifice everything in order to share the beautiful gospel in a hostile world. May it be so. Truth is immortal.

Summary of Islamic Beliefs

Doctrine	Islamic Teaching
God	Deny the Trinity; believe Allah is the only god (monotheistic) and that Jesus is not the Son of God, but a prophet; Allah is transcendent and removed from mankind
Authority/ Revelation	The Bible is viewed as a revelation from God that has been corrupted, but the revelations of Muhammad in the Koran supersede the Bible; the Hadith are revered as traditions that tell of Muhammad's life and act as a sort of authorized commentary on the Koran
Man	Man is the highest creature made by Allah and is able to do good with his free will, though he needs guidance from Allah's prophets.
Sin	Transgression of Allah's will as revealed in the Koran and Hadith; no concept of original sin corrupting mankind; following the guidance of prophets will help you avoid sin and do good; the Five Pillars give a framework for obeying Allah
Salvation	Each person will be judged by Allah for his or her own actions; Allah will allow some into Paradise (Heaven) and send others to hellfire based on the balance of how many good and bad deeds they have done; there is no concept of a mediator or Savior and they deny that Jesus died on the Cross; martyrs receive entrance into Paradise

30. Emir Fethi Caner and H. Edward Pruitt, *The Costly Call, Book 2* (Grand Rapids, MI: Kregel Publications), p. 168–173.

| Creation | The Koran speaks of creation in six days, but many modern scholars allow for an allegorical interpretation and evolutionary views; conservative scholars would reject evolutionary ideas and hold a view very similar to the biblical timeline. |

Chapter 8

Jehovah's Witnesses

Got Questions Ministries

They're at your door again — Jehovah's Witnesses — with their smiles and their literature and their claims about Jesus and how He's been misunderstood all this time. So you open your door to talk to them. What do you say? What do Jehovah's Witnesses believe, and what makes them so dedicated to spreading their ideas about God?

Jehovah's Witnesses believe we are living in the last days, which gives impetus to their mission. They consider their time is short for spreading Jehovah's message. They also paint an appealing picture of eternal life. For example, they teach that virtually everyone who has died will be resurrected and given a second chance to be saved and inherit paradise — and who wouldn't like a second chance? They will cheerfully admit that they are not in the New Covenant, that Jesus is not their mediator, and what's more, there's no need to be born again in order to enter the kingdom (more on this in a moment).

Distribution and Basic Facts

The Watchtower Bible and Tract Society, commonly called the Jehovah's Witnesses, is an international religious organization based in Brooklyn, New York. Often labeled as a Christian denomination, the Watchtower Society is non-trinitarian and differs from orthodox Christianity in several other ways. It takes the name "Jehovah's Witnesses" from Isaiah 43:10, "'You are my

Watchtower Bible and Tract Society headquarters in Brooklyn, New York

witnesses,' declares Jehovah, 'Yes, my servant whom I have chosen' " (New World Translation).

In 2014, the Jehovah's Witnesses reported nearly 20 million members in over 113,000 congregations worldwide. Every month, the Jehovah's Witnesses conduct 9.2 million home Bible studies. Every day, hundreds of thousands of copies of their two magazines, *Watchtower* and *Awake!* are printed and distributed in nearly two hundred languages.

Overseeing the Watchtower Society is the Governing Body, a group of men known as "the faithful and discreet slave." This title comes from one of Jesus' parables: "Who really is the faithful and discreet slave whom his master appointed over his domestics, to give them their food at the proper time? Happy is that slave if his master on coming finds him doing so! Truly I say to you, he will appoint him over all his belongings" (Matthew 24: 45–47; NWT).

History

In the late 19th century, in Pittsburgh, Pennsylvania, 18-year-old Charles Taze Russell started a Bible class that he called "the Millennial Dawn Bible Study" in which he promulgated some aberrant doctrines that would later be part of the corpus of Jehovah's Witnesses' theology. Russell drew many of his ideas from Adventists and others who speculated about Bible prophecy, and he rejected many biblical doctrines that he found problematic. Intent on distributing his ideas as widely as possible, Russell published the first editions of the magazines *Watch Tower* and *Herald of Christ's Presence* in July 1879. In 1881, Russell formed Zion's Watch Tower Tract Society, incorporated in 1884 and renamed the Watch Tower Bible and Tract Society, and subsequently to Watchtower Bible and Tract Society.

Charles Taze Russell

Russell died in 1916, and the second president, Joseph Franklin Rutherford, began implementing some changes in the Society. By 1930, some 75 percent of the original Bible students had dropped out, citing conflicting doctrinal positions. It was during Rutherford's tenure that the name "Jehovah's Witnesses" was first applied to those who remained in the organization. Also under Rutherford's watch, several of the group's distinctive doctrines appeared, including the idea that Jehovah's Witnesses had replaced the Jewish people and the requirement that every Witness take part in literature distribution.

Joseph Franklin Rutherford

From humble origins, the Watch Tower Bible and Tract Society has grown into a worldwide organization. The Jehovah's Witnesses' expansion program is ambitious. To finance their worldwide outreach, each congregation is instructed to commit to regular monthly contributions, even though they themselves have no legal or financial control over the buildings they pay for or construct. The closer "the end of this wicked system of things"[1] draws, the more money pours into Society coffers. The "publishers" (door-to-door distributers of the literature) are admonished to work even harder in the interests of the kingdom because time is running out. The Governing Body stresses the imminence of the Tribulation and the need for Witnesses everywhere to do even more to prove their loyalty.

---

1. "But Jehovah's servants already belong to the only organization that will survive the end of this wicked system of things," *Watchtower*, Dec 15, 2007, p.14, http://jwfacts.com/watchtower/salvation-only-for-jehovahs-witnesses.php.

Means of Worship

Jehovah's Witnesses meet twice a week for worship and Bible study in King-dom Halls. They do not call these buildings "churches," because that term is associated with Christianity, a false religion in their eyes. There are no stained glass windows, no images or statues, no candles, and absolutely no crosses, occupied or empty (Jehovah's Witnesses consider the Cross to be a pagan symbol). Kingdom Halls have no pews, no choir, and no organ. There is no baptistery, no altar or communion table, and no liturgical garb. The hall is plain and functional, with perhaps a lectern from which talks are delivered. The Jehovah's Witnesses do not sing hymns but have their own "Kingdom Song Book." Each meeting starts and ends with a prayer to Jehovah, asked in Jesus' name.

Distinctive Doctrines

- Their own translation of the Bible, the New World Transla-tion (NWT), is the only version that can be trusted.

- Jesus was created by Jehovah as a spirit creature named Mi-chael the Archangel.

- Jesus is not divine and has always been subordinate to His heavenly father, Jehovah.

- Jesus was a perfect man, but He could have sinned and failed in His mission.

- Jesus only became the "Son of God" at His baptism.

- Since He is not God, Jesus must not be worshiped or prayed to.

- Jesus died to atone only for the sin of Adam (inherited sin).

- Jesus was raised from the dead as a spirit creature — His body disappeared.

- Jesus started ruling God's Kingdom (invisibly, from heaven) in October 1914.

- Jesus chose the Jehovah's Witnesses to be Jehovah's earthly or-ganization in 1919.

- The Jehovah's Witnesses have replaced Israel, and the 144,000 mentioned in Revelation 14:1 are "spiritual Jews."

- Only 144,000 persons since the time of Jesus can enter the New Covenant and go to heaven, there to rule with Jesus.

- Only 144,000 persons needed to be born again or anointed with Jehovah's impersonal "holy spirit."

- The Trinity is a pagan, polytheistic teaching.

- There is no such thing as an immortal soul — the dead know nothing (a doctrine related to soul sleep and annihilationism).

- Jehovah would never punish people for eternity — there is no such place as hell or the lake of fire.

- Jehovah exercises selective foreknowledge — He chose not to know that Adam and Eve would sin.

- Death acquits a person of his personal sin.

- After Armageddon, the dead will be physically resurrected to live on the earth.

- After their resurrection, the unsaved dead will get a second chance to be saved and live forever in a paradise on earth.

- Salvation depends upon works and being faithful and obedient to the end.

- There is no salvation apart from membership in the Jehovah's Witnesses' organization.

- There is no assurance of salvation, even for those with a "heavenly hope."

- Jehovah's revelation to His chosen representatives is progressive — the light keeps getting brighter. This accounts for changes made to previously held interpretations regarding the end times. Whenever those in the Governing Body modify a former belief, they attribute the change to "increased light."

Authority

Jehovah's Witnesses claim their authority comes from the Bible, the divinely inspired Word of God. However, the Bible can only be properly interpreted and applied "with the help of publications prepared by 'the faithful and discreet slave.' "[2] In fact, according to the Watchtower Society, a mature Christian "does not advocate or insist on personal opinions or harbor private ideas when it comes to Bible understanding. Rather, he has complete confidence in the truth as it is revealed by Jehovah God through His Son, Jesus Christ, *and* 'the faithful and discreet slave.' "[3] Thus, all of Scripture is filtered through the group's corporate leaders, and no other interpretation is given the least consideration, so they rely on the fallible ideas of men as their true authority.

Jehovah's Witnesses also claim their authority comes from Jehovah God through Jesus, because Jesus appointed them as His sole channel of communication to the world. The Society is Jehovah's one-and-only earthly organization, and it is only through a small group of men (the faithful and discreet slave) that spiritual food is dispensed from Jehovah to His people.

According to the April 15, 2013, *Watchtower*, "the earthly part of Jehovah's organization" is structured in this way:

1. The Governing Body

2. Branch Committees

3. Traveling Overseers

4. Bodies of Elders

5. Congregations

6. Individual Publishers (those who personally distribute the literature)

Such is the power and authority of the men who make up the Governing Body that no Witness dares challenge or question them. The Governing Body is perceived as Jehovah's representative on earth. A Jehovah's Witness cannot disagree with what he is told; he must accept the published literature and the word of the elders whose job it is to enforce loyalty. If he does disagree and

---

2. *Watchtower*, February 15, 2003, p. 31.
3. Ibid., August 1, 2001, p. 14.

makes his objection known, he will be disciplined. The ultimate punishment is to be disfellowshiped.

A disfellowshiped member is shunned by all Witness friends and family, sometimes resulting in decades of estrangement. Those still in the organization are advised not to have anything to do with shunned individuals: "Really, what your beloved family member needs to see is your resolute stance to put Jehovah above everything else — including the family bond. . . . Do not look for excuses to associate with a disfellowshipped family member."[4]

The Jehovah's Witnesses maintain a high level of control over what their congregations learn, and independent study is anathema: "All who want to understand the Bible should appreciate that the 'greatly diversified wisdom of God' can become known only through Jehovah's channel of communication, the faithful and discreet slave."[5] Submission to the Governing Body is seen as submission to Christ.

Foundations and Beliefs: Creation and Evolution

Jehovah's Witnesses claim to believe the creation account as recorded in the Book of Genesis. They have always rejected atheistic evolution, believing that Jehovah, through Christ Jesus, is the Creator of the universe. However, they are not young-earth creationists. While they reject Darwinian evolution, they accept astronomical and geological evolution (i.e., billions of years).[6] They do hold to a form of evolution, believing that God created the various "kinds" that were then allowed to diversify within their kind, though they mean, "remarkably different from one another."[7] Charles Taze Russell in *Studies in the Scripture,* VI, states:

> In the beginning we have merely the physical forces out of which the grand structure is made by a gradually unfolding, or if one prefers to say so, an 'evolutionary' process. . . . that there is a divine plan of evolution, appears on the face of the whole chapter.[8]

4. Watchtower Study Edition, January 15, 2013, p. 16.
5. Ibid., October 1, 1994, p. 8.
6. Watch Tower Bible and Tract Society of Pennsylvania, "Do Jehovah's Witnesses believe in Creationism?" 2015, http://www.jw.org/en/jehovahs-witnesses/faq/creationism-belief/.
7. Watch Tower Bible and Tract Society of Pennsylvania, "The Untold Story of Creation," *Awake!* March 2014, http://www.jw.org/en/publications/magazines/g201403/untold-story-of-creation/.
8. Charles Taze Russell, *Studies in the Scriptures*, Volume VI, In the Beginning, "Creation Was Gradual," 1904, p. 53.

This is denoted twice in a footnote on the same page that states: "As already indicated, it is only in respect to man's creation that the Evolution theory conflicts with the Bible — and only to attack this point does that theory exist or find advocates."

Jehovah's Witnesses believe that the six days in the creation account are actually "epochs" — each one a period of 7,000 years.[9] In addition, they believe the earth existed for an indefinite period of time before the creation of life began. This allows for the idea that the earth is millions of years old. The March 2014 *Awake!* states, "The Bible does not support fundamentalists and creationists who claim that the creative days were literal 24-hour days" ("The Untold Story of Creation").

A recent article in *Awake!* magazine takes the old-earth creationist position: "God created the universe, including the earth, in the indefinite past — 'in the beginning,' as Genesis 1:1 says. Modern science agrees that the universe had a beginning. A recent scientific model suggests it to be almost 14 billion years old."[10] The same article speaks of "the false ideas of creationists" that could lead one "to dismiss the Bible altogether" and never benefit from "its storehouse of 'practical wisdom.' "

The length of each creative day being 7,000 years long is so central to Jehovah's Witnesses' chronology that they have calculated that Adam was created in 4026 B.C. They reckon that the year 1975 marked 6,000 years since Adam was created, and from this they reckon that Jehovah's seventh day of rest must now have little more than 1,000 years left to go. This is hugely significant to Jehovah's Witnesses because they believe that the Millennial reign of Christ will take place during the final 1,000 years of Jehovah's 7,000-year-long "day of rest."

Jehovah's Witnesses claim to present "the real Bible story of creation," one that contains "a very logical and credible explanation of the beginning of the universe" that "harmonizes with scientific discovery."[11]

Foundations and Beliefs: The Character of God

Jehovah's Witnesses acknowledge that God is holy (Isaiah 6:3), loves justice (Psalm 37:28), and is all-powerful. And they make much of the fact that "God is love" (1 John 4:8). Jehovah is "merciful and compassionate, slow

9. *Watchtower*, February 15, 1970; Russell, *Studies in the Scriptures*, Volume VI, "In the Beginning, 'The Creative Week,' " 1904, p. 29–51.
10. *Awake!* "Creation," January 2014.
11. *Awake!* March 2014, "The Untold Story of Creation."

to anger and abundant in loyal love" (Exodus 34:6; NWT). Jehovah God created all things (Revelation 4:11). Jehovah alone is the Most High, the Almighty, righteous and true, and the King of eternity (Revelation 15:3). He alone has always existed. The view held by Jehovah's Witnesses denies the existence of a personal Holy Spirit and the truth of the pre-incarnate Christ as the eternal Word of God (John 1).

Apparently, Jehovah is so loving that He would never punish people for eternity. This belief makes the character of God *unjust*, which is in opposition to Witnesses' view that God loves justice. The idea of a place of eternal torment is abhorrent to Jehovah's Witnesses. They teach that the Bible does not provide any basis for a belief in hell fire — in spite of Jesus' warning in Luke 16:19–31 (and elsewhere). To support their view of a "loving" God, they teach that souls are not immortal and that the dead know nothing — the dead are in a state of "soul sleep." Thus, God does not punish sin justly.

Jehovah's Witnesses also refuse to acknowledge that God is omniscient or that He knows the end from the beginning. They think it would have been wrong for Jehovah to create Adam and Eve knowing they would sin and bring terrible consequences into the world. Their belief is that Jehovah exercised selective foreknowledge — He commanded Adam and Eve not to eat of the tree of the knowledge of good and evil, but He chose not to know how they would respond. When they disobeyed, God was surprised.

Jehovah's Witnesses try to constrain God, to make Him fit their view of how He should be. Whenever they come against a biblical teaching about God that they dislike, they reinterpret (or "retranslate") the Bible and assign to God the characteristics they want Him to have. In so doing, they have created a God in their own image.

Foundations and Beliefs: Life after Death

Jehovah's Witnesses base their belief that the soul is not immortal on Ezekiel 18:4: "Look! All the souls — to me they belong. . . . The soul who sins is the one who will die" (NWT). Jehovah's Witnesses say that someone who has died is simply a "dead soul" (Leviticus 21:11). Although the spirit, or "life-force," returns to Jehovah God, it does not actually travel to heaven; rather, "returning to Jehovah" means that any hope of future life rests with God. Only by God's power can the spirit return and a person be made to live again. At the resurrection, the dead will be given a new body, and Jehovah will bring it to life by putting the life-force into it. Jehovah's Witnesses use

Ecclesiastes 9:5–6, 10, and Psalm 146:4 to show that the dead know nothing at all and we mortals do not survive the death of the body. The dead simply cease to exist.

Jehovah's Witnesses also believe that death acquits a person from his own personal sin, so they reckon that billions of people will be brought back to life on earth with a new body into which Jehovah will place that person's personality. Some, however, will not be resurrected; Jehovah's Witnesses take Luke 12:5 to mean that some of the dead are currently in Gehenna, which they consider a symbol of everlasting destruction or non-existence.

Another aspect of Witness theology that does not align with biblical teaching is their view that those who are resurrected will be given a second chance to be saved. They suppose the "day of judgment" will last for 1,000 years, and during that time people who never knew about Jehovah will be physically resurrected and given time to learn how to serve Him. This teaching directly contradicts Hebrews 9:27, which says that man is destined to die once and after that to face judgment. The Bible does not teach a second chance after death.

In Jehovah's Witnesses' theology, there is no interim place of suffering or bliss and no place of eternal torment or joy — just soul sleep until the resurrection, and soul annihilation if you fail the final test. Many people find this an attractive proposition. They are comforted in thinking that no one will suffer after death and that virtually every person who has died will be resurrected (or re-created) and given a second chance to be saved.

Foundations and Beliefs: View of Christ

The person of Christ is the single most important issue in Christianity. Jesus is the cornerstone of our faith (Ephesians 2:20). Get the truth about Jesus Christ wrong, and the foundation of faith will collapse. Unfortunately, the Jehovah's Witnesses miss the truth about Jesus.

Jehovah's Witnesses believe that Jehovah created the pre-human Jesus as a spirit creature, Michael the Archangel (contradicting the whole of Hebrews 1). After the Virgin Mary was impregnated, the spirit of Michael the Archangel entered Jesus. They teach that Jesus lived a perfect life, although He could have sinned and failed in His mission. Jesus has always been subordinate to His Heavenly Father, and Jesus must not be worshiped or prayed to. Jesus died on a "torture stake" (not a cross) to atone for the sin of Adam. After Jesus died, His body disappeared, and what came out of the tomb was, again, a spirit creature. Although Jehovah's Witnesses say that Jesus is the Son of God, they deny He was fully man and fully God, and they deny His bodily Resurrection.

Foundations and Beliefs: Salvation — Grace, Faith, and Works

The Bible says that salvation is deliverance, by the grace of God, from eternal punishment for sin, granted to those who accept by faith God's conditions of repentance and faith in the Lord Jesus. Salvation is the result of faith in Jesus' substitutionary death and bodily Resurrection (Romans 5:10; Ephesians 1:7). Scripture is clear that salvation is the work of God, His gracious, undeserved gift (Ephesians 2:5, 2:8). Salvation is only available through faith in Jesus Christ (Acts 4:12). This faith involves repentance (Acts 3:19) and calling on the name of the Lord (Romans 10:9–10, 10:13).

Jehovah's Witnesses have a different view of salvation, one that relies on human works and careful obedience. For this reason, Witnesses promote high standards of morality and adhere to a strict set of rules. Some of their directives uphold the moral stance of the Bible; they forbid lying, sexual immorality, gambling (avoiding the love of money), etc. In those areas, the Witnesses are acting biblically. However, other rules, such as their prohibition against celebrating birthdays and holidays or their injunction against saluting flags, have no basis in Scripture.

Jehovah's Witnesses call Jesus the Son of God, and they believe in His atoning death — but with some twists. They clearly teach a works-based salvation and that only Jehovah's Witnesses will be saved. And they deny three foundational tenets of the Christian faith: that Jesus is God Incarnate, that Jesus died to cleanse us of our personal sins, and that Jesus rose bodily from the dead. The Bible says that "if Christ has not been raised, your faith is futile; you are still in your sins" (1 Corinthians 15:17; NIV). Thus, the Jehovah's Witnesses' denial of Jesus' actual Resurrection contradicts the very foundation of biblical faith.

Jehovah's Witnesses believe that Jesus was a perfect man who laid down His life as a ransom sacrifice to atone for Adam's sin. "Since a perfect human life [Adam's] was lost, no imperfect human life could ever buy it back. What was needed was a ransom equal in value to what was lost. . . . In a sense, Jesus stepped into Adam's place in order to save us. By sacrificing, or giving up,

His perfect life in flawless obedience to God, Jesus paid the price for Adam's sin. Jesus thus brought hope to Adam's offspring."[12] This sounds good at first, until one realizes the parameters they place on Jesus' atonement: *only* Adam's sin was atoned for. Our personal sin is still our responsibility. That's why the Witnesses say, "Those who in faith accept God's provision for atonement through Jesus Christ can gain salvation."[13] Note, according to this, faith does not *guarantee* salvation; it simply opens the *possibility* of salvation.

Jehovah's Witnesses believe that a person is acquitted of his sins when he *dies*, not when he believes in Christ. Romans 6:7 in the New World Translation says this: "He who has died has been acquitted from his sin." Of course, the whole chapter is talking about a *spiritual* death to sin, but Jehovah's Witnesses take verse 7 to mean that their personal debt of sin is paid when they die *physically*. They say that Jesus only died to take care of inherited sin, to give people *hope* of being saved. The Witness must still earn the right to be declared righteous, not by anything Jesus did, but by his own works.

Jehovah's Witnesses have to *prove* they have faith by doing everything the Governing Body tells them to do — attend the meetings, spend a minimum amount of time each month distributing literature and conducting home studies, and pledge to support the worldwide building program financially. And another stipulation: "We show that we appreciate the ransom by . . . attending the Lord's Evening Meal."[14] This meal is the annual memorial service of the death of Jesus, where only those of the "anointed remnant" partake of the bread and the wine. Everyone else is a mere spectator.

Not a single Jehovah's Witness has any assurance of salvation. They must all remain faithful and obedient until they die. Any Witness could stumble and fall and thereby lose the hope of living forever in the restored earthly paradise. Even the "anointed remnant" do not have any assurance of salvation because they, too, could fail to cross the finish line.

Sadly, this faith is placed entirely in man, a governing body that demands works, and not on the Lord God and His Word, the 66 books of the Bible. The Jehovah's Witnesses' view of salvation could be summed

---

12. Watchtower Editors, *What Does the Bible Really Teach?* (Brooklyn, NY: Watchtower Bible and Tract Society of New York, Inc., 2005, 2014), chapter 5. It is provided as part of a worldwide Bible educational work supported by voluntary donations.

13. Watchtower Editors, *Insight on the Scriptures*, Vol. 1 (Brooklyn, NY: Watchtower Bible and Tract Society of New York, International Bible Students Association, 1988), p. 212.

14. Watch Tower Bible and Tract Society of Pennsylvania, *What Does the Bible Really Teach?* p. 56.

up by this short statement: "Yes, to gain salvation it is not enough to have faith."[15]

Arbitrariness, Inconsistencies, and Refutations: Regarding Authority

For many years, Jehovah's Witnesses were taught that all "anointed" Christians were part of the faithful and discreet slave. However, the Governing Body has recently changed that. The *Watchtower*, July 15, 2013, article "Who Really Is the Faithful and Discreet Slave?" begins by sweeping aside the previous understanding that the slave was appointed in A.D. 33. The article then explains how Jesus' words only *began* to be fulfilled after 1914. The faithful and discreet slave is now identified specifically as "a small group of anointed brothers" that includes the Governing Body as a "composite slave." Thus, the Governing Body has more authority now than ever. It's strange that Jehovah's anointed channel of communication managed to get the interpretation of Jesus' Words so wrong for so long — unless their authority does not come from God but instead from the men who currently make up the Governing Body. However, this group still insists on total obedience:

> We need to obey the faithful and discreet slave to have Jehovah's approval.[16]

> All of us must be ready to obey any instructions we may receive [from Jehovah's organization], whether these appear sound from a strategic or human standpoint or not.[17]

There is no biblical basis for any of these claims of a right to rule over the people of God.

Arbitrariness, Inconsistencies, and Refutations: Regarding Salvation

According to the *Watchtower*,[18] there are four basic requirements for salvation that Jehovah's Witnesses must meet:

1. Take in knowledge of God and Jesus by studying the Bible.

2. Obey God's laws, especially with regard to being moral.

---

15. *Watchtower*, June 1, 2000, p. 12.
16. *Watchtower*, July 15, 2011, p. 24, Simplified English Edition.
17. *Watchtower*, November 15, 2013.
18. Ibid., February 15, 1983, p. 12–13.

3. Associate with God's channel, His organization (there is only one), and serve God as part of it.

4. Support God's government by loyally advocating God's Kingdom rule to others.

In regard to items 3 and 4, we rightly question whether these instructions come from God or men. Here is what the Jehovah's Witnesses say:

> Genuine Christians are now being gathered into a united brotherhood earth wide. Who are they? They are the Christian congregation of Jehovah's Witnesses.[19]

> We will be impelled to serve Jehovah loyally with his organization if we remember that there is nowhere else to go for life eternal.[20]

Nowhere in Scripture does it suggest that God is using Jehovah's Witnesses as His sole channel of communication or that the Society is His exclusive earthly organization or that you must belong to this organization to be saved. Such exclusivism is a mark of a cult. To the contrary, the Scripture says in 1 Timothy 2:5, "For there is one God and one mediator between God and mankind, the man Christ Jesus" (NKJV).

Arbitrariness, Inconsistencies, and Refutations: Regarding Core Teachings and Chronology

From its founding, the Watchtower Society has always proclaimed that the end is near. Yet their proclamations of just how near are constantly shifting. They have predicted the end of the world to happen in 1914, 1925, and 1975. Of course, they were wrong every time.

Here is a clearly false prophecy made in 1969: "If you are a young person . . . you will never grow old in this present system of things. Why not? Because all the evidence in fulfillment of Bible prophecy indicates that this corrupt system is due to end in a few years. . . . Therefore, as a young person, you will never fulfill any career that this system offers. If you are in high school and thinking about a college education, it means at least four, perhaps even six or eight more years to graduate into a specialized career. But

---

19. Ibid., July 1, 1994, p. 7.
20. Ibid., "Serve Jehovah Loyally," November 15, 1992, p. 21.

where will this system of things be by that time? It will be well on the way toward its finish, if not actually gone!"[21] The same line was still being touted in 2012: "No doubt, school counselors sincerely believe that it is in your best interests to pursue higher education and to plan for a secular career. Yet, their confidence lies in a social and financial system that has no lasting future."[22]

One of the Jehovah's Witnesses' core teachings is that Jesus took up His throne and started ruling (invisibly) from heaven in 1914. The outbreak of World War I "proved" that Satan had been ousted from heaven, which was supposed to be the first act of the new King. World War I was interpreted to be the Tribulation. However, since that time, the Society has been receiving huge quantities of "increased light."

Significantly, they admit they got a lot of things wrong about the Tribulation: "In the past, we thought that the great tribulation began in 1914 when World War I started. We thought that Jehovah 'cut short' those days in 1918 when the war ended so that the remaining anointed ones on earth could preach the good news to all nations. Then we realized that a part of Jesus' prophecy about the last days has two fulfillments. So we needed to change the way we understood some parts of the prophecy."[23] This revision is significant, given their claim that since 1919 they have been God's sole channel of communication. Why did Jehovah allow them to get the message wrong in the first place, and why did it take almost 100 years for them to realize they got it wrong?

Another core teaching that has been altered through the years concerns their view of "this generation" mentioned by Jesus in Matthew 24:34, Mark 13:30, and Luke 21:32. Originally, the Jehovah's Witnesses taught that this was the generation alive in 1914 — the World War I generation would live to see Armageddon. They openly taught that "Millions Now Living Will Never Die" (first proclaimed in 1920). Later, the Watchtower Society declared that 1975 marked 6,000 years since the creation of Adam, pointing to an imminent Armageddon. But the date of that final battle kept moving back. Such adjustments to previous teaching are explained away by saying, "The light gets brighter," and using Proverbs 4:18 as a proof text.

Other examples of Watchtower Society prophecies that were later modified include an assertion in 1989 that the Christian missionary work begun

21. *Awake!* May 22, 1969, p. 15.
22. *Watchtower*, June 15, 2012, p. 23.
23. Ibid., July 15, 2013.

in the first century would "be completed in our 20th century." However, when the *Watchtower* was republished in bound volumes, the phrase "in our 20th century" was replaced with the less specific "in our day." Another subtle change was made in Society literature in 1995. Up until October 22 of that year, the *Awake!* mag-azine declared its purpose was to proclaim "the Creator's promise of a peaceful and secure new world before the generation that saw the events of 1914 passes away." That was changed on November 8 to read, "The Creator's promise of a peaceful and secure new world that is about to replace the present wicked, lawless system of things."

1907 cover of *Watchtower* magazine

In the November 1, 1995, *Watchtower*, the previous under-standing of "this generation" (the generation alive in 1914) was modified to say, "In the final ful-fillment of Jesus' prophecy today, 'this generation' apparently refers to the peoples of earth who see the sign of Christ's presence but fail to mend their ways." All mention of 1914 was dropped. According to the current interpretation, Jesus' words refer to people born *after* 1914 who will comprise a "wicked generation" — "wicked" because they see the signs of Jesus' invisible presence but fail to become Jehovah's Witnesses.

Arbitrariness, Inconsistencies, and Refutations: Regarding Their Translation of the Bible

The New World Translation of the Holy Scriptures is the Jehovah's Wit-nesses' official Bible. The NWT is an anonymous work of a Watchtower Society committee. Jehovah's Witnesses claim that the anonymity ensures the credit for the work will go to God alone. Of course, it has the added benefits of shielding the translators from accountability for their errors and preventing independent scholars from checking their academic credentials.

The New World Translation is unique in that it is the first intentional, systematic effort to produce a complete version of the Bible edited and revised for the specific purpose of agreeing with one group's doctrine. The Watchtower Society realized that their beliefs contradicted the Bible. But rather than conform their beliefs to Scripture, they altered Scripture to agree with their beliefs.

For example, the New World Translation inconsistently translates the Greek for "Lord" or "God" as "Jehovah." In fact, the Watchtower adds the word *Jehovah* to the New Testament 237 times, even though it has no textual authority for doing so.

They also consistently add words to the Bible in order to make it fit their theological bias. One of the most glaring examples is John 1:1, which should read ". . . and the Word was God." The NWT adds the article *a*: ". . . and the Word was a god." There is absolutely no basis for adding this extra word. It is a blatant attempt to change the meaning of the verse and deny the deity of Christ.

Another egregious example of an added word meant to alter doctrine is found in the NWT translation of Colossians 1:16. In the NIV, this verse reads, "For in him all things were created. . . ." The NWT inserts the word *other* after *all,* despite its being completely absent from the original Greek text. The Jehovah's Witnesses make the verse say, "Because by means of him all other things were created . . ." (NWT). This wording gives the impression that Christ himself is also a created thing, which, of course, is exactly what the Jehovah's Witnesses teach. It is only the pre-conceived, heretical rejection of the deity of Christ that forces the Watchtower Society to translate the Greek text as they do, thus allowing their error to gain legitimacy in the minds of their followers.

Arbitrariness, Inconsistencies, and Refutations: Regarding Blood Transfusions

The Old Testament forbids consuming blood (Genesis 9:2–6) and says that the life of the flesh is in the blood (Leviticus 17:11). Jehovah's Witnesses use this truth to forbid their members from participating in blood transfusions. We know that blood transfusions aid in the preservation of life. When we use someone's blood to keep life going, we uphold the principle of the sanctity of life. However, Jehovah's Witnesses turn the *symbol* of life (blood) into something more important than what it symbolizes.

Furthering their error is the Jehovah's Witnesses' warped interpretation of Acts 15:20, which admonishes Gentiles in the early Church to "abstain . . . from blood." The passage is clearly speaking of eating meat with the blood still in it. But Jehovah's Witnesses apply this to blood transfusions as well. A blood transfusion is simply a transplant of blood; the blood is not absorbed, ingested, or taken as food in any way. It is transplanted just as a kidney would be. But the Jehovah's Witnesses see it differently. The Governing Body used to teach that organ transplants were a form of cannibalism; that vaccinations were useless, sinful, and caused demonism; and that blood transfusions and organ transplants would transmit the personality of the person it came from. Tragically, on the basis of these unscientific and uninformed opinions, many Jehovah's Witnesses have died. Here is a partial record of how the Jehovah's Witnesses have changed their view on this issue over the past 70 years:

> 1940 — Blood transfusions are acceptable
> 1945 — Blood transfusion are not acceptable
> 1956 — Blood serums should be treated as blood and are banned
> 1958 — Blood serums and fractions are acceptable
> 1959 — Storage of one's own blood is unacceptable
> 1961 — Blood fractions are not acceptable
> 1964 — Blood fractions are acceptable
> 1967 — Organ transplants are not acceptable
> 1974 — Blood serums are a personal choice
> 1975 — Hemophilia treatments (Factor VII and IX) are not acceptable
> 1978 — Hemophilia treatments (Factor VII and IX) are acceptable
> 1980 — Organ transplants are acceptable
> 1982 — Albumin is acceptable
> 1983 — Hemodilution is acceptable
> 1990 — Hemodilution is not acceptable
> 1995 — Hemodilution is acceptable
> 2000 — Blood fractions are acceptable
> 2004 — Hemoglobin is now acceptable

Again, we ask, if the Governing Body is the mouthpiece for God in this world, how is it that their decrees are so changeable?

In the past, any Witness accepting a blood transfusion faced disciplinary action at the hands of a judicial committee. Any unrepentant Witness was disfellowshiped and shunned by every other Witness, including members of his own family. Recently, the Society has withdrawn the overt threat of punishment for disobeying these rules. They now say it is a matter of conscience and sanctions will not be applied. Yet the prohibition against transfusions is still a *de facto* rule. There exist "hospital liaison committees" who intervene on behalf of Witnesses facing major surgery. These committees apply a great deal of pressure to the family of Witnesses who may face a life-or-death decision about blood transfusions. So the threat of being disfellowshiped is still implied, if not stated.

The Gospel for Jehovah's Witnesses

First, we should understand that Jehovah's Witnesses have been deceived. They have been taught a false gospel, and they do not know who Jesus really is. They have no assurance of salvation and must constantly strive to work harder to prove their loyalty and obedience to the organization. Make no mistake, they are sincere people who honestly believe they alone have "the truth," and they genuinely think Armageddon is imminent. They feel compelled to share their version of the gospel with anyone who will listen. They are sincere, but sincerely wrong.

Witnessing to the Witnesses must be done in Christian love and compassion. Let them know how much you care about their eternal salvation. Share your Christian testimony with them. It comes as a surprise to them to meet people who love the Lord, display the fruit of the Spirit, and use the Bible as the basis for their faith (Hebrews 4:12). Speak the truth in love (Ephesians 4:15). Lead your conversation to the person of Christ and the need to put total faith in what He has done. Focus on the gospel. Above all else, pray for them.

Here is the testimony of a former Jehovah's Witness:

> When nothing happened after 1975, I left the organization. So did thousands of other disillusioned Witnesses. The awful thing was I still believed Armageddon was just round the corner, and so I lived in fear that I would be destroyed. Also, I had nowhere else to turn because I had believed every other Christian denomination was part of a false religion, soon to be destroyed. For many years, I wandered in a spiritual wilderness. I still believed in God, in Jesus, and in the Bible, but I wanted

nothing to do with Jehovah's Witnesses in particular and with religion in general.

Years later I discovered my twin sister had also left the organization, and she had become a Christian. I had many questions for her, and she answered them in full. Unknown to me, she had been praying for me for many years because she knew the spiritual danger I was in. Praise God, her prayers were answered, and on March 30, 1996, the Lord broke down the last of my barriers and brought me to the foot of the Cross where I repented and was forgiven.

I finally understood what Jesus had endured to save a sinner such as I. It took several years before I came to understand that Jesus was not just a man and that He was not Michael the Archangel but the eternal Word of God who became flesh and dwelt with us — God incarnate. From that wonderful moment when I finally capitulated and gave myself to Him, my life was transformed. No longer do I fear Armageddon or feel the need to obey an organization. I now belong to Christ Jesus, who has given me rest. He is gentle and humble, his yoke is easy, and his burden is light (Matthew 11:29–30). He is the good shepherd, and I recognize His voice. It is God who draws people, and many Jehovah's Witnesses have come out of the dark into the light because Christians have prayed for them and gently shown them the true gospel, which is all about Christ.

People in a cult seldom realize they are in a cult until they try to leave. The price to be paid for walking out is sometimes so great that Witnesses will keep their fears and thoughts to themselves and go through the motions just to avoid being disfellowshiped and shunned. Christians can help such people by persistent prayer — and by being willing to be the answer to their own prayers. Rather than shut the door on Jehovah's Witnesses when they call, we should present the true gospel to them in love and gentleness. A key to helping Jehovah's Witnesses is to always point them to Christ Jesus because they do not understand who He really is. They must see the significance of Jesus' death and why they must be born again in order to have their sins forgiven.

The example of Christian love in action speaks volumes, and it is the work of the Holy Spirit to bring people to repentance and saving faith. For our part, we should be sensitive to the prompting of the Spirit and always be ready to be the Spirit's voice in presenting the gospel of salvation.

Summary of Jehovah's Witness Beliefs

Doctrine	Jehovah's Witness Teaching
God	Deny the trinity; Jehovah is the only god; Jesus was created as Michael the Archangel and became the Son at His baptism; the "holy spirit" is an impersonal force of Jehovah
Authority/ Revelation	The New World translation of the Bible; the Governing Body and its publications, which contain new revelations ("increasing light")
Man	A created being with a free will who must choose to obey Jehovah
Sin	Transgression of Jehovah's commands as well as other legalistic restrictions announced by the Governing Body; an individual's sins are removed at death
Salvation	Salvation comes from obeying laws and by doing good works; Jesus died to atone only for Adam's sin, not the sins of individuals; there is no concept of hell or eternal punishment; eternal paradise will be obtained by only a select few while others will have their souls annihilated
Creation	The Genesis account is acknowledged, but with a day-age understanding; the earth and universe are billions of years old; biological evolution to some extent is allowed, but man was specially created

Chapter 9

Judaism

David Abrahams

A Brief Historical Introduction

Have you ever wondered why there is so much strife between Jews and Muslims in the Middle East (and abroad)? The truth is, the Middle East has rarely been stable since the events that occurred at the Tower of Babel in Genesis 11.

There was the brotherly feud between Isaac (father of the Israelites and Edomites) and Ishmael (father of many Arabs), the two eldest of eight sons of Abraham whose progeny now dominates much of the Middle East (1 Chronicles 1:32). Abraham was also involved in a war where there were four kings against five in the Middle East (Genesis 14:7–16). Further conflicts arose due to strife between two more brothers, the sons of Isaac — Jacob (Israel) and Esau (father of the Edomites). And so it continues.

Needless to say, there have been problems brewing in the Middle East for ages. But why are the issues between Jews and Muslims so vicious today? They are clearly not on friendly terms. I suggest there was a culminating event that has triggered much of this aggression.

Two thousand years ago, the Jews, by and large, did not receive Jesus Christ as Messiah, the ultimate Passover Lamb, Savior, and deliverer who paid for sin once and for all. Because of this, they were still anticipating a messiah well after the time of Christ. In the days of Muhammad (late A.D.

500s and early A.D. 600s), some local Jews were familiar with the supposed prophet in Arabia, and some thought that he might be the long-awaited Messiah.[1]

Muhammad, favoring this idea, raised his hopes of being the Jewish Messiah and had many favorable things to say about the Jews (and Christians) in his dictated Koran. In time, however, the Jews realized that Muhammad did not fit the prophecies of the Messiah. When tested against the many messianic prophecies in Scripture, Muhammad wasn't even close (e.g., not born in Bethlehem [Micah 5:2], not a descendant of Judah [Genesis 28:14], etc.).

So, because of this (as well as for other reasons), Muhammad's attitude turned from one of kindness toward the Jews to hostility. From that time forward, there has been aggression toward the Jews (and Christians) from the Muslims because Muhammad labeled the Jews as "cursed" (Koran 4.46) and wanted his followers to "not take the Jews and the Christians for friends" (Koran 5.51). (Note that the Koran is not written in chronological order but from longest chapter to shortest chapter.)

Judaism in History

The words *Jew* and *Judaism* come from the name Judah, one of the 12 sons of Israel. Judah was one of the larger tribes that became dominant as its own country when the nation of Israel split into two kingdoms. The northern kingdom retained the name Israel (with 10 tribes), and the southern kingdom took the name Judah (with two tribes, one being Judah, naturally).

Although Judaism shares the same foundational history in the Old Testament with Christians — going back to God creating in six days and resting on the seventh — there is a stark contrast between what Judaism *has become* in comparison to what the Old Testament teaches. Judaism couldn't properly be named "Judaism" until after Judah came into being![2] Let me state this more succinctly: Judaism is an off-shoot, or deviation, from the Old Testament.

In Old Testament days, when Israelites followed the clear teachings of the Old Testament Scripture, they were following the true religion. Obviously, if

---

1. Mesbah Uddin, "Prophet Muhammad Was Revered as the Jewish Messiah in Medina," Media Monitors Network, March 3, 2008, http://usa.mediamonitors.net/Headlines/Prophet-Muhammad-was-Revered-as-the-Jewish-Messiah-in-Medina.

2. The name Jew/Jews was first used in the Book of 2 Kings 16:6 and 25:25, being men of Judah. If one tries to use this argument about Christianity not coming into being until Christ, then there is a flaw, as Christ is the Creator and preeminent to all things.

they were not following the Old Testament, they were not being godly and thus were not following the true religion!

In the first century, however, there was a division among those who followed the Old Testament: those of the Way (i.e., Christianity — e.g., Acts 19:23, 24:14) who followed Christ as the Jewish Messiah and all the implications thereof, and those who did not follow Jesus and were finally organized into the Jewish religion of Judaism, based on traditions as opposed to finding true freedom in the Messiah.

What Are the Holy Books in Judaism?

Where Christians follow the Old and New Testament Scriptures, those holding to Judaism follow the Old Testament and the Talmud (meaning the Babylonian Talmud).

The Talmud is defined by the World Book Encyclopedia as the following:

> A collection of legal and ethical writings, as well as Jewish history and folklore. It serves primarily as a guide to the civil and religious laws of Judaism. Orthodox Jews believe the laws in the Talmud were given to Moses by God and passed down orally from Generation to Generation. About A.D. 200, scholars wrote down these oral laws in a work called the *Mishnah*. Later scholars explained and interpreted the Mishnah. Their comments were recorded in the *Gemara*, which was written between 200 and 500. The Mishnah and Gemara together make up the Talmud.[3]

There is also a less authoritative Talmud that was compiled by about A.D. 400 called the Talmud of the Land of Israel (or the Jerusalem Talmud). It also contains two parts, a Mishnah and Gemara, but is shorter overall than the Babylonian Talmud.

The Talmud is made up of the traditions that were often spoken of in the New Testament (e.g., Matthew 15:3; Colossians 2:8; etc.). Of course, they were still in oral form at the time of Christ. There were times when Jews elevated these traditions above the Scriptures of the Old Testament (e.g., Matthew 15:4–9; Mark 7:3–13), hence they came to the wrong conclusions on certain issues such as, "Sabbath was made for man, and not man for the Sabbath"(Mark 2:27). This is why interpretation of Scripture is best done by

---

3. World Book Encyclopedia, Volume 11, Entry: Judaism, World Book, Inc., 1990, p. 178.

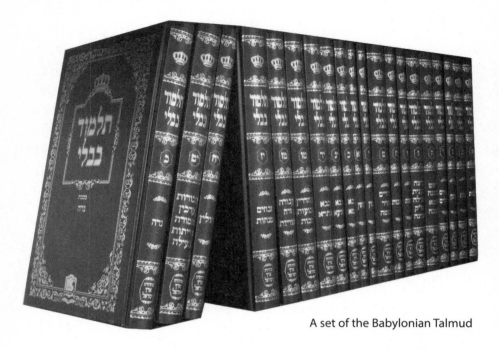

A set of the Babylonian Talmud

Scripture itself, as God is the best interpreter of His own Word, instead of relying strictly on the ideas of "scholars."

The infiltration of man's ideas has been a major issue in the history of the Israelite nation. How often does the Old Testament record deviations from the Word of God where Israelites began worshiping Baal or setting up high places to false gods? How many times did the Lord send prophets to call the Israelites back to His Word? Even the wise Solomon himself succumbed to the worship of false gods!

These types of seeds finally flourished into a version where man's interpretations of the Old Testament (in the form of the Talmud's Gemara) began to supersede the very Word of God. It becomes a major problem when man's ideas are elevated to be greater than the Word of God. Consider the words of Isaiah:

> Stop regarding man, whose breath of life is in his nostrils; for why should he be esteemed? (Isaiah 2:22; NASB).

What Are the Beliefs within Judaism?

Of course, it would require extensive time to develop all the beliefs within Judaism. So I will be concise in this section. But something must be stated up front: many who are Jews do not hold to Judaism. There are many who are secular (that is, the primary humanistic religion) and are of Jewish heritage. So just because someone says they are Jewish doesn't necessarily mean they hold to the tenets of Judaism. However, for the sake of simplicity, when I say "Jew" in this chapter on Judaism, I mean those who hold to the religion of Judaism, unless the context warrants otherwise.

Judaism is a set of informal beliefs about the world and how people should live their lives. Although Jewish beliefs vary, they can be summed up by medieval Jewish scholar Moshi ben Maimon's (Maimonides) 13 articles:

1. God alone exists and is Creator
2. God is one and unique
3. God is incorporeal and incomparable
4. God is eternal (both first and last)
5. We are to pray to God alone and to no other
6. The words of the prophets are true
7. Moses was the chief prophet, and Moses' prophecies are true
8. The Torah (first five books of the Bible) and oral Torah (Talmud) were given to Moses and divinely preserved
9. There will be no other Torah since it cannot be changed
10. God knows all things including the thoughts and deeds of men
11. God will reward the righteous and punish the wicked
12. The Messiah will come
13. The dead will be resurrected.[4]

Take note that Christians easily agree with most of these points. However, a Christian would disagree with the idea that the Talmud is of divine origin. Replacing the Talmud with the New Testament (along with the remaining Old Testament books) in point 8 would make this statement accurate. And in point 12, we would change "The Messiah will come" to "The Messiah has come, and He is Jesus of Nazareth."

In addition, although true, I would clarify point 11. All have sinned and fall short of God's glory (Psalm 116:11; Romans 3:23, 5:12), thus all

4. Tracey R. Rich, What do Jews Believe? Jewfaq.org, 1995–2011, http://www.jewfaq.org/beliefs.htm; John Parsons, Sheloshah-Asar Ikkarim, Hebrew for Christians website, Accessed April 15, 2015, http://www.hebrew4christians.com/Scripture/Shloshah-Asar_Ikkarim/shloshah-asar_ikkarim.html.

would be classed as sinful, hence wicked in God's eyes. The only way to be *made* righteous would be for God to assign the righteousness of His Son, the Messiah, to us so that we are seen as righteous and pure (clean) in the sight of God. More on this later.

Divisions in Judaism

There are several divisions within modern Judaism. The main divisions in religious outlook are Reform, Conservative, and Orthodox Judaism. This is not to be confused with cultures and traditions of various Jewish groups.

Allow me to explain the history of Jewish groups so that we can better understand the terms. Let's go back about 2,000 years to see the division that existed then. At the time of Christ, there were already divisions in Jewish thought.[5] These groups included Pharisees, Sadducees, Essenes, Scribes, and Zealots. Here are some of their views and differences.[6]

- Pharisees — those who held to strict adherence of the Law of Moses and the Old Testament, but *also* held to oral tradition as the truth. Interestingly, they set aside the divisions set up by God in the Law of Moses (i.e., Levites were required to do certain things for worship and priestly service, but the Pharisees proclaimed these things could be performed by any and all Jews). Positively, they held to the resurrection of the dead. This movement traces its roots back to the Maccabean revolt around 150 B.C. The Pharisaical view became the basis for modern Rabbinic Judaism after the fall of Jerusalem in A.D. 70.

- Sadducees — they trace their roots back to Zadok/Tzadok the priest (1 Kings 1:8) in David and Solomon's day. Their name actually is a variation of Zadok (think "s"adok or Sadoksees) and means "the righteous ones of Zadok." They held the priestly and ruling responsibilities at the Temple with prestigious positions. They did not believe in the resurrection of

---

5. One prior division before the first century that is worthy of note is the Samaritans. They, though not properly Jews, were a group of Israelites that had intermarried with pagans and had a form of primeval Judaism mixed with idolatry. They held to the Books of Moses and no other. They rejected the prophets and the oral traditions but often held to false gods.

6. For more on these groups please see: Daniel Sweet, *Who were the Pharisees, Sadducees, Scribes, Essenes, and Zealots?* God's Word First International Biblical Research & Teaching Ministry, 2010, http://www.gods-word-first.org/jesus-christ/pharisees-sadducees-scribes-zealots.html.

the dead (i.e., no afterlife, Matthew 22:23) and welcomed Roman rule.

- Essenes — they flourished for about 300 years ending prior to A.D. 100, likely due to the Romans. The Essenes may have been a division of the Sadducees and had become one of the three major divisions of the Jews around the first century. They lived in communes and abstained from worldly desires; they lived lives of poverty with very strict rules (think of something like monks and nuns within the Roman Catholic worldview). They were famous for the Dead Sea Scrolls, which were preserved in caves and not found for nearly 2,000 years.

- Scribes — these were highly trained scholars of their day who were often devoted to copying the Scriptures, but also had responsibilities as bankers, judges, governing authorities, and those sought for wisdom on some matters. There are still a few modern-day "Sofers," as they are called, who are scribes that still do work like those in the first century. The Masoretes who meticulously copied the Hebrew Old Testament until the tenth century were Scribes.

- Zealots — these people were often fanatic for the nation of Israel and wanted to try to do away with Roman rule. This group goes back to the Maccabean revolt against Rome that failed in about 150 B.C. They likely influenced many Jews to wage war against Rome, which led to the utter destruction of Jerusalem, the Temple and Sanctuary, and much of Judea (e.g., synagogues) by the Romans from A.D. 66 to 73.

Out of all these divisions, the Pharisaical system basically took over after the destruction of the Temple in A.D. 70 when the Jews were scattered or put into bondage. The added oral traditions, which were seen as Scripture, began to be put into written format about A.D. 200.

After the war with Rome that left millions dead in Judea, those Jews who survived were basically in two groups: those who fled from the grip of Rome and those who were taken captive by Rome. Of course, there were some who were left, but most in the region would fit into these two categories. Many of those taken captive by Rome became slaves that were sent to various parts of the Empire.

Sephardic Jews

Groups of captive Jews were taken by Rome to Spain, Portugal, North Africa, and the Middle East (while some fled "under the radar"). In subsequent years when tensions were reduced, they became their own people known as the Sephardic Jews. This group is divided into two groups. The first is the *Sephardim* in Iberia, or Spain and Portugal, and the *Mazrachim*, which include those in North Africa and the Middle East. Many Sephardic Jews in Spain were expelled in 1492 and made their way to communities among the Mazrachim.

Ashkenazi Jews

The *Ashkenazi* Jews are those who fled to the land of Germany. Ashkenaz was one of Noah's great-grandsons (Genesis 10:3), and it was his progeny that populated Germany.[7] Hence, many Jews refer to this land as "Ashkenaz," and the Ashkenazi Jews were those who lived in Ashkenaz, or Germany.

It makes good sense for Jews fleeing the grip of Rome to go to Germany, since Germany, which is relatively close to Rome, was never fully subdued by Rome. This was the ideal place to reach if you could make your way across the mountainous terrain to get to safety. Germany was also safer for Jews to stretch out to many other places in Europe as Rome's power diminished.

As a side note, this occurrence may be one reason for the tensions we still see today. Consider that these new German hosts were likely bitter about the massive numbers of new arrivals, and it might explain much of the tension between Jews and the Germans that has existed since that time. There were conflicts during the Crusades, and during the Reformation. And one cannot forget the utter devastation at the hands of the evil Nazis. Sadly, there are still tensions in Europe today between Europeans and Jews.

Messianic Jews

Another group called the *Messianic Jews* should really be mentioned at this point. Many Jews who *have* received Jesus Christ as Savior and Messiah in modern times take this name. In many ways, they are merely Christians with Jewish backgrounds or converted Gentiles, but in another respect, they

---

7. Bodie Hodge, *The Tower of Babel* (Green Forest, AR: Master Books, 2012), p. 151–157.

still retain certain aspects of Judaism (e.g., feasts, celebrations, and so on). They hold to the Old and New Testament as Scripture and Christ as the Son of God (one person of the one triune God; see appendix A).

Orthodox, Conservative, and Reform Judaism

As we have seen from our historical review, the modern groups within Judaism are primarily born out of Pharisaical teaching that held the Old Testament and the Talmud (traditions) as supreme authority. Even within this modern Judaism, there are divisions with three being the main groups:

- Orthodox Judaism — a movement holding traditional beliefs and practices such as kosher diets, Sabbath rest, and distinctive dress codes.

- Reform Judaism[8] — a modern movement begun in the 1800s that takes many liberal viewpoints and does away with conservative values and practices that are inherent to Orthodox Judaism.

- Conservative Judaism — a group that tries to balance between Orthodox Judaism and Reform Judaism.

There is one more group that is very prominent today that should be added to this section:

- Secular Judaism — those who still identify as Jews, most often by heritage, but are actually secular humanists (the popular religion of today). They have taken one more step beyond the Reform Judaist position to be purely secular in their religious outlook. They just retain the name for the sake of their ancestry.

Discussion

Now that we are familiar with the names, divisions, and some history of Judaism, let's proceed with the discussion. But before I go any further, let me speak my heart on this issue. I love the Jews, and I have a fondness for

---

8. In Christianity, the term "reformed" means that you go back to the Bible to reform your theology and beliefs to get it close to what God teaches (hence the name "Reform"). Reform Judaism is really the opposite. It seeks to take Judaism and reform it to modern, secular practices and beliefs.

them and have often defended them. But I still have the hope, as the Apostle Paul did (Romans 11:13–14), that they would repent of their sin and receive Jesus as Christ and Lord.

The Jews are loved on account of the patriarchs (Romans 11:28), and so I echo this same love. But like atheists, Muslims, and so many others, the Jews are enemies of the gospel of Jesus Christ, which is the good news that can set them free and guarantee eternal life (John 3:36, 10:28, 17:3; 1 Timothy 1:16; 1 John 5:11). Now that Gentiles have been offered the gospel, this puts Jews and Gentiles under the same need in equal fashion in the eyes of God (Romans 10:12). And with that, there is only one name under heaven that men must be saved (Acts 4:12) and only one way to peace with God for Jew or Gentile, and that is through Jesus Christ (Isaiah 9:6; John 14:6).

Even with many similarities, the differences between Judaism and Christianity are stark. And there is no reason we cannot be open about them.

Arbitrariness and Inconsistency

The Old Testament is the Word of God, and to say otherwise would be arbitrary opinions of man compared to the absolute of God's Word. Christians applaud those in Judaism who hold to the Old Testament as the truth. But at the same time, Judaists deny that the New Testament is the Word of God, based on their own arbitrary opinions.

Furthermore, adding oral traditions to the Word of God is also arbitrary. Naturally, these oral traditions are attributed to Moses by the Jews. But after 1,500 years of oral transmission in the hands of fallible and sinful men who were often in disobedience to the written Word, how can anyone know for sure that they are accurate? In the Old Testament, there were times when most Israelites knew precious little about the *written* Word due to so much false worship, let alone the *oral* traditions.

To prove this point, we could ask why is it that the Jerusalem Talmud and the Babylonian Talmud do not contain the same teachings when certain topics are discussed (e.g., agricultural laws or sacrificial rites and laws at the Temple)? Why do they disagree with each other (one being rather anti-Gentile [Babylonian] and one not so much [Jerusalem])? This shows they were not preserved as the Word of God.

In the two Talmuds, there are opinions of rabbis that disagree with each other concerning Bible passages — too many to cite! Such inconsistencies show that it is not the Word of God nor should it be elevated to a position of being greater than God's Word in the Bible. To cap the debate, Jesus Christ, who is God, affirmed that the traditions of men were not the Word of God and should not to be equated as such (Matthew 15:3–6; Mark 7:8–13).

To summarize, the Word of God was entrusted to the Jews. This is an honorable position — one that should not be taken lightly. All traditions should be judged by the written Word of God rather than allowing the written Word of God to be judged by oral traditions.

Borrowing from the Word of Christ

Obviously, those in Judaism have regarded much of the Bible as the truth, especially the Old Testament. Since Jesus, Immanuel, is God with us (Isaiah 7:14; Matthew 1:23), the Old Testament is His Word. Therefore, Judaists borrow from Jesus' Word for their religion. This helps clarify a misconception. Often, we hear that Christianity was born out of Judaism, but this is not the case. Judaism emerged as a response to Christianity.

The Old Testament is a Christian document that points to Jesus Christ who is the ultimate author of Scripture (Luke 24:27; John 5:46). Professor of Church History Dr. Phillip Schaff rightly states that the Old Testament Jewish religion "was the true religion before Christ but not perfect, or final."[9]

The New Testament, with Christ as the centerpiece, is like a blossomed flower with the Old Testament patriarchs, such as Abraham and Moses and the prophets as the stem, leaves, and roots. But where the New Testament perfected or finalized the Old Testament in God's perfect timing, the Pharisees deviated and held man's ideas in the oral traditions to be greater than God's Word. Judaism is just that: a deviation from the clear teachings of the Old Testament caused by elevating the traditions of men and rejecting the New Testament of God.

In other words, Judaism was born out of an improper understanding of Christ's religion (Old Testament) and a rejection of God's Word in the New Testament, particularly the rejection of the Messiah, Jesus. This happened because they misunderstood the promise, which led to a misunderstanding of its fulfillment.

But since Jews and Christians have the Old Testament in common, there will be some beliefs on which they agree. In fact, Christians and Jews share many similar doctrines because they draw many of them from the same pages of Scripture.

9. Philip Schaff, *Theological Propaedeutic* (New York: Charles Scribner's Sons, 1904), p. 55.

As a side note, Christians break the Old Testament books into 39 while the Jews have a listing that contains about 24. For example, where we split Kings, Chronicles, and Samuel into two books each, the Jews have one book for each of these. Ezra and

Orthodox Jewish men praying in Jerusalem

Nehemiah are put together into a single book, while all 12 of the minor prophets are combined as well. Nevertheless, it is the same content.

As Christians, we share the same foundation in Genesis as the Jews do, as well as draw from the patriarchal roots on up to the final prophets of the Old Testament. We both believe in one God (Genesis 1:1; Deuteronomy 6:4; Ephesians 4:6), hold to marriage as defined by God in the Garden of Eden (Genesis 1:27, 2:24), and have a basis for logic, knowledge, and the truth since we are made in the image of a logical, truthful God (Genesis 1:26–27). We both understand that we live in a sin-cursed and broken world (Genesis 3) and have a need for a Messiah (Deuteronomy 18:15; Daniel 9:25) and an everlasting covenant (Jeremiah 32:40).

There are many other doctrines in common, of course. But the differences begin where we start to see the outworking of the Old Testament as it flows into the New Testament (versus flowing into the Talmud). The Old Testament does not flow in two directions, so one direction must be wrong. The Old Testament naturally flows into the New Testament — its fulfillment. Because of this, there are many differences in doctrines, too many to discuss in one chapter, so we will focus on a few significant ones.

Obviously, diet is one well-known difference. In the New Testament, Jesus Christ (who is God) declared all foods clean in Mark 7:19. This initially shocked Peter, who was devout in his kosher diet (Acts 10:13–16)! The Judaists still maintain strict dietary restrictions (Colossians 2:16; 1 Timothy 4:3).

Christians recognize Jesus as the Messiah, or Christ — God who came in the flesh and dwelt among us (John 1:1, 1:14). But the Judaists still wait for a messiah and have a much lower view of who he will be. Their hope is that he will be a military leader to help free the Jews from some earthly crisis. Consider if the Jews had received Christ as Messiah the first time. Would they still have considered Muhammad to possibly be the Messiah? There would have been no reason to. Would there still be the conflicts with those of the Islamic faith? Only the Lord knows.

Of course, God's Messiah did so much more than the Judaists are looking for. He set us free for all eternity from sin and the cares of this world. The Messiah was put to death — the punishment that we all deserve for sin — to set us free forever. And those in the Messiah (Christ) have nothing to fear when the resurrection comes. Here are just 20 of the many Messianic prophecies in the Old Testament and where they were fulfilled in Jesus:

	Messianic Prophecy	**OT Reference**	**NT Reference**
1	Seed of the Woman	Genesis 3:15	Matthew 1:20; Galatians 4:4
2	Line of Abraham	Genesis 12:3, 22:18	Matthew 1:1–16; Luke 3:23–34
3	Line of Isaac	Genesis 17:19, 21:12	Matthew 1:1–16; Luke 3:23–34
4	Line of Israel	Numbers 24:17	Matthew 1:1–16; Luke 3:23–34
5	Line of Judah	Genesis 28:14	Matthew 1:1–16; Luke 3:23–34
6	Heir of David	2 Samuel 7:12–13; Isaiah 9:7	Matthew 1:1–16; Luke 3:23–34
7	Eternal throne and everlasting Kingdom	2 Samuel 8:13–16; Psalm 45:6–7; Daniel 2:44, 7:13–14	Luke 1:33; Hebrews 1:8–12; 1 Peter 5:11; Jude 1:25; Revelation 1:6
8	He will be a prophet	Deuteronomy 18:18	John 8:28–29
9	Savior of both Israel and Gentiles	Isaiah 49:6	Luke 2:29–32; John 8:12; Acts 13:46

10	Called the Son of God	2 Samuel 7:14; Psalm 2:7	Matthew 3:16–17
11	He will be King	Psalm 2:6; Zechariah 9:9	Matthew 27:37; Revelation 7:14, 19:16
12	He will resurrect	Psalm 16:10, 49:15	Matthew 28:2–7; Acts 2:22–32
13	Sits on the throne of God	Psalm 68:18, 110:1	Matthew 22:44; Mark 16:19
14	He would be a sacrifice for sin	Isaiah 53:5–12	Romans 5:6–8
15	He would be pierced in His side	Zechariah 12:10	John 19:34
16	As in a proper Passover sacrifice, His bones would not be broken	Exodus 12:46; Psalm 34:20	John 19:33–36
17	His hands and feet would be pierced	Psalm 22:16	John 20:25–27
18	Born in Bethlehem	Micah 5:2	Matthew 2:1; Luke 2:4–6
19	Born of a virgin*	Isaiah 7:14	Matthew 1:22–23
20	Called Immanuel (God with us)	Isaiah 7:14	Matthew 1:22–23

---

* The Judaist often professes that this doesn't mean "virgin" but merely "young woman." Refuting this, famed reformer John Calvin wrote in his commentary on Isaiah 7:14, "Although the word המלע, (gnalmah,) a virgin, is derived *from* םלע, (gnalam,) which signifies to hide, because the shame and modesty of virgins does not allow them to appear in public; yet as the Jews dispute much about that word, and assert that it does not signify virgin, because Solomon used it to denote a young woman who was betrothed, it is unnecessary to contend about the word. Though we should admit what they say, *that* המלע (gnalmah) sometimes denotes a young woman, and that the name refers, as they would have it, to the age (yet it is frequently used in Scripture when the subject relates to a virgin), the nature of the case sufficiently refutes all their slanders. For what wonderful thing did the Prophet say, if he spoke of a young woman who conceived through intercourse with a man? It would certainly have been absurd to hold out this as a sign or a miracle. Let us suppose that it denotes a young woman who should become pregnant in the ordinary course of nature; everybody sees that it would have been silly and contemptible for the Prophet, after having said that he was about to speak of something strange and uncommon, to add, A young woman shall conceive. It is, therefore, plain enough that he speaks of a virgin who should conceive, not by the ordinary course of nature, but by the gracious influence of the Holy *Spirit*."

Where Jews have looked to sacrifice and their good works for the possibility of salvation, Christians have looked to the ultimate sacrifice of Jesus in whom they believe and have faith and the assurance of salvation. Faith, or belief in God and what He has done, has always been the means of salvation. Those prior to Jesus looked forward to Him for their salvation in the same way Christians now look back to Christ for our salvation.

But salvation has always been of God alone. This is a major point of disagreement between Judaism and Christianity. The Judaist holds works to be essential, but the Christian holds faith in Christ through grace as the means of salvation. Christians do good works to please God, not to gain salvation. Leading modern Jews Dennis Prager and Joseph Telushkin write,

> Judaism stresses action more than faith.[10]

> The major difference between Judaism and Christianity lies in the importance each religion attaches to faith and actions. In Judaism, God considers people's action to be more important than their faith; acting in accordance with biblical and rabbinic law is the Jews' central obligation.[11]

This naturally has implication for theology. Consider what Prager and Telushkin continue to say:

> According to Judaism, one can be a good Jew while doubting God's existence, so long as one acts in accordance with Jewish law.[12]

> It is not, of course, our intention to deny the centrality of God in Judaism, but merely to emphasize that Judaism can be appreciated and practiced independently of one's present level of belief in God.[13]

Where Jews look to works for the *possibility* of salvation, the Bible teaches that works can't save a person. Sin still needs to be punished by an infinite and perfectly holy and just God. Josh McDowell pointed out the crux of the difference when he wrote:

---

10. Dennis Prager and Joseph Telushkin, *The Nine Questions People Ask About Judaism* (New York, NY: Simon & Schuster, 1975), p. 18.
11. Ibid., p. 78.
12. Ibid., p. 18.
13. Ibid., p. 19.

Judaism, while admitting the existence of sin, its abhorrence by God, and the necessity for atonement, has not developed a system of salvation teaching as found in Christianity. Atonement is accomplished by sacrifices, penitence, good deeds, and a little of God's grace. No concept of substitutionary atonement (as in Christianity in the person of Jesus Christ) exists.[14]

Yes, sin still needs to be dealt with properly — going back to the first sin in Genesis 3. Just as the coats of skins in Genesis 3:21, Abel's fat portions in Genesis 4:4, and Noah's sacrifices of clean animals after the Flood in Genesis 8:20, each pointed forward to the sacrificial laws given by Moses, so these sacrifices, as well as the Levitical sacrifices, ultimately pointed to Christ's final and eternal sacrifice once and for all (Hebrews 7:27, 9:12, 10:10). The sacrifices before the Law, and as a result of the Law, were still not sufficient to satisfy God's full wrath upon sin. They were mere shadows of what was to come in the blood of the ultimate Lamb of God, the Lord Jesus Christ.

The Bible makes it clear that the blood of bulls and goats are not sufficient to satisfy the wrath of God upon sin (Hebrews 10:4). An even better sacrifice, a sufficient sacrifice, was needed. And Christ, who is God, was that all-sufficient sacrifice (2 Corinthians 5:21). The Old Testament sacrifices pointed to the ultimate sacrifice of Jesus Christ on the Cross.

We (and the animals used in sacrifice) are only created beings — far less than the eternal God. No created being could take the punishment we deserve from an uncreated, infinite God. God Himself was the only one in a position to remedy His punishment upon sin. God, the infinite Son, Jesus, became a man fulfilling the promised seed of the woman (Genesis 3:15) and was the fulfilled seed of Abraham, Isaac, Jacob, Judah, and heir of David. The infinite Son, Jesus, took the infinite punishment from God, the infinite Father, when He was offered up as our ultimate Passover Lamb by the high priest of Israel nearly 2,000 years ago (Matthew 26:62–66; 1 Corinthians 5:7).

This is what makes salvation possible — not by our works, but by the necessary work of God so that He alone receives the glory. Salvation comes as a person repents of sin and receives Jesus Christ as Lord and Savior. And then Christ's righteousness is imputed to the sinner — whether Jew or Gentile. This is why sacrificial and ceremonial laws have been done away with

---

14. Josh McDowell, *A Ready Defense*, compiled by Bill Wilson (Nashville, TN: Thomas Nelson Publishers, 1993), p. 301.

— they are no longer necessary because they've been fulfilled in Christ. This is also why the Temple is no longer necessary. The body of the believer is now the new temple of the Holy Spirit (1 Corinthians 3:16, 6:19).

Where Judaists still hope for a new covenant (Jeremiah 31:31), Christians have recognized the coming of the new covenant (an eternal covenant) already in Christ's blood (Luke 22:20). He is our ultimate Passover Lamb (1 Corinthians 5:7). And we want those raised in Judaism to realize that they, too, need to receive Jesus the Messiah to be saved (Acts 4:12).

Although not a uniquely Jewish symbol before the 19th century, the Star of David, or Shield of David as it is known in Hebrew, has become a modern symbol of Judaism and the Jewish state of Israel.

Conclusion

Few realize that Christians have been among those who have supported the Jews for many years in their plight, not only because of their love for the ethnic Israelites, but for the sake of the biblical patriarchs. Even though many Israelites have been saved over the last 2,000 years, it seems that many Jews have been blind to the gospel for so long, yet the door seems so open for Gentiles. Why is that?

To answer this question, we first need to remember that God is the God of both the Jew *and* the Gentile (Romans 3:29)! What has happened is that Gentile believers have been grafted into the root of Israel in the same way that Ruth (a Moabite) and Rahab (a Canaanite) were grafted into Israel.

Sadly, by the rejection of God's Redeemer, Jesus the Christ, many Jews have been pruned from the tree of Israel. An Israelite Pharisee, Saul (Paul), who became a Christian nearly 2,000 years ago, writes about this mystery of why many Jews have been blinded to the truth (and only a remnant saved) and why the miracle of Gentiles being saved is so significant. He writes in the Book of Romans:

> So then faith comes by hearing, and hearing by the word of God. But I say, have they not heard? Yes indeed: "Their sound

has gone out to all the earth, and their words to the ends of the world." But I say, did Israel not know? First Moses says: "I will provoke you to jealousy by those who are not a nation, I will move you to anger by a foolish nation." But Isaiah is very bold and says: "I was found by those who did not seek Me; I was made manifest to those who did not ask for Me." But to Israel he says: "All day long I have stretched out My hands to a disobedient and contrary people."

I say then, has God cast away His people? Certainly not! For I also am an Israelite, of the seed of Abraham, of the tribe of Benjamin. God has not cast away His people whom He foreknew. Or do you not know what the Scripture says of Elijah, how he pleads with God against Israel, saying, "LORD, they have killed Your prophets and torn down Your altars, and I alone am left, and they seek my life"? But what does the divine response say to him? "I have reserved for Myself seven thousand men who have not bowed the knee to Baal." Even so then, at this present time there is a remnant according to the election of grace.

And if by grace, then it is no longer of works; otherwise grace is no longer grace. But if it is of works, it is no longer grace; otherwise work is no longer work. What then? Israel has not obtained what it seeks; but the elect have obtained it, and the rest were blinded. Just as it is written: "God has given them a spirit of stupor, eyes that they should not see and ears that they should not hear, to this very day." And David says: "Let their table become a snare and a trap, a stumbling block and a recompense to them. Let their eyes be darkened, so that they do not see, and bow down their back always."

I say then, have they stumbled that they should fall? Certainly not! But through their fall, to provoke them to jealousy, salvation has come to the Gentiles. Now if their fall is riches for the world, and their failure riches for the Gentiles, how much more their fullness! For I speak to you Gentiles; inasmuch as I am an apostle to the Gentiles, I magnify my ministry, if by any means I may provoke to jealousy those who are my flesh and save some of them. For if their being cast away is the reconciling of the world, what will their acceptance be but life from the dead?

For if the firstfruit is holy, the lump is also holy; and if the root is holy, so are the branches. And if some of the branches were broken off, and you, being a wild olive tree, were grafted in among them, and with them became a partaker of the root and fatness of the olive tree, do not boast against the branches. But if you do boast, remember that you do not support the root, but the root supports you. You will say then, "Branches were broken off that I might be grafted in." Well said. Because of unbelief they were broken off, and you stand by faith. Do not be haughty, but fear. For if God did not spare the natural branches, He may not spare you either.

Therefore consider the goodness and severity of God: on those who fell, severity; but toward you, goodness, if you continue in His goodness. Otherwise you also will be cut off. And they also, if they do not continue in unbelief, will be grafted in, for God is able to graft them in again. For if you were cut out of the olive tree which is wild by nature, and were grafted contrary to nature into a cultivated olive tree, how much more will these, who are natural branches, be grafted into their own olive tree? For I do not desire, brethren, that you should be ignorant of this mystery, lest you should be wise in your own opinion, that blindness in part has happened to Israel until the fullness of the Gentiles has come in. And so all Israel will be saved (Romans 10:17–11:26; NKJV).

As Christians, we need to remember that we, too, were enemies of God until the Holy Spirit saved us (1 Corinthians 12:3; Colossians 1:21). This is why our prayer is for those caught in Judaism to be set free by the promised Messiah, Christ Jesus our Lord. Our hope is for those in Judaism to receive the final Passover Lamb, Jesus, to have peace with God once and for all.

Just as God often left a remnant in the Old Testament, so a remnant of Israelites joined the firstfruits of the fulfillment of the Old Testament, such as Peter, Paul, John, Matthew, and many others. But the door is still open, as both Jews and Gentiles are called upon to receive Christ to be saved by the same measure (Acts 15:3–9; Romans 10:12). Gentiles, who were seen as unclean sinners by the Jews, are now made clean by the work of the Lord.

Is anything too hard for God (Jeremiah 32:27)? Is it too hard for God to take a pruned, natural branch and re-graft it in? Not at all! By receiving the Messiah, Jesus Christ, the natural branch will be made fruitful again.

Summary of Jewish Beliefs

Doctrine	Judaism's Teaching
God	Deny the Trinity; there is only one God; Jesus is not the Son of God or the Messiah; the Holy Spirit is not a person
Authority/ Revelation	39 books of the Old Testament; Talmud; various rabbis and traditions
Man	Man is created in the image of God; mankind is fallen as a result of Adam's sin; man is able to attain perfection
Sin	Disobeying the laws prescribed in the Old Testament
Salvation	Salvation is possible through the obedience of the individual to biblical and rabbinical laws; atonement is accomplished through personal acts of sacrifice and penitence; some see the future Messiah or the future restoration of the Temple sacrifices as a means of atonement
Creation	The universe and all that is in it was created out of nothing in six, 24-hour days about 6,000 years ago; all living things were created according to their kinds in supernatural acts of God; mankind was specially created by God in supernatural acts; many modern groups would accept certain forms of evolution

Chapter 10

Mormonism

Roger Patterson

As the story goes, a young man named Joe in upstate New York in 1820 was seeking after the right church to join. Seeing such strife and contention in the local churches — specifically the Methodists, Baptists, and Presbyterians — the 14-year-old was torn over the claims that each church was the true church. Longing to know the truth, Joe turned to the Bible where he read from the Epistle of James that those who ask God for wisdom would be given it.

Revival was breaking out in the area where Joe lived, but how could he know which church looked to the Bible to know the truth? Finding a secluded spot in the woods near his home, young Joe knelt down to ask God for wisdom about which church to join.

As Joe began to pray, an overwhelming force bound his body and tongue, and thick darkness enveloped him! Just as he thought he was about to die, a pillar of light descended from heaven delivering him from the power. Before him stood the Heavenly Father and His beloved Son engulfed in light. In answer to Joe's question, the Son told him that all of the creeds of these denominations were an abomination and their professors were all corrupt and that he should join none of them.

After three years of living a rebellious lifestyle, Joe sought another revelation. That night an angel named Moroni appeared to him and told young Joe that God had a great work for him and that he would receive a book written on plates of gold that contained the fullness of the everlasting gospel. Joe was to found a new church and restore the truth to the world — an answer to his prayer and the beginning of a legacy that continues almost 200 years later.[1]

History of the Church

Portrait of Joseph Smith Jr., circa 1842

You probably know the followers of young Joseph Smith Jr. as the Mormons. While officially called the Church of Jesus Christ of Latter-day Saints, or LDS, the common name comes from one of the books they consider to be "another testament of Jesus Christ," *The Book of Mormon*. The LDS Church claims to have over 15 million members spread across the globe and gathering in 29,000 local congregations (known as wards). They send missionaries to hundreds of countries and publish their literature in nearly 200 different languages. In 2014, there were a reported 84,000 Mormon missionaries actively spreading the faith on six continents. There are nearly 150 temples used for religious rituals, with more being built each year. Additionally, the church runs three universities named after Brigham Young, an early prophet, in Utah, Idaho, and Hawaii.[2]

The Mormon Church was originally established in April of 1830 in Palmyra, New York, after Joseph had received golden plates from the angel Moroni and translated it to produce *The Book of Mormon*. As the message of the "restored gospel" spread, Joseph gained followers in New York, and soon there were followers and missionaries spreading the religion. It was necessary to restore the gospel because the true gospel laws and ordinances

1. For the full account of the First Vision in Joseph's own words, see "Joseph Smith — History," chapter 1, at https://www.lds.org/scriptures/pgp/js-h/1. It is also worth noting that the account of what happened during the First Vision changed over time, and there are discrepancies in the various accounts. The official version was recorded in 1839, almost 20 years after the original event.
2. "Facts and Statistics," accessed March 3, 2015, http://www.mormonnewsroom.org/facts-and-statistics.

had been lost shortly after the Apostles died — a time known as the great Apostasy.[3] Commanded to gather in Kirtland, Ohio, the LDS temple was built in 1836 as missionaries continued westward, establishing a community in Independence, Missouri, and proselytizing in Europe. A prophecy by Smith identified a valley near Independence as the original location of the Garden of Eden and the future site of the New Jerusalem, so the cornerstone of a temple was placed there but not completed.

Brigham Young

Eventually forced out of these areas by persecution, including the killing of many Mormons, Brigham Young led the growing congregation to establish the city of Nauvoo, Illinois, while Joseph Smith was imprisoned. Eventually escaping to Nauvoo, Joseph Smith took over as mayor and military leader, directing the building of the town and a large temple completed in 1846. However, the temple was completed only after Joseph Smith had been killed in a battle with a mob while he was under arrest in Carthage, Illinois, for treason. It was during this period in Missouri and Illinois that the doctrines most identified with the early Mormons, including baptisms for the dead and polygynous[4] marriage, were proclaimed by Joseph Smith (though plural marriages had been occurring since the time in Kirtland, Ohio).

After Smith's death, there was a dispute over the succession of leadership. This led to the eventual formation of several sects with various church leaders claiming authority. The largest surviving offshoot today is the Reorganized Church of Jesus Christ of Latter Day Saints (now known as The Community of Christ) under the eventual leadership of Smith's eldest son, Joseph Smith III, who was 11 at the time of his father's death. At the time of this succession crisis, other smaller sects led by prominent leaders formed and moved to different areas of the country, but the main denomination

---

3. "Apostasy," LDS.org, accessed April 8, 2015, https://www.lds.org/topics/apostasy.
4. While the practice is commonly referred to as polygamy, the Mormon doctrine only allowed men to marry multiple wives, so polygyny is a more accurate term. Within Mormonism, the euphemistic term "plural marriage" is generally used to avoid the stigma of polygamy.

that survives today was led by Brigham Young. After the Mormons had migrated to the Utah Territory in waves beginning in 1846, the mainline church was established. Since that establishment, various groups have split from the main branch over issues such as the doctrine of plural marriage. The groups identify themselves as Fundamentalist LDS groups (FLDS), believing that they are remaining faithful to the teachings of Joseph Smith that were abandoned by the leadership in Salt Lake City.

The Salt Lake Temple

Once they arrived in the Great Salt Lake valley, the pioneers began constructing a temple and the city that became Salt Lake City, Utah. The temple remains today, and the headquarters for the church are located just across the street. It is from here that the office of the president passed from Brigham Young through 13 other men to the current president, Thomas S. Monson. The president is the head of the church and is a modern prophet, seer, and revelator along with the two members of the First Presidency and the Quorum of the Twelve Apostles. Along with these 15 leaders, there are Quorums of Seventy, each with a president, to fulfill different functions of leadership and counsel over various church organizations. At the local level, stake presidents govern the various bishoprics, which serve the local groups called wards. The structure and function of these authorities are laid out in *Doctrine and Covenants* (*D&C*) section 107. These positions do not receive any direct compensation and are considered service positions.

Worship Practices

The typical Mormon attends a worship service and Sunday school classes on a Sunday. These meetings take place in the ward chapels, where several local wards make up a stake (similar to a presbytery or diocese). Meetings of the ward and the stake are held regularly. On a Sunday, the service and meetings would look very much like a typical evangelical church. There is a sacrament meeting of the whole ward where hymns are sung, communion of bread and water is offered, prayers are spoken, and speakers present teaching. Other classes are offered for separate ages and teach on topics from the Mormon scriptures. There are also meetings of the stake and biannual general conference meetings in Salt Lake City, which are broadcast around the world.

Additionally, Mormons have temples all over the world. As of 2015, there were 144 temples on six continents with more under construction. While the ward chapels are used for Sabbath worship by anyone, entrance into the temples is generally restricted to members of the church in good standing. Certain portions of the temples are restricted to those holding certain levels of the Mormon priesthood and those they are ministering to, and an identification card, called a temple recommend, is necessary for entrance. This is only granted to those who are living a faithful life as a Mormon as determined by the ward bishop.

The temples are used to practice the various ordinances that Joseph Smith received in his revelations and visions. One of the primary rituals is the endowment ceremony where doctrines are taught and certain ceremonies are performed. This ceremony typically happens just before young people go on their mission or before they are married. Converts can also receive this endowment. Marriages of Mormons are performed in the temple, and there are also special ceremonies where families are sealed to one another so that they can be together in eternity forever. The other main activities that happen in the temples are ordinances for the dead. Proxy baptisms are performed for dead family members and others (hence the emphasis on genealogical study among Mormons) so that they may participate in eternal life even if they were not baptized on earth. Sealing ordinances are also performed by proxy on behalf of other people so that their marriages and families may also continue in life after death.

Authority

When we talk about any worldview or religious system, it is important to understand where the authority in that system is drawn from. Mormonism is a relatively young religious system founded less than 200 years ago in 1830. In the vision that Joseph Smith claimed to see God the Father and

Jesus, he was told that there were no true churches on the earth. In light of that, Joseph claimed that he was told that he would be shown the truth so that the gospel could be restored to the earth. Mormons believe that it is under the direction of God the Father, typically referred to as Heavenly Father, through visions and revelations given to Joseph Smith that the fullness of the gospel has been revealed to mankind. Mormons claim that the God of the Bible is their ultimate authority, but because they believe in modern revelation through prophets and individual revelation through messengers from heaven, it is hard to justify that claim on a practical level.

The Mormons look to four written revelations as their scriptures (see section below), but they hold to the teaching that God has different plans in effect during different dispensations. Unfortunately, this becomes an arbitrary device by which any contradictions between their scriptures or the pronouncements of their prophets can be written off as God employing different rules at different times. For example, *The Book of Mormon* (*BoM*) condemns the polygamous relationships of David and Solomon (Jacob 2:23–29) and tells the readers not to participate in such abominations. In the early printings of the *Doctrine & Covenants* from 1835 to 1876, there was a strict condemnation of polygamy: "Inasmuch as this Church of Christ has been reproached with the crime of fornication, and polygamy: we declare that we believe, that one man should have one wife; and one woman but one husband, except in the case of death, when either is at liberty to marry again."[5] Later, under pressure of the U.S. Federal Government, polygamy was disavowed by Mormon President Wilford Woodruff after he claimed to have had a new revelation about the damage that would come to the church if polygamy continued.[6] Since that declaration in 1890, the LDS Church has officially forbidden polygamy, though there have been hidden instances within the church. The changing nature of these revelations, and other doctrinal changes, makes true authority an elusive and ever-moving target for the followers. Peering in from the outside, it is hard to see anything other than a system that constantly changes to fit new situations in the culture as new "revelations" are received.

---

5. This prohibition against polygamy was included in the original section 101:4 in printings up to 1876. At this point, the new revelation about the allowance for polygamy was included in sections 132:51–66, so the contradictory passage was removed. Jerald and Sandra Tanner, *The Changing World of Mormonism* (Chicago, IL: Moody Press, 1980), p. 205–207.

6. The declaration can be read in full at "Official Declaration 1," LDS Website, accessed March 16, 2015, https://www.lds.org/scriptures/dc-testament/od/1.

For the modern Mormon, the ultimate authority is vested in the current president of the church, since he is the "prophet, seer, and revelator" of the current dispensation. Elder Merrill C. Oaks, a member of the Council of the Seventy, presents the case for obedience to the modern prophet:

> Just over two years before his death, the Prophet Joseph Smith published the Articles of Faith. The ninth article of faith states, "We believe all that God has revealed, all that He does now reveal, and we believe that He will yet reveal many great and important things pertaining to the Kingdom of God." I will speak concerning the final sentence, "He will yet reveal many great and important things pertaining to the Kingdom of God." This principle of continuing revelation is an essential part of the kingdom of God. In the fourth and fifth verses of the Doctrine and Covenants section 21, the Lord declared to the Church their obligation to heed the guidance of His prophet: "Wherefore, meaning the church, thou shalt give heed unto all his words and commandments which he shall give unto you as he receiveth them, walking in all holiness before me; For his word ye shall receive, as if from mine own mouth, in all patience and faith."[7]

This continuing revelation denies the Christian doctrines of the inerrancy, sufficiency, and authority of the Bible as the source of authority for all areas of life. The Bible is not the ultimate authority for the LDS faithful, but instead it is the changing ideas of man as they receive ongoing revelations.

Mormon Beliefs

While the LDS Church would claim to be a part of the wider Christian tradition, the beliefs that they hold place them outside of traditional and biblical orthodoxy. Of late, the LDS church has made a significant effort to be included in the broad community of Christianity. This has not always been the case. Early prophets and teachers in the church sought to distinguish Mormons from Christians, teaching that all of the other expressions of Christianity had been corrupted beyond salvage. Modern media campaigns have sought to reverse this previous attempt at distinction, calling Christians to embrace Mormons as brothers and sisters in Christ. However, from their

---

7. Merrill C. Oaks, "The Living Prophet: Our Source of Pure Doctrine," *Liahona*, January, 1999, https://www.lds.org/liahona/1999/01/the-living-prophet-our-source-of-pure-doctrine.

understanding of who God is to their understanding of what awaits individuals in the afterlife, the majority of Mormon doctrines do not pass the test of being consistent with what is revealed in the Bible. Let's examine some of these key doctrines to expose the differences and make clear the chasm that separates Mormonism from biblical Christianity.

The Godhead

At a fundamental level, the Mormon view of the Godhead denies the biblical trinitarian explanation. In contrast to the biblical view of trinitarian monotheism, with God the Father, God the Son, and God the Holy Spirit as three persons in one God, Mormonism teaches that there are many gods. In its truest sense, Mormonism is a polytheistic religion since they believe that there are many gods occupying different sections of the universe. More accurately, Mormonism is henotheistic — they acknowledge many Gods but worship only the gods connected with this planet. The first Article of Faith sates: "We believe in God, the Eternal Father, and in His Son, Jesus Christ, and in the Holy Ghost." Notice the distinction of three beings rather than the trinitarian expression from confessions such as the Athanasian Creed. The online resources of the LDS church describe their view of God:

> These three beings make up the Godhead. They preside over this world and all other creations of our Father in Heaven. The Mormon view of the members of the Godhead corresponds in a number of ways with the views of others in the Christian world, but with significant differences. Latter-day Saints pray to God the Father in the name of Jesus Christ. They acknowledge the Father as the ultimate object of their worship, the Son as Lord and Redeemer, and the Holy Spirit as the messenger and revealer of the Father and the Son. But where Latter-day Saints differ from other Christian religions is in their belief that God and Jesus Christ are glorified, physical beings and that each member of the Godhead is a separate being.[8]

While Mormons deny that God is a Trinity, the gods they worship are described as being united in their purpose: "Although the members of the Godhead are distinct beings with distinct roles, they are one in purpose and

---

8. "Godhead," LDS.org, accessed March 19, 2015, https://www.lds.org/topics/godhead.

doctrine. They are perfectly united in bringing to pass Heavenly Father's divine plan of salvation."[9] The Mormon godhead is three divine persons united in purpose, not in being.

Heavenly Father

The Heavenly Father of Mormonism, called Elohim, was once a man who was created by another god (who was created by another god) and earned his status as a god by being glorified through obedience to his spiritual father. Unlike the biblical doctrine of the eternal nature of the triune God, the chief god of Mormonism is a created being who progressed through degrees of sanctification to eventually become exalted as a god. This is known as the law of eternal progression and applies to all spiritual beings in the universe. Humans can achieve godhood by being obedient to the "laws and ordinances of the gospel" defined by Heavenly Father. Additionally, Heavenly Father is a man of flesh and blood who has been exalted. He is not a spirit, but a man with a physical body. He is said to currently reside on a planet near the star Kolob (Abraham 3:1–4). In this doctrine, the LDS deny the biblical doctrine of omnipresence.

Joseph F. Smith, the sixth LDS president, wrote the following about Heavenly Father:

> I do not believe in the doctrine held by some that God is only a Spirit and that he is of such a nature that he fills the immensity of space, and is everywhere present in person, or without person, for I can not [sic] conceive it possible that God could be a person . . . . God the Eternal Father, whom we designate by the exalted name-title "Elohim," is the literal Parent of our Lord and Savior Jesus Christ, and of the spirits of the human race. Elohim is the Father in every sense in which Jesus Christ is so designated, and distinctively He is the Father of spirits.[10]

Even though the Mormon prophets constantly refer to the Father as an eternal being, there is no normal sense in which he can be eternal if he was once a man who was exalted to godhood. The teaching of god as an exalted man was an explicit teaching of Joseph Smith and has been perpetuated by all of

---

9. Ibid.
10. "Teachings of the Presidents of the Church: Joseph F. Smith," chapter 40, "The Father and the Son," https://www.lds.org/manual/teachings-joseph-f-smith/chapter-40

the LDS prophets. In a sermon delivered to the LDS gathered at a conference in 1844, Smith gave what is commonly called the King Follett sermon where he plainly described the character and origin of his god:

> God himself was once as we are now, and is an exalted man, and sits enthroned in yonder heavens! That is the great secret. If the veil were rent today, and the great God who holds this world in its orbit, and who upholds all worlds and all things by His power, was to make himself visible — I say, if you were to see him today, you would see him like a man in form — like yourselves in all the person, image, and very form as a man; for Adam was created in the very fashion, image and likeness of God, and received instruction from, and walked, talked and conversed with Him, as one man talks and communes with another. . . . for I am going to tell you how God came to be God. We have imagined and supposed that God was God from all eternity. I will refute that idea, and take away the veil, so that you may see. These ideas are incomprehensible to some, but they are simple. It is the first principle of the gospel to know for a certainty the character of God, and to know that we may converse with Him as one man converses with another, and that He was once a man like us; yea, that God himself, the Father of us all, dwelt on an earth, the same as Jesus Christ Himself did; and I will show it from the Bible.[11]

Lorenzo Snow, the fifth president, coined a well-known couplet to portray the law of eternal progression: "As man now is, God once was: As God now is, man may be."[12] While the Bible teaches that Christians are increasingly conformed into the image of Jesus Christ in godly character and will be ultimately glorified (Romans 8:28–30), to become a god with the same nature as God is far from orthodox biblical teaching.[13]

The natural extension of believing that Heavenly Father is a man of flesh and bones is to understand that he has at least one wife with whom

---

11. Joseph Smith, Jr., "The King Follett Sermon," *Ensign*, April 1971, https://www.lds.org/ensign/1971/04/the-king-follett-sermon.
12. "Becoming Like God," LDS.org, https://www.lds.org/topics/becoming-like-god.
13. The teaching of *theosis* or *divinization* has had various expressions in Christianity, but the idea that humans will become gods is not taught in the Bible. Humans are creatures that will never fully exhibit the divine nature of God.

he created the spirit children who would receive bodies to become humans. While the Mormon teaching on the Heavenly Mother is limited, she does not receive worship. Some in the LDS church, including President Brigham Young, have taught that there are multiple mothers, in line with polygamous earthly and celestial marriages, but this idea is not official doctrine of the church.

Table 1: A Comparison of the Mormon and Biblical Views of God the Father

Mormon God the Father	Biblical God the Father
A created being produced as a spirit child of another god and his wife	An eternal being of the same substance as the Son and the Spirit
Exalted to godhood by obedience to his father	Eternally God
Father of all spiritual beings, including Jesus	The Creator of all other beings outside the Trinity
One of three persons who are gods over earth	One of the three persons of the trinitarian Godhead
Seeks counsel from other gods to make his plans	Exercise absolute sovereign rule over the universe
A product of Joseph Smith described in contradictory ways in various revelations	Reveals Himself consistently in the Bible

Jesus

The Mormon view of Jesus diverges from the biblical Jesus in many of the same ways as God the Father. Jesus, also referred to as Jehovah, is believed to be the firstborn spirit child of Heavenly Father and Mother in a period and state known as the preexistence. Thus, the Mormon can affirm that Jesus is the firstborn over all creation (Colossians 1:15), but they must deny that He is the Creator of all things (Colossians 1:16), since He Himself is a created being and did not create other spiritual beings. But Jesus is not alone as a creature; there have been billions of spirit beings sired by the Heavenly Father who were all together in the preexistence, Jesus being the eldest spirit brother of all. The second-born was Lucifer, making the two spiritual brothers and siblings of all the other spirits. Jesus offered a plan of testing the worthiness of the spirit children that was favored by Elohim over Lucifer's plan. This led to a war in which Lucifer and those spirits who followed him were banished and doomed to exist as demonic spirits until they will be cast into outer darkness (the Mormon notion of hell).

While the Bible teaches that Jesus was born of Mary as a virgin and conceived of the Holy Spirit (Luke 1:26–38), LDS prophets and apostles have taught a different origin. Brigham Young was the first prophet to declare that the Heavenly Father directly sired Jesus with Mary in the flesh and not in a supernatural way: "When the time came that His first-born, the Saviour, should come into the world and take a tabernacle, the Father came Himself and favoured that spirit with a tabernacle instead of letting any other man do it."[14] President Orson Pratt later acknowledged the truth, teaching, "Each God must have one or more wives. God, the Father of our spirits, became the Father of our Lord Jesus Christ according to the flesh. . . . it was the personage of the Father who begat the body of Jesus. . . . The fleshly body of Jesus required a Mother as well as a Father. Therefore, the Father and Mother of Jesus, according to the flesh, must have been associated together in the capacity of Husband and Wife; hence the Virgin Mary must have been, for the time being, the lawful wife of God the Father."[15] In a more modern context, LDS apostle Bruce R. McConkie asserts, "Christ was begotten by an Immortal Father in the same way that mortal men are begotten by mortal fathers."[16] In this, the Mormon can affirm that Jesus is the only begotten Son of the father in the flesh, but not in the biblical sense of being the Son of God.

While many modern Mormons would reject the teaching as authoritative, the prophets and leaders of the church proclaim that Heavenly Father had normal sexual intercourse with Mary to conceive the earthly body of Jesus. This changes the biblical doctrine of the virgin birth into the idea of a virgin conception — the latter is no miracle, as virgins conceive children regularly through intercourse. With these things in mind, the Mormon view

---

14. "To Know God Is Eternal Life," Brigham Young, *Journal of Discourses*, vol. 4:42; available online at http://journalofdiscourses.com/4/42.

15. "Celestial Marriage," Orson Pratt, *The Seer*, (1853), 158. Facsimile available at http://mit.irr.org/files/imagecache/node-gallery-display/seerp158.gif.

16. Bruce R. McConkie, *Mormon Doctrine* (Salt Lake City, UT: Deseret Book, 1966), p. 388. Available in PDF at https://ia601505.us.archive.org/17/items/MormonDoctrine/mormon_doctrine.pdf.

of Jesus might be classified as some form of Arianism since Jesus is a created being that shares some of the nature of God.

Table 2: A Comparison of the Mormon and Biblical View of Jesus

Mormon Jesus the Son	Biblical Jesus
A created being produced as a spirit child of Heavenly Father and Mother	An eternal being of the same substance as the Father and the Spirit
Exalted to godhood by obedience to his father	Eternally God
Spiritual brother of Lucifer and all other beings	The Creator of all other beings outside the Trinity
One of three persons who are gods over earth	One of the three persons of the trinitarian Godhead
Provided a sacrifice that was not sufficient to pay for sins and offer full righteousness	Provided a sufficient sacrifice for sin once and for all to secure perfect righteousness
A spirit who entered a body formed by the sexual union of Elohim and Mary; conceived with a virgin	God who took on flesh; born to a virgin
Organizer of the earth from existing matter	Creator of the universe from nothing

The Holy Ghost

Following the language of the KJV, Mormons typically refer to the Holy Ghost, but also the Holy Spirit, as a third member of the Godhead. The concept of the Spirit is much more orthodox, though they still deny Him as a person of the Trinity. Rather than possessing a physical body, He is only a spirit who works in perfect unity with the Heavenly Father and Jesus to bring about their plans. Mormons believe that the Holy Spirit can influence people to do good and protect from spiritual and physical harm. After baptism, members of the Melchizedek priesthood can lay hands on an individual to impart the gift of the Holy Spirit to them (one of the ordinances of the gospel). This confirmation allows continual companionship of the Spirit if the person is obedient to the ordinances and commandments of the church, and allows them to experience various spiritual gifts.

Mankind

In Mormon thinking, all of humanity are children of the Heavenly Father and Mother(s). Believing that Heavenly Father is a man of flesh and bones, the natural extension is to understand that he has at least one wife with whom he created the spirit children who would receive bodies to become humans. It is the role of families on earth to provide bodies for the spirit children to inhabit and go through the probationary testing here on earth to determine their worthiness to return to live with Heavenly Father.

Because Heavenly Father is an exalted man, Mormons understand that mankind was created in the image of God in a most literal sense — having human form. There is great controversy within the LDS teachings about the nature of the creation of Adam and Eve, since some of the early prophets taught that Adam was Elohim — known as the Adam-God Doctrine. Most modern Mormons reject these inspired teachings of the early prophets as they were instructed to do by later prophets, particularly President Spencer W. Kimball in a 1976 address at the fall General Conference. (Here we find a prime example of the conflicting doctrines taught by the modern LDS prophets who both claim to be directed by their god.)

While the Bible teaches that all of mankind is fallen and damned in Adam (Romans 5:12–19; 1 Corinthians 15:20–28), Mormons acknowledge the consequence of physical death for all of Adam's descendants but not spiritual death. They believe that there is spiritual enmity against God, but that man has an autonomous will (called "free agency") that can strive after holiness and "yield to the enticings of the Holy Spirit."[17] "The Articles of Faith" 1:2 states: "We believe that men will be punished for their own sins, and not for Adam's transgression." Mormons deny any condemnation from original sin, focusing on individual disobedience as the source of any loss of rewards in the afterlife. Therefore, the Fall of man is a positive idea in Mormon theology, since without it the spirits could not be tested and learn and progress toward godhood (2 Nephi 2, *Book of Mormon*).

Salvation

While Jesus Christ appears in the church's name, the "restored gospel" of Joseph Smith is not a biblical expression of the gospel. From "The Articles of Faith," Mormons affirm: "We believe that the first principles and ordinances

---

17. Mosiah 3:19, *The Book of Mormon*.

of the Gospel are: first, Faith in the Lord Jesus Christ; second, Repentance; third, Baptism by immersion for the remission of sins; fourth, Laying on of hands for the gift of the Holy Ghost." And the article that comes just before this states: "We believe that through the Atonement of Christ, all mankind may be saved, by obedience to the laws and ordinances of the Gospel."

As these principal articles of faith are compared to Scripture, a glaring error becomes apparent. At its core, the Mormon view of salvation is one that is based on the works of man, not solely on the perfect life and substitutionary death of Jesus Christ. In 2 Nephi 25:23, the ancient Mormon prophet taught: "For we labor diligently to write, to persuade our children, and also our brethren, to believe in Christ, and to be reconciled to God; for we know that it is by grace that we are saved, after all we can do." The prophet Moroni related grace and works when he said, "Yea, come unto Christ, and be perfected in him, and deny yourselves of all ungodliness; and if ye shall deny yourselves of all ungodliness, and love God with all your might, mind and strength, then is his grace sufficient for you, that by his grace ye may be perfect in Christ; and if by the grace of God ye are perfect in Christ, ye can in nowise deny the power of God" (Moroni 10:32). In both of these citations, grace is only effective in addition to works of personal righteousness and not sufficient for the believer.

While Mormons are fond of talking about the peace they find in the atonement of Jesus, their concept of atonement is an unbiblical one. The Bible repeatedly affirms that the sacrifice of Jesus on the Cross was an act of substitutionary atonement that covered sins completely and requires no work on our part to complete (Ephesians 2:8–10; Titus 3:3–7; Hebrews 9:11–15). In this sense, *atonement* has a different meaning to a Mormon than it does to a Bible-believing Christian. Additionally, Mormons teach that the atoning sacrifice occurred during the suffering in the garden of Gethsemane only to be completed on the Cross.

Degrees of Glory in Heaven and Hell

To claim that Mormonism promotes a form of works-righteous salvation is clear from their teachings, but most Mormons would reject this claim. This is partly because they believe that almost all people will be saved from condemnation that leads to punishment in hell, known as outer darkness, and enter into one of the three levels of heaven (*D&C* 76:31–37, 76:40–45). However, salvation is only possible if a person exercises faith, repents, receives baptism by immersion, and the laying on of hands by someone with the proper priesthood authority — only then are you born again. Their right standing before God is maintained by their obedience to the laws and ordinances of the gospel and making and keeping covenants in the temple. Only those who obey the Mormon teachings will achieve the ultimate salvation and exaltation to the highest level of heaven known as the Celestial kingdom where Heavenly Father will be (*D&C* 76:50–70, 76:92–96). The concept of three Kingdoms of Glory is drawn from 1 Corinthians 15:40–41, and ignores the biblical understanding of these three heavens referring to the atmosphere of the earth, space where the planets and stars reside, and the heavenly realm where God's presence exists. Based on this passage, the Celestial kingdom has the glory of the sun, the Terrestrial the glory of the moon, and the Telestial the glory of the stars. This is reflected in the architecture of some Mormon temples and the ornamentation on their exterior.

The spirits of those who have been obedient to the gospel rules and principles and have participated in rituals in the temple will proceed to Paradise in the Spirit World and be resurrected with a body of flesh and bone into the Celestial kingdom at the final judgment. Within the Celestial kingdom, there are three degrees of glory available based on obedience (*D&C* 131:1–4). It is generally taught that only those who have participated in temple marriage — sealed for time and all eternity — are eligible for the highest degree and can ultimately be exalted to godhood.

After death, the spirits of those who have not responded to the gospel or continued in the gospel rules and principles (being obedient Mormons) will enter into a place known as the Spirit Prison (*D&C* 138:32). There, the spirits in prison are "taught faith in God, repentance from sin, vicarious baptisms for the remission of sins, the gift of the Holy Ghost by the laying on of hands, and all other principles of the gospel that [are] necessary for them to know" (*D&C* 138:33–34). Those who respond with acceptance to this "second chance and have accept[ed] the principles of the gospel, repent of their sins, and accept ordinances performed in their behalf in temples, they will be welcomed into paradise."[18] At the judgment and resurrection, they will be conveyed into the Celestial kingdom at one of three levels.

---

18. "Death, Physical," LDS.org, accessed April 8, 2015, https://www.lds.org/topics/death-physical.

People who have died without these essential gospel ordinances [baptism, laying on of hands (confirmation), temple marriage, and family sealing] may receive those ordinances through the work done in temples. Acting in behalf of ancestors and others who have died, Church members are baptized and confirmed, receive the endowment, and participate in the sealings of husband to wife and children to parents.[19]

The practice of baptisms for the dead is claimed to be one of the restored elements of the gospel that was lost in the Great Apostasy after the Apostles had died. Biblical justification for this practice is drawn from 1 Corinthians 15:29. Apart from baptism, no one will enter the Celestial kingdom, so this work is very important to Mormons as they seek to offer their spirit brothers and sisters the chance of the highest level of heaven.[20]

From the Spirit Prison, salvation to the lower kingdoms of glory, the Telestial being the lower and the Terrestrial being the middle, is possible for almost all people, even those who have never heard the gospel or responded to it on earth. Those who refuse the offer to repent after death and instead reject the fundamentals of the gospel, or have not received proxy baptism by someone on earth, will enter into the lower kingdoms after the judgment and resurrection. The Terrestrial is reserved for those who were moral (i.e., being good people) during the mortal probation, including unfaithful Mormons, and they will "receive of the presence of the Son, but not of the fullness of the Father. Wherefore, they are bodies terrestrial, and not bodies celestial, and differ in glory as the moon differs from the sun" (D&C 76:71–80). The Telestial is for those who were wicked on earth and continue to reject the gospel (D&C 76:81–90, 76:98–106). There will be no glory of any god in the Telestial kingdom, but even its glory "surpasses all understanding."[21]

What the Bible would call "hell" is typically referred to as outer darkness or perdition. This realm is reserved for Lucifer and those who fought with him in the battle in the preexistence (Satan and the demons). Along with these will

19. "Temples," LDS.org, accessed April 8, 2015, https://www.lds.org/topics/temples.
20. "Baptisms for the Dead," LDS.org, accessed April 8, 2015, https://www.lds.org/topics/baptisms-for-the-dead.
21. Some have claimed the Joseph Smith taught that the Telestial kingdom was so glorious that if one could get a glimpse of it they would commit suicide to get there. However, this is at best a third-hand idea in a journal of a man who heard President Wildrow Woodruff say it at a funeral 33 years after Smith's death. It is likely an apocryphal addition and is not found anywhere in Smith's own writings.

be those Mormons who have turned from the faith and denied the Mormon teaching, receiving resurrected bodies to rule in hell (*D&C* 76:30–49).

Eternal Progression

Those Mormon men who have been faithful in their probationary lives on earth and achieve the Celestial kingdom have the opportunity to progress toward godhood. Eventually, they use a special name to call their wife (or wives) whom they have been sealed to in the temple ceremony of celestial marriage to be goddesses with them. Smith taught:

> Here, then, is eternal life — to know the only wise and true God; and you have got to learn how to be gods yourselves, and to be kings and priests to God, the same as all gods have done before you, namely, by going from one small degree to another, and from a small capacity to a great one; from grace to grace, from exaltation to exaltation, until you attain to the resurrection of the dead, and are able to dwell in everlasting burnings, and to sit in glory, as do those who sit enthroned in everlasting power.[22]

By this law of eternal progression, a man may become a god, earning the privileges and powers of Elohim and being granted the ability to organize his own planet, where his wives will produce spirit children to continue the cycle of the four stages of existence — premortal existence, mortal life, spirit life, and resurrected life. The teaching that God was once a man and that men can become gods runs afoul of many biblical passages, but let's consider one in particular.

> "You are My witnesses," says the LORD, "and My servant whom I have chosen, that you may know and believe Me, and understand that I am He. Before Me there was no God formed, nor shall there be after Me. I, even I, am the LORD, and besides Me there is no savior (Isaiah 43:10–11).[23]

In concert with other passages (Deuteronomy 4:35; Isaiah 44:6–8), the Mormons must admit that their teaching on the nature of God and the exaltation of man is contrary to the Bible.

---

22. Joseph Smith, Jr., "The King Follett Sermon," *Ensign*, April 1971, https://www.lds.org/ensign/1971/04/the-king-follett-sermon.

23. Quoted Scripture in this chapter is from the New King James Version of the Bible.

Modern Prophets

Joseph Smith understood himself to be the first modern prophet who was to bring the restoration of the fullness of the gospel. As he gradually received revelations through various messengers, he identified these functions as prophet, seer, and revelator. These terms are used in various ways throughout his writings, but he taught the importance of a modern prophet to lead the church and speak on behalf of God.

Eventually, Smith was directed to reestablish the office of Apostle in the same form as the 12 Apostles who walked with Jesus. These modern apostles are said to have the keys of the kingdom of God and serve as modern prophets. Further, councils of 70 are called to serve the church in ways similar to the Jewish council of elders (Exodus 24:9; Numbers 11:16). Today, the Mormon leader, specifically the president, is designated a prophet, seer, and revelator.

Throughout the decades of the LDS church, the prophets have received revelations that have contradicted the Bible, *The Book of Mormon*, or one another.[24] These contradictions are prime examples of the arbitrary nature of a religious system that is based on the ongoing revelation given modern men. They depart from the authority of the Bible and cannot help but contradict the truth of Scripture and one another. One of these is the Adam-God doctrine taught by Brigham Young and early prophets, but rejected by the church's later prophets as false doctrine. If the first prophet was speaking authoritatively for God as a modern prophet, seer, and revelator, how could he have been in error? Which prophet is a true prophet who has the keys to the restored gospel?

> Brigham Young (2nd LDS President) — When our father Adam came into the garden of Eden, he came into it with a celestial body, and brought Eve, one of his wives, with him. He helped to make and organize this world. He is Michael, the Archangel, the Ancient of Days! about whom holy men have written and spoken — He is our Father and our God, and the only God with whom we have to do. . . . Jesus, our elder brother, was begotten in the flesh by the same character that was in the garden of Eden, and who is our Father in Heaven. Now, let all

---

24. For an extensive treatment of these contradictions and changes, see Jerald and Sandra Tanner, *The Changing World of Mormonism* (Chicago, IL: Moody Press, 1980). These references can also be found on various online resources that deal with apologetics to Mormons.

Mormon Worldview

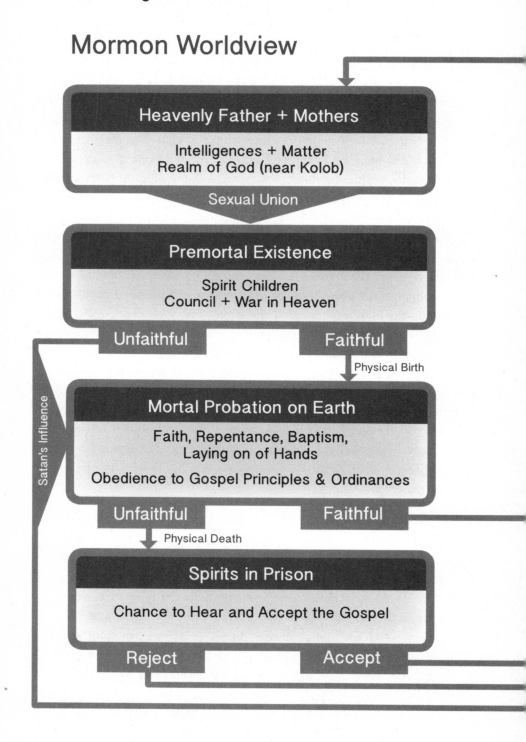

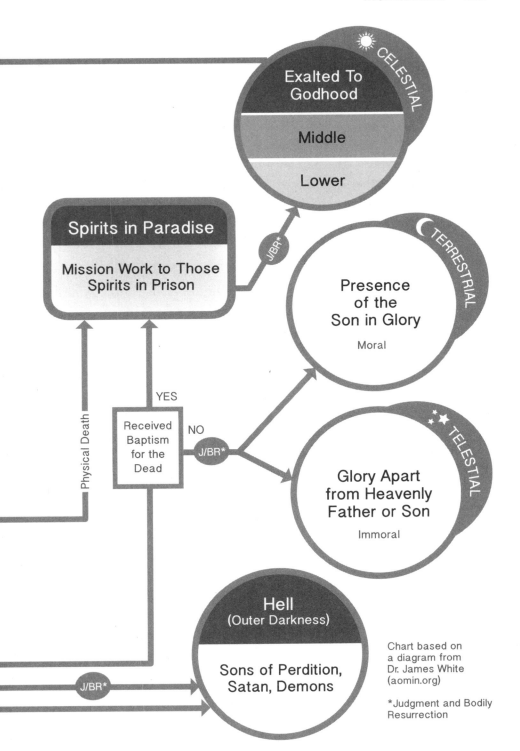

CELESTIAL

Exalted To
Godhood

Middle

Lower

Spirits in Paradise

Mission Work to Those
Spirits in Prison

J/BR*

TERRESTRIAL

Presence
of the
Son in Glory

Moral

YES

Physical Death

Received
Baptism
for the
Dead

NO

J/BR*

TELESTIAL

Glory Apart
from Heavenly
Father or Son

Immoral

Hell
(Outer Darkness)

Sons of Perdition,
Satan, Demons

J/BR*

Chart based on
a diagram from
Dr. James White
(aomin.org)

*Judgment and Bodily
Resurrection

who may hear these doctrines, pause before they make light of them, or treat them with indifference, for they will prove their salvation or damnation. (Journal of Discourses, 1852)[25]

Spencer W. Kimball (12th LDS President) — We hope that you who teach in the various organizations, whether on the campuses or in our chapels, will always teach the orthodox truth. We warn you against the dissemination of doctrines which are not according to the scriptures and which are alleged to have been taught by some of the General Authorities of past generations. Such, for instance, is the Adam-God theory. We denounce that theory and hope that everyone will be cautioned against this and other kinds of false doctrine. (General Conference, October 1976)[26]

Additionally, there are failed prophecies of future events pronounced by Joseph Smith and other Mormon prophets. In one case, Smith announced that the building of a temple in Missouri would be completed within a generation of the revelation received in 1832:

Yea, the word of the Lord concerning his church, established in the last days for the restoration of his people, as he has spoken by the mouth of his prophets, and for the gathering of his saints to stand upon Mount Zion, which shall be the city of New Jerusalem. Which city shall be built, beginning at the temple lot, which is appointed by the finger of the Lord, in the western boundaries of the State of Missouri, and dedicated by the hand of Joseph Smith, Jun., and others with whom the Lord was well pleased. Verily this is the word of the Lord, that the city New Jerusalem shall be built by the gathering of the saints, beginning at this place, even the place of the temple, which temple shall be reared in this generation. For verily this generation shall not all pass away until an house shall be built unto the Lord, and a cloud shall rest upon it, which cloud shall be even the glory of the Lord, which shall fill the house. . . . For the sons of Moses

---

25. Brigham Young, "Self-Government — Mysteries — Recreation and Amusements, Not in Themselves Sinful — Tithing — Adam, Our Father and Our God," *Journal of Discourses*, vol. 1:8, http://journalofdiscourses.com/1/8.

26. Spencer W. Kimball, "Our Own Liahona," General Conference talk delivered October 1976, LDS.org, https://www.lds.org/general-conference/1976/10/our-own-liahona.

and also the sons of Aaron shall offer an acceptable offering and sacrifice in the house of the Lord, which house shall be built unto the Lord in this generation, upon the consecrated spot as I have appointed (*D&C* 84:2–5, 84:31).

While no temple has been built by the LDS church in Independence, Missouri (the designated spot), there has been a temple built by The Community of Christ (formerly the RLDS) and there is a visitor center run by the LDS church. While some Mormons would reinterpret "generation" to mean an indefinite period of time, a plain reading of Smith's prophecy shows that it failed to come to pass in the time he designated.

Applying the principle from Deuteronomy 18:20–22, Joseph Smith was a false prophet, and his teachings should not be followed nor his threats taken to heart. If the founder of the religious system was a false prophet, the foundation for the entire system crumbles and the church is exposed as fraudulent.

To make this point in a stronger way, Joseph Smith claimed that the gospel had been lost and that there was need for a restored gospel — a different gospel than the one preached by Paul and others as recorded in the Bible. Further, the messages were delivered to Smith by angels who appeared as beings surrounded by bright light. As we look at the Bible, we see that Paul warned the Galatian churches to reject any other gospel that came to them, whether from himself or an angel, describing those who would teach a different gospel as damned (accursed) by God (Galatians 1:6–9). The nature of the "restored gospel" given to Smith becomes apparent when we read in 2 Corinthians 11:13–15:

> For such are false apostles, deceitful workers, transforming themselves into apostles of Christ. And no wonder! For Satan himself transforms himself into an angel of light. Therefore it is no great thing if his ministers also transform themselves into ministers of righteousness, whose end will be according to their works.

Taken together, these verses help us understand the demonic origins of Mormonism and how Satan influences people to believe in counterfeit gospels that look like the genuine article on the surface, but are based on works rather than grace.

Modern Priesthood

Smith and his companions claim to have received visitations from various apostles and prophets who restored the laws and ordinances of the priesthood to the earth. In 1829, Smith and Oliver Cowdery claim that John the Baptist appeared to them and laid hands upon them to confer the Aaronic priesthood on them. This had been lost during the Great Apostasy that followed the death of the Apostles, but is now available to worthy Mormon men beginning at age 12. At some later point, Smith claims that Peter, James, and John appeared to him to confer on him and Cowdery the Melchizedek priesthood. Those who receive the Aaronic priesthood prepare to receive the greater Melchizedek priesthood by faithful service in the local wards. Then they can be considered for service as priests in the temples, service in higher offices, and they become eligible for exaltation. The particulars of these offices are described in *D&C* 107 and other writings.

Contrary to this Mormon teaching, only Jesus has the Melchizedek priesthood according to Hebrews 7, and He alone holds that priesthood forever, so this is a direct contradiction of biblical teaching. Further, the Aaronic (Levitical) priesthood was reserved by God only for those of the line of Levi, not Gentiles in New York in the 19th century.

Baptism and Laying on of Hands

Mormons are typically baptized at age 8 when they are believed to be able to make such a decision to follow the church's teachings willingly and of their own "free agency." Baptism must be performed by someone holding the proper priesthood authority and by absolute immersion. This act of baptism is one of the four key parts of the Mormon gospel (as described above). Additionally, they pursue baptisms on behalf of the dead. Apart from baptism, no one is eligible to enter into one of the levels of heaven. Therefore, Mormons see it as a duty to participate in these proxy baptisms (drawing on genealogical work) so that those who did not have that opportunity on earth might receive its benefits to be transferred from the Spirit Prison to Paradise by accepting this work done on their behalf.

After baptism, individually or by proxy, Mormons practice the laying on of hands for the receiving of the Holy Spirt as an essential part of the gospel ordinances.

Scriptures

For Mormons, the scriptures include the four "stand-ard works" of the Bible, *The Book of Mormon* (*BoM*), *Doctrine & Covenants* (*D&C*), and *The Pearl of Great Price* (*PGP*). In *The Pearl of Great Price* we find a 13-point creed known as "The Articles of Faith." Regarding revelation, Articles 7–9 state:

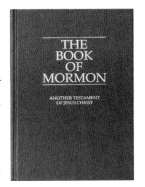

> 7) We believe in the gift of tongues, proph-ecy, revelation, visions, healing, interpretation of tongues, and so forth.

> 8) We believe the Bible to be the word of God as far as it is translated correctly; we also believe the Book of Mormon to be the word of God.

> 9) We believe all that God has revealed, all that He does now reveal, and we believe that He will yet reveal many great and important things pertaining to the Kingdom of God.

Bible

The Bible has a tenuous relationship to Mormon doctrine. While most Mor-mons in the West would use the KJV translation, as you will find posted on the LDS.org website and officially published by the church, the standard teaching is that the Bible has been corrupted to some degree over the ages. This is reflected in the phrase "as far as it is properly translated" in Article 8. With these errors in mind, Joseph Smith sought to "translate" the Bible correctly. His work was not a translation from the manuscripts, but simply a rewriting of the sections of text he believed were in error. In Mormon teaching, *translation* has a much broader meaning and includes receiving direct revelation audibly or in visions.[27] Smith's translation, referred to as the JST, was never completed, but includes what he believed to be corrections to texts and the removal of contradictions. However, these corrections added content to the Bible that sought to make sense of Mormon doctrines.

---

27. This broader view of *translation* and *translator* is discussed with respect to the Book of Abraham in the *PGP* in this article: "Translation and Historicity of the Book of Abraham," LDS.org, accessed March, 30, 2015, https://www.lds.org/topics/translation-and-historic-ity-of-the-book-of-abraham.

For example, Smith added to John 4:26 to remove the contradiction of Elohim having a body of flesh and bones when the Bible says "God is spirit": *For unto such hath God promised his* Spirit. And they *who* worship him, must worship in spirit and in truth (JST changes italicized). This alternate reading has no foundation in any Greek manuscript and is an entire fabrication of Smith to accommodate his peculiar teachings. The Mormon sect known today as The Community of Christ (formerly the RLDS) has published the most complete form of the JST, while most Mormons have only a portion of the JST in their scriptures and some of the changes in footnotes. Smith never finished the rewriting of the Bible, and it is a great curiosity as to why future prophets did not take up the work as the modern prophet, seer, and revelator of the church that claims to be the only true church on earth.

The Book of Mormon

For Mormons, *The Book of Mormon* is "the most correct of any book on earth, and the keystone of our religion, and a man would get nearer to God by abiding by its precepts, than by any other book."[28] The *BoM* is said to have been translated from a set of golden plates that Joseph Smith received after their location was revealed to him by the angel Moroni. After several years, Smith was allowed to take the plates. He also received a breastplate and spectacles, which are sometimes referred to as the Urim and Thummim. These spectacles allowed him to translate "by the gift and power of God." As Smith received the text, it was recorded by Oliver Cowdery who acted as principal scribe and one of 11 witnesses who testified to seeing the plates. Cowdery describes that Smith "translated his book, two transparent stones, resembling glass, set in silver bows. That by looking through these, he was able to read in English, the reformed Egyptian characters, which were engraven [*sic*] on the plates."[29] Other sections were recorded by Smith's wife Emma as he peered into a hat containing a seer stone. Interestingly, Smith did not look at the plates while he was "translating." David Whitmer describes the process:

> Joseph Smith would put the seer stone into a hat, and put his face in the hat, drawing it closely around his face to exclude

---

28. "What the Church Teaches about the Book of Mormon," LDS.org, accessed March 31, 2015, https://www.lds.org/topics/book-of-mormon/what-the-church-teaches-about-the-book-of-mormon.
29. "Book of Mormon Translation," LDS.org, accessed March 31, 2015, https://www.lds.org/topics/book-of-mormon-translation.

the light; and in the darkness the spiritual light would shine. A piece of something resembling parchment would appear, and on that appeared the writing. One character at a time would appear, and under it was the interpretation in English. Brother Joseph would read off the English to Oliver Cowdery, who was his principal scribe, and when it was written down and repeated to Brother Joseph to see if it was correct, then it would disappear, and another character with the interpretation would appear. Thus the Book of Mormon was translated by the gift and power of God, and not by any power of man.[30]

The confusion over the seer stone, the spectacles, the Urim and Thummim, and the breastplate in the various accounts of the translation process is further evidence of the spurious nature of the book that claims to be "Another Testament of Jesus Christ."

The *BoM* is supposed to be a collection of writings from two ancient groups recorded in Reformed Egyptian. The first group is said to have traveled to Central America in barges at the time of the dispersion at Babel and are called the Jaredites. A second group of writings in the *BoM* are supposed to be from a group of Jews who left Israel in 600 B.C. under the leadership of Lehi at the time of King Zedekiah. This line also comprised Native Americans of North America and ended with the prophet Moroni burying these plates of gold in upstate New York on the Hill Cumorah in A.D. 421. Significantly, 3 Nephi 11–28 describes Jesus appearing to the group of people known as the Nephites and teaching and performing miracles for them during the days He was believed to be buried in the tomb in Jerusalem before His Resurrection.

The archaeological and anthropological details of the *BoM* have had no external confirmation and have been contradicted on many levels, the most important of which are the contradictions with the Bible and tests that have confirmed that there is no genetic connection between the Jewish people and the Native Americans. All of the cities, temples, armies, and weapons described across Central and North America in the *BoM* are absent. On the other hand, there have been a multitude of archaeological and other historical confirmations of the things recorded in the Bible.

A portion of the plates were said to have been sealed and untranslated, with the anticipation of their translation at some future point. Conveniently,

30. David Whitmer, *An Address to All Believers in Christ* (Richmond, MO: n.p., 1887), p. 12.

the golden plates were returned to Moroni and are currently under his charge, not available for examination and verification as are the early manuscripts of the Bible. Some of the witnesses say that they are reserved in a cave in the Hill Cumorah awaiting a future time when they will be revealed. If the LDS church wanted to corroborate the 11 witnesses who claim to have seen the plates, all they need to do is conduct exploration and excavations on this small hill to produce the plates and verify their translation.

Doctrine and Covenants

In the introduction to this work we read, "The Doctrine and Covenants is a collection of divine revelations and inspired declarations given for the establishment and regulation of the kingdom of God on the earth in the last days."[31] D&C primarily includes revelations, noted in sections not chapters, given to Joseph Smith about specific points of doctrine as well as explanations of passages (section 74 explains 1 Corinthians 7:14). There are also a few revelations to other modern prophets near the end. Most of Mormon doctrine is found in this book as Smith formulated the various teachings over time. Earlier sections are contrary to later sections as Smith received new guidance for the dispensation of the church. For example, polygamy was condemned in early revelation (the original Section 101) and then commanded in later revelation (Section 132). Each of the sections includes headings that describe the time and setting of the revelations and brief explanatory notes.

The Pearl of Great Price

The Pearl of Great Price is the most interesting and eclectic book in the standard works. It was a collection of writings that was added to the LDS canon in 1880. The Book of Moses includes what Smith claimed to be a translation of writings of Moses, though what is written is not found in any form of the Hebrew Bible. The Book of Abraham is claimed to be a translation of a set of Egyptian papyri purchased by Smith in 1835. Smith "translated" these papyri and "discovered" they contained writings of Abraham. In these translations, Smith fabricated details of Abraham's life and revelations he received to validate doctrines such as the existence of Kolob (Abraham 3:3) and the spirits (intelligences) in the pre-existence (Abraham 3:22).

The papyri were lost for a time after being sold by Smith's family in 1856, but were discovered in a museum in New York in 1967 so the originals could

---

31. Introduction, *Doctrine and Covenants*, available online at https://www.lds.org/scriptures/dc-testament/introduction.

be examined to verify Smith's translation. Included in the papyri were diagrams that are printed as facsimiles in the *PGP*. As early as 1856, these printed facsimiles were recognized by a French Egyptologist as funerary scripts — a book of the dead for an Egyptian. Facsimile 1 supposedly shows the sacrifice of Isaac, but has actually been interpreted by Egyptologists as the burial rites of a man named Hor with the canopic jars where his organs would be placed.[32] Regardless of the clear fabrication of the translation, the Mormons accept these writings as coming from the prophet.[33] Ironically, the same textual criticism that has proven the Bible to be true is used to disprove the Book of Abraham and demonstrate it is a fabrication, not a translation. All the while, Mormons claim that the Bible has been corrupted and mistranslated, even when we have thousands of manuscripts that can affirm its modern accuracy.

The next two portions of the *PGP* contain a translation of a part of the Gospel of Matthew from Smith and an excerpt of the Joseph Smith History, which is the testimony and official history of Smith's life. The final section is the creed of Mormonism known as "The Articles of Faith." These 13 articles are typically memorized as a form of catechesis by young members and affirmed as true by all faithful Mormons.

Other Authoritative Writings and Teachings

Other works commended by the Mormons for study include: *Joseph Smith History*; *History of the Church*; *Journal of Discourses*; *Teachings of the Presidents of the Church*; *Mormon Doctrine* by Bruce R. McConkie; *Encyclopedia of Mormonism*; *Jesus the Christ* Teaching Manual; various teaching manuals and handbooks; messages from the apostles and prophets delivered biannually at General Conferences.

Official LDS magazines include *Ensign*, *New Era*, *Liahona*, and *Friend*.

At the LDS.org website you can find electronic versions of all of the Standard Works of Scripture as well as many other resources that describe Mormon teaching. You can also find many of the works referenced in this chapter in digital form for your own reference. I have attempted to use as many of the resources from the official LDS website as possible so that there

---

32. For a detailed analysis of the problems with the Book of Abraham translation, see: "The Book of Abraham," MormonThink.com, accessed April 6, 2015, http://mormonthink.com/book-of-abraham-issues.htm.

33. For the LDS response to these discoveries, see: "Translation and Historicity of the Book of Abraham," LDS.org, accessed April 6, 2015, https://www.lds.org/topics/translation-and-historicity-of-the-book-of-abraham.

may be no doubt about the source of the materials referenced to describe Mormon beliefs, as the reader can access them directly.

Various Doctrines of Mormonism

Creation and Evolution

As mentioned briefly above, the Mormon view of creation is not a creation out of nothing as the Bible teaches. Orthodox Christianity has understood the opening chapters of the Bible to describe the triune God creating the entirety of the universe out of nothing in a span of six days, resting on the seventh. In Mormonism, Elohim, with the cooperation of Jehovah and others, organizes the matter that we know as our solar system. This is described in detail, in a fashion similar to Genesis 1, in the Book of Abraham in chapters 3 and 4 (as well as in Moses 1–3). Working with a counsel of spirits in the premortal existence identified as Gods, Elohim sent Jehovah:

> And there stood one among them that was like unto God, and he [Jehovah/Jesus] said unto those who were with him: We will go down, for there is space there, and we will take of these materials, and we will make an earth whereon these may dwell; And we will prove them herewith, to see if they will do all things whatsoever the Lord their God shall command them. . . . And then the Lord said: Let us go down. And they went down at the beginning, and they, that is the Gods, organized and formed the heavens and the earth. And the earth, after it was formed, was empty and desolate, because they had not formed anything but the earth; and darkness reigned upon the face of the deep, and the Spirit of the Gods was brooding upon the face of the waters. And they (the Gods) said: Let there be light; and there was light (Abraham 3:24–25, 4:1–3).

As described, these gods took preexisting matter and organized it in a portion of the universe that was empty, forming earth. The verses that follow describe the rest of the creation over six days and rest on the seventh "time." Chapter 5 describes the creation of Adam and Eve and their placement in the garden in Eden.[34]

---

34. For a detailed explanation of Mormon views on the timing of creation, see: *Encyclopedia of Mormonism Online*, s.v. "Creation, Creation Accounts," accessed April 9, 2015, http://eom.byu.edu/index.php/Creation,_Creation_Accounts.

As mentioned above, there have been differing doctrinal positions on who Adam and Eve were. Brigham Young taught that Adam was Elohim and Eve was one of his wives, but the descriptions in the books of Moses and Abraham and declarations from other presidents contradict Young's teaching.

Most Mormons would reject the idea that biological evolution was involved in any sense in the formation of life on earth, but those views vary as they do in various religions. There is no official position from the leadership of the church on other forms of evolution, but the First Presidency has repeatedly affirmed the special creation of Adam and Eve. Under the heading "Evolution," the Mormon Encyclopedia, endorsed by the church, reads:

> The position of the Church on the origin of man was published by the First Presidency in 1909 and stated again by a different First Presidency in 1925:
>
> The Church of Jesus Christ of Latter-day Saints, basing its belief on divine revelation, ancient and modern, declares man to be the direct and lineal offspring of Deity. . . . Man is the child of God, formed in the divine image and endowed with divine attributes (see appendix, "Doctrinal Expositions of the First Presidency").
>
> The scriptures tell why man was created, but they do not tell how, though the Lord has promised that he will tell that when he comes again (D&C 101:32-33). In 1931, when there was intense discussion on the issue of organic evolution, the First Presidency of the Church, then consisting of Presidents Heber J. Grant, Anthony W. Ivins, and Charles W. Nibley, addressed all of the General Authorities of the Church on the matter, and concluded,
>
> Upon the fundamental doctrines of the Church we are all agreed. Our mission is to bear the message of the restored gospel to the world. Leave geology, biology, archaeology, and anthropology, no one of which has to do with the salvation of the soul of mankind, to scientific research, while we magnify our calling in the realm of the Church. . . .
>
> Upon one thing we should all be able to agree, namely, that Presidents Joseph F. Smith, John R. Winder, and Anthon H.

Lund were right when they said: "Adam is the primal parent of our race" [First Presidency Minutes, April 7, 1931].[35]

Missionary Work

You have probably seen the stereotypical Mormon missionary team riding their bikes or walking through a neighborhood. Their goal is to share their message of the Mormon gospel and make converts to Mormonism. These young people work in pairs, typically a first-year and a second-year missionary, and pay for their own expenses. While missionary work is not required in the church, it is considered an act of faithfulness and merits favor with God and the Mormon community as they seek exaltation. For males ages 18–25, they must be worthy to receive the Melchizedek Priesthood, receiving the title of elder, and be living lives of purity, chastity, and faithfulness to the teachings of Mormonism. Young women can begin mission service at 19 and are called Sisters while on their mission. These missionaries will ask to present a series of lessons about the teachings of the church as well as perform acts of service to those they contact.

Other mission work includes work within LDS organizations, at various visitor's centers and temples, and at food production facilities. People of all ages are involved in these missions, and the length of service varies.

Missionary work continues in the Spirit World when those faithful spirits in Paradise go to preach to those who are in the Spirit Prison. There, the spirits in prison who did not hear or did not respond to the gospel are offered the opportunity to accept the gospel and the proxy temple work done on their behalf.

Blacks and the Priesthood

Beginning with direction from Brigham Young in 1852 until 1978, men of black African descent (not just dark skin) were not allowed to hold the priesthood, though they could be baptized and considered members. Following Young's death, successive prophets also denied temple endowments and marriages to African blacks. There is no official church teaching as to why this was the case, but the most typical explanations involved the curse of Cain and the premortal existence. It was commonly taught in Christian circles that the curse of Cain in Genesis 4:10–15 involved black skin.

---

35. *Encyclopedia of Mormonism Online*, s.v. "Evolution," accessed April 9, 2015, http://eom.byu.edu/index.php/Evolution.

Additionally, the curse on Ham in Genesis 9:24–25 is suggested by some to include black skin (though the curse was actually on his son Canaan). From Mormon teaching, it was suggested that those who were less valiant during the premortal existence, and especially the war against Lucifer and his followers, were cursed with dark skin. This prohibition was removed in 1978 when President Spencer W. Kimball claimed to have received a new revelation. This is now included as Official Declaration 2 in *D&C*.[36] Most fundamentalist Mormon groups maintain the exclusion of black Africans from the priesthood and marriage to whites.

Native Americans

According to the various accounts in the *BoM*, there were two groups of people that traveled across the ocean to what we know as the Americas. The first group was called the Jaredites, and this group left from the Tower of Babel to a promised land in a group of barges. The book of Ether in the *BoM* gives their account, ending in their destruction after a civil war. Interestingly, no archaeological evidence has confirmed this group in Central America. The second group came at the time of King Zedekiah, leaving Jerusalem with a copy of the Torah and other writings under the direction of the prophet Lehi (1 Nephi 1–9). This initial group who traveled to North America is considered to include the ancestors of the current Native Americans. A group known as the Lamanites was cursed with dark skin (2 Nephi 5:20–25) for their disobedience, while the Nephites remained white. Those Lamanites who turned to follow God would have their curse removed, and their skin would become white and fair (3 Nephi 2:12–16).

About 200 years after Jesus is claimed to have visited them in North America, the Lamanites exterminated the Nephites and are considered the ancestors of Native Americans. Mormon prophets continued to teach that the conversion of the Native Americans would result in their skin changing color, leading to an adoption program of Native children into Mormon homes and claims of these becoming "white and delightsome" in supposed partial fulfillment of the prophecy of *D&C* 49:24.[37] Despite these claims, DNA analysis has shown that no Native American groups are descendants of

---

36. "Race and the Priesthood," LDS.org, accessed April 13, 2015, https://www.lds.org/topics/race-and-the-priesthood.

37. Bill McKeever and Eric Johnson, "White and Delightsome or Pure and Delightsome? A Look at 2 Nephi 30:6," Mormon Research Ministry, accessed April 13, 2015, http://www.mrm.org/white-and-delightsome.

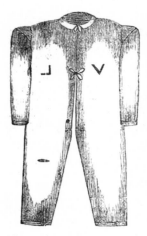

The Church of Jesus Christ of Latter-day Saints temple garments. Post-1979 two-piece temple garments end just above the knee for both sexes. Women's garments have cap sleeves with either a rounded or sweetheart neckline. Male tops are available in tee-shirt styles.

The early Mormon temple garments bore the square and compass symbol, demonstrating the link between Mormonism and Freemasonry.

Jewish ancestors, but rather of Asian descent as we would expect from migrations through Asia and across the Aleutian land bridge during the Ice Age.

Temple Garments

When a Mormon is deemed faithful and eligible to receive the temple endowments, they begin the practice of wearing special undergarments both day and night. The style has changed over time from one-piece to two-piece, and these are worn as symbols of purity and to promote modesty day and night. Symbols on the garments include a carpenter's square and compass (among other marks) that likely come from Smith's connection with Freemasonry. The garments are seen as a reminder to keep the covenants made in the temple, of God's protection, and to promote modesty. To mock these garments is very offensive to Mormons and is not a wise way to help LDS members to consider the true gospel.

Temple Work

Faithful Mormons are encouraged to participate in the various works and covenant ceremonies that take place in the temples. Beginning at age 12, young people begin participating in baptisms for the dead. Families can be involved in sealing ceremonies so that they will be "forever families" in the eternal realm. Likewise, Mormon marriages do not include the language "till death do us part," but rather "for time and all eternity," since they are sealed together in the temple to remain married in the afterlife. A man may be sealed to multiple wives in the case of the death of a wife or other circumstances. These and other ceremonies are considered sacred by the Mormons and are not shared publicly. When a temple is first constructed, non-Mormons can take a tour, but after the dedication non-members are only allowed in certain waiting areas. The exact nature of the covenants, vows, clothing, and ceremonies has changed over time, so many younger Mormons are not familiar with some of the older rituals. With that in mind, take care when discussing these issues with Mormons so that you do not accuse them of participating in something they have not done or do not believe.

Masonic Influence

Both Joseph Smith and Brigham Young were involved in the society of Freemasonry. The influence of the rituals and symbolism of Freemasonry in Mormon temple construction and rituals is evident. Some have made claims that the connection was much stronger than it is, but the connections cannot be denied. Joseph's father was a Master Freemason enrolled in a lodge in New York, and his older brother was also a Mason. While the relationship between the two groups has changed, the handshakes, oaths, and ritual dress of the LDS temple ceremonies are similar to those of the Masons and their progression from one level to the next in the society. Most notably, the square and compass markings on the temple garments are borrowed from the symbol of Freemasonry.

Occult Influence

Before finding the golden plates, the Smith family was involved in treasure seeking through occult practices known as "money digging." Part of this practice involved a seer stone which Smith would place in a hat to "see" the location of buried treasure. Smith was convicted of being a "glass looker" in a New York court on March 20, 1826. This occult practice continued even after Smith claimed to have received visits from the angel Moroni. Seeing the spirits that guarded the buried treasures was part of evading the evil spirits and claiming the treasure. Having opened himself to these occult influences, the deception of Satan in providing a different gospel was easy to accomplish. Remember that Smith did not claim to translate the golden plates directly, but he placed his seer stone into a hat where he saw the words appear. The same technique he used to "locate" buried treasure was used to "translate" *The Book of Mormon.*

Polygamy

As mentioned above, the teaching on polygamy changed over time and was practiced both openly and secretly at different times. Joseph Smith had approximately 40 wives, which were either married to him or sealed to him in temple ceremonies to be his wives in eternity if not on earth. At least 14 of these wives were married to other men at the time of their sealing or marriage to Smith.[38]

Tithing and Fasting

Mormons are directed to give 10 percent of their income, since the modern prophets have restored the ordinance of tithing for support of the work of the church (*D&C* 119). Failure to pay this tithe is seen as unfaithfulness to the ordinances of the church and a lack of trust in God to provide. Additionally, during fasting, Mormons are instructed to go without food or water for two consecutive meals during a 24-hour period, contributing the money that would have been spent to a special offering for those in need and devoting extra time to prayer and study. This is typically done during the first Sunday of each month and is accompanied by a testimony service in the local ward chapel.

Word of Wisdom

Mormons adhere to a dietary standard called the Word of Wisdom as a sign of honoring the bodies their god has given them. In general, the revelation instructs them to avoid alcohol, caffeine, various narcotic and hallucinogenic drugs, tobacco, and tea and coffee, and to eat meat sparingly and grains in abundance (*D&C* 89). Through obedience to these food laws, they are promised blessings of body, mind, and spirit. Biblically, these prohibitions run counter to Paul's instructions to the Galatian and Corinthian churches and brings to mind the warning to guard against those false teachers who

---

38. For the official LDS explanation of Smith's many wives, see: "Plural Marriage in Kirtland and Nauvoo," LDS.org, accessed April 15, 2015, https://www.lds.org/topics/plural-marriage-in-kirtland-and-nauvoo.

command people to abstain from certain foods which God gave to be received with thanksgiving (1 Timothy 4:3; Colossians 2:20–23).

Genealogical Work

In order to complete the work of proxy baptism and other temple ordinances, Mormons are devoted to studying genealogies. In order to do ordinances like sealing families "for time and all eternity," the names and relationships of families must be known.

Families

Large families are generally encouraged, as this allows physical bodies for those spirit children who are still waiting to enter their probation. Family unity is encouraged through various activities including family home evenings (often on Mondays) where there is teaching and time together as a family. Family prayer is also practiced. While the happy faces on many Mormons may make it seem that all is well, the high expectations of obedience and adherence to the church's teachings can create an environment of unrealistic expectations and standards. As with any legalistic religion, this can lead to depression, seeking to please others, and rebellion within the family. The claim of oppressive social and family structures within Mormonism are often dismissed as anecdotal, but various social surveys support these claims and they are consistent with my personal experience growing up as a Mormon and living in northern Utah and southern Idaho.[39]

Angels

Mormons believe in the continued communication with those who have died and entered into the Spirit World. To Mormons, angels are not spiritual beings created by God as distinct from humans, but spirit children along with all offspring of Heavenly Father. *D&C* 129:1–3 informs us that "There are two kinds of beings in heaven, namely: Angels, who are resurrected personages, having bodies of flesh and bones . . . [and] the spirits of just men made perfect, they who are not resurrected, but inherit the same glory." *D&C* 130:5 says that "there are no angels who minister to this earth but those who do belong or have belonged to it." These messengers were once

---

39. To be clear, an oppressive family life is not unique to Mormon families, but the doctrines of personal growth and the demands of obedience to such a high level of performance to achieve exaltation provide a justification for this high set of expectations. This type of dynamic can be experienced in any legalistic religious system.

people who lived on the earth and are now spirits. These messengers can communicate with those in the mortal existence. The angel Moroni was the prophet Moroni; the angel Gabriel was Noah; the angel Michael was Adam,[40] (*D&C* 107:54, "And the Lord appeared unto them, and they rose up and blessed Adam, and called him Michael, the prince, the archangel.") Other angels are said to have delivered the keys of the modern priesthood (as described above). Today, Mormons offer accounts of receiving messages in the form of visions from angels who offer them guidance.

Bearing Testimony / Burning in the Bosom

Knowing whether or not *The Book of Mormon* and the claims of Joseph Smith are true is not promoted through reasoned study and comparison to the Bible, but by an emotional response. Those who have interacted with Mormon missionaries on a doorstep or a Mormon friend have experienced the hearing of the person's testimony: "I bear you my testimony that this is the only true church, that Joseph Smith was a true prophet, that *The Book of Mormon* contains the restored gospel, and that there are modern prophets today to guide the church." They often invite you to read *The Book of Mormon* and then tell you to pray to God asking for a revelation of its truthfulness. If it is true, God will give you a "burning in the bosom" and a peace of mind that will make it clear. The absolutely subjective nature of this feeling leaves the individual open to personal and demonic influence.

This bearing of testimony is important for LDS members as only those who acknowledge Smith as a prophet of the only true church will be able to enter the Celestial kingdom. Brigham Young taught:

> . . . no man or woman in this dispensation will ever enter into the celestial kingdom of God without the consent of Joseph Smith. From the day that the Priesthood was taken from the earth to the winding-up scene of all things, every man and woman must have the certificate of Joseph Smith, junior, as a passport to their entrance into the mansion where God and Christ are — I with you and you with me. I cannot go there without his consent. He

---

40. If Adam was Elohim, as Young taught in the Adam-God doctrine, then Michael the archangel is also God and could not have been a spirit child. Again, the man-made doctrines of Mormon prophets contradict one another, demonstrating their falsehood and their satanic origin.

holds the keys of that kingdom for the last dispensation — the keys to rule in the spirit-world; and he rules there triumphantly, for he gained full power and a glorious victory over the power of Satan while he was yet in the flesh, and was a martyr to his religion and to the name of Christ, which gives him a most perfect victory in the spirit-world. He reigns there as supreme a being in his sphere, capacity, and calling, as God does in heaven. Many will exclaim — "Oh, that is very disagreeable! It is preposterous! We cannot bear the thought!" But it is true.[41]

Contrary to the Bible where Jesus Himself instructs us that all judgment has been given to Him by the Father (John 5:19–30), the Mormons rely on access to the highest degree of glory granted by a man named Joseph Smith. Again, Mormon doctrine shows itself contrary to the Word of God.

A Religion with a False Foundation

I trust that from the limited description above (entire volumes have been written on the details of Mormon doctrine and worldview) it is clear to the reader that Mormonism bears some resemblance to an orthodox view of Christianity based on the Bible, but it is not a Christian religion. Mormonism is focused on a god who used to be a man and has a physical body, a Jesus who is the spiritual brother of Lucifer and every other person, a Savior who does not provide a satisfactory atonement for sins once and for all to obtain eternal redemption (Hebrews 9:27–28). It is a religion based on human additions to the true Word of God that have been shown not only to contradict the Bible, but also one another.

The Mormon faith contains so many internal inconsistencies that it cannot provide a coherent framework for a worldview. If there are multiple gods who are all omniscient and omnipotent, how can we be sure that we should be worshiping one and not the other? How can we be sure that another god will not rise up to overthrow and disrupt Elohim's plans for the future? On top of this contradiction, the concept of eternal progression to godhood produces a great quandary — where did the first god come from, and why don't we worship him? Which of these gods determines what is true and establishes the laws of nature and morality? If Elohim was created by a

---

41. Brigham Young, "Intelligence, etc." *Journal of Discourses*, vol. 7:45; available online at http://journalofdiscourses.com/7/45.

god, who was created by a god, who was created by a god, we enter into an illogical condition called infinite regression. Just as the Hindu cannot answer what the lowest turtle which is holding up the world is standing on, neither can the Mormon answer who the first god was. From a biblical worldview with one triune God, He is the uncreated Creator who has created everything in the universe — the I AM who announced Himself to Moses.

Mormonism is built on a foundation that is arbitrary because it came from the mind of one man — and no man can speak authoritatively on his own. It is evident that Joseph Smith and the Mormon prophets who followed him were not speaking on behalf of God, but on their own arbitrary authority. That is why the doctrines and stories have changed so much over the years. Not only have the stories and doctrines changed, they are contrary to what God has revealed to us in the Bible and in the person of Jesus Christ. Mormonism offers a shifting and contradictory revelation and an insufficient Savior. The Bible offers us a perfect revelation telling us of a perfect Savior.

Keys to Reaching Mormons

As Christians seek to share the hope of a Savior who is able to save to the uttermost those who are perishing through the perfect sacrifice on the Cross and acknowledged in the Resurrection, we must do so prayerfully, boldly, and patiently. Having grown up in the Mormon Church, I have experienced the teaching, baptism, priesthood, and temple work up to age 14. After a period of rebellion and running far from God, He was pleased to draw me to Himself and has granted me salvation in Christ. I have experienced the burden of the yoke of seeking to be good enough to be accepted by those in my community and church and, ultimately, Heavenly Father. But that yoke is heavy. Having been conveyed out of that power of darkness and into the kingdom of God's beloved Son, I now know the freedom that comes from trusting in Jesus Christ alone for my right standing before the Father. I have traded the yoke of man-made legalism for the yoke of Jesus Christ — and it is light and easy because He is my righteousness, not my own works (Ephesians 2:1–10; Titus 3:4–7). As you talk with Mormons, begin to share with them about the rest offered by Christ (Matthew 11:25–30).[42]

---

42. Roger Patterson, "Every Mormon's Need for Rest," Answers in Genesis, https://answersin-genesis.org/world-religions/every-mormons-need-for-rest/.

While discussions over specific points of illogical or contradictory points of doctrine can expose contradictions, do not forget that it is by the convicting work of the Holy Spirit and the drawing of the Father that anyone will repent of their sins, and trust in Christ (John 6:44, 16:5–11). Those involved in Mormonism are involved in a culture that dominates their life. How would you respond if someone tried to persuade you to abandon Christianity and become a Mormon? Jesus taught that those who respond to the gospel message should count the cost (Luke 14:25–33). That cost can be very high for those involved in Mormonism as they will likely face being ostracized by friends and family. However, the benefits are eternal, and God's grace is available to them by the work of the Spirit, enabling them to take up their cross and follow Jesus as a perfect Savior. Be willing to invest time and love in this person who is perishing, knowing that God can use you as an instrument of His redemptive grace.

One of the most important things to consider when talking about Mormon doctrine is the use of terms. While Mormons will use the same language as Christians, their meanings are usually different. Mormons are fond of talking about the atonement, but the atonement they know is an incomplete atonement that only makes it possible for them to achieve ultimate exaltation if they work hard. Become skilled in asking good questions that draw out what they believe and why they do what they do:

- You talk a lot about the atonement. What does that mean to you?

- Have you ever been baptized for a dead person? Why do you do that? Where do you see that in the Bible?

- Can you explain to me why you think there are modern prophets? Why don't they always agree?

- I know some Mormon prophets have taught that Adam was Elohim (God). Do you believe that?

By asking questions rather than making rash accusations, you draw out the person's heart and help to expose the falsehoods and contradictions they are clinging to (Proverbs 20:5). Making accusations or telling them what they believe may put them on the defensive, especially if they don't believe those particular doctrines. For example, many Mormons may not have heard the teaching that Heavenly Father had sexual relations with Mary to prepare a body for Jesus. To announce, "Well, you guys believe God had sex with Mary, and that is weird" can be counterproductive, especially if they don't hold to that doctrine.

However, asking these types of questions can allow you to explain to them the contradictions in their worldview and point them to the truth that is found in the Bible (Proverbs 26:4–5). Help them to understand that if one prophet contradicts another, then they cannot both be speaking for God. Point them to the only omnipotent Creator and Savior who created and rules over the entire universe, not just this planet.

Another advantage to asking questions is that you don't have to remember every point of Mormon doctrine. You can ask them what they believe happens after someone dies, listen to their response, and then share what the Bible teaches on that topic. When they tell you there is a second chance to hear the gospel after death, point them to Hebrews 9:27 and ask them to explain why their teaching is different from the Bible. You should know your own doctrine and where to find those truths in the Scripture much better than you should understand any other worldview. You are not responsible to know every false teaching, just to be able to recognize them as false and point to the truth in Scripture. First Peter 3:14–17 instructs us to set apart Christ as Lord over our hearts as we seek to give a reasoned defense for the hope that we have in Christ, doing it with meekness and fear.

I leave you with the words of Paul to his disciple Timothy, and pray that God will use you to share the hope of Christ with truth, boldness, and love:

> But avoid foolish and ignorant disputes, knowing that they generate strife. And a servant of the Lord must not quarrel but be gentle to all, able to teach, patient, in humility correcting those who are in opposition, if God perhaps will grant them repentance, so that they may know the truth, and that they may come to their senses and escape the snare of the devil, having been taken captive by him to do his will (2 Timothy 2:23–26).

Table 3: This table describes the key events in the supposed restoration of the fullness of the gospel. Various angelic beings appeared to Smith and his associates to convey certain messages and ordinances. Revelations continued until Smith's death in 1844.

Date	Event	Agents	"Restoration"
1820	First Vision	Heavenly Father and Jesus	Message of the corruption of modern churches and the future restoration of the gospel
1823	Golden Plates	Moroni	Plates of gold that record "the fullness of the everlasting gospel"
1824–27	Joseph's mission	Moroni	Joseph visits the site where the plates are buried to receive further instruction until they are given to him on the fourth visit
1827–30	*The Book of Mormon* translated and published	Joseph Smith, Emma Smith, Martin Harris, and Oliver Cowdery using special seer stones	The testimony of Jews who lived on the American continents and their testimony of Jesus
1829	The first elders	John the Baptist	The Aaronic priesthood is given to Joseph Smith and Oliver Cowdery by John the Baptist, and they baptize one another, becoming the first elders of the restored church
1830 (?)		Peter, James, and John	The Melchizedek priesthood is given to Joseph Smith along with the authority to rule the church
1831	Bible translation	Joseph Smith	Work on retranslating the Bible begins to correct errors in the KJV

1833	New revelations	Joseph Smith	Joseph Smith receives 65 new revelations to direct the restored church, including the building of temples
1835–44	New revelations	Joseph Smith	A total of 138 revelations to direct the restored church are recorded as the *Doctrine and Covenants*
1836	Keys given	Jesus, Moses, Elijah, and Elias	At a temple service, the keys of the dispensation are given to Joseph Smith and Oliver Cowdery
1843	New revelation	The Lord	Baptism for the dead is instituted as a temple ceremony
1843	New revelation	The Lord	Eternal progression of man toward godhood is recorded

Summary of Mormon Beliefs

Doctrine	Teachings of Mormonism
God	Deny the Trinity One god (Elohim) rules this planet, but there are many gods (henotheistic) Elohim was once a man and has a body of flesh and bone Jesus (Jehovah) is a created being and our spirit brother The Holy Spirit is a god without a body The Godhead are three different gods who are united in purpose
Authority/ Revelation	Four standard works: Bible, *The Book of Mormon*, *Doctrine & Covenants*, *The Pearl of Great Price* *The Book of Mormon* is the most perfect book ever The Bible is correct only as far as it is translated correctly Modern prophets lead the church and determine doctrine
Man	All men are spirit children of Heavenly Father and his wives Man is sinful since the Fall of Adam Man has "free agency" to obey God Man can become a god by obedience to the gospel and other ordinances

Sin	Sin is disobedience to Heavenly Father's will Additional commandments not in the Bible (e.g., Word of Wisdom)
Salvation	The four ordinances of the gospel are faith, repentance, baptism by immersion, and the laying on of hands for the Holy Spirit Additional ordinances and covenants made in the temple are necessary for exaltation to godhood in the Celestial Kingdom All except Satan and the demons and a few "sons of perdition" will inherit one of three levels of glory in heaven
Creation	Jesus, with the assistance of others, organized matter in an empty part of the universe to form our solar system Generally reject biological evolution with varying views on cosmological (big bang) and geological evolution Believe the "days of creation" were phases

Chapter 11

The Baha'i Faith

Dr. Nagy Iskander

The Baha'i faith is arguably the youngest of the independent world religions. It was founded by Mirza Husayn Ali Nuri (1817–1892), who was given the title *Baha'u'llah*, which means "the manifestation of the glory of Allah" (the god of Islam). He is regarded by Baha'is as the most recent in the line of messengers from Allah.

Bahaullah claimed to be "he whom Allah will manifest" — not merely a teacher or prophet, but divine. Hence, his words were considered to be "of Allah" himself. He claimed to have knowledge no one else possesses or is even able to possess. And no one has the right to oppose him:

> The essence of being a Baha'i is boundless devotion to the person of the manifestation and a profound belief that he is divine and of different order from all other beings.[1]

It is estimated that there are about five million Baha'is worldwide. Baha'is believe that all previous religions lost their spirit; therefore, a new cycle must begin to enlighten the world. They believe that the great cycle that began in Adam had reached its culmination in Mirza Husayn Ali Nuri, known as "Baha'u'llah," the founder of their faith.

---

1. James Hastings, ed., *Encyclopedia of Religion and Ethics* (Edinburgh: T&T Clark Publishers, 1908–1927), ref "Bab."

The Historical Background of the Baha'i Faith

In order to understand the Baha'i faith, we need to understand its Islamic background. Although modern Baha'is would like to think of Baha'ism as a universal faith, this religion is considered to be an offshoot of Shi'ite Islam.

The Islamic faith was started by Muhammad, the prophet of Islam, in the year A.D. 570 and spread over the Arabian Peninsula. After the death of Muhammad, the Muslims chose Abu Bakr as *caliph*, or "successor." Abu Bakr ruled the state of Islam in Muhammad's place and was succeeded, in turn, by Umar, Uthman, and Ali. These four are known as the rightly guided caliphs who were all chosen by the majority of the known Muslim world.

Within the first century of Islam, a party developed whose members believed that the caliph, the successor of the prophet who rules the Islamic world, must be chosen by Allah rather than by the people. This sect is called *Shi'ite*, or "separatists." Though there were many divisions among the Shi'ites, they all held firmly to the belief that their leader, or the *imam*, must be a descendant of the prophet Muhammad and must be nominated explicitly by his predecessor.

The Shi'ites held that the first imam of the prophet Muhammad was Ali — the cousin and son-in-law of Muhammad. Thus the Muslim world was, from early times, divided between the Shi'ites and their opponents, the Sunnis (who differ on who should have succeeded Muhammad). This division has remained until the present day.

Though the Shi'ites have always been a minority in the Muslim world and were often divided among themselves as to who was the rightful imam of their time, they have often shown the most passionate devotion to their beliefs and to their leaders. The majority of the Shi'ites live in Iran where most Iranians believe in the doctrine of the divine right of kings, considering their rulers to be divine beings. Therefore they believe the imam has the divine right to rule over them in both civil and spiritual affairs.

The Shi'ites acknowledge 12 imams. The followers of this form of Islam affirm that Ali and ten of his descendants, who succeeded him one after another, suffered violent deaths at the hands of the Sunnis and are counted as holy martyrs. The fate of the 11 imams was bloody: Ali was assassinated with a dagger; Husain was killed after battle; and nine others were poisoned. The last one is believed to have mysteriously disappeared as a child in Iraq after the death of his father in the year A.D. 873.

However, the Shi'ites also believe that this 12th imam (also called *Imam Mahdi*) was given the titles "Lord of the Age" and the "Proof of Allah" and came from the family of Muhammad, the prophet of Islam; and it is believed that he is still alive and will appear again on earth.

For a period of 70 years after his disappearance, the 12th imam communicated his will to men through four leaders called *babs*, which means "gates" in Arabic. A bab is considered to be a channel of grace to mankind. When the fourth bab died, no one succeeded him, and so the Shi'ites thereafter were cut off from direct communication with the Lord of the Age.

Shi'ites earnestly look for the appearance of the hidden 12th imam. They believe that all of the former prophets and imams will return to earth to aid this Mahdi, or "Guided One." It is believed that the Mahdi (12th imam) will bring all oppression to an end and will fill the earth with justice. Only Shi'ites will then be found on the earth, and at last, the religion and government of all mankind will become one.

The Manifestation of the Bab

This brings us to the religious movement of Baha'i. Sayyid Ali Muhammad (1820–1850), known as the *Bab* (Bab means gate in Arabic), was born in Shiraz in the southern part of Iran on October 9, 1820. He was a descendant of the family of Muhammad, the prophet of Islam.

As he grew up, Sayyid was interested in religious matters, so he made a pilgrimage to the shrines of the Shi'ite imams near Bagdad in Iraq. Long meditation and much prayer brought him to the conviction that he himself had been chosen by Allah to bring a special message to mankind.

On May 23, 1844, at the age of 24, Sayyid made an historic declaration in his native city of Shiraz, marking the beginning of the Babi-Baha'i movement. He believed himself to be a major manifestation of deity — the "Gate of Allah" — greater than anyone who had preceded him.

Sayyid traveled through different parts of Iran, was opposed by the government, was imprisoned and then was executed on July 9, 1850, in the public square of the city of Tabriz. And some 20,000 of his followers perished in a series of massacres throughout Persia.

While the Bab, Sayyid Ali Muhammad, was imprisoned in Iran, his followers were busy traveling around the country calling upon the Shi'ites to accept him as their long-expected Mahdi.

Among the followers of the Bab was a young man named Husain Ali who was called *Mirza*, or "nobleman," from the village of Badasht in Iran. He was given the title of *Baha,* or "splendor" and later called himself *Bahaullah*, which means the "splendor, or the glory, of Allah." Those who followed him became known as *Baha'i.*

Baha'is believe that the Bab, Sayyid Ali Muhammad(1820–1850), was an independent messenger of Allah whose message was to start a new cycle in humanity's spiritual development and whose writings prepared the way for the mission of Bahaullah.

Who Is Bahaullah?

Bahaullah is an Arabic title meaning "the manifestation of the glory of Allah." He was born on November 12, 1817, in Tehran, Iran, and his given name was Husain Ali. He was the son of a wealthy government minister from the nobles of Persia. But instead of pursuing a life of power and leisure, Husain Ali chose to give all his energy to religious matters.

In 1844, when Sayyid Ali Muhammad declared himself to be the Bab and proclaimed the arrival of the "great day of Allah awaited by all religions," Husain Ali became one of the most active followers of the Bab.

In 1848 at the village of Badasht, Husain Ali hosted a gathering of the most eminent followers of the Bab known as the *Babis*. This led to Husain Ali's arrest. Most of the followers of the Bab who were arrested were put to death by the ruling Iranian authorities. But Husain Ali was spared the fate of his companions and was punished by being beaten with a rod on the soles of his feet.

The Babi movement swept Iran like a whirlwind and stirred intense persecution from the religious establishment. Its founder, the Bab, was executed in 1850.

Two years later, in 1852, Husain Ali was arrested and falsely charged with an attempt on the life of the shah of Iran. He was brought in chains and on foot to Tehran where influential members of the court and the clergy demanded a death sentence. Husain Ali, however, was protected by his personal reputation and his family's social position, as well as protests from Western embassies. So Husain Ali was cast into a dungeon known as the "black pit." The black pit had foul air, filth, and pitch darkness. Authorities hoped this would result in Husain's death.

Instead, the dungeon became the birthplace of a new religious revelation. Husain Ali spent four months in the black pit. During that time, he contemplated the full extent of his mission. Upon his release, Bahaullah, Husain Ali, was banished from his native land — the beginning of 40 years of exiled persecution. He was sent first to neighboring Baghdad. But after about a year, he left for the mountainous wilderness of Kurdistan where he spent two years. In 1856, Bahaullah returned to Baghdad where his reputation as a spiritual leader spread throughout the city.

Before leaving Baghdad, Bahaullah and his companions camped in a garden on the banks of the Tigris River. From April 21 to May 2, 1863, Bahaullah shared with the Babis in his company that he was the promised one foretold by the Bab and by all the world scriptures. The garden became known as the Garden of *Ridvan*, which indicates "paradise" in Arabic. The anniversary of the 12 days spent there is still celebrated by the Baha'is as the most joyous holiday, known as the Ridvan Festival.

On May 3, 1863, Bahaullah rode out of Baghdad on his way to the imperial capital, Constantinople, accompanied by his family and selected companions. After four months in Constantinople, Bahaullah was sent as a virtual state prisoner to Adrianople (modern Adrian), arriving in December of 1863. During the five years he spent there, Bahaullah's reputation continued to grow, attracting the intense interest of scholars, government officials, and diplomats.

Beginning in September 1867, Bahaullah wrote a series of letters to the world leaders of his time. In these letters, Bahaullah openly proclaimed his station as "the splendor of the glory of Allah."

Soon the continued agitation of opponents caused the Turkish government to send the exiles to Akka where Bahaullah and his family arrived in August of 1868. This was the final stage in his long exile. He spent the rest of his life — 24 more years — in Akka and its surrounding area.

Bahaullah's most important work was written in Akka, known more commonly among Baha'is by the Persian name *Katb-ul-Aqdas*, or "the most holy book." In it, Bahaullah outlined the essential rules and principles that are to be observed by his followers, laying the groundwork for the Baha'i administration.

In the late 1870s, Bahaullah was given the freedom to move outside Akka's city walls and his followers were able to meet with him in relative peace and freedom. Bahaullah passed away on May 29, 1892. His remains were laid to rest in a garden room next to his mansion known as *Bahji*, which means "joy." For Baha'is, this spot is the most holy place on earth.

Bahaullah's Son

Born Abbas Effendi (1844–1921), Abdul-Baha was Bahaullah's eldest son of his first wife. He was appointed by his father to be the successor — the one,

authorized interpreter of the Baha'i teachings and head of the faith after his father's passing. Abbas assumed the title of *Abdul-Baha*, or "the servant of Baha" being the "servant of Allah," and also called himself the "centre of the covenant."

Abdul-Baha

From earliest childhood, Abdul-Baha shared his father's sufferings and his mission. He was imprisoned in Akka. But upon his release in 1908, he started traveling, reaching Europe and America in 1911 and 1913 to proclaim the message of the Baha'i faith to the West. Abdul-Baha wrote that he was the "interpreter of all the works and books of the blessed perfection," and therefore, no believer has any right to criticize. If someone does not understand the hidden secret of one of his commands or actions, they ought not to oppose it.

When Abdul-Baha died on November 29, 1921, thousands of people gathered on Mount Carmel to mourn his death. After his passing, the leadership of the Baha'i community entered a new phase evolving from that of a single individual to an administrative order.

The grandson of Abdul-Baha, Shogi Effendi, was designated "Guardian" of the Baha'i faith. His main task was to appoint the Universal House of Justice, which became the supreme authority over the Baha'i community. Although he did not have the authority to alter in any way what Bahaullah or Abdul-Baha had revealed, he performed the crucial tasks of clarifying points that may not have been clear before.

The Universal House of Justice

The Universal House of Justice, ordained by Bahaullah as the legislative authority of the Baha'i faith, finally came into existence in 1963. It has legislative, judicial, and administrative functions through a nine-member body elected at five-year intervals by the entire membership of the national government institutions of the Baha'i. It is believed that the House of Justice inherited both the position and the spirit of the "infallible guardian of the faith" and considers "divine agents" as representative of Allah.

The Baha'is International Centre

The Baha'i World Centre is established in the Haifa-Akka area of Israel, which is the location of Bahaullah's exile in 1868 and his death in 1892. Today the area is the site of the faith's most sacred shrines — the resting places of Bahaullah and his forerunner, the Bab — and is the seat of the international governing body.

The Universal House of Justice at the Baha'i World Centre, Haifa, Israel

Babi-Baha'i Scriptures and Customs

Sayyid Ali Muhammad, known as the Bab, wrote the book called the *Bayan*, which means "declaration" in Arabic. In it he explained the principles and customs of the Babi community, such as dividing the year into 19 months. Each month is 19 days (19 by 19 equals 361, almost being a year). The 19th month is the month of the fast. Immediately following the fast is the ancient Iranian festival of Nowruz, the Iranian New Year, which is to be observed with joy and gladness. The book also describes inheritance rules and many other aspects of social life for the Babis.

Bahaullah adopted what the Bab had prescribed in the Bayan, but he also wrote many other books and epistles in both Arabic and Persian, the most important being *Kitab-ul-Aqdas*, or the "most holy book." It was written at Akka in Palestine in the Arabic language. This is a book of laws — ceremonial, moral, civil, and criminal.

It's important to note that in Bahaullah's writings, he relegated the Bab to the background, putting the Bab into a position as a forerunner of himself. In fact, the fundamental assertion of Baha'ism is that Bahaullah is the manifestation of Allah. The Baha'is begin their writings with the phrase, "In the name of our lord El Baha," instead of "In the name of Allah."

In the development of the Baha'i faith, Abdul-Baha also added yet a third condition to the previous two conditions for being a true Baha'i. The first two conditions were the acceptance of Mirza Husayn Ali Nuri, known as Bahaullah, as the manifestation of Allah, and following him in complete obedience. The third condition that has been added since the death of Baha-ullah is the adherence to Abbas Effendi, known as Abdul-Baha, as supreme head — the center of the covenant. What's more, whoever rejects Abdul-Baha is cut off — no longer of the kingdom.

This is very similar to how most cults elevate their leaders, which is why the Baha'i religion is like a cult of both Islam and Christianity! The ethics of this religion permit polygamy (having multiple spouses). Their philosophy affirms the eternity of matter — which then begs the eternality of God in their view, unless matter is their God, which is self-refuting. The Baha'is have even aimed to create a new alphabet unlike the Arabic and Persian alphabets because their House of Justice must select one tongue out of the present languages — or a new language — to teach the children in the schools of the world.

Baha'ism Is Inconsistent with Christianity

If we were to ask a believer of the Baha'i faith what he thinks of God, he would most likely say that God is impersonal and "beyond the understanding of any mortal mind, though we may find expressions of His attributes in every created thing."[2] Though they believe God is unknowable, Baha'ism asserts:

> He has sent a succession of Divine Messengers, known as Manifestations of God, to educate and guide humanity, awakening in whole populations capacities to contribute to the advancement of civilization to an extent never before possible.[3]

So, unlike the God of the Bible who reveals Himself to mankind through His Word and His Son, the god of Baha'i can only send messengers to guide us, and has no interest in a personal relationship with us.

Baha'ism asserts that the promises and prophecies given in the Holy Scriptures have been fulfilled by the appearance of the prince of the universe,

2. http://www.bahai.org/beliefs/god-his-creation/.
3. Ibid.

the great Bahaullah, and of Abdul-Baha. Of course, those familiar with biblical prophecies understand that these have precious little to do with Bahaullah! But the Bible warns of such persons:[4]

> For false christs and false prophets will rise and show signs and wonders to deceive, if possible, even the elect (Mark 13:22).

> But there were also false prophets among the people, even as there will be false teachers among you, who will secretly bring in destructive heresies, even denying the Lord who bought them, and bring on themselves swift destruction (2 Peter 2:1).

> Beloved, do not believe every spirit, but test the spirits, whether they are of God; because many false prophets have gone out into the world (1 John 4:1).

To accept Bahaullah and Abdul-Baha is to deny and forsake Christ. It is impossible for Christians to exchange the clear, consistent plan of salvation through the death and Resurrection of the Lord Jesus Christ for the mystical claims of Baha'ism simply because this man says so.

Baha'i is a religion that relies on the story of a man and the absolute adherence to that man without question. When Baha'i is judged by previous revelation, such as the Old and New Testaments in God's Word, we find contradictions on many fronts, including contradictions of itself, which shows that it is not from the God of the Bible. For example, compare the following two Baha'i quotes from their Messenger of God:

> God in His Essence and in His own Self hath ever been *unseen, inaccessible, and unknowable* (emphasis added).[5]

> Having created the world and all that liveth and moveth therein, He, through the direct operation of His unconstrained and sovereign Will, chose to *confer upon man* the unique distinction and capacity to *know Him* and to *love Him* (emphasis added).[6]

So the issue is simply whether to trust in God or trust in this man. The answer should be obvious: Christ came back from the grave to prove He

---

4. Quoted Scripture in this chapter is from the New King James Version of the Bible.
5. http://www.bahai.org/beliefs/god-his-creation/revelation/quotations; *Epistle to the Son of the Wolf.*
6. Ibid; *Gleanings from the Writings of Bahá'u'lláh*, XXVII.

was correct, whereas Bahaullah remains in his grave. This further shows that Bahaullah was not God incarnate but is himself subject to inescapable death, which is the punishment for sin since the Garden of Eden. Only Jesus Christ, being God, has power over life and death.

Finally, consider these stark differences between the words of the Messenger of Baha'i and Jesus Christ:

> The different religions have one truth underlying them; therefore, their reality is one.[7]

Now read what Jesus says about this claim:

> "Most assuredly, I say to you, I am the door of the sheep. All who ever came before Me are thieves and robbers, but the sheep did not hear them. I am the door. If anyone enters by Me, he will be saved" (John 10:7–9).

> Jesus said to him, "I am the way, the truth, and the life. No one comes to the Father except through Me" (John 14:6).

Jesus did not say there are many ways to God; there is only one way — and that is the truth of the gospel.

Summary of Baha'i Beliefs

Doctrine	Baha'i's Teaching
God	Allah; believe that all descriptions of gods from different religions reveal part of the truth about Allah
Authority/ Revelation	Writings of Bahaullah and his son; writings of other prophets sent by Allah; modern prophets and the House of Justice
Man	Man is generally good and is working to obtain his divine potential and harmony
Sin	Bringing injustice or disharmony to humanity
Salvation	Seeking enlightenment and connection with the divine; religions are all a part of achieving unity of the human race
Creation	Genesis gives a spiritual account of creation, but modern scientific theories provide details; accepting of all forms of evolution

---

7. Ibid.; *The Promulgation of Universal Peace.*

Chapter 12

Deism

Dan Fisher

Dust particles dance in the shaft of light penetrating the dirty window-pane as the soothing tick-tock of numerous clocks fills the small work-shop. Tiny springs, gears, and screws glisten in the morning sun as they lay scattered across the watchmaker's workbench, while the welcome heat from the crackling fire in the woodstove drives the chill from the morning air.

Softly whistling a favorite tune, the watchmaker carefully plies his trade, adding the finishing touches to his latest masterpiece. One by one, he meticulously assembles the individual pieces until he has crafted a beautiful work of mechanical timekeeping ingenuity. With a few tweaks here and a slight adjustment there, the job is finished. Polishing the crystal to a shiny luster, he holds the piece at arm's length and surveys his work. Nodding his approval, the great craftsman sets the hands, winds the spring, and then presses the piece to his ear to listen to the smooth sound of the steady ticking of the works. His job now complete, the watchmaker places the sparkling new pocket watch on the workbench, puts on his coat, and steps outside, locking the door behind him. The cold air forces a shiver from his body as he walks down the street, leaving the watch to run all alone.

Anyone who has studied anything about deism has no doubt heard the watchmaker story. Even though the simple story of a watchmaker who makes a watch only to leave it functioning on its own cannot fully explain what deists believe, it does, in a very general sense, state the core of their faith. At its basic level, deism teaches that God made the universe and its natural laws, and then left it running on its own, free from any divine interference or interaction.[1]

Deism often compares God to a watchmaker.

Admittedly, there is no uniform belief among deists on this point and their beliefs range from viewing the Creator as a distant, uninvolved deity to accepting the possibility that He can and does (although rarely) interact with His creation. As deist Brutus Tipton explains it:

> . . . the Creator, if he acts upon the manifest world at all, does so rarely and according to his own purpose . . . that is assuming he is "concerned" at all. That's not to say, of course, that some people and events are not possibly "acted" upon by the Creator.[2]

All Alone

Many struggle to understand why deists so eagerly embrace the concept of a distant and uninvolved Creator/God. Most people find the idea of being left all alone, for all practical purposes, in this vast universe incredibly unappealing. By nature, we humans crave social interaction, and the long history of human civilization certainly suggests that the interaction we most crave is that with our Creator. Civilizations from the earliest recorded periods of Mesopotamia, from the Greeks and Romans to modern times, all fashioned gods with whom they could interact. Distinct among those is Christianity, which teaches that the God of the Bible fulfilled the spiritual craving in the person of Jesus Christ, which is consistent, since we are made in the image of an interacting God in Genesis 1.

---

1. By affirming this position, the deist runs into a serious problem. If God upholds the universe's existence, then God is interfering and interacting. If God doesn't uphold the universe, then how can it remain in existence?
2. Brutus C. Tipton, "Deism: A New Beginning," World Union of Deists, http://www.deism.com/deismbeginning.htm.

On the opposite side of the religious spectrum is deism, which teaches that a personal, intimate relationship between man and his Creator is a practical impossibility, insisting instead, that all that can be known about God is revealed by the cold, impersonal laws of physics alone. Armed only with his sheer logic and reason, the deist hacks his way through the spiritual wilderness of life in his quest to understand a God who refuses to speak directly. Rejecting all divine revelation as spurious, deists rob themselves of any possibility of the deeply satisfying experience of actually "knowing" their Creator.

A Short History

Deism's relatively short story began when the term "deist" first surfaced in the middle 1500s in the writings of a Swiss theologian by the name of Pierre Viret. It appeared a few decades later in England in the early 1600s in Lord Herbert of Cherbury's work, *De Veritate*. Although not a deist in the truest sense (since deism would not become a distinct philosophy until years later), many consider Herbert the "father of deism" in the English world. In *De Veritate*, which means "concerning truth," Herbert postulated that man could use his human reason and other innate human fac-

Swiss theologian Pierre Viret first used the term "deist."

ulties to discover truth, and by extrapolation, God. Extremely revolutionary for that time, his writings helped to ignite a firestorm of progressive thought that swept over Europe and led to the eventual development of deism as a distinct philosophy.

Spurred on by unending wars in Europe, many of which were fought over religion, and the many advances in science, especially in astronomy, deism's star continued to rise into the late 17th and early 18th centuries. With the corruption that had taken hold in the "established" Christian Church of this time (which in many instances was far from the traditional, biblical Christian Church), many became disillusioned with traditional religion.

As the pendulum began to swing the other way, many of these disillusioned seekers turned to human reason (apart from the Scriptures or autonomous human reason) as an alternative to a faith that, in their view, had failed. Rejecting the idea of divine revelation altogether, deism became their default "religion." Finding a welcome home among these "seekers," deism spread to France, and with the efforts of men like Montesquieu, Voltaire, and Rousseau, it became a powerful engine of the age of enlightenment. Eventually jumping "the pond," this new "religion of reason" made its way to the shores of America. Once introduced to the American intelligentsia, numerous notables such as Thomas Jefferson[3] and Benjamin Franklin embraced deism, or at least were heavily influenced by it. Foremost among America's deists was Thomas Paine who, though not a Founding Father, did become deism's primary American evangelist and whose teachings continue to be heralded by deists to this very day.

A Working Definition

When studying any philosophy/religion, establishing a working definition is crucial. In his 1755 *A Dictionary of the English Language*, the English writer and literary giant Samuel Johnson defined deism as "the opinion of those that only acknowledge one God, without the reception of any revealed religion."[4] Seventy-three years later in his own dictionary, Noah Webster defined deism as:

> The doctrine or creed of a deist; the belief or system of religious opinions of those who acknowledge the existence of one God, but deny revelation: or deism is the belief in natural religion only, or those truths, in doctrine and practice, which man is to discover by the light of reason, independent and exclusive of any revelation from God. Hence deism implies infidelity or a disbelief in the divine origin of the scriptures.

---

3. There is still some debate over Jefferson's views to this day. In a letter to Charles Thomson on January 9, 1816, Jefferson openly proclaimed to be a Christian, which was clearly not the mark of a deist. Though he was likely influenced by deism to say the least and struggled in particular with the supernatural in the Bible, showing the influence of naturalism and deism. For all practical purposes, we will treat him as a deist in this chapter

4. Samuel Johnson, LL.D., *A Dictionary of the English Language* (London: 1755, 1785) Sixth Edition, accessed from http://publicdomainreview.org/collections/samuel-johnsons-dictionary-of-the-english-language-1785/.

Although numerous nuances have developed within deism since the time of Johnson and Webster, at its core, its basic tenets remain essentially the same. The World Union of Deists, a leading deist organization founded in 1993 by Robert Johnson, confirms this with their modern definition:

> . . . the recognition of a universal creative force greater than that demonstrated by mankind, supported by personal observation of laws and designs in nature and the universe, perpetuated and validated by the innate ability of human reason coupled with the rejection of claims made by individuals and organized religions of having received special divine revelation.[5]

So at the very heart of deism lies the emphatic declaration that, other than creation itself, there is no divine revelation of God. According to deists, not even the Holy Bible has a valid claim to divine inspiration. Thomas Paine, the "patron saint" of many deists, said:

> The creation is the Bible of the Deist. He there reads, in the handwriting of the Creator himself, the certainty of his existence and the immutability of his power, and all other Bibles and Testaments are to him forgeries.[6]

Adding insult to injury, The World Union of Deists harshly declares that the Bible ". . . paint[s] a very evil and insane picture of God."[7]

No Divine Revelation, No Divine Intervention

Rejecting all "spiritual truths" that cannot be substantiated by physical science, deists contend that any talk of sin, judgment, redemption, etc., is irrelevant, since creation teaches nothing of these concepts and can only be found in inspired writings like the Bible — a book they vehemently reject. Void of any divine revelation, the deist must resort to his imperfect reason/logic when attempting to understand God. Stating it succinctly, The World Union of Deists declares, "God gave us reason, not religion."[8]

In drastic contrast to Christianity, which teaches that the God of the Bible longs to have a meaningful and personal relationship with humans, deism

---

5. http://www.deism.com.
6. Thomas Paine, *The Age of Reason, In Two Parts* (New York: G.N. Devries, 1827), p. 173.
7. World Union of Deists, www.deism.com.
8. Ibid.

leaves man to make assumptions about a God who refuses to interact with His creation. Believing the Bible to be the divinely inspired Word of God, Christians base every belief concerning God's nature and His will on the clearly articulated doctrines laid down in Scripture. Relying on passages such as 2 Timothy 3:16–17, Christians believe the Bible to be the literal breath of God:[9]

> All Scripture *is* given by inspiration [*theopneustos /Greek/* — God-breathed] of God, and *is* profitable for doctrine, for reproof, for correction, for instruction in righteousness, that the man of God may be complete, thoroughly equipped for every good work.

Unlike deists, Christians, do not speculate about God; they believe men can know with absolute certainty the things God has revealed about Himself in His Word.

At one level, Christians wholeheartedly agree with deists that creation does "scream" the existence of a God who *intelligently designed* and created a universe of space, time, and matter. Paul declared as much in Romans 1:20:

> For since the creation of the world His invisible attributes are clearly seen, being understood by the things that are made, even His eternal power and Godhead, so that they are without excuse.

Therefore, it is biblically correct to say that the creation is proof that there is a Creator/God. But this knowledge alone does not provide answers to such important questions as: "How did the universe come to be? How did mankind come to be? How should man relate to his Creator? What about the concepts of sin, righteousness, eternal life, and eternal judgment?" In short, a long list of questions essential to man's spiritual understanding and wellbeing cry out for answers that creation alone cannot provide.

For example, when Lord Herbert Cherbury articulated his early deistic postulations about truth, he summarized them with five "common notions":

1. There is a supreme deity.

2. This deity ought to be worshiped.

3. Virtue combined with piety is the chief part of religious practice.

---

9. Scripture in this chapter is from the New King James Version of the Bible.

4. Men are wicked and must repent of their sins.

5. There is reward and punishment from God, both in this life and after it.[10]

It is impossible to imagine how creation alone could have revealed all of that to Herbert. But let's take this one step further. From the creation alone, how can the deist know that logic and reason really exist? Reason has no mass and is conceptual (nonmaterial), so how can a *physical* creation reveal the *nonphysical* notion of reason? Even though this is devastating to the deist, let's grant that he can use reason and with that, it is easy enough to see how he might have conceived the first two notions from a "reasoned" study of the universe; but how could he possibly have understood the concepts of sin, repentance, and eternal punishment/reward without some additional source of divine revelation?

Formulating explanations to these deep spiritual issues without an authoritative, divine revelatory source is certainly a tall order indeed. Left to himself, the seeker of truth must either resort to his imagination for answers or he must simply ignore these critical issues altogether, hoping all eventually turns out well in the end; hence, this religion is purely arbitrary and left to the whims of each individual. What a terrible way to deal with such serious issues. Even more serious is the terrifying proposition of "guessing" incorrectly about these eternal questions or of completely ignoring them only to discover in the end that there actually was a divine revelation that provided answers to these critical queries. The eternal consequences will be catastrophic (Matthew 25:46).

Additionally, if man is left to develop his own explanations about spiritual essentials, what happens when these many explanations end up contradicting each other, as they no doubt will? Who decides which answers are correct? Can all positions be correct even if they contradict with each other? How can two opposing views of the same thing both be correct in the same sense at the same time? Wouldn't that contradict the law of non-contradiction?

This is the dilemma with which deists have grappled since the birth of their "religion" in the 1600s. Brutus C. Tipton, once an orthodox Christian and now leading deist, admits:

---

10. Accessed from christiandeistfellowship.com/truth.htm, cited 1/9/15.

As a Deist I must allow that there are very many things that are not currently known to us through scientific inquiry and perhaps there is much that will never be known. . . . As a Deist I am very much content to say that I just don't know when it comes to questions such as the existence (or lack thereof) of an afterlife. . . . Perhaps science will someday validate the belief in an afterlife (or at least some form of consciousness which continues after physical dewoath) and perhaps it may someday validate the power of prayer and other spiritual and religious practices. Nothing would please me more and although I personally stop short of faith I believe in keeping an open mind.[11]

Even the famed deist Thomas Paine was forced to admit his inability to possess any real certainty concerning his own afterlife:

I consider myself in the hands of my Creator, and that He will dispose of me after this life consistently with His justice and goodness. I leave all these matters to Him, as my Creator and friend, and I hold it to be presumption in man to make an article of faith as to what the Creator will do with us hereafter.[12]

Of course, if Paine was correct when he *reasoned* that the Bible is not God's divine revelation, then eternity may turn out well for him (this is what he hopes and placed his faith in). But, since he was wrong and the Bible is correct, then Paine is in for quite a rude awakening on Judgment Day. Interestingly, for those who believe and obey Scripture, right or wrong, eternity turns out well for them. This is a rehash of Pascal's Wager, but it leaves the truth of the God as a probability. Let's take this one step further for the readers: the God of the Bible does exist and we have certainty of that (e.g., 1 John 5:20).

Thomas Paine

---

11. Ibid., Brutus C. Tipton, "Deism: A New Beginning."
12. Thomas Paine, *The Theological Works of Thomas Paine* (London: R. Carlile, 1824), p. 261.

In spite of this eternal risk, deists remain adamant that their impersonal and disconnected God has provided no divine revelation of Himself short of creation. Since creation is subject to interpretation, then really the deist can't know anything for certain: not even their claim that creation is the only revelation, which is self-refuting. Sadly, the rank and file deist concludes that he is left with little or no hope of receiving any assistance or illumination from God. What a depressing and lonely existence this must be — especially in those moments of personal crisis when a personal, interactive God is what one needs most.

Deists and Revealed Religions

With their rejection of any valid source of divine revelation, it comes as no surprise that deists also reject all revealed religions as unreasonable, corrupt, and even insane. They argue that if these religions ever possessed any significant truth, centuries of human manipulation and myth have tainted and tarnished them beyond usefulness. And yet so often, deists fail to realize the human manipulation of their own religion! Even so, according to many deists, mankind would actually be much better off had he not been beguiled by the deceptive myths and superstitions of religion in the first place. The Union of World Deists implies as much when it declares:

> Much of the evil in the world could be overcome or removed if humanity had embraced our God-given reason from our earliest evolutionary stages.[13]

Deist Robert Johnson goes on to blame religion, especially Christianity, for much of the suffering in the world:

> I believe the Christian mind-set that is so eager to accept guilt and original sin, as well as the additional unnatural idea of redemption by proxy, is much to blame for the suffering of millions of people who allow themselves to be victims of negativity.[14]

Johnson even insinuates that had deism been the dominant religion centuries ago, life for mankind would be a virtual utopia by now:

> Every invention and discovery we have today could have been in effect 2,000 to 5,000 years ago. . . . We could be enjoying a

13. Ibid., World Union of Deists.
14. Robert Johnson, "The Beauty of Deism," http://www.deism.com/beautyofdeism.htm.

virtually disease free, peaceful progressive society extending well beyond our planet Earth. . . . As we generate a peaceful worldwide religious revolution through Deism and the World Union of Deists we will bring about the emancipation of the individual's mind and spirit. The soul of society will then be lifted to a new level, never before thought possible. A level of progress and international cooperation that will make warfare just an archaic oddity of the dark, superstitious past.[15]

Of course, Johnson and most other deists fail to mention the good that religions, particularly Christianity, have brought to the human experience (despite the fact that a true deist cannot state if something is really good or bad as their god has not revealed what is good or bad!). They fail to mention the massive humanitarian efforts performed throughout history mainly by Christians. They fail to mention that most hospitals and medical missions in America, and around the world for that matter, were originally founded and operated by Christian organizations. They seem not to notice that in every country where Christianity has become the dominant faith, those citizens experience the greatest amount of liberty, enjoy the most prosperous economies, have the greatest opportunity for personal advancement, and have, generally, enjoyed the best living conditions of all peoples. Like Johnson, Christians also wonder where mankind would be without these pesky "revealed religions" — Christians simply draw a much different conclusion than do Johnson and his like-minded deists.

Deism and America's Founding Fathers

(Editor's note to our international readers: this section dives into deism's influence in the founding of the United States. Though you may not think this is important, it could still be very valuable to understand what is occurring in the United States today and why certain debates occur in the United States that are often seen on news sources around the world.)

"America was founded mostly by atheists and deists!" This is the incessant mantra that is peddled by the media/educational elites of our day. In this post Christian era, rarely do these "authorities" mention our Founding Fathers without insinuating or emphatically declaring that the majority of them were either deists or atheists. Are they correct? Certainly not — but

---

15. Ibid.

most will not know this if they listen to the majority of today's commentators and educators. Those dining on a steady diet of their anti-Christian ranting are commonly quite surprised to learn that very few of our Founders even claimed to be deists. Accomplished historian Greg Frazer says that after some thirty years of research, he can only identify two Founders who were definitely deists.[16]

But does it even matter here in 21st-century America what religion our Founders embraced, if any? As it so happens, it matters a great deal — especially if we want to properly understand the philosophical roots of our form of government

George Washington
(Portrait by Gilbert Stuart Williamstown)

and if we are to properly interpret our founding documents. To our Founding Fathers, religion was essential to self-governance. Consider the sentiments of George Washington. Though it is unknown whether or not he was a "born-again" Christian (reasonable arguments concerning his faith can be made both ways), Washington considered "religion" vital to the survival of our Republic:

> Of all the dispositions and habits which lead to political prosperity, religion and morality are indispensable supports. In vain would that man claim the tribute of patriotism, who should labor to subvert these great pillars of human happiness. . . . And let us with caution indulge the supposition that morality can be maintained without religion.[17]

According to the "Father of Our Country," religion (most believe he was referring to Christianity) is the primary pillar that upholds our Republic;

16. Frazer/Mohler interview, "What Did America's Founders Really Believe? A Conversation with Historian Gregg Frazer," transcript, interview with Al Mohler on *Thinking in Public*, September 10, 2012, accessed from http://www.albertmohler.com/2012/09/10/what-did-americas-founders-really-believe-a-conversation-with-historian-gregg-frazer-transcript/, cited 1/7/15.

17. George Washington, Farewell Address, September 17, 1796, The George Washington Papers at the Library of Congress , 1741–1799.

therefore, any "ism" that would seek to strike at that pillar (as deism obviously does) would pose a real threat to our Republic's existence. Historian Greg Frazer observes:

> . . . for them [the Founders], the critical element in religion was morality. And this is where the left is wrong with their wall of separation notion and the idea that the founders wanted to keep religion out of public life. . . . they were creating a republic, a free society, without the iron fist of the government controlling people. And so the question they then had to deal with was, "How do you control such people? How do you get them to behave?" And their answer was that you get them to behave, you control them, through morality. And where do you get morality? You get it through religion. So they did not want to divorce or separate religion from public life; . . . they believed that morality was indispensible for a free society and that religion was the best source for morality. . . .[18]

This statement starkly contrasts to the common emphatic claim that our Founders intended to create a totally secular government completely free from religion and its influence (that is with the exception of the secular religions of course!).

It is important, though, to remember that these men were, among many things, also politicians. They were not attempting to lead a church or a denomination; they were attempting to create a new country with a form of governance (representative republic) that was a radical departure from the prevalent form of government for that time (monarchy). They understood that the success of self-governance would hinge on Christian morality — not necessarily Christian doctrine. For example, Benjamin Franklin said, "Only a virtuous people are capable of freedom."[19] In 1776, John Adams declared, ". . . it is religion and morality alone, which can establish the principles upon which freedom can securely stand. The only foundation of a free constitution is pure virtue."[20]

18. Frazer/Mohler interview.
19. Benjamin Franklin, *The Writings of Benjamin Franklin* (London: Macmillan & Co., 1906), Albert Henry Smyth, ed., Volume 9, Letter to Messrs. The Abbes Chalut and Arnaud, April 17, 1787, p. 569.
20. John Adams, letter to Zabdiel Adams, June 21, 1776, accessed from national archives, http://founders.archives.gov/documents/Adams/04-02-02-0011, cited 1/27/15.

Charles Carroll, signer of the Declaration of Independence, warned, "Without morals a republic cannot subsist any length of time . . . the solid foundation of morals, [is] the best security for the duration of free governments."[21] In 1798, John Adams, in commenting on the importance of morality to the effectiveness of our Constitution, said, "Our Constitution was made only for a moral and religious people. It is wholly inadequate for the government of any other."[22] Summing up this concept, Robert Winthrop, Speaker of the U.S. House of Representatives, declared in 1849, "Men, in a word, must necessarily be controlled, either by a power within them, or by a power without them; either by the word of God, or by the strong arm of man; either by the Bible, or by the bayonet."[23]

In defense of those who claim that deism greatly impacted our Founders, they are partially correct. By the middle of the 18th century, deism was definitely on the rise in America, due mainly to the influence of the French Enlightenment. Devout Christian and Founding Father Patrick Henry lamented the wave of deism sweeping over America:

> The view which the rising greatness of our country presents
> to my eyes is greatly tarnished by the general prevalence of deism,
> which, with me, is but another name for vice and depravity.[24]

Historian Greg Frazer argues that many of our Founders, who are today labeled as deists, actually embraced a "mixture of Christianity, natural religion (deism), and rationalism."[25] Coining the term "theistic rationalism" to describe their faith, Frazer says they "took elements of Christianity and elements of natural religion and then, using rationalism, kept what they considered reasonable and rational while rejecting everything else."[26] Unfortunately for some like Thomas

21. Bernard C. Steiner, *The Life and Correspondence of James McHenry* (Cleveland, OH: The Burrows Brothers, 1907), p. 475, letter from Charles Carroll to James McHenry, November 4, 1800.

22. Charles Francis Adams, *The Works of John Adams, Second President of the United States: with a Life of the Author, Notes and Illustrations* (Boston, MA: Little, Brown and Co., 1856), Vol. 9. Chapter: "To the Officers of the First Brigade of the Third Division of the Militia of Massachusetts, October 11, 1798."

23. Robert Winthrop, *Addresses and Speeches on Various Occasions* (Boston, MA: Little, Brown & Co., 1852), "An Address Delivered At The Annual Meeting Of The Massachusetts Bible Society In Boston, May 28, 1849," p. 172.

24. William Wirt, *Sketches of the Life and Character of Patrick Henry,* third ed. (Philadelphia, PA: James Webster, 1818), p. 836.

25. Mohler/Frazer interview.

26. Ibid.

The official presidential portrait of Thomas Jefferson. The debate continues over whether Thomas Jefferson was a deist.

Jefferson, that meant rejecting many of the supernatural parts of the Bible, especially in the New Testament. For example, Jefferson was willing to accept Jesus as a good moral teacher but refused to fully accept His claim to deity — denying that He had the power to work miracles defying the laws of physics.[27]

But even with deism's growing acceptance among America's ruling class, there remained a friendly coexistence between deists and Christians. Historian Gordon Wood claims that the major difference in the rivalry between deism and Christianity then and now is that "Enlightened rationalism and evangelical Calvinism were not at odds in 1776 . . ."[28] — certainly not to the extent they are today. Still, in the face of this rising tide of deism, Christianity remained by far the primary religious force in early America and was the religion of the masses and many of the Founders.

So how have the revisionist historians been able to convince a significant number of Americans that the Founders were mostly deists and atheists? Easy. They simply restrict their discussions to the views of the Founders who were mainly deistic — Thomas Jefferson and Benjamin Franklin. In a sound byte age when most people know little about our history, the results are predictable: these two Founders end up being the only ones most know anything about. From there, the next step is simple. Americans with a shallow view of their history are then easily led to believe that the spiritual views of Jefferson and Franklin were representative of most of the other Founders — when the exact opposite is actually true. Even conceding the point that Franklin was probably a deist and Jefferson a "theistic rationalist," it is worth

27. Miracles do not always defy natural law; some are by timing, and some may well be within the laws of nature, as we simply do not know all the laws of the physical creation. The fact that Christ did miraculous things was a testimony to His deity regardless; for more see Paul S. Taylor, "Did Miracles Really Happen?" Answers in Genesis, June 7, 2011, https://answersingenesis.org/apologetics/did-miracles-really-happen/.

28. Gordon Wood, *Creation of the American Republic 1776–1787*, "Republicanism," (Chapel Hill, NC: University of North Carolina Press, 1969), p. 60.

noting that they both retained a healthy respect for Scripture and certainly seemed to believe in an interactive God.

Consider Benjamin Franklin. Even though he was raised an Episcopalian by devout Christian parents and later attended a Presbyterian church for some time, in his own autobiography he called himself a "thorough deist" and said that, the "Arguments of the Deists . . . appeared to me much stronger [than the arguments of the Christians.]"[29] His deistic beliefs are clearly evident in a 1790 letter to Rev. Ezra Stiles, president of Yale:

> As to Jesus of Nazareth, my Opinion of whom you particularly desire, I think the System of Morals and his Religion, as he left them to us, the best the world ever saw or is likely to see; but I apprehend it has received various corrupt changes, and I have, with most of the present Dissenters in England, some Doubts as to his divinity; tho' it is a question I do not dogmatize upon, having never studied it, and I think it needless to busy myself with it now, when I expect soon an Opportunity of knowing the Truth with less Trouble. . . .[30]

Yet this same Benjamin Franklin, when the Constitutional Convention was gridlocked in Philadelphia during the summer of 1787, made the following appeal, which, sadly, was never officially adopted:

> In the beginning of the Contest with G. Britain, when we were sensible of danger we had daily prayer in this room for the divine protection. Our prayers, Sir, were heard, and they were graciously answered. . . . And have we now forgotten that powerful friend? I have lived, Sir, a long time, and the longer I live, the more convincing proofs I see of this truth — that God governs in the affairs of men. And if a sparrow cannot fall to the ground without his notice, is it probable that an empire can rise without his aid? We have been assured, Sir, in the sacred writings, that "except the Lord build the House they labor in vain that build it." I firmly believe this; and I also believe that without his concurring aid we shall succeed in this political building no better than the Builders of Babel: . . . I therefore beg leave to move,

29. Benjamin Franklin, *The Autobiography of Benjamin Franklin* (New Haven, CT: Yale University Press, 1964), p. 113–114.
30. Carl Van Doren, *Benjamin Franklin* (New York: The Viking Press, 1938), p. 777.

that henceforth prayers imploring the assistance of Heaven, and its blessings on our deliberations, be held in this Assembly every morning before we proceed to business, and that one or more of the Clergy of the City be requested to officiate in that service.[31]

These are hardly the words of a man who believed God was unconcerned and uninvolved in the activities of men. He was even quoting Scripture (e.g., Psalm 127:1, Matthew 10:29)!

Although not an orthodox Christian himself, Thomas Jefferson was certainly no enemy to Christianity. Con-

Benjamin Franklin, circa 1785
(Portrait by Joseph-Siffrein Duplessis)

sider the design for our national seal that he, John Adams, and Benjamin Franklin proposed to Congress. Although it unfortunately was not adopted, it was a circle with the words "Rebellion To Tyrants Is Obedience to God" written around its circumference with a drawing of Moses and the Children of Israel looking on as the Egyptians are drowning in the Red Sea, with God's presence depicted by a pillar of smoke and fire in its center, as described in the Bible. This is quite amazing considering the fact that these three supposedly rejected the Bible, all revealed religions, and an interactive God.

When serving as president, Jefferson exhibited no inclination to slight or diminish the importance of religion's role in America. For example, three times he signed into law extensions of a 1787 act that ordained special lands "for the sole use of Christian Indians" and reserved lands for the Moravian Brethren "for civilizing the Indians and promoting Christianity."[32] On April 10, 1806, he approved the rules and regulations for the Armies of the United

---

31. Library of Congress, "Religion and the Founding of the American Republic, Religion and the Federal Government, Part 1," http://www.loc.gov/exhibits/religion/rel06.html#obj145.

32. *The Laws of the United States of America, From the 4th of March, 1789, to the 4th of March, 1815, Including the Constitution of the United States, The Old Act of Confederation, Treaties, With Many Other Valuable Ordinances and Documents; With Copious Notes and References* (Philadelphia, PA: John Bioren and W. John Duane and Washington City: R.C. Weightman, 1815), Vol. 1, p. 569.

States, of which the second of the 101 articles began with the admonition, "It is earnestly recommended to all officers and soldiers diligently to attend divine service. . . ."

Clearly, even though Jefferson and Franklin were deistic in their thought, they harbored no hostility toward revealed religions and apparently embraced a God who was involved in the affairs of men. Though prominent among the Founders, their religious views were by no means predominant. Tragically, because of today's almost exclusive focus on the two, many Americans are led to the mistaken notion that the majority of our Founders were deists like Franklin and Jefferson.

In taking a closer look at the faith of our Founders, it is significant to note that most of them attended Christian churches that were orthodox in their teaching. Of course, this fact alone does not prove that they were true believers, but it does seem to strongly indicate that most of them were far from being deists. But there is an even greater source that reveals the authenticity of their faith — their official writings. Though imperfect and sometimes inconsistent, as all humans are, many of our Founding Fathers gave strong indications of the sincerity of their Christian faith. Consider:

- Charles Carroll, signer of the Declaration of Independence — "On the mercy of my Redeemer I rely for salvation and on His merits; not on the works I have done in obedience to His precepts."[33]

- Robert Treat Paine, signer of the Declaration of Independence — "I desire to bless and praise the name of God most high for appointing me my birth in a land of Gospel Light where the glorious tidings of a Savior and of pardon and salvation through Him have been continually sounding in mine ears. . . . in full belief of [H]is providential goodness and [H]is forgiving mercy revealed to the world through Jesus Christ,"[34]

---

33. The Last Will and Testament of Charles Carrollton, Life of Charles Carrollton, p. 226, accessed from https://play.google.com/books/reader?id=FkYSAAAAYAAJ&printsec=frontcover&output=reader&hl=en&pg=GBS.PA226, Kate Mason Rowland, *Life of Charles Carroll of Carrollton* (New York: G.P. Putnam's Sons, 1890), Vol. II, p. 373–374, will of Charles Carroll, Dec. 1, 1718 (later replaced by a subsequent will not containing this phrase, although he re-expressed this sentiment on several subsequent occasions, including repeatedly in the latter years of his life).
34. Robert Treat Paine, *The Papers of Robert Treat Paine*, Stephen Riley and Edward Hanson, editors (Boston: MA Historical Society, 1992), Vol. I, p. 98, March/April, 1749, https://books.google.com/books?id=-vcWuNWxNkwC&pg=PA98#v=onepage&q&f=false.

- Benjamin Rush, signer of the Declaration of Independence — "My only hope of salvation is in the infinite, transcendent love of God manifested to the world by the death of His Son upon the cross. Nothing but His blood will wash away my sins. I rely exclusively upon it."[35]

- Richard Stockton, signer of the Declaration of Independence — "I bequeath my Soul to the Lord that gave it me trusting in his mercies that he will Receive it again. . . ."[36]

- John Witherspoon, signer of the Declaration of Independence — "Believe it, there is no salvation in any other than in Christ. His atoning blood will reconcile you to God: His grace and love will captivate your souls; His holy and blessed Spirit will write His laws in your hearts. Believe in Him. . . ."[37]

- John Hart, signer of the Declaration of Independence — "Thanks be given unto Almighty God — therefore, and knowing that it is appointed for all men once to die and after that the Judgment. . . . first and principally I give and recommend my Soul into the Hands of Almighty God who gave it, and my Body to the Earth to be buried in a decent and Christian like manner . . . not doubting but to receive the same again at the General resurrection by the mighty power of God. . . ."[38]

- Roger Sherman (Signer of the Declaration of Independence & the U.S. Constitution) — "I believe that there is one only living and true God, existing in three persons, the Father, the Son, and the Holy Ghost. . . . that the Scriptures of the Old and

35. Benjamin Rush, *The Autobiography of Benjamin Rush*, George Corner, editor (Princeton, NJ: Princeton University Press for the American Philosophical Society, 1948), p. 166, accessed from http://books.google.com/books/about/The_Autobiography_of_Benjamin_Rush.html?id=g3IrAQAAMAAJ.

36. Richard Stockton's will, July 21st 1775, Albemarle County, Virginia, Will Book 2, page 324, accessed from http://www.genealogy.com/forum/surnames/topics/stockton/2235/, cited 4/2/15.

37. John Rogers, *The Works of John Witherspoon* (Philadelphia, PA: William W. Woodward, 1800), Vol. I, p. 256, accessed from http://books.google.com/books/about/The_works_of_the_Rev_John_Witherspoon_D.html?id=7kUVAAAAYAAJ, cited 4/2/15.

38. John Hart's last will and testament, attested April 16, 1779, which is in the custody of the State of New Jersey Library, Archives and History, Trenton, accessed from http://www.laurellynn.com/genealogy/hart/john_hart_marriage_children.htm, cited 4/3/15.

New Testaments are a revelation from God. . . . that God did send His own Son to become man, die in the room and stead of sinners, and thus to lay a foundation for the offer of pardon and salvation to all mankind so as all may be saved who are willing to accept the Gospel offer."[39]

- William Samuel Johnson, signer of the U.S. Constitutuion — "Remember, too, that you are the redeemed of the Lord, that you are bought with a price, even the inestimable price of the precious blood of the Son of God. . . . Acquaint yourselves with Him in His word and holy ordinances."[40]

- George Mason, member of the Constitutional Convention and called the "Father of the Bill of Rights" — "My soul I resign into the hands of my Almighty Creator, whose tender mercy's are all over his works, who hateth nothing that he hath made, and to the Justice and Wisdom of whose Dispensations I willingly and chearfully submit humbly hopeing from his unbounded mercy and benevolence, thro the Merits of my blessed Savior, a remission of my sins."[41]

- Patrick Henry, Governor of Virginia and leading patriot — "This is all the inheritance I can give to my dear family. The religion of Christ can give them one which will make them rich indeed."[42]

Though this is but a small sampling of our Founders' declarations of faith, it sufficiently reflects the beliefs of a good number of them and certainly refutes the notion that most of them were deists and atheists.

39. Lewis Henry Boutell, *The Life of Roger Sherman* (Chicago, IL: A.C. McClurg and Company, 1896), p. 272–273, accessed from http://books.google.com/books/about/The_life_of_Roger_Sherman.html?id=RVQCZ9VD0lIC, cited 4/2/15.

40. Beardsley Edwards, *Life and Times of William Samuel Johnson, LL.D.* (New York: Hurd and Houghton; Cambridge: The Riverside Press, 1876), William S. Johnson's address to the graduating class of Columbia Univ., 1789, p. 141–143, accessed from http://books.google.com/books/about/Life_and_times_of_William_Samuel_Johnson.html?id=rdm-fGCDg6YIC, cited 4/2/15.

41. George Mason, Last Will and Testament, March 20, 1773, accessed from http://www.virginia1774.org/GeorgeMasonWill.html; http://www.consource.org/document/george-masons-last-will-and-testament-1773-3-20/, cited 4/3/15.

42. Patrick Henry, Last Will and Testament, November 20, 1798, accessed from http://www.redhill.org/last_will.htm, cited 4/3/15.

What Really Motivates Deists?

Like all other religious/philosophical persuasions, there is a core conviction that drives deists to believe what they believe. In the final analysis, their rejection of divine revelation appears to be propelled by a deep desire to avoid any possibility of the unpleasant prospect of having their reason "shocked" by a faith-based religion. Essentially, deists adamantly refuse to embrace anything that offends human reason. Thomas Paine clearly articulated this when he wrote:

> There is a happiness in Deism, when rightly understood, that is not to be found in any other system of religion. All other systems have something in them that either shock our reason, or are repugnant to it, and man, if he thinks at all, must stifle his reason in order to force himself to believe them.[43]

In his search for God, the deist looks in two directions: outward at creation and inward to his own logic. His reliance on human reason alone to guide him to the truth makes him, in the words of Albert Einstein, a "religious nonbeliever":

Albert Einstein
(Photo by Oren Jack Turner)

> I cannot conceive of a personal God who would directly influence the actions of individuals, or would directly sit in judgment on creatures of his own creation. . . . My religiosity consists of a humble admiration of the infinitely superior spirit that reveals itself in the little that we can comprehend about the knowable world. That deeply emotional conviction of the presence of a superior reasoning power, which is revealed in the incomprehensible universe forms my idea of God. . . . I am a deeply religious nonbeliever. This is a somewhat new kind of religion.[44]

---

43. Thomas Paine, "Of the Religion of Deism Compared with the Christian Religion," *Age of Reason*, 1794-1796.
44. Walter Isaacson, *Einstein: His Life and Universe* (New York: Simon & Schuster, 2007), p. 387-388, 536.

Even though Einstein could not conceive of a god like the God of the Bible, billions of people across the centuries have (1 Corinthians 12:3). They have chosen to trust the most verified book in human history rather than "the little that we can comprehend about the knowable world."

Admittedly, the gospel is indeed "repugnant" to the natural man and its message definitely "shocks his reason." Paul taught this in 1 Corinthians 2:14 when he warned that human reason/logic cannot, on its own, comprehend the infinite God:

> But the natural man does not receive the things of the Spirit of God, for they are foolishness to him; nor can he know *them,* because they are spiritually discerned.

In Romans 9:33, Paul acknowledged to the Christians in Rome that God's message of redemption is indeed offensive to the unbeliever:

> Behold, I lay in Zion a stumbling stone and rock of offense, and whoever believes on Him will not be put to shame.

But before discounting Paul's teachings, one should seriously consider the strong words of Jesus to all who would ignore this "rock of offense." In Luke 20:18, Jesus warned: "Whoever falls on that stone will be broken; but on whomever it falls, it will grind him to powder."

No Faith, Just Reason

On the 1960s television series *Dragnet,* Sergeant Friday was famous for wanting only the facts. Similarly, deists also claim to be interested in only the "facts." In their search for the facts, they reject faith altogether, convinced that faith and fact are mutually exclusive. It is ironic that they have such faith in what they perceive as fact! The suggestion of a "factual faith" is anathema to them. They insist on seeing everything in life through the filter of human logic/reason (and human sense perception), thus eliminating any place for faith in their system of belief. Voltaire, the French philosopher and deist, put it this way:

> It is perfectly evident to my mind that there exists a necessary, eternal, supreme, and intelligent being. This is no matter of faith, but of reason.[45]

---

45. Voltaire, *Philosophical Dictionary*, "Faith," I, accessed from https://ebooks.adelaide.edu.au/v/voltaire/dictionary/chapter196.html.

Deists condemn faith as nothing more than the suspension of God-given reason for a subjective, experiential leap into a logical vacuum. Deist Stephen Van Eck put it like this: "When propagating a religion where proof is not available, one that contains logical absurdities, it is essential that the logical processes of the mind be short-circuited."[46] To them, faith masquerades as truth when it is actually nothing more than superstition/myth and is the bait spiritual hucksters in the church use to reel in the gullible to accept "such insane and unreasonable claims and ideas as original sin, walking on water, healing the sick without medical care, splitting the Red Sea, etc."[47] Deists naively believe that there is no objective proof to substantiate the "insane claims" of revealed religions. Of course, we can ask, what objective proof do they have of the contrary?

Although deists are certainly correct when they claim that most spiritual truths and absolutes cannot be proved using the laws of nature, this in no way means that the Bible's claims are completely without evidence or that faith and reason are mortal enemies.[48] After all, it was Jesus who said, "You shall love the LORD your God with all your heart, with all your soul, and with all your *mind*" (Matthew 22:37). Human reason, when illuminated by the Holy Spirit, can aid us in our search for truth. In spite of what deists claim, Christians are not required to "check their minds at the door" when they enter the faith.

Christians would argue that logic exists because God exists, and we are made in the image of this logical and reasoning God (Genesis 1:2–27). This is what makes logic possible for a person in the first place. In a deistic worldview, man is not made in the image of a logical God, so how can the deist really know that logic and reasoning really exist and that they are in a position to be able to do it and use it? Even so, are deists correct when they insist that there is no concrete proof to validate the claims of Scripture?

Consider the historical integrity of the Bible. It is no stretch to say that practically every time an archeologist sinks his spade into the sands of the Middle East, he unearths some new evidence that verifies the historical narrative of Scripture. Millar Burrows, biblical scholar and leading authority on

---

46. Stephen Van Eck, "Dissecting Christianity's Mind-Snaring System," accessed from http://www.deism.com/christianhype.htm.
47. World Union of Deists, www.deism.com.
48. Jason Lisle, "Faith versus Reason," *Answers* magazine, September 13, 2010, https://answersingenesis.org/apologetics/faith-vs-reason/.

the Dead Sea scrolls, put it quite simply: "More than one archaeologist has found his respect for the Bible increased by the experience of excavation in Palestine."[49]

Many are the historians who have eaten a huge piece of humble pie, admitting they were wrong in doubting the historicity of Scripture. As archeologist Dr. Joseph P. Free aptly said:

> Archaeology has confirmed countless passages which have been rejected by critics as unhistorical or contradictory to known facts. . . . Yet archaeological discoveries have shown that these critical charges . . . are wrong and that the Bible is trustworthy in the very statements which have been set aside as untrustworthy. . . . We do not know of any cases where the Bible has been proved wrong.[50]

Renowned archaeologist and Bible scholar William F. Albright said, "There can be no doubt that archaeology has confirmed the substantial historicity of the Old Testament tradition."[51] The famous Jewish Rabbi and archeologist Nelson Glueck echoed:

> It may be state[d] categorically that no archaeological discovery has ever controverted a biblical reference. Scores of archaeological findings have been made which confirm in clear outline or exact detail historical statements in the Bible.[52]

Given that Scripture has been repeatedly confirmed by the historicity test with flying colors (and every other apologetic test that can be employed to scrutinize its message), it is reasonable to say that the Bible and its message, though the most critiqued and attacked literary work in history, remains the most enduring account ever given to man. Compared to all other religions, Christianity, rather than being a "suspension of our God-given reason/ logic," is uniquely a faith accompanied and confirmed by logic and reason.

If deists would only embrace the claims of God's Word, they would discover that rather than taking a huge leap of faith into intellectual darkness,

---

49. Millar Burrows, *What Mean These Stones?* (New York: Meridian Books, 1956), p. 1.
50. Dr. Joseph P. Free, *Archaeology and Bible History* (Wheaton, IL: Scripture Press, 1969), p. 1.
51. William F. Albright, *Archaeology and Religion of Israel* (Baltimore, MD: Johns Hopkins Press, 1953) p. 176.
52. Nelson Glueck, *Rivers in the Desert* (New York: Farrar, Strous and Cudahy, 1959), p. 31.

they would, instead, be taking an illuminating step of faith into the wonderful light of God's truth. The renowned physicist/cosmologist Robert Jastrow put it this way:

> For the scientist who has lived by his faith in the power of reason, the story ends like a bad dream. He has scaled the mountain of ignorance; he is about to conquer the highest peak; as he pulls himself over the final rock, he is greeted by a band of theologians who have been sitting there for centuries.[53]

Summary of Deistic Beliefs

Doctrine	Deistic Teaching
God	A distant deity or force that has no intimate interaction with the world
Authority/ Revelation	Deny any special revelation from God; acknowledge natural law discerned by human reason and practice
Man	A rational being who directs his own destiny
Sin	Varies by individual; generally rejected as any absolute standard
Salvation	Varies by individual; some acknowledge an afterlife
Creation	Generally evolutionary explanations instigated by a deity

---

53. Robert Jastrow, *God and the Astronomers*, chapter 6, "The Religion of Science" (New York: Reader's Library, Inc., 1992), p. 107.

Chapter 13

Satanism

Bodie Hodge

The mere name of it rings out as a blasphemy against God. The conjuring of the name Satan, which literally means "adversary," often strikes fear in the hearts of many believers and unbelievers alike. Why does it strike the nerve of a Christian more than many other religions? I would suggest it is because, unlike other religions where supposed gods Zeus, Odin, and Vishnu are not really real, *Satan is real* and he is cleverly and viciously evil!

Many Christians are unfamiliar with what Satanism is. To a certain degree, this makes sense. For hundreds of years, many things have been labeled "satanic" or "Satanism," yet they are not the same thing. "Satanism" is a form of religion, whereas "satanic" is used to describe things that are characteristic of Satan, cruelty, or viciousness; however, that definition is changing in our modern day to include things that are merely atheistic.

The religion of Satanism has been difficult to document for one simple reason — Satanists were not out in the open but kept their secrets to themselves. Therefore, it has been tough to ascertain their specific doctrines and beliefs. With the dominance of Christianity in the Western world, few Satanists would have shouted from their rooftops, "I am a Satanist."

Collectively, it has been estimated that at the time of this writing, Satanism is a relatively small religion of less than 100,000 people in the world between all groups of those calling themselves Satanists. Precise numbers are hard to come by, due to the high number of unaffiliated Satanists. Regarding Satanism in recent years though, things have changed. Christianity's influence, though still quite strong in the Western world, has declined in politics and education, where the religion of secularism (with its many forms) has dominated. As a result of the culture becoming so relative (a product of secularism), anything seems to go, and this has been a springboard for Satanism to "come out of the closet."

The "coming out" of this religion has made it easier for Christians to refute it. Instead of relying on sketchy accounts of certain Satanists over the past few centuries, Christian apologists are now able to analyze Satanist publications to discover what Satanists believe. And that is what is being done here; taking a few moments to refute some of these Satanist religious forms (two in particular) collectively known as Satanism.

The Two Major Forms of Satanism

In the past, there have been various forms of Satanism, but today two forms have risen to dominance: Theistic (Traditional) Satanism and Modern or Symbolic Satanism (Church of Satan; or LaVeyan Satanism).

Theistic (Traditional) Satanism

In Theistic (Traditional) Satanism, Satan is real and is seen as a deity, in many cases to be worshiped. This is the group that has been known as "devil worshipers" or "Satan worshipers." Most hold to Satan by devotion, and some also partake of rituals. Some hold that magic really does exist (being channeled through Satan and his fallen angels).

There are various forms of traditional Satanism including: *Theistic Satanism* —Church of Azazel, Order of the Nine Angels, and Temple of the Black Light; *Theistic Luciferianism* with its unique differences and goals; and *Satanas* Ophite Cultus Satanas/Our Lady of Endor Coven founded in post-WWII era in Ohio. In a general sense, these variations each hold that Satan or Lucifer is a real being. Goals and specifics vary where some view Satan alone as *the* god, and some hold to pantheism, polytheism, or other popular pagan gods of the past.

Modern or Symbolic Satanism (Church of Satan; or LaVeyan Satanism)

LaVeyan or Modern Satanism was founded in the mid 1960s by Anton LaVey (1930–1997), hence, the name "LaVeyan Satanism." Its roots could be traced to occultist Aleister Crowley (1875–1947) who led a perverse life in opposition to Christian morality. Though Crowley was not seen as a Satanist, his influence set the stage for modern Satanism.[1]

LaVeyan Satanism (the Church of Satan) is a modern form that is massively different from Theistic Satanism. In fact, there is often strife between these two groups where Theistic Satanists often accuse the LaVeyan Satanists of being false Satanists or disguising themselves as Satanists but who are not true Satanists. Likewise, the LaVeyans lash out at Theistic Satanists saying "there is no such thing,"[2] since the LaVeyans hold to an atheistic position (more on this in a moment). LaVeyans are new to the scene of Satanism when compared to Theistic Satanists.

In a nutshell, Modern or LaVeyan Satanism is held in organization by the Church of Satan and adheres to Anton LaVey's teachings in his books *The Satanic Bible, The Satanic Rituals,* and *The Devil's Notebook* as well as other teachings imposed by the Church of Satan. Unlike Theistic Satanism, LaVeyan Satanism is an atheistic religion where people are seen as the absolute authority and their own desires are to be expressed and not inhibited, particularly in the area of lust. This means that even though the Law of God is written on their hearts (Romans 2:15), LaVeyan Satanists are fine with allowing their sin nature to rule supreme without an absolute moral code to rein them in from their sin. Anton LaVey writes in *The Devil's Notebook*, "Atheism wasn't tolerated when scriptural dictates were in fashion and accepted as the Word. Now, thanks to Satanic infiltration, it's safe to say, 'I don't believe in God.' "[3]

Even the Church of Satan website affirms, "Satanists are atheists. We see the universe as being indifferent to us, and so all morals and values are subjective human constructions. Our position is to be self-centered, with ourselves being the most important person (the "God") of our subjective universe, so we are sometimes said to worship ourselves."[4]

Furthermore, the LaVeyan form does not really believe in Satan, God, or any other alleged deities. "Satan" or the "Devil," to the LaVeyan, is likened metaphorically to the drives and desires within a person to do evil and unacceptable

---

1. George Mather and Larry Nichols, *Dictionary of Cults, Sects, Religions and the Occult* (Grand Rapids, MI: Zondervan Publishing House, 1993), p. 242–243.
2. Church of Satan Website, FAQ: Fundamental Beliefs, What is "Theistic Satanism"? Poughkeepsie, NY, 1999–2015, http://churchofsatan.com/faq-fundamental-beliefs.php.
3. Anton LaVey, *The Devil's Notebook*, (Port Townsend, WA: Feral House, 1992), p. 86.
4. Church of Satan Website, FAQ: Fundamental Beliefs, "Why do Satanists Worship the Devil?" Poughkeepsie, NY, 1999–2015, http://churchofsatan.com/faq-fundamental-beliefs.php.

things. For example, their ritual chant of "Hail Satan" doesn't reflect that they believe in Satan, but is merely a chant of rebellion to honor themselves.

Satanism Is Another Form of Man's Religion

In the grand scheme of religions, where there are two overarching religions — God's and not God's — obviously Satanism (in any form) is not God's, but man's. Both Theistic and LaVeyan forms of Satanism are "dedicated to the antithesis of the God of the Christian Bible."[5]

Some people might argue that this religion doesn't come from man, but comes from Satan. However, they need to realize that either way, it came through man and man's rebellious sinful nature to oppose God. For example, LaVeyan Satanism came from Anton LaVey, a man with roots back to another man, Aleister Crowley; hence, it is man's religion.

Theistic Satanism comes from men as well, each to their own individual forms. Sadly, these Theistic Satanists would rather "worship" Satan, a created and fallen entity, than the Creator. This warping of the mind is a result of what God reveals would happen in Romans 1, where people worship the creation rather than the Creator and are thus struck with a debased mind and given over to unnatural lusts, which is exactly what Satanism's fruit is. Consider Romans 1:20–28:[6]

> For since the creation of the world His invisible attributes are clearly seen, being understood by the things that are made, even His eternal power and Godhead, so that they are without excuse, because, although they knew God, they did not glorify Him as God, nor were thankful, but became futile in their thoughts, and their foolish hearts were darkened. Professing to be wise, they became fools, and changed the glory of the incorruptible God into an image made like corruptible man — and birds and four-footed animals and creeping things.
>
> Therefore God also gave them up to uncleanness, in the lusts of their hearts, to dishonor their bodies among themselves, who exchanged the truth of God for the lie, and worshiped and served the creature rather than the Creator, who is blessed forever. Amen.
>
> For this reason God gave them up to vile passions. For even their women exchanged the natural use for what is against

5. Mather and Nichols, *Dictionary of Cults, Sects, Religions and the Occult*, p. 241.
6. Scripture in this chapter is from the New King James Version of the Bible.

nature. Likewise also the men, leaving the natural use of the woman, burned in their lust for one another, men with men committing what is shameful, and receiving in themselves the penalty of their error which was due.

And even as they did not like to retain God in their knowledge, God gave them over to a debased mind, to do those things which are not fitting.

LaVeyan Satanism is exactly this — debased minds following after their own unnatural sexual lusts (it seems that anything goes, except godly marriage!). Theistic Satanism also illustrates Romans 1 where people worship the creation (i.e., Satan) instead of God, the Creator; they exchange God for a lie! Theistic Satanists have replaced Satan as the transcendent eternal being (i.e., God), and demoted the eternal Creator God as the created entity who is causing problems (Isaiah 5:20).

In either form, what these Satanists fail to realize is that when they do these sinful things, it proves they are under judgment by God and are merely waiting for death — the next judgment where an *eternal* punishment awaits them unless they repent and turn to God in the person of Jesus Christ and His death, burial, and Resurrection.

Satanism and Evolution

LaVeyan Satanism and Evolution

The Church of Satan and its atheistic stance is heavily influenced by the materialistic (atheistic/humanistic) view or origins, namely Darwinian evolution. Recall that Satanism is a form of atheism and atheism is a form of humanism. An early priest in the Church of Satan wrote in the introduction to *The Satanic Bible* in 1976:

> Satanism is a blatantly selfish, brutal philosophy. It is based on the belief that human beings are inherently selfish, violent creatures, that life is a Darwinian struggle for survival of the fittest, that only the strong survive and the earth will be ruled by those who fight to win the ceaseless competition that exists in all jungles — including those of urbanized society.[7]

---

7. Anton Szandor LaVey, *The Satanic Bible* (New York: Avon Publishing, 1976), introduction by Burton H. Wolfe, author and priest in the Church of Satan.

This echoes the exact sentiment of Anton LaVey, which is found in *The Satanic Bible*:

> Are we not all predatory animals by instinct? If humans ceased wholly from preying upon each other, could they continue to exist?[8]

> Satan represents man as just another animal, sometimes better, more often worse than those that walk on all-fours, who, because of his "divine spiritual and intellectual development," has become the most vicious animal of all![9]

Clearly, the Church of Satan or Modern Satanism is merely another form of a humanistic, atheistic religion. So any refutations of atheism and humanism can be applied to Modern Satanism. Specific refutations will be discussed later in this chapter.

Theistic Satanism and Evolution

Theistic Satanism is different. Where the Modern Satanists (LaVeyan) hold to atheism and its tenets of naturalism and materialism (prerequisites for evolution), Theistic Satanism is not so limited. Within the various forms of Theistic Satanism, some hold to much of the Bible being true, while others disavow much more. So you can have a broad range of origins accounts such as Satan being seen as "the creator."

Consider also that many Satanists of this vein hold to pagan forms of Satan or polytheism (e.g., Church of Azazel) so the range of origins options of this religion broadens. But based on the research that I've done, it seems evolution holds the most popular form of origins. For example, the Theistic Satanism website commented:

> Unlike the people in Bible times, scientists today do know quite a bit about the likely evolution of both the human species in particular and the Earth in general. Most likely, our species came into existence through natural evolution. Perhaps one or more gods had a hand in the evolution of humans now and then,

---

8. Ibid., p. 25.
9. Ibid., p. 33, reiterated: Church of Satan Website, The Nine Satanic Statements, http://churchofsatan.com/nine-satanic-statements.php.

too, at one or more times during the many millions of years that life has existed on this Earth.[10]

Evolution is a false philosophy that is often disguised as science. True science is based on repeatable observations. Evolution, big bang (cosmic evolution), and long ages (like millions and billions of years, which is geologic evolution) have neither been observed nor repeated. Clearly, evolution is not good science but rather an embarrassing view of origins. So having Theistic Satanists jump on board with the false view, and trying to tack Satan or other "gods" as the director of evolution is mere story-telling.

Satanism Is Not Particularly Special to Satan

One might think that Satanism is Satan's favorite religion as he receives "worship" by some, but I would suggest that it is merely one of many religions that Satan uses to distract people from the truth. You see, all false religions are religions that Satan uses to deceive people to miss the truth of biblical Christianity in Jesus Christ. Satan's goal is not necessarily for people to follow him; it is to keep them from following the Bible and particularly the Jesus Christ of Scripture. Keep in mind that Satan is fine if you follow Jesus, as long it is not the Jesus Christ of Scripture. Satan is fine with people following the Jesus of Islam (merely a prophet) or the Jesus of Mormonism (one of many people who became gods) or the Jesus of Jehovah's Witnesses (the created archangel Michael) and so on. So any religion that deviates from the Christ of Scripture and the 66 books of God's Word is a favorite of Satan.

Sadly, if Satan worshipers were aware that Satanism isn't necessarily that special to Satan, they might realize they are wasting their time, as their worship is really no different from someone worshiping a rock! Even Satan would be happy with that, as long they were not worshiping the Lord Jesus Christ.

For those who may entertain the idea of worshiping Satan so that they too may have a higher position in hell (favoritism), this is absurd. Satan has no power in hell, but will also be punished for all eternity in hell. Hell is likened to a fire in the Bible. One person in a fire is not ruling the other people in a fire. Sadly, I've heard people say, "I *want* to go to hell." Of course, their

---

10. Diane Vera, "The Here-and-Now Principle in Theology," Theistic Satan Website, 2004, http://theisticsatanism.com/CoAz/belief/here-now.html.

actions betray this. We don't observe these same people casting themselves into a fire to burn themselves up!

Refutations

How Do You Know about Satan and the Spiritual World?

One popular Theistic Satanism group, the Church of Azazel, states about knowledge (epistemology):

> What can we humans possibly know about the spirit world? Not much. And it is all too easy for us humans to deceive ourselves. We humans cannot really know the spirit world. At best, we can make educated guesses, based on our own and other people's spiritual and paranormal experiences, if any, and based on our knowledge of the history of religion and current religious trends.[11]

From their own viewpoint, they really can't know anything about the spirit world. But it is worse than that. They can't know *anything*. Theistic Satanists can't know that Satan exists; and yet as religious people, they are still devoted to a being that they can't know exists. It is purely arbitrary. Even knowledge itself breaks down at a fundamental level in this religion. They merely appeal to their own thoughts and whims (mere opinions). It is no different from a person arbitrarily saying, "I believe 3+7=8"! They obviously can't know it, but blindly believe it anyway.

Since people are not made in "Satan's image," and there is no inerrant personal revelation from an "all-knowing" Satan to mankind, people can't even be sure that their senses are reliable because nothing can be known about this Satan character. So Satanists can't even know that what we see, feel, smell, taste, and hear is actually real.

Consider also that the laws of nature might change tomorrow. Perhaps in the Satanic view, gravity might change tomorrow. After all, there is no revelation from an "all-knowing" Satan who knows the future that promised to uphold the world in the same fashion each day like the God of the Bible did (e.g., Genesis 8:22, etc.).

As for LaVeyan Satanists, how can they know anything either? They are atheists, which are *materialistic* by their very nature. In other words,

---

11. Diane Vera, "Epistemology: What Can We Know about the Spirit World, and on What Basis?" Theistic Satanism website, 2010, http://theisticsatanism.com/CoAz/belief/epistemology.html.

in atheism, only material things exist — nothing immaterial. But for that to be the case, then knowledge, which is not material, can't exist in their religion. So ultimately nothing can be known, which defeats the purpose of everything the LaVeyans have ever said.

Logic, reason, love, truth, or happiness are not material either. So why did LaVey write books or the Church of Satan run a website when their religion dictates that knowledge, logic, and reason can't exist? The only way they could do it is *by betraying the religion they claim to follow* because it cannot make sense of truth, logic, and knowledge. Neither should they involve themselves in anything that utilizes reason or logic or truth because such things are meaningless in their religion.

Refutations of False Nativities

During the Christmas season of 2014, The Satanic Temple (of the New York-based Church of Satan) did a public display in Florida to counter Christian nativity scenes. In it, Satan was falling from heaven into flames. On the display, it said, "Happy Holidays from The Satanic Temple" and quoted Isaiah where Satan (Lucifer, "Son of the Morning") fell from Heaven (Isaiah 14:12).

I found it quite interesting that they would say "happy," since their religion has nothing to do with happiness. Happiness is not material, so it is inconsistent for followers of a materialistic religion like this to discuss happiness. They say "holidays" (i.e., holy days), yet there is nothing holy in Satanism. Furthermore, apparently they felt they didn't have anything within their own religion to display so they had to borrow from the Bible. For those who claim to think independently, it is sad that they had to borrow from God's Word when they quoted Isaiah. Plus their Scripture quoting is very arbitrary, since they studiously avoid Revelation 20:10, which foretells Satan's final defeat.

Another false nativity was placed by Satanists (The Satanic Temple) in Detroit that had a snake with a book, a cross that had an inverted star in a circle (pentacle), and dead animal image affixed in the star. The display said, "The greatest gift is knowledge." As we learned in the previous section, Satanists have no basis for knowledge. These Satanists must give up their atheistic view and grab hold of the Christian worldview to even make sense of knowledge.

Furthermore, atheistic Satanists once again had to borrow from the Bible for the cross, snake (Genesis 3), and star (Numbers 24:17) used in their display. They had to borrow from Christianity in order to criticize Christianity!

Borrowing from the Bible: Marriage in Satanism

Believe it or not, even Anton LaVey got married at one point. But the origin of marriage comes from a literal Genesis where God created the first man (Adam) and first woman (Eve) in a perfect world. Today there are marital problems as well as sin and death in the world, thanks to Satan and the first couple's sin. But marriage comes out of a literal Genesis, and our Lord Jesus Christ defended this in Matthew 19 and Mark 10.

So in other religions, like Satanism, why get married? Getting married is a denial of one's own religion and openly affirms Genesis is true since it is a biblical doctrine. Each form of Satanism adheres, for the most part, to evolutionary origins, not a literal Genesis. So there is no need to get married. Mice don't wake up and say, "Let's get married." Marriage is strictly a Christian institution (instituted by Christ in the Garden of Eden), and yet religions all over the world have borrowed it. Satanism is no different.

In the Theistic Satanism perspective, they can't know anything about the spiritual world, so how can they know marriage exists? In the LaVeyan form, which is atheistic, immaterial institutions like marriage cannot exist. Again, they must give up their religion to make sense of marriage or love or happiness.

Inconsistency and Arbitrariness

Inconsistency

The Church of Satan makes it clear that they view people (i.e., themselves) as their own god and there is no other "god" in their view. "In Satanism each individual is his or her own god — there is no room for any other god and that includes Satan, Lucifer, Cthulhu, or whatever other name one might select or take from history or fiction."[12]

But then the Church of Satan goes on to give certain rules to its members such as: "Do not take that which does not belong to you."[13] "Do not

12. Church of Satan Website, FAQ: Fundamental Beliefs, "What is 'Theistic Satanism'?" Poughkeepsie, NY, 1999–2015, http://churchofsatan.com/faq-fundamental-beliefs.php.
13. Anton LaVey, "The Eleven Satanic Rules of the Earth," 1967, http://churchofsatan.com/eleven-rules-of-earth.php.

harm little children."[14] "Do not kill non-human animals unless you are attacked or for your food."[15] Naturally, this is inconsistent because if you are your own god and there is no other god, then why do they have rule-givers who have god-like status above you to make rules and impose them on you? If you are your own god, then you set your own rules. If you are your own god and there are no others, then other Satanists cannot be a "god" either and are not in any position to set authoritative rules over you.

Satan (yes, the biblical one who exists) is indeed clever. Do you realize that he has convinced these people they are their own "god"? The President of Puritan Reformed Theological Seminary Dr. Joel Beeke writes in the context of Satan's skill at matching his suggestions with our own corrupt reason, "Satan is a master at suggesting that we believe what we want to believe rather than believe the truth."[16]

In Satanism, people are seen as their own gods following their own evil desires. And yet, the atheistic Satanists still don't realize they have been deceived. This has been Satan's tactic since sin in Genesis 3 to convince people they can become their own "god" and thus neglect God's Word.

Interestingly, there is another inconsistency. In 1967, Anton LaVey wrote in *The Eleven Satanic Rules of the Earth*: "Do not give opinions or advice unless you are asked."[17] Yet LaVey was never asked for his opinion on Christianity by Christians. However, he openly gives it. So, by his own standard, he has refuted himself. No one asked for the Satanists' opinion at nativity scenes, and yet they gave it and betrayed their own inconsistent rules.

Another blatant inconsistency is when the Church of Satan states: "The Church of Satan does not condone illegal activities. If the use of certain drugs is illegal in your country of residence, they are just that: illegal."[18] Yet they openly advocated illegal activities such as homosexuality and adultery since 1966 which *was* illegal during much of that time. They openly admit this:

---

14. Ibid.
15. Ibid.
16. Joel Beeke, *Striving Against Satan* (Bryntirion, Bridgend, Wales, UK: Bryntirion Press, 2006), p. 72.
17. LaVey, "The Eleven Satanic Rules of the Earth."
18. The Church of Satan's Policy on Drug Abuse, Poughkeepsie, NY, 1999–2015, http://churchofsatan.com/policy-on-drug-abuse.php.

> We fully accept all forms of human sexual expression between consenting adults. The Church of Satan has always accepted gay, lesbian and bisexual members since its beginning in 1966.[19]

As previously seen, Theistic Satanism has no basis to know anything (epistemology), so for them to claim to know anything would be self-refuting due to its inconsistency. One popular independent Theistic Satanist, writing to Satanists who have left Christianity, advises:

> Learn the value of independent thinking, and introspection. Be inquisitive and don't accept everything at face value. These practices will help you to develop *independent thinking*, a method of living that I believe is necessary for experiencing life as a Satanist. You will wonder if what you have left behind, was the "real truth." In reality, there are no absolute truths in religion because there are so many beliefs and ideals that to accept one as an absolute truth is to be blind to the reality that ALL religions sanctimoniously claim to be the truth.[20]

There are a few glaring inconsistencies here. The first is that it is quite ironic for someone to be an independent thinker just because *someone else* says so. It defeats the purpose. The consistent independent thinker should reject someone telling him to be an independent thinker. Otherwise, it is a contradiction. Furthermore, when this Satanist writes, "Be inquisitive and don't accept everything at face value," then you shouldn't accept this Satanist's words either, for they are self-refuting.

Next are the claims of truth. Satanists are suppressing the truth in unrighteousness, as God said in Romans 1. There is really only one way to suppress the truth and that is to deny the truth and particularly its existence. This is precisely what this Satanist has done. She claims truth doesn't really exist when she blatantly states, ". . . there are no absolute truths in religion." This becomes a huge problem because she is stating as absolute truth that there are no absolute truths, which is a contradiction.

---

19. The Church of Satan Website, F.A.Q. Sexuality, Poughkeepsie, NY, 1999–2015, http://churchofsatan.com/faq-sexuality.php.
20. Venus Satanas (self-proclaimed name), Spiritual Satanist Website, "My Advice on Leaving Christianity," 2004, http://www.spiritualsatanist.com/articles/satan/exchristian.html.

Arbitrariness

Both Theistic Satanism and Modern Satanism (Church of Satan) hold to man's ideas about reality being the supreme authority. Hence, they are opinions, and thus, they are arbitrary. Arbitrariness is devastating for the *foundation* of a belief system. Mere human opinions show the bankruptcy of such a worldview at its very start.

Concluding Remarks

Satanism, in either form discussed here, is simply united in one purpose: to oppose God's religion as authoritative.[21] Satanists must borrow doctrines from the Bible to make sense of the world, all the while denying the God who owns them.

Yet so often Theistic Satanists and LaVeyan Satanists use terms like Satan, hell, devil, Lucifer, church, and temple, which ultimately have no meaning in their religion. But why? Did you ever stop to think why they spend so much time utilizing Christian terms and symbols (the upside-down cross of Peter,[22] a star, snake, and so on)? Because deep down they know the true religion is biblical Christianity. It is by their sin nature that they oppose Christianity, which is clearly their main target. Let's be frank here — Satanists don't run around chanting "Hail *Care Bears*" or have "The Temple of the Easter Bunny." They have chosen Satan to show their opposition to Jesus Christ.

In either Atheistic or Theistic Satanism, there is no absolute God, no ultimate right or wrong, and no salvation. Both religious forms lead nowhere. There is no hope and one is merely part of an illusionary evolutionary fairy tale that leads to utter meaninglessness. Any form that holds to Satan being real is purely arbitrary, unless they borrow that from the Bible.

---

21. The Church of Satan Website writes: "Anton Szandor LaVey never expected to be the founder of a new religion, but he saw a need for something publicly opposing the stagnation of Christianity, and knew that if he didn't do it, someone else, probably less qualified, would." Blanche Barton, Church of Satan website, Church of Satan History: Modern Prometheus, Poughkeepsie, NY, 2003, http://churchofsatan.com/cos-modern-prometheus.php. The Theistic Satanism Website also actively opposes Christianity as a requirement for members in Diane Vera, "Church of Azazel: Who We Are and How to Join," Theistic Satanism website, accessed January 8, 2015, http://theisticsatanism.com/CoAz/who.html.

22. Church fathers affirmed that Peter was crucified upside-down. This symbol has been part of the church for nearly 2,000 years.

Yes, There Is Hope . . . But Not in the Name of Satan

But there is hope. There have been many Christians saved out of Satanism. If you know people involved in Satanism, be praying that the Lord opens them up to salvation in Jesus Christ and further opens their hearts to the truth. Second Timothy 2:24–26 says:

> And a servant of the Lord must not quarrel but be gentle to all, able to teach, patient, in humility correcting those who are in opposition, if God perhaps will grant them repentance, so that they may know the truth, and that they may come to their senses and escape the snare of the devil, having been taken captive by him to do his will.

Although this chapter is designed for Christians, there may be some who have had satanic tendencies who are reading this. If you have been involved or dabbled in Satanism, it is time to stop running and realize that God does exist, and you know this in your heart of hearts (Romans 1). Logic, truth, reason, love, and knowledge also exist, which cannot in an atheistic and materialistic worldview (e.g., the Church of Satan). Knowledge, even about the spiritual and Satan, can be known (unlike Theistic Satanism or LaVeyan Satanism), because an all-knowing God made us in His Image and He has revealed what is sufficient to know Him and about spiritual things in His Inerrant Word.

I took note in this research that one of the main reasons Satanists deny God and Jesus Christ is that they see the world and the people in it as imperfect and broken, and they do not want to even consider that a God who may have made the world and people this way. Instead of finding out more about God and why the world and people are this way, they just reject Him outright and go for atheism (the popular religion of the day) or Satan (God's fallen adversary) or anything else they think can justify the world as it is.

But let's address this simple misconception. Originally, God made the world perfect (Deuteronomy 32:4) and very good (Genesis 1:31). There was no sin, bad things, suffering, anguish, brokenness, disasters, death, and so on. But Satan, who was also created perfect, sinned of his own accord with his pride to try to rise above God.[23] Hence, his fall into sin. He immediately went after mankind. He cleverly used a serpent (as a pawn) to

---

23. Bodie Hodge, *The Fall of Satan* (Green Forest, AR: Master Books, 2011), p. 27–28.

deceive mankind to sin, resulting in death, suffering, and pain entering the creation. This is the world in which we now live.

We are all fallen beings subject to a taste of punishment from God for sin. This world, full of sin and death, became a fallen domain, or as we say, "Satan's kingdom." A perfect God must punish sin. If not, He would not be perfectly just, since we are all sinners (Romans 3:23). We deserve eternal punishment. So, not only do we experience pain, death, and suffering on earth, we should be eternally punished after we die. But God made a way of escape because He loved us. Jesus Christ, who is God, came in the flesh to become one of us (also remaining 100 percent God). As a man, He lived a perfect life. (Romans 8:3). When Christ was offered up as a sacrifice by the Jews (Matthew 27:25; John 19:15; Acts 2:23, 3:13–15, 5:30, 7:52, 10:39), the Infinite Son of God (Jesus Christ, who is the second person of the one eternal triune God) took the infinite punishment that we deserve by the infinite Father (first person of the one triune God), which satisfied the wrath of God upon sin. The debt was paid entirely.

But Christ, our great God and Savior, did not remain in the grave but had the power to take up His life again to prove that salvation was possible unto eternal life (John 10:17; Acts 10:40; 1 Corinthians 15:11–24). So those who repent of their sin (Acts 17:30), no matter how many sins they have committed, and receive Christ (Colossians 2:6) and His Resurrection (Romans 10:9) will be saved for the new heavens and new earth when this sin-cursed world is finally done away with (Revelation 21–22).

And with salvation possible, the gospel (good news of Jesus Christ) is going forward. Pastor Warren Wiersbe wrote:

> Christ invaded Satan's kingdom when he came to this earth as a man. Satan, of course, knew that he was coming, and he did all in his power to prevent it. Satan even tried to kill Jesus after he was born. When he invaded Satan's kingdom, Christ also overcame Satan's power. "The strong man" came face-to-face with One who is stronger! In his life, death, and Resurrection, Jesus Christ has completely overcome Satan's power. Today he is claiming the spoils. He is rescuing sinners from Satan's dominion and then using those changed lives to defeat Satan's forces.[24]

---

24. Warren Wiersbe, *The Strategy of Satan* (Carol Stream, IL: Tyndale House Publishers, Inc., 1979), p. 149.

For those who may have been involved in Satanism, you and you alone must receive Christ to be saved; I cannot do it for you, and neither can anyone else. Please consider the claims of our Lord and Savior Jesus Christ who alone has all power and authority (Matthew 28:18):

> Therefore submit to God. Resist the devil and he will flee from you (James 4:7).

Summary of Satanist Beliefs

Doctrine	Satanist Teaching
God	Views vary, but some are atheists and others view Satan as a god
Authority/ Revelation	The Bible is rejected as a revelation from God, but there is no formal revelation from Satan. Many would look to writings of various leaders like Anton LaVey as instructive.
Man	Atheistic Satanists view man as an animal with primal urges that should be followed; Theistic Satanists have varying views but generally deny the biblical view of man as a sinner in need of redemption.
Sin	Relativistic views of right and wrong based on the individual's beliefs
Salvation	There is no formal concept of an afterlife in most versions of Satanism, though some would believe in the continuation of life after death. Their unbiblical view of man does not require salvation from sin.
Creation	Most would believe in evolutionary views from the big bang to biological evolution, while some Theistic Satanists would assert that Satan or other gods were involved in the evolutionary process or see Satan as the creator.

Chapter 14

Freemasonry

Ryan McClay

The startled gathering raised their heads as the sharp rap of heels cut through the solemnness of the funeral home. Perfectly silent other than their walking, 16 men entered and marched to the front of the room. Each bearing a sprig of acacia and wearing white aprons over their black suits, they passed by and carefully placed the evergreen on the casket as they lined up along it. After all were in position, they performed a sharply executed salute, crossing both arms across their breast and in the process striking their shoulders. Then raising their hands above their heads with palms to the front, they let them fall down to the thighs.[1]

Such an experience is often the only exposure most people have to the religion of Freemasonry. Free Masons, Freemasons, or simply "the Masons" are a secretive organization that goes far beyond fraternal characteristics of social, professional, or honorary principles. Not to be confused with the building trade of a stone mason or a brick mason, Freemasonry is an elaborate, allegorical religion steeped in mystery. Given the secret nature of the religion and the infrequent, intriguing public displays, it is not surprising

---

1. Adapted from personal experiences and Grand Lodge of Iowa Handbook for Masonic Memorial Services, retrieved from http://grandlodgeofiowa.org/docs/ObituaryRites/MasonicMemorialHandbook.pdf.

that public perception of Freemasonry ranges widely from harmless benevolence to cautious suspicion to outright fear.

These perceptions have resulted in a voluminous amount of both "for" and "against" papers, books, articles, blogs, and websites. This chapter will not attempt to summarize or comment on these works, but for those interested in further study, be aware that these perceptions often color the material presented in a way that one must be cautious when evaluating various claims. The best way to evaluate any religion or claim is under the scrutiny of the lens of Scripture.

In order to better understand Freemasonry, a definition is in order, and what better source than Freemasonry itself. On page 26 of the Heirloom Masonic Bible — Master Reference Edition, "Freemasonry has been well defined as, 'A peculiar system of morality veiled in allegory and illustrated by symbols.' "[2] Since allegories by definition convey abstract or spiritual meanings through concrete or material forms, the exploration of Freemasonry must be handled with the knowledge that it has allegory as its basis.

Many religions use symbol and allegory, but the Freemasonry borrows from Christianity and specifically the Old Testament for much of its apologue. However, the fact that Freemasonry is a non-Christian religion becomes evident when carefully examined.

Status as Religion

Some may object that Freemasonry is not actually a religion, but is a harmless, benevolent fraternal organization. In order to evaluate that objection, consider the following definition of a religion:

> A set of beliefs concerning the cause, nature, and purpose of the universe, especially when considered as the creation of a super-human agency or agencies, usually involving devotional and ritual observances, and often containing a moral code governing the conduct of human affairs.[3]

We've already seen that Freemasonry defines itself as a system of morality and have seen evidence of its ritual nature in the funeral right, and more of the ritual will be explored later in this chapter. That, in and of itself, does not make Freemasonry a religion — after all, many non-religious social groups

2. http://www.emfj.org/dbr.htm.
3. http://dictionary.reference.com/browse/religion.

participate in funeral processes and have their own rituals and formality. However, Freemasonry goes much further. Consider the following statement one might hear in the liturgy that accompanies the ritual in the funeral:

> As Masons we put our trust in a Higher Power, a Supreme Being whom we call God, and we believe that He gives us each a task to do and looks down upon us, his children. We call ourselves builders because each one of us is trying to build his own spiritual temple of character, and because we believe that each one of us may have some little part in the building of that larger temple which is the sum of all human achievement, that great structure rising slowly through the ages according to the plans drawn by the Great Architect of the Universe on his Trestle-board, a temple whose foundations were laid in the beginning of time, and which will last through eternity — the great plan of the Supreme Builder of the Universe.[4]

One would hardly be able to read these statements without concluding that the Masonic funeral right fully expresses the nature of Freemasonry as a religion. It speaks of the natural ("human achievement") and supernatural ("a Supreme Being"), devotion ("a temple," "the Great Architect of the Universe"), and governance ("the building of that larger temple").

However, even with the components of a religion being present, some may argue that it still lacks some of the other characteristics of a religion. For instance, UCLA History Professor Margaret Jacob made this statement on CBS News:

> "Freemasonry is not a religion. Freemasonry has the look of a religion," said Jacob. "You think of religion as ritual, there's also this ritual element. But there are no priests, there are no ministers, there are no rabbis, there's no system of clergy of any sort. Everybody's their own thinker."[5]

The assertion by Professor Jacob is that somehow the presence of clergy is the defining nature of religion. Even if that were the case, Jacob's claim that Freemasonry does not have structure is simply not true. However, the key item

---

4. Grand Lodge Of Iowa A.F. & A.M. Masonic Memorial Handbook, p. 29.
5. http://www.cbsnews.com/news/9-things-you-didnt-know-about-freemasonry/.

in this statement is that "Everybody's their own thinker." This gives us a hint as to the true nature of Freemasonry and its relationship with another religion — that of humanism, which will be discussed in greater detail later in the book series.

One additional characteristic of a religion is its use of symbols. Freemasonry makes substantial use of symbols, and its members often have public display of these symbols either in the form of a ring, license plate, or other regalia. The square and the compass often combined with the letter G is the universal emblem of Freemasonry.

Freemason square and compass

The use of these symbols will be explored later in this chapter.

Despite all of this, many would still argue that Freemasonry is not a religion. Their rebuttal would be that structure, professed belief in a higher being, symbolism, and ritual do not make a religion and by that definition organizations such as the Boy Scouts of America are a religion. Furthermore, the argument points to other characteristics of a religion supposedly missing from Freemasonry: having a priesthood, teaching theology, ordaining clergy, defining sin and salvation (which Freemasonry does anyway), performing sacraments, publishing or specifying a holy book, or describing or defining the Deity. Of course, the religion of atheism doesn't have this either! But this type of rebuttal is a logical fallacy as it attempts to define religion in solely monotheistic characteristics common to a few religions such as Christianity or Islam and then attempts to show how Freemasonry does not fit that model. By comparing to such a specific example, the argument ignores addressing the actual practices of Freemasonry that are supposed to be secret and can't be talked about openly anyway.

In fact, if comparison is the metric for the definition of religion, Freemasonry has many similarities to the mystery religions associated with the Greco-Roman world. Those religions have the common characteristics of secrecy in their rituals and initiation of members. Freemasonry shares many similar characteristics with Rosicrucianism, another esoteric, secret society religion that arose out of the same school of thought as those ancient mystery religions.

Yes, Freemasonry is much more than a fraternal, social organization. In some of its own documents, it declares that it is not merely a social organization. The Masonic Declaration of Principles from the 1940s states, "It is a social organization *only so far as* it furnished additional inducement that men may forgather in numbers, thereby providing more material for its primary work of education, of worship, and of charity."[6] The education referred to is education in the religion. Worship would hardly be mentioned if Freemasonry wasn't religion, and charity doesn't make sense without the moral code ostensibly underlying the entire structure. Freemasonry is indeed a religion, but many of its own adherents may not realize that fact . . . after all, many Christians have even joined!

History, Structure, and Distribution

As with many religions, Freemasonry has a vague history along with its various sects and splinter groups. One undeniable fact is that it originated in Western Europe and was formalized in London in the early 18th century. Some histories of Freemasonry profess ties back to stonemason guilds of the Middle Ages, with one possible written reference in the late 14th century.[7] The closest thing to a "founding date" would be the year 1717 where the keeping of records became more formal with the formation of the first Grand Lodge in London, England,[8] although other public documents from the 1600s clearly reference (and often condemn) Freemasonry practices.

Freemasonry is organized in regional groups called "Lodges." A Masonic Lodge is analogous to a local Christian congregation and does not represent a physical building, but often has a physical building where adherents gather. Each Lodge has its own self-determined operating principles. Larger organizational structures called Grand Lodges represent amalgamations of the smaller Lodges and adapt standards by which all Lodges in the Grand Lodge operate albeit with local variations permitted.

Masonic Lodges in the Anglo-American tradition require a monotheistic belief in a "supreme being."[9] Despite the presence of the Bible in many Masonic Lodges, this does not necessarily mean that this "supreme being" is the God of the Bible. In fact, Masons in a given Lodge likely do not believe

---

6. Emphasis mine. Retrieved from http://masonicgenealogy.com/MediaWiki/index.php?title=GMMJohnson#DECLARATION_OF_PRINCIPLES.
7. The Regius Poem or Halliwell Manuscript c. 1390 seems to indicate the structure of Freemasonry. History prior to that is at best circumstantial.
8. http://www.masonicsourcebook.com/grand_lodge_of_england.htm.
9. This is not true of "Continental Freemasonry," the liberal split of the religion based in France with adherents largely in mainland Europe and Latin America.

in the same "supreme being." Freemasonry teaches that there is one God and men of all religions worship that one God using a variety of different names. In a Masonic Lodge, Masons join in corporate prayer to the Great (or Supreme) Architect of the Universe (GAOTU) to refer to the "supreme being." However, when a Mason prays, he is praying to his own view of that "supreme being" individually, but within the corporate prayer. This is consistent with a deist philosophy, but not a Christian one.

Within each Lodge, a type of clergy and governance does indeed exist. There are usually at least eight offices in each Lodge, with several others possible depending on the local jurisdiction.[10] Titles such as Deacon and Warden are progressive toward the highest office in a Lodge — the Worshipful Master. That role is analogous to the Chief Executive Officer (CEO) of a corporation rather than a spiritual leader, but the role does come with its own shepherding responsibilities. The leadership manages the affairs of a Lodge and is key in the instruction and advancement of its members through a series known as "degrees."

The degree of a Mason determines his rights and standing in a Lodge — also known as a Blue Lodge. There are three basic degrees through which an adherent progresses: Entered Apprentice, Fellowcraft, and Master Mason. Attainment of a degree marks advancement through the Masonic brotherhood. All Masonic Lodges have these three degrees in common. There are, however, degrees above Master Mason, but what those degrees are and represent will vary from region to region. These are often, but not always, referred to as "Rites" and have degrees that proceed from the fourth degree up to the 33rd degree and higher.[11] These degrees are often awarded by associated, but separate, Masonic bodies a Master Mason can join.

Another characteristic of this base level of Freemasonry or Blue Lodge Freemasonry is that it is limited to men only and is often referred to as a brotherhood.[12] There are several groups that are not Free Masons per se, but are appended or offshoot organizations. The Order of the Eastern Star and the Rainbow Girls are female-oriented groups affiliated with Freemasonry, for example. Another well-known all-male group is the Shriners, known for their children's hospitals, whose members must be a Free Mason.

---

10. http://en.wikipedia.org/wiki/Masonic_Lodge_Officers.
11. Higher degrees do not necessarily represent "rank" as they do in the 3 Blue Lodge degrees.
12. Some female-oriented lodges do exist in the Continental form of Freemasonry.

Although Freemasonry has its strongest presence in the British Isles and the United States, it is a global religion with over four million participants.[13] Given its London roots, it is not surprising that it is most prevalent in countries of the British Empire — most of North/South America, Western Europe, India, Australia, and sub-saharan Africa. It does not have a strong presence in Southeast Asia, with none in China.

Freemasonry arose in the early 1700s and spread rapidly across Europe. And although there is alignment with the language and terminology of Christianity, the Catholic Church and distrustful political leaders resisted its growth. *In eminenti apostolatus specula* was a papal bull issued by Pope Clement XII on April 28, 1738, banning Catholics from becoming Freemasons. As for Masonic involvement in the public square, a number of theories have emerged linking Freemasonry to major events such as the French Revolution. Whether or not these links are valid, they have occasionally led to restrictions on joining Freemasonry by other religious bodies or governments.

Fundamentally, there is no denying the philanthropic nature of Freemasonry and its associated organizations. Given its distributed nature, it is difficult to quantify the amount and nature of charitable support. The Shriner's Hospitals are a good example of public display of charity. There are two forms of Freemasonry charity: aid to non-Masons and mutual aid for fellow Masons. For example, one of the promoted benefits to new recruits is the care for a widow or orphans of a deceased Mason. These incentives, and the lack of government-sponsored social security in the 18th century, may have contributed to its rapid growth. These member benefits may extend into various societal benefits such as preference in hiring or promotion, lenience in legal issues, and similar things where a Freemason may be in a position of influence.

As Freemasonry has grown and spread, differences have developed. Although the three degrees of the Blue Lodge are common, several different Rites or advancement paths have developed. While difficult to quantify, there may have been over 100 Rites, and at least 1,500 Degrees or grades connected directly and indirectly with Freemasonry.[14] For example, The Ancient and Accepted Scottish Rite bends its efforts toward advancing individual freedoms and citizenship rights as well as responsibilities. On the other hand, York Rite Masonry, in its concluding Degrees or Orders of the Knights Templar, is said

13. http://www.msana.com/historyfm.asp.
14. http://www.masonicdictionary.com/rites.html.

to be a Christian organization.[15] Adding to these complexities, there are two key forms of Freemasonry — the Anglo-American Form that requires belief in a supreme being and the Continental Form that has no such requirement, and thus can include atheists. The Continental Form often takes a more liberal stand on social issues such as same-sex "marriages," but the Anglo-American Form is the most widely adopted and the primary subject of this chapter.

Authority

The diversity and complexity of Freemasonry is not surprising given that it is fundamentally a form of deistic humanism. While this may seem to be an oxymoron, it does capture the fundamental essence of Freemasonry. Freemason theology could be summed up as belief in a "supreme being" combined with layered allegories in which each adherent finds their own "truth." It is deistic in its belief in an agnostic supreme being, and humanistic in its belief that mankind is ultimately the source of truth. This is best captured in the following quote:

> In his private petitions a man may petition God or Jehovah, Allah or Buddha, Mohammed or Jesus; he may call upon the God of Israel or the First Great Cause. In the Masonic Lodge he hears petition to the Great Architect of the Universe, finding his own deity under that name. A hundred paths may wind upward around a mountain; at the top they meet.[16]

With such a wide possibility for interpretation of the practices and rituals in Freemasonry, it is not unusual that this diversity should exist and possibly extend to self-worship, demon or Satan worship, nature worship, or any other form of deity that one would like to ascribe.[17] This is not to say that all or even a majority of Free Masons seek their truth in one of these ways, but it is to point out that fundamentally the *primary* source of truth in Freemasonry is the individual and his interpretation of his religious experience.

---

15. http://srjarchives.tripod.com/1997-09/Duncan.htm.

16. Carl H. Claudy, *Introduction to Freemasonry* (Washington, DC: The Temple Publishers, c1931), p. 38.

17. One may attempt to argue that these are not "supreme beings," but if an individual accepts the tenets of Freemasonry as defining one's own truth, then why could these not be supreme beings?

The basis for much of the allegory and symbolism in Freemasonry comes from the Old Testament account of the building of Solomon's Temple. The central figure in Masonic allegory is Hiram Abiff, purported Grand Master at the temple project. Note, while there are several mentions of Hiram (or Huram) in the Old Testament, none precisely matches that of the allegorical Hiram Abiff (also Abif, Abi-ff, or Abiv among others). One such biblical reference is found in 2 Chronicles.[18]

> And now I have sent a skillful man, endowed with understanding, Huram my master *craftsman* (the son of a woman of the daughters of Dan, and his father was a man of Tyre), skilled to work in gold and silver, bronze and iron, stone and wood, purple and blue, fine linen and crimson, and to make any engraving and to accomplish any plan which may be given to him, with your skillful men and with the skillful men of my lord David your father (2 Chronicles 2:13–14).

While there may be a historical basis for the builder of Solomon's Temple, all connection to actual history and biblical teaching ends there.

To summarize the basic allegory, Hiram Abiff went to visit the Temple. Entering the Temple from the West, Hiram — himself a Master Mason — was accosted by three Fellowcrafts. These Fellowcrafts wanted the secrets (or secret word) of a Master Mason. Hiram attempted to leave, each time attempting a different side of the Temple, going from South, back to West, and finally to the East and refused the Fellowcrafts who stopped him at each turn. The first two times he was wounded, but the third time he was killed by the assailant. The murderers fled after burying the body, but it was found after a search. In the end the assailants were found by searchers who overheard their lamentations coming in the form, "I wish that I had been killed in *such and such a manner*, rather than that I had been the cause of the death of our Master Hiram." The murderers were brought to Jerusalem and before Solomon, who sentenced them according to the punishments they had wished for themselves. The allegory concludes with Hiram interred in the Temple with great ceremony.[19]

---

18. Scriptures in this chapter are from the New King James Version of the Bible.
19. Many details and variations are omitted here for brevity. An interesting discussion of the variations is *The Evolution of the Hiramic Legend in England and France* by Joannes A.M. Snoek, himself a 32 degree mason (http://204.3.136.66/web/heredom-files/volume11/snoek.pdf).

In addition to the allegory above, the Blue Lodge draws allegorical symbolism from aspects of stonemasonry in their Lodge proceedings. Participants don aprons and participate in dialogue with references to the compass, square, gauge, plumb, and level to convey moral messages symbolically. The Entered Apprentice must go through a ceremony where he is led blindfolded around the Lodge ostensibly following the path of Hiram Abiff. During the Fellowcraft ceremony, initiates are taken into a room said to represent one of the chambers in Solomon's temple and the Master Mason's degree revolves around the Hiram Abiff allegory itself.

Advanced degrees may expand and expound on all of the above. For example, *Morals and Dogma* was published in 1872 by Alexander Pike of the Scottish Rite as an extensive commentary of the minutia of Masonic ritual. While an esoteric work, it does contain an emphasis on religious and cultural tolerance common to the thinking of his day. Philosophically, it expounded upon the idea that the root of all religion was the same. Concepts from ancient Egypt, Greece, and Phoenicia are linked with Buddhist, Hindu, Jewish, Islamic, and Christian doctrines to show the common traits in detail. Even though it was often given to a Master Mason upon attaining that degree, the work was not widely

Albert Pike

read (or understood) given its esoteric nature and immense size. *Morals and Dogma* nevertheless has had an influence on Masonic ritual as it has evolved through the past couple of centuries.

Although the source of authority in Masonic worship is ultimately oneself and the worshiper's own interpretation of the Hiram Abiff allegory, there is another major influence — that of the Lodge. Adherents to Freemasonry are required to make very serious oaths in order to advance in the three degrees of the Blue Lodge. These oaths are similar to the laments made by the three Fellowcrafts as they were discovered and summarily punished, and thus are the basis of the Lodge's authority over a Freemason.

Ostensibly a candidate has the opportunity to refuse these oaths because before he is given the obligation of the Entered Apprentice degree a candidate hears these words from the Worshipful Master:[20]

> Mr. _____, before you can proceed further in Freemasonry, it will be necessary for you to take an Obligation appertaining to this degree. It becomes my duty as well as pleasure to inform you that there is nothing contained in the Obligation that conflicts with the duties you owe to God, your country, your neighbor, your family, or yourself. With this assurance on my part, are you willing to take the Obligation? (Nevada ritual, circa 1984)

This same question is asked of the candidate before he proceeds with the obligation of the Fellow Craft degree, and likewise with the Master Mason degree.

Consider the penalties of the obligations (Nevada ritual, circa 1984):

> "To all of which I do solemnly and sincerely promise and swear, without any hesitation, mental reservation, or secret evasion of mind in me whatsoever; binding myself under no less a penalty than that of having . . .

> Entered Apprentice Degree: ". . . my throat cut across, my tongue torn out, and with my body buried in the sands of the sea at low-water mark, where the tide ebbs and flows twice in twenty-four hours, should I ever knowingly or willfully violate this, my solemn Obligation of an Entered Apprentice."

> Fellow Craft Degree: ". . . my left breast torn open, my heart and vitals taken thence, and with my body given as a prey to the vultures of the air, should I ever knowingly, or willfully, violate this, my solemn Obligation of a Fellow Craft.";

> Master Mason Degree: ". . . my body severed in twain, my bowels taken thence, and with my body burned to ashes, and the

20. Taken from http://www.emfj.org/oaths.htm

ashes thereof scattered to the four winds of Heaven, that there might remain neither track, trace nor remembrance among man or Masons of so vile and perjured a wretch as I should be, should I ever knowingly or willfully violate this, my solemn Obligation of a Master Mason."

And the ending for each of these obligations is:

"So help me, God, and make me steadfast to keep and perform the same."

These oaths represent a strong tie to the Lodge and the Freemason religion. Many Freemasons argue that the oaths themselves are allegorical, but regardless of whether they have any strength of validity or not, they clearly go against the teachings of Jesus in the Sermon on the Mount (Matthew 5:33–37):

Again you have heard that it was said to those of old, "You shall not swear falsely, but shall perform your oaths to the Lord." But I say to you, do not swear at all: neither by heaven, for it is God's throne; nor by the earth, for it is His footstool; nor by Jerusalem, for it is the city of the great King. Nor shall you swear by your head, because you cannot make one hair white or black. But let your "Yes" be "Yes," and your "No," "No." For whatever is more than these is from the evil one.

This warning should be a red flag against the religion of Freemasonry for anyone who professes faith in Jesus Christ.

Foundations and Beliefs

Fundamentally, the story of Hiram Abiff is the basis for most Masonic ritual, and many books have been devoted to sharing the story and associated rituals (despite the aforementioned oaths).

However, underlying the allegories is the true end of Masonic worship — pursuing Light. What is meant by the search for Light in the Masonic sense? It is not to be equated or confused with pursuing the Light of the World (Jesus), nor seeking absolute Truth, nor Christian salvation.[21] Recall

---

21. Many pro-masonic writings make the argument that it cannot be a religion because it does not offer a path to salvation — this is frankly untrue.

a portion of the funeral liturgy quoted earlier "We call ourselves builders because each one of us is trying to build his own spiritual temple of character. . . ." With that statement in mind, Freemasonry can be seen as fundamentally about the individual defining his own truth. After the vows, rituals of the Lodge, and the rules of Masonic body, there is a great amount of latitude to the adherent to interpret, visualize, and evaluate the allegories. At some point, the "truth" found in the allegories becomes a revelation and the Mason can be said to have gained more Light. No matter how confusing this may sound, all of Masonic teaching and ritual is a framework by which a Mason defines his own truth.

Given this premise and the growth of Freemasonry in the 17th and 18th centuries, it is reasonable to conclude that Freemasonry shares much of its religious basis with that of the intellectual movement from the same period known as the Enlightenment. The Enlightenment philosophy was characterized by "thinking for oneself" (as opposed to religious leaders for instance) and the employment and reliance on an individual's intellectual capacity in determining what to believe and how to act. These philosophies are very consistent with what is observed in Freemasonry. They are, however, contrary to biblical teachings of Christianity where the Word of God is the source of truth.

Use of Symbols

It is interesting to note the Freemasonry use of symbols in their allegorical exploration of truth. We've already seen the use of the square and the compass in the masonic emblem. These are used to express two of the three "Great Lights" in Freemasonry. A Wiccan Freemason, Robert Fisher, describes it like this:

> The Square means morality, honesty and fair dealing, whilst the Compasses are Freemasonry's most prominent symbol of truth and loyalty. The Compass, which is used to draw circles, can also be seen as representing the realm of the spiritual while the square, the symbol of earth and the realm of the material. Together, the compass and square represent the convergence of matter and spirit, and the convergence of earthly and spiritual responsibilities.[22]

---

22. Robert Fisher, http://pagantheologies.pbworks.com/w/page/13622064/Freemasonry.

Thus, Freemasonry symbols are used to illustrate the link between the material and the spiritual.

Before proceeding, one revealing quote by Mr. Fisher says:

> I can only say that as someone who was initiated as a Freemason first and as a Wiccan second I can honestly say that the Wiccan training and initiation opened my eyes to the magical potential that Freemasonry has and I think it so sad that in the main Freemasons are concerned with the externals of rite or organization rather than deeper content.[23]

There is also one other "Great Light" in Masonic ritual, the Volume of Sacred Law as it is referred to. In many cases, the Bible proper is used, but it does not necessarily need to be. In countries that are not predominantly Christian, the dominant religious text may be used. Whichever is used, it is displayed prominently with the other two "Lights" displayed upon it.

Rather than being an actual source of truth, like much in Freemasonry, the presence of the Volume of Sacred Law is symbolic.

> Like most other things in Freemasonry, the Holy Bible is itself a symbol of Divine Truth in every form. When viewed as a symbol, it represents that divine truth or knowledge from whatever source derived.[24]

Again, this appeal to truth from "whatever source" shows that the individual, not the true and living God and Creator, defines the truth. Also note in the quote the reference to "Divine Truth in every form." The emphasis is on many forms of truth, and ultimately centered upon the Mason's own interpretation.

Given the secret nature of Freemasonry, it is often tied to another secret society of the same era, the Illuminati. Illuminati symbolism and ties to revolutionary thought, conspiracy theory, and the relationship to Freemasonry are far beyond what can be described or addressed in this short chapter. For instance, it is widely believed that the pyramid on the U.S. dollar

---

23. Most Freemasons would argue that this is evidence of the individual truth that each one of them seeks. However, it illustrates the underlying influence of the allegories in leading men away from real truth.

24. http://www.themasonictrowel.com/Articles/degrees/degree_1st_files/the_great_light_of_fremasonry_gltx.htm.

bill, topped with the all-seeing eye is based on either Masonic or Illuminati symbolism or both. Regardless, there are undeniable ties to the Founding Fathers of the United States as James Madison, James Monroe, Benjamin Franklin, and George Washington were all Freemasons.

Theory of Origins

Since adherents to Freemasonry worship a "generic" god and reference a holy book symbolically, they do not necessarily have a consistent story of the origin of the universe. The Great Architect of the Universe is given credit for putting things in motion, and mankind is building upon that foundation (much like deism). The details of the origin of the universe are not important to developing Masonic allegory. However, an individual may draw upon their particular religious text or upon whatever individual experience one may have for the basis of their understanding of the origins of the universe.

This is an interesting consistency with Enlightenment principles of scientific thought growing rapidly during the same time that Freemasonry was building its philosophical underpinnings. In the Enlightenment, mankind — as the source of truth — rejected the revelations of Scripture, especially when it addressed the material world. Principles of geologic uniformitarianism (based on naturalism) arose during this same time. Observations surrounding the deposition of rock into layers over time led to an extrapolation and acceptance of millions or billions of years as to the age of the earth.[25] Secular "science" came in conflict with the authority of the Word of God. Theological and religious leaders at that time embraced the antiquity of the earth as a scientific fact. All of these factors combined to result in a rejection of the biblical account of origins. This type of thought aligns with the philosophical tenet of Freemasonry of a "supreme being," but denying that the Supreme Being is the ultimate source of truth.

Freemasonry has its influences in the growth and acceptance of evolutionary thought. Erasmus Darwin was a Mason as was Richard, Charles Darwin's father.[26] There is no formal record that Charles Darwin himself was a Mason, but there is no denying the influence of Enlightenment and Masonic thought on him. When Darwin observed the diversity in the

25. See Terry Mortenson, *The Great Turning Point* (Green Forest, AR: Master Books, 2012).
26. William R. Denslow, *10,000 Famous Freemasons* (Richmond, VA: Macoy Publishing & Masonic Supply Co., Inc., 1957). For mother lodge, cf. H.L. Haywood, *Supplement to Mackey Encyclopedia of Freemasonry* (1966), p. 1198, retrieved from http://freemasonry. bcy.ca/biography/darwin_e/darwin_e.html.

Galapagos, rather than interpret it in light of the revelation of God's Word, he chose to interpret it in the mind of his own truth and the anti-[Christian-based]-religious, anti-establishment nature of the Enlightenment.

Arbitrary Doctrines and Salvation

Some historical records of Freemasonry actually refer to the Trinity[27] and in particular "The Son," but as the religion has grown and evolved, that level of alignment with Christian teaching has been deemphasized or completely removed. This may explain why many Christians were part of it in the past, but today, there is no excuse for Christians to be part of this anti-Christian religion.

The religion of Freemasonry has changed and is continuing to change into something that is opposed to Christianity. Fraternal organizations, for example, are not necessarily a bad thing for a Christian, but when doctrines of such an organization change to oppose biblical doctrines, then should Christians be part of that organization . . . especially when they become a religion of themselves?

In fact, the recognized uniqueness of Christianity — Jesus Christ — is not mentioned in any Masonic teachings. Outside religion and politics as topics are forbidden in a Lodge, but this is quite odd given that Freemasonry is a religion itself. In reality, the prohibition is in reference to sectarianism and the fact that Masons worship the GAOTU generically and one member could not call out a particular deity or doctrine at the potential offense of another.

There are many, many sources, including ex-Masons, that claim that the underlying "god" of Freemasonry is demonic or satanic. It is true that making oneself the source of truth is absolutely consistent with satanic tactics (e.g., the Garden of Eden), but this may not be universally the case since each Freemason determines for himself who is his god. One biblical basis for why man was created was to worship God the Creator, not some generic Great Architect of the Universe. However, any religion that goes against this is in reality not worshiping Satan, but is advocating the worship of the individual. By denying the Creator, and more importantly the sacrifice by the Creator for the creation, one could be considered to be "worshiping Satan," but not as a deity per se. In this, I agree with Masons who say they do not worship demons or Satan or Lucifer. They simply agree with the tactics of the original liar.

27. http://www.rgle.org.uk/RGLE_Tenet.htm.

Let us consider the view of Freemasonry toward Scripture. The following excerpt details well the underlying basis of Freemasonry. Note the inconsistency in the insistence upon the existence of a Supreme Being, but denying that a common source of truth exists.

> Freemasonry invites men of all faiths to its teachings, requiring only a belief in a Supreme Being, knowing that we all pray to the God and Father of the Universe regardless of the actual name one uses to address Him. Thus, the Bible is often referred to as the Volume of Sacred Law, allowing men of differing faiths to use the Sacred Writings of their faith as the Volume of Sacred Law.
>
> What does this mean to the Freemason? The fact that the Holy Bible or some other Volume of Sacred Law rests open upon the Altar of Freemasonry means the Freemason must have some Divine Revelation. The Freemason must seek truth and wisdom from a source greater than that from human minds. Freemasonry makes no attempt at a detailed interpretation of the Bible. The Volume of Sacred Law lies upon the Altar open for all to read, open for all to study and interpret for himself. The tie that unites Freemasonry is strong, but it provides for the utmost liberty of faith and thought. It unites men not by creed or dogma, but upon the broad truth of a belief and faith in God, the Supreme Grand Architect of the Universe. Freemasonry is truly a Brotherhood of Man under the Fatherhood of God.[28]

Again, many Masons are strong in their statements that Freemasonry is not a religion and is not because it does not offer a plan of salvation or have specific doctrines. However, evaluate the concluding statements from the Master Mason Degree ritual:

> Then, finally my brethren, let us imitate our Grand Master, Hiram Abiff, in his virtuous conduct, his unfeigned piety to God, and his inflexible fidelity to his trust; that, like him, we may welcome the grim tyrant, Death, and receive him as a kind messenger sent by our Supreme Grand Master, to translate us from this

28. http://www.themasonictrowel.com/Articles/degrees/degree_1st_files/the_great_light_of_fremasonry_gltx.htm

imperfect to that all-perfect, glorious, and celestial Lodge above, where the Supreme Architect of the Universe presides.

Much of Masonic allegory does emphasize the sureness and inevitability of death. While it does not speak of the need for salvation per se, salvation is assumed by the acceptance of the Freemason by the "Supreme Grand Master . . . in the celestial Lodge above" through the process of death. In order to obtain that salvation, you are instructed to imitate Hiram Abiff so that you can get into heaven. The nature of the salvation message within Freemasonry is hard to deny given these statements.

So, how does one go about imitating Hiram Abiff? Think back to the allegory. Hiram traveled through the compass directions of West, South, and East. In much of Masonic allegory and ritual, the Light is "in the East," and adherents go through a sequence and eventually are "brought to the light" in the East which is where the Worshipful Master (CEO of the Lodge) sits.

Regardless of symbolism, there is an appeal that the Worshipful Master is the light or at least sits in the place of the light. The Worshipful Master holds the position that can bring the light to the adherent or at least get them on the path. The journey to the light embodies much of Masonic thought, and theoretically you cannot obtain all of the light that can be conferred in a lodge of Master Masons until you become the Worshipful Master yourself.[29] Of course, the Worshipful Master is the head of Blue Lodge Masonry and "additional light" can be gained through its many attached organizations. Unfortunately, this light is founded upon self-determination of truth and not the ultimate truth as revealed by the Holy Bible.

The problem is that this is a false gospel, one based on imitation of Hiram Abiff, rather than faith in Jesus Christ. Salvation is obtained through the efforts of imitating Hiram Abiff and becomes a works-based salvation. Also, in 1 Corinthians 15:26, "The last enemy that will be destroyed is death," but in Masonic teachings, death is a "kind messenger." These are just a few examples of the disparity between grace-based salvation through faith in Christ and the nature of salvation and death as described in Freemasonry.

Good News for Freemasons

A friend of mine asked me what I knew about the Masons, as he was considering joining. As a young Christian, he didn't see anything inherently

---

29. http://www.nj-freemasons.org/masoniclight.php.

wrong with joining a group that is known for its community service and its spirit of brotherhood. At the time, I didn't know a lot about the Masons and their beliefs, so rather than give uninformed advice, I simply asked this question: "Why do you want to join? What is it about the Masons that is appealing to you?"

His response was typical in a world today where faith in the sustaining power of the Creator has been lost and the Church, by and large, has failed to serve its people. "I want to have assurance that if something happened to me, my widow would be taken care of and if I ended up in court, I could count on my fellow Mason's to take care of

Stained glass window at St. John's Church, Chester, England, depicting Hiram Abiff

things for me." I was shocked at his response. Here was a young Christian looking to a secular group to serve his needs in an area that typically would fall to faith in Christ and the Body of Christ. My, how far the Church has fallen from influence, even among its own!

Even so, what would be the problem with a Christian also being a Freemason? Let's examine this question further. A Christian (assuming that he was worshiping Jesus) walking into a Hindu temple to take part in the worship service and joining in corporate prayer to Vishnu is not unlike a Masonic ceremony where there is corporate prayer to GAOTU where you may have Christians, Muslims, Hindus, and Buddhists all together. Would Jesus Christ be willing to accept worship in this manner? The answer is found in Paul's first letter to the church at Corinth.[30] Paul wrote in 1 Corinthians 10:20–22:

---

30. http://www.emfj.org/mensclub.htm.

> I do not want you to have fellowship with demons. You cannot drink the cup of the Lord and the cup of demons; you cannot partake of the Lord's table and of the table of demons. Or do we provoke the Lord to jealousy? Are we stronger than He?

In this passage, Paul warns believers about mixing religions, especially those that are demonic in nature. As we have discussed, Freemasonry could be considered demonic in its approach to authority. This Scripture clearly warns against engaging in this kind of behavior.

Joining in a group prayer to a generic, self-determined God could be considered a heresy. And the acceptance of the Master Mason that he is to imitate Hiram Abiff for salvation is a false gospel. The penalty for teaching a false gospel is eternal in nature as Paul wrote in Galatians 1:8–10:

> But even if we, or an angel from heaven, preach any other gospel to you than what we have preached to you, let him be accursed. As we have said before, so now I say again, if anyone preaches any other gospel to you than what you have received, let him be accursed.
>
> For do I now persuade men, or God? Or do I seek to please men? For if I still pleased men, I would not be a bondservant of Christ.

Rather than imitate Hiram Abiff in order to gain salvation, Christians are to trust in the sacrifice of Jesus Christ and the truth of His Resurrection. As we see in 1 Corinthians 15:1–4:

> Moreover, brethren, I declare to you the gospel which I preached to you, which also you received and in which you stand, by which also you are saved, if you hold fast that word which I preached to you — unless you believed in vain.
>
> For I delivered to you first of all that which I also received: that Christ died for our sins according to the Scriptures, and that He was buried, and that He rose again the third day according to the Scriptures.

Paul repeatedly appeals to the authority of the Scriptures as his source of truth for the sacrifice of Jesus Christ. How much more should Christians do the same?

Additionally, the Scriptures document that Jesus, not Hiram Abiff, is the only way to salvation and reconciliation with God. In John 14:6, Jesus said:

> Jesus said to him, "I am the way, the truth, and the life. No one comes to the Father except through Me.

Even with the overwhelming weight of the words of Christ, some Masons may be concerned about their allegiance to the Lodge and the oaths that they took to join. Trust in Christ, and the oaths that you took are null and void. Leviticus 5:4–5 teaches that if something is hidden from a man and he takes an oath thoughtlessly, he is guilty of sin:

> Or if a person swears, speaking thoughtlessly with his lips to do evil or to do good, whatever it is that a man may pronounce by an oath, and he is unaware of it — when he realizes it, then he shall be guilty in any of these matters.
>
> And it shall be, when he is guilty in any of these matters, that he shall confess that he has sinned in that thing.

However, once he recognizes it and confesses it as sin, he can claim the promises of 1 John 1:8–9:

> If we say that we have no sin, we deceive ourselves, and the truth is not in us. If we confess our sins, He is faithful and just to forgive us our sins and to cleanse us from all unrighteousness.

If you are a Christian who has become ensnared in Freemasonry, I suggest that you confess your involvement in Freemasonry as sin, resign from your Lodge, and renounce your involvement. Scripture is clear that you are not to remain in such a state of dualistic allegiance. Second Corinthians 6:14–17 gives godly advice in this area:

> Do not be unequally yoked together with unbelievers. For what fellowship has righteousness with lawlessness? And what communion has light with darkness? And what accord has Christ with Belial? Or what part has a believer with an unbeliever? And what agreement has the temple of God with idols? For you are the temple of the living God. As God has said: "I will dwell in

them and walk among them. I will be their God, and they shall be My people." Therefore "Come out from among them and be separate," says the Lord. "Do not touch what is unclean, And I will receive you."

There are many resources to assist you in this process.[31] Forgiveness in Christ is available for those who repent and trust in Christ, but our repentance must be accompanied by works befitting that repentance (Acts 26:20).

Summary of Freemason Beliefs

Doctrine	Freemason Teaching
God	Whichever deity you choose to refer to as the Great Architect
Authority/ Revelation	There is a diverse tradition, but all based on man's ideas and personal religious interpretations; local Lodge leaders hold authority and teach the allegorical symbolism
Man	A being who has a duty to do good
Sin	Transgression of individual ethical codes
Salvation	Varies by individual; progressing through various degrees within the religious system
Creation	Varies by individual; generally a deistic view of origins that would accommodate evolutionary views

---

31. http://www.emfj.org/leave.htm.

Chapter 15

Zoroastrianism

Dr. Carl Broggi

Origins of Zoroastrianism

The founder of Zoroastrianism was a man named *Zarathushtra*, written in Greek as *Zoroaster*, from which comes the name *Zoroastrianism*. Most scholars say that Zoroaster lived around 650 years before Christ, though there is some debate as to precisely when and where he was born. One scholar in the field of world religions writes:

> The early history of Zoroastrianism is much in dispute. The religion was founded by Zoroaster, but it is not certain when he lived, where he lived or how much of later Zoroastrianism came from him. Tradition puts him in western Iran in the sixth century B.C., a little earlier than the Buddha in India, but it is now thought that he lived in northeastern Iran, in the area on the borders of modern Afghanistan and Turkmenistan. An alternate theory dates him much earlier, somewhere from 1700 to 1500 B.C., and places him in the plains of Central Asia, perhaps before the first groups of Aryans moved south from the plains into Iran and India.[1]

---

1. Richard Cavendish, *The Great Religions* (New York: Arco Publishing Company, 1980), p. 125.

Church historian Dr. Philip Schaff wrote about 100 years ago regarding Zoroastrianism:

> Zoroastrianism, or Fire-worship, is the ancient Persian religion, and traced to Zoroaster (Zarathustra), a priest in the temple of the Sun, who lived about B.C. 1300. It was the religion of Cyrus, Darius, Hystaspis, and Xerxes, and of the Wise Men from the East who came to worship the new-born Messiah at Bethlehem. . . . . It is a system of dualism with a monad behind and, possibly a reconciliation in prospect. Ormazd is the good principle (the sun, the light), and Ahriman, the evil principle (darkness, winter), who corresponds to the Devil of the Scriptures; yet both were created by Zerana-Akerana. They are in constant antagonism, and hosts of good and bad angels under their banners. There is an incessant war going on in heaven as well as on earth. At last Ormazd sends his prophet (a kind of Messiah) to convert mankind; then follows a general resurrection, and separation of the just from sinners . . . the followers of this religion worship with the face turned towards the sun or the fire upon the altar; hence they are called fire-worshipers.[2]

This religion obviously has aspects similar to Christianity and may have been influenced by events from Genesis forward as they were passed down from generation to generation.

The Zoroastrian View of God

Regardless, Zoroastrianism is considered one of the world's oldest monotheistic religions — the doctrine or belief that there is only one God. However, while Zoroastrians say they believe there is one supreme God whom they call Ahura Mazda, they also recognize another immortal deity, known as Angra Mainyu, who represents the epitome of evil. So using the traditional definition of monotheism, many religious scholars would say it is more accurate to describe this religion as polytheistic. Polytheism is the belief or worship of more than one God, taken from the Greek word *poly*, meaning many and *theos*, meaning God. Polytheism is in contrast to the term "monotheism," derived from the Greek word *mono*, meaning one.

---

2. Philip Schaff, *Theological Propaedeutic* (New York: Charles Scribner's Sons Publisher, 1904), p. 49–50.

Nineteenth-century depiction of Zoroaster derived from a figure in a 4th-century sculpture, extracted from *Persia by a Persian* (Isaac Adams, 1906)

As Christians, it is important to understand that when God created us in His image, He wrote monotheism into our "spiritual DNA." In helping us to understand this reality, the Apostle Paul explains in the first two chapters of the Book of Romans that the existence of only one true God is evident to everyone in one of two ways. First, it is evident by the creation around us: "For since the creation of the world His invisible attributes are clearly seen, being understood by the things that are made, even His eternal power and Godhead, so that they are without excuse" (Romans 1:20).[3] The Bible reminds us that everything God has created in this world — every leaf, every flower, every drop of water — bears the stamp, "Made by God."

In addition to this outward revelation found in the visible creation, people also possess an inward knowledge of God known as the conscience. Romans 2 says that people of the world who have never even read a Bible instinctively understand certain moral parameters because God has "the law written in their hearts" (Romans 2:15). So when one reads in Zoroastrian literature of two deities who exist side by side, we immediately know that error has entered into this religion. Since people are born with a monotheistic view of God, it is only when they suppress the truth — seen outwardly in the creation and felt inwardly by the conscience — that they become polytheistic.

According to God's Word, people who believe in many gods are not displaying an earnest search for God, but are giving evidence of their rebellion against God (Romans 1:21–23). Having traveled to many countries of the world to share the good news, I understand that there are individuals

---

3. Scripture in this chapter is from the New King James Version of the Bible.

raised from birth in false religious systems like Zoroastrianism. Nevertheless, I have also witnessed that many people caught up in a polytheistic religion know that it is not true. Therefore, it is our responsibility as Christians to reason with them that there is only one God, who has revealed Himself in Jesus Christ.[4] People who practice Zoroastrianism are lost, and like everyone else in this world, they need to receive the forgiveness found in Jesus Christ.

The Zoroastrian View of Creation

Zoroastrians say that their supreme deity, Ahura Mazda, created the world. Their religions literature states:

> In the beginning, there was nothing in the world except Ahura Mazda, the Wise Lord, who lived in the Endless Light. And the Evil Spirit, Ahriman, who lived in the Absolute Darkness. Between them lay only emptiness.
>
> One day, Ahura Mazda decided to make different creations. First He shaped the sky made of metal, shinning and bright. Second, He made the pure water. Third, the Wise Lord created the Earth, flat and round with no mountains and valleys. Fourth, He made the plants, moist and sweet with no bark or thorn. Fifth, he created the animals, big and small. Then he created the First Man, Gayomard, bright, tall, and handsome. And lastly, he created Fire and distributed it within the whole creation. The Wise Lord ordered Fire to serve the mankind in preparing food and overcoming cold.[5]

Anyone who has read the opening chapters of Genesis can quickly see that there are major differences between the creation account in Genesis and the creation story in Zoroastrian literature; however, there are a few vague similarities. Because of these similarities, some liberal scholars have argued that Zoroastrianism predates the biblical record of Genesis and influenced the writings of Moses.

---

4. For some timeless lessons on how to reason with polytheistic people, study the Apostle Paul's interchange with the people of Athens on Mars Hill (Acts 17:16–34).

5. This creation account is taken from the *Book of Creation*, the *Bundahishn*, dating from the 6th century A.D. While this book draws on the Avesta, the official sacred text used by Zoroastrians, because it reflects Zoroastrian scripture, today it is also considered authoritative by those in this cultish religion. Zorastriankids.com/creation.html.

Others argue that there was one common myth as to how the creation of the world took place and with time it gave birth to many different creation accounts. This view is very similar to those of liberal scholars who point out that there are over 200 different flood accounts found in ancient cultures. From these, it is contended that the different (but sometimes similar) accounts reflect commonly held ancient myths, but not historical fact. Commenting on this fallacious argument, Ken Ham writes:

> When I attended university in Australia (many years ago!), I remember one of my professors stating that there were Babylonian stories about a flood similar to the account in the Bible. Therefore he concluded, the Jews borrowed their "story" from the Babylonians! But I say it's really the other way round! There are flood legends in cultures all over the world because there really was an actual global Flood — Noah's Flood. As the account of the Flood was handed down (and particularly as people spread out around the world after the Tower of Babel), it was changed by many cultures. Yet many of these legends (including the Babylonian ones) have similar elements to the Bible's account. Because the Bible is God's inspired Word, it gives us the true account.[6]

This same line of reasoning could be used in helping to sort out the different, (but sometimes similar) creation accounts. On the one hand, even if one subscribes to the earlier and much highly debated date that places Zoroaster 1,700 years before Christ, this does not change the fact that in the early chapters of Genesis, Moses is writing of historical events that took place approximately 4,000 years before Christ.

On the other hand, if one ascribes to the founding of Zoroastrianism held by most scholars to be the 6th century B.C., the Bible still predates the writings of Zoroastrianism. Most historians and scholars, liberal and conservative alike, place the writing of the Torah (Genesis–Deuteronomy) between 1446 and 1406 B.C. when Moses and the children of Israel wandered in the desert for 40 years.

This would mean that the Old Testament pre-dates the oral traditions of Zoroaster, later recorded in the Avesta (the official religious text of

---

6. Ken Ham, Blog, January 27, 2014, answersingenesis.org/blogs/ken-ham/2014/01/27/was-noahs-ark-round/.

Zoroastrianism), by close to 900 years. Since the Bible predates the religious teachings of the false prophet Zoroaster, one should expect some similarities in Zoroastrianism and other ancient cultures concerning the creation of the world.

As with the Flood of Noah's day, the different creation accounts began with one authoritative account written by God through Moses and later disseminated through the peoples of the world after the Tower of Babel (Genesis 10–11).

The Zoroastrian Source of Revelation

The false prophet Zoroaster, purportedly at the age of 30, received a vision that he recorded in the Avesta. He was drawing water from the Daiti River and supposedly saw a "Shining Being," who called himself Vohu Manah. Most Zoroastrian scholars concur that this was an angel. According to Zoroaster, Vohu Manah led him into the presence of Ahura Mazda, the Zoroastrian god. This supposedly was the first in a series of visions in which Zoroaster asked questions and received answers from Ahura Mazda. The answers he received became the foundational tenets for the Zoroastrian faith. From these visions given uniquely to him, Zoroaster became the sole human author of the Zoroastrian religious literature.

Of course, as Christians, we know that Satan describes himself as "an angel of light" and that he uses fallen angels to communicate false doctrine (2 Corinthians 11:13–15; 1 Timothy 4:1). Typical in virtually every religious cult, there is some vision, some angelic messenger, or some revelation, usually given to a single person. I find it interesting that Zoroaster's method of enlightenment was very similar to Mohammed's enlightenment in Islam. Mohammed also supposedly received a vision from an angel, and this "revelation" became Islam's religious text, the Quran.

In both Zoroastrianism and Islam, the source of the religious revelation that is held to be authoritative is given to just one man, and in both instances it is given by an angel. By comparison, the revelation found and recorded in the Bible is so very different.

One of the amazing facts about the Bible is that although it was written by a wide diversity of authors (as many as 40), over a period of 1,600 years, from many different locations and under a wide variety of conditions, the Bible is uniquely one book, not merely a collection of 66 books.

The authors of the Bible lived in a variety of cultures, had different life experiences, and often were quite different in their personal make-up. They wrote their material from three continents (Africa, Asia, and Europe), in very diverse places — Moses in a desert, Solomon in a palace, Paul in a prison, John in exile, etc. — while employing three languages in their writings (Hebrew, Aramaic, and Greek). In addition, they represented a wide variety of backgrounds and professions. For instance, Moses was a political leader; Joshua a military leader; David a shepherd; Nehemiah a cupbearer; Solomon a king; Amos a herdsman; Daniel a prime minister; Matthew a tax collector; Luke a medical doctor; Paul a rabbi; and Peter a fisherman. And what is so amazing is that while most of the human authors never met each other and were unfamiliar with each other's writings, the Bible is still a unified whole, without a single contradiction! There is a perfect unity that runs from Genesis to Revelation. The only explanation is that the Bible is the Word of God. The only explanation is that behind the 40 human authors, there was one Divine Author, God the Holy Spirit.[7]

The Zoroastrian View of Good and Evil

Zoroastrianism teaches that there is a "cosmic dualism" that is unfolding in the universe. "Cosmic dualism" is a term used to summarize Zoroaster's belief that there is an ongoing battle, an ongoing tension, between good and evil. The "good power" is represented in their supreme being, Ahura Mazda, while the "evil power" is represented in Angra Mainyu. They believe that Ahura Mazda is responsible for the best in the world, while Angra Mainyu, existing alongside their supreme deity, infiltrates the universe with evil, making it impure. Therefore, Zoroastrians would attribute aging, sickness, famine, natural disasters, and death to this evil power. Zoroastrianism teaches that these two co-equal powers existed side by side from the beginning of time.[8] Furthermore, this "cosmic dualism" is reflected in man's "moral dualism" where he too makes both good and evil choices.

Of course, this teaching of moral dualism is contradictory to the revelation of God found in the Bible. When God created the world, "God saw

---

7. "Why Is the Bible Unique," Dr. Carl J. Broggi, p. 53, found in Ken Ham and Bodie Hodge, eds., *How Do We Know The Bible Is True*, Volume 2 (Green Forest, AR: Master Books, 2012).

8. For a helpful discussion on this topic with direct quotations from their religious writings, see *Early Zoroastrianism* by James Hope Moulton (London: Constable and Company, 1913), p. 344–349.

everything that He had made, and indeed it was very good" (Genesis 1:31). The Bible is clear that all of God's creation was very good, but sin entered into His creation through both the fall of Satan and the Fall of man.[9] The Bible does not present two cosmic powers dueling against each other from the beginning. There is one sovereign God who rules and reigns, who at a point in time made both angels and men with the capacity to choose. One-third of the angels (now called demons) rebelled, as did all of humanity since Adam (Revelation 12:4; Romans 5:12). The one true God of the Bible is very clear that it was not some cosmic evil force that brought aging, sickness, famine, natural disasters, and death into this world; it was man's sin (Romans 8:20–22). The Zoroastrian good god Ahura Mazda is co-eternal to the evil god Angra Mainyu. By contrast, the God of the Bible is sovereign over all. Furthermore, Satan is not the opposite of God; rather he is a created being and has limited power and by God's grace, limited time (Ezekiel 28:15; Job 1:12).

The Zoroastrian View of Salvation

Zoroastrianism teaches that man has a free will, and in the end he will be rewarded for his choices. Ahura Mazda, the "good power," is perfect and abides in heaven, as will all who live righteously. Alongside this "good power" is Angra Mainyu, the "evil power," who is wicked and dwells in the depths of hell, as will all who live wickedly. Zoroastrianism teaches that when a person dies he goes to heaven or hell depending on his deeds during his lifetime.[10] This religion is really no different from all the different "isms" found around the world: Confucianism, Mohammedism, Taoism, Sikhism, or Shintoism. All these religions teach that people are ultimately received by a Supreme Being or into some afterlife on the basis of what they have accomplished.

Why Should I Care about Zoroastrianism?

Why should you care about a subject that most of us can hardly pronounce? We should care because God has called us to reach the world for Christ, and tens of millions of people are trapped either directly or indirectly in this false religion of Zoroastrianism. Jesus Christ commissioned His followers to

---

9. To study the fall of Satan read Isaiah 14 and Ezekiel 28. To study the Fall of man read Genesis 3.

10. The above summary of these doctrines can be found in the following Zoroastrian scripture (Yasna 30:2, 4, 9-11; 31:8, 9; 43:12; 46:12; 51:6; 53:7-9). The Yasna is considered by Zoroastrians to be the most important portion of the Avesta.

"Go into all the world and preach the gospel to every creature" (Mark 16:15).

The U.S. Center for World Mission is an organization that, among other endeavors, catalogues all of the unreached people groups in the world. It continually stresses to Christians living in the West that most people who need to hear the gospel of Jesus Christ are located in the part of the world that missiologists refer to as the 10/40 window. The 10/40 window can be defined simply as, "the rectangular area of North Africa, the Middle East, and Asia, approximately between 10 degrees north and 40 degrees north latitude. This section of the world is often called 'The Resistant Belt' and includes the majority of the world's Muslims, Hindus, and Buddhists."[11]

The god Ahura Mazda on the rock relief of Shapour II at Taq-e Bustan The rock relief of Sasanian king Shapur II (309-379 CE) at Taq-e Bostan, also known as Taq-e Bustan I, shows a double scene of investiture and victory.

While this geographical region of the world comprises only about one-third of earth's total land area, nearly two-thirds of the world's people reside here. Included in this mass of humanity are the majority of those who practice Zoroastrianism. People groups found in India, Iran, Afghanistan, and Azerbaijan currently practice pure, undiluted Zoroastrianism. But there are also tens of millions who do not necessarily practice Zoroastrianism in its purest form, but who have adopted aspects of this cultish religion.

For instance, when describing the 650,000 Yazidi people of Iraq, many of whom have been attacked and slaughtered by ISIS,[12] Dan Scribner of the U.S. Center for World Mission writes: "The Yazidi people follow an

---

11. "What is the 10/40 Window?" by the Joshua Project, A ministry of the U.S. Center for World Mission.

12. The *Islamic State of Iraq and Syria* (ISIS), also translated as the *Islamic State of Iraq and the Levant* (ISIL), and known too by the self-proclaimed title of *Islamic State* (IS), is a Sunni, extremist, jihadist rebel group controlling territory in Iraq, Syria, eastern Libya, the Sinai Peninsula of Egypt, parts of Pakistan, and parts of India.

old religion which has remnants of Zoroastrianism, Hinduism, Judaism, and Christianity."[13] Those practicing the purest expression of Zoroastrianism number approximately 11,000 in the United States and approximately 300,000 worldwide. However, those practicing component parts of Zoroastrianism, mixed in with some other religion, number in the millions.

Americans might possibly meet someone living here who is practicing Zoroastrianism in its purest form.[14] God is bringing many different unreached peoples from around the world to our own land. Under current immigration law, the United States often grants refugee status to those who are persecuted for their religious beliefs.[15] This includes a people group known as the Parsis, who originate from the Bombay region of India and practice Zoroastrianism.[16] In addition, many of the Kurdish people of Turkey, Syria, Iraq, and Iran trace their religious roots to Zoroastrianism. Most Kurds in these nations are only nominally Muslims, of the Sunni branch.[17] "It has been said that Kurds hold their Islam lightly, due to several factors, one being that many Kurds still feel some connection with the ancient Zoroastrian faith. They feel it is an original Kurdish spirituality that far predates the seventh century A.D. arrival of Muhammad."[18] Overall, as more and more of the peoples from countries found in the 10/40 window come and take up residence in our own nation, we will meet an increasing number of individuals who embrace Zoroastrianism.

---

13. Dan Scribner, newsletter of the U.S. Center for World Mission, June 9, 2014.
14. According to the Federation of Zoroastrian Associations of North America, this number is small, estimated at approximately 11,000. For a demographic breakdown for North American, go to www.fezana.org.
15. For a helpful article explaining the *1951 United Nations Convention Relating to the Status of Refugees* which the United States bases its immigration policy on, see the University of Minnesota's Human Rights Library article on "Study Guide: The Rights of Refugees," Human Rights Education Associates 2003, http://www1.umn.edu/humanrts/edumat/studyguides/refugees.htm.
16. The Parsis, whose name means "Persians," are descended from Persian Zoroastrians, having immigrated to India in the last century to avoid religious persecution by the Muslims. They live chiefly in Bombay and in a few towns and villages mostly to the north of Bombay, but also in places like Karachi (Pakistan), Bangalore (Karnataka, India), and now in the United States.
17. Shiite Muslims are known for persecuting Sunni Muslims. The Sunni branch believes that the first four caliphs — Mohammed's successors — rightfully took his place as legitimate religious leaders of Muslims. Shiites, in contrast, believe that only the heirs of the fourth caliph, Ali, are the legitimate successors of Mohammed. See more at historynewsnetwork.org/article/934.
18. US Center for World Mission, article, "The Kurds" at www.http://joshuaproject.net/peoplegroups.

Increasingly, Christians in America who are faithful to share the gospel are discovering that religious beliefs once foreign to us have now moved into the American religious landscape. I recently baptized three individuals from India who have come to faith in Jesus Christ. Witnessing their conversions has heightened my awareness of other people from India who live in our community. India currently has a population of 1.3 billion people, and it is expected to pass China in population growth by 2025.[19] If Christ has not returned by that time, there will be more people from India alive on planet Earth than any other single people group. Being aware of this phenomena is important, because India is the primary nation where Zoroastrianism has been syncretized into Hinduism and the other religions found there.

According to *Operation World*, Hinduism is the principal religious faith of India, practiced by nearly 1 billion people living there.[20] So when you speak to Hindu people living here in America, you may be talking to people who knowingly or unknowingly embrace a number of the tenets of Zoroastrianism.

In addition, since Zoroastrianism has often been syncretized into many other world religions, and with the East moving West, being able to understand the beliefs of this false religion will better equip a Christian to win these people to Christ. All these factors combined should be enough motivation for any believer who takes the Great Commission seriously to want to reach a Zorastrian with the gospel.

Reaching a Zoroastrian with the Gospel

While there seems to be endless other issues in the Zoroastrianism cult that one could examine, like the manner in which they bury their dead, the so-called fire temples they worship in, or the allegiance they give to their seven archangels, to name just a few of dozens of topics we could have covered, we have nonetheless examined the principal components of Zoroastrianism. As

---

19. "India to Pass China in Population" by Sam Roberts, *The New York Times*, December 15, 2009.
20. *Operation World* is a wonderful resource to help Christians understand the religious climate of every nation in order to intelligently pray for the unevangelized. Their website (operationworld.org) indicates that the world's least-evangelized peoples are concentrated in India. Of 159 people groups of over 1 million people, 133 are unreached. Hundreds more groups of fewer than 1 million are unreached. Also, 953 ethnic groups have populations greater than 10,000; of these, 205 have no church and little to no outreach from Christians. About 700,000 of these people practice pure Zoroastrianism. However, nearly one billion people practice some form of Hinduism in which you will find components of Zoroastrianism. Only about 2.2 percent of the population is considered to be evangelical Christians.

in the study of any religious cult, what is critically important is not necessarily knowing every point of doctrine the religious cult ascribes to, but at least knowing the major points in order to be able to springboard into a discussion of the truth.

One should never be intimidated by the "strangeness" of so many new religions entering America. People are people, usually looking for meaning in life, and trying to find some way in which to relieve a guilty conscience. Never forget that no matter what people may tell you about their so-called god or even multiple gods, you can still appeal to what Christian theologians refer to as "general revelation."

General revelation is that truth that God has revealed about Himself to all people, wherever one may live in the world. People outwardly are able to understand that there is one Creator God who made the world we live in. God's fingerprints are all over His creation, and God wrote His moral dictates on each person's heart (Psalm 19:1–6; Acts 14:17; Romans 1:20, 2:14–15). God's laws are a reflection of God's character, which is why man innately knows what is right and wrong, and what is just and unjust. Certainly, people can sin against their conscience and develop a calloused conscience (1 Timothy 4:2; Titus 1:5; Hebrews 10:22), but they still know that they have sinned against a holy God (Romans 1:32). Our responsibility remains the same, and that is to make a defense for the truth found in the Bible. We are to share the forgiveness that is offered in Jesus Christ.

Remember, most other major religions in the world, including Zoroastrianism, claim that a person can achieve, on his own, some kind of afterlife by how he lives. However, the Bible alone teaches man cannot save himself, because the penalty for sin is death (Romans 6:23).

If You Have Been Influenced by Zoroastrianism

We have good news to share, how God in Christ took that death penalty for us, when He became a man and died on the Cross in our place (2 Corinthians 5:19). Jesus Christ then proved His sinless perfection, and therefore His ability to take our punishment as a sinless person, when He was raised from the dead (Romans 1:4, 4:25). The message of the Bible is that no one can possibly earn salvation, but each one must receive salvation by placing his or her faith in Jesus Christ alone (Ephesians 2:8–9).

God does not spell salvation "DO" — and God does not spell salvation "DON'T" — God spells salvation "DONE" (John 19:30). For this reason, with kindness and compassion, knowing that the Holy Spirit works with us as we share this message of forgiveness (John 16:8), we can boldly declare that Jesus Christ is the only way to heaven. We must never forget that Christ did not claim to be a good way to God. He did not even claim to be the best way to God. He claimed to be the only way to the Father (John 14:6).

Wherever you go in this country or this world, people need forgiveness. People need release from the wrong things they have done and the relief that only a clear conscience can bring. As Bible-believing Christians, we have the only message that both works and is true (Acts 4:12).

So look around the community you live in. You will probably find someone from Iran or Iraq or India or some place that either knowingly or unknowingly has embraced some tenet of Zoroastrianism. Share the good news of Christ with them.

Possibly before reading this chapter you were under the impression that your good deeds could save you, or at least they helped to save you. But maybe now you understand that it is only by the gospel, defined as the death, burial, and Resurrection of Christ, that you can be forgiven (1 Corinthians 15:1–3; Romans 1:16). It really does not matter what you may be guilty of in your past. God can forgive you, and He will forgive you, but He will only forgive you if you will call on His Son Jesus Christ to save you (Romans 10:13) I invite you to do that right now.

Summary of Zoroastrian Beliefs

Doctrine	Zoroastrian Teaching
God	Ahura Mazda is the supreme god who is worshiped, but there is also another immortal deity who represents evil, Angra Mainyu.
Authority/ Revelation	The Avesta is the scriptural record of the revelation announced by the prophet Zoroaster. Various sects hold to different sections as authoritative.
Man	The first man was created by Ahura Mazda but evil entered the universe and corrupted man; man must use his free will to choose to do good

Sin	Sin has physical and spiritual aspects and is not well-defined apart from doing good or evil.
Salvation	Those who do good deeds can earn their salvation; there is no concept of a mediator or Savior though all will ultimately be purged of sin to be in heaven.
Creation	Ahura Mazda is eternal and created the universe, including earth, plants, animals, and humans in a way that echoes Genesis.

Chapter 16

Worldwide Church of the Creator (The Creativity Movement)

Pastor Chuck Hickey

> Dedicated towards developing the tremendous potential of nature's finest — the white race. May this book give our great race a religion of its own that will unite, organize, and propel it forward towards a whiter and brighter world. — Ben Klassen, P.M.E.
>
> *The White Man's Bible*

On February 21, 1973, a book was published titled *Nature's Eternal Religion*. The author was Ben Klassen and the publisher was The Creativity Movement. This was the initial written work of a newly launched religious sect following a long line of Aryan cults that have dotted recent history. The above quote from *The White Man's Bible* (the second major publication of The Creativity Movement published in 1981)[1] encapsulates the essence of The Creativity Movement.

In the following pages, I will expose the teachings of The Creativity Movement, contrast those teachings with Christianity, and call those who have embraced the errors and heresies of The Creativity Movement to

---

1. The publication date of *The White Man's Bible* does not appear in the publication but does appear on The Creativity Movement website. The publication can be found at http://creativitymovement.net/Holy%20Books.html.

repentance. In endeavoring to accomplish these goals, a contrast between Christianity and Creativity will be undertaken under four philosophical headings: Epistemology (the study of how we know truth), Theology (the study of the transcendent being), Anthropology (the study of the nature and purpose of man), and Teleology (the study of the created order being directed toward an end or shaped by a purpose).

Throughout this writing, The Creativity Movement will be referred to as a cult. In Walter R. Martin's helpful book *The Kingdom of the Cults*,[2] Dr. Martin cites Dr. Charles Braden's definition of a cult: "A cult, as I define it, is any religious group which differs significantly in some one or more respects as to belief or practice, from those religious groups which are regarded as the normative expressions of religion in our culture."[3] As will become evident on the following pages, the beliefs of The Creativity Movement differ significantly from religious groups throughout North America, particularly Christianity. In fact, The Church of the Creator claims in its own documents (*The White Man's Bible, Nature's Eternal Religion*, and *Salubrious Living*)[4] that Creativity is a unique religion unlike all other religions. In many respects this is true, but in other respects, Creativity is as Solomon wrote in Ecclesiastes 1:9: "nothing new under the sun"[5]

The "sameness" of The Creativity Movement is found in its humanistic/evolutionary origins. These humanistic/evolutionary origins inculcate virtually every society throughout the world. When mankind is elevated to a position of the highest known creature and his origins are attributed to evolutionary processes, the uniqueness of The Creativity Movement is all but lost. In the case of The Creativity Movement, a third element is introduced that makes its humanistic/evolutionary beliefs a bit unique — the presumed superiority of the white race.[6]

2. Walter R. Martin, *The Kingdom of the Cults* (Minneapolis, MN: Bethany House Publishers, 1981).
3. Ibid., p. 1.
4. Each of these publications can be downloaded from The Creativity Movement website at http://creativitymovement.net.
5. In this chapter, Scripture quotations are from the New King James Version (NKJV) of the Bible.
6. "The whole objective and purpose of our religion, Creativity and the CHURCH OF THE CREATOR, is to advance the interests of the White Race, the finest creation in Nature's universe," Ben Klassen, *Nature's Eternal Religion* (New York: The Creativity Movement, 1973), Book II, paragraph 15. (This document is not paginated but appears on The Creativity Movement website www.creativitymovement.net in PDF format. The PDF document page is 274.)

Epistemology: Origins of the Creativity Cult

The beginnings of The Creativity Movement are somewhat muddled. It could be said that it began in 1973 as the Church of the Creator with the publication of Ben Klassen's first book, *Nature's Eternal Religion*. In Klassen's mind, the structure of religion is "eternal" and it is part of "nature." Thus, for Klassen, truth resides in nature alone. It is not revealed; it is merely observed. Klassen wrote, "When we reflect on the source of all our knowledge, we find that *the only real truths are in Nature and in Nature's laws. All that we know is rooted in the natural laws* that surround us. It is the White Man's uncanny ability to observe, to reason and to organize his knowledge of that small part of Nature's secrets from which he has lifted the veil"[7] (emphasis added).

It is interesting to note that although truth exists throughout nature for Creativity and its followers, it is only in the last 40-plus years that this "eternal" religion is distinguishable from all other religions. Furthermore, only "white" mankind is intelligent enough to discern this religion that is presumably eternal.

By way of contrast, Christianity asserts that truth is revealed to mankind by the eternal Creator/God who has codified His truth in the Bible. Therein we learn that God created all things in the space of six days, and all very good, by the power of His Word.[8] In John 17:17, Jesus Christ asserts without equivocation, when speaking of God the Father's revelation, "Your word is truth." This is really the heart of the issue — the arbitrary opinions of man versus the absolute truth of God.

Epistemology is the study of knowing truth. It endeavors to answer the question, "How do we know what we know?" Every religion or philosophy endeavors to answer this question. For The Creativity Movement, you must be of the white race to know and understand truth, and truth only exists in nature.[9] Truth has no other origin. For the Christian, truth is of two kinds, which are completely compatible with one another. Those two kinds of truth

---

7. Klassen, *Nature's Eternal Religion*, PDF p. 18.
8. "In the beginning was the Word, and the Word was with God, and the Word was God. He was in the beginning with God. All things were made through Him, and without Him nothing was made that was made. In Him was life, and the life was the light of men. And the light shines in the darkness, and the darkness did not comprehend it" (John 1:1–5).
9. "All truth and all knowledge originates from our observations of the laws of Nature." Klassen, *Nature's Eternal Religion*, PDF p. 140.

are "general" and "special" revelation. In the strict sense, God's revealed Word, the Bible, is His special revelation and is, in all its parts in the original autographs, the essence of truth. Additionally, Christian theologians have rightly asserted that God's revelation includes the "general" revelation of God's creation. From that "general" revelation, all mankind, including all peoples, regardless of skin shade, can observe things about God because He has created all that exists.[10]

Creation Movement logo

Thus, Creativity is at odds with the Christian understanding of the origins of "truth" and consequently "knowledge."

Theology: The Church of the Creator Rejects the Notion of a Creator God

All philosophies and religions deal with the concept of "God." Either they accept the concept of "God" and then endeavor to explain His person and character, or they reject the concept of a "God" and endeavor to explain why they reject any notion of "God." The Creativity Movement is no different. This movement rejects any notion of God while at the same time asserts that it is a "Church of the Creator."

In *Nature's Eternal Religion,* Klassen asserts the following:

1. The universe is governed by the laws of Nature.

2. The laws of Nature are fixed, rigid and eternal.

3. The laws of Nature apply to living creatures just as firmly and relentless as they do to inanimate objects.

4. The human race, too, is a creature of Nature.

5. Nature is interested only in survival of the species, and not the individual.

---

10. "For since the creation of the world His invisible attributes are clearly seen, being understood by the things that are made, even His eternal power and Godhead, so that they are without excuse" (Romans 1:20).

6. Only those species survive that can compete in the hostile face of all others and either hold their own or increase.

7. Nature continually tries to upgrade the species by the law of the "Survival of the Fittest." It ruthlessly culls out, generally before reproduction, all the misfits, the sickly and the weak.

8. In the struggle for the survival of the species Nature shows that she is completely devoid of any compassion, morality, or sense of fair play, as far as any other species is concerned. The only yard stick is survival.

9. Nature favors and promotes the inner segregation of each species and causes the sub-species to compete against each other.

10. Nature frowns upon mongrelization, cross-breeding or miscegenation. She has given not only each species, but each sub-species, the instinctive drive to mate only with its own kind.

11. Nature has evolved for each particular species a particular pattern in its life cycle which that species must follow. This is called instinct, a very important and vital part of its makeup. Any deviation, deadening or dulling of its instincts usually results in the extinction of that particular species. The White Race should note this well.

12. Not only has Nature usually assigned a particular lifecycle for each species, but usually also a certain type of environment that the species is limited to, such as fish can only live in water, polar bears in the Arctic regions, etc.

13. Nature is completely impartial as to which species survives, each being on its own, in the hostile faces of all others.

14. Each species is completely indifferent to the survival of any other species, and Nature tells each species to expand and multiply to the limit of its abilities. Love and tenderness are reserved exclusively to its own kind.

15. There are many species that realize the importance of territory and stake out limits of the territory that they need for the survival and raising of their families.

16. Many animals, birds, insects, and other categories have a well-developed social structure.

17. The leadership principle is instinctively ingrained and utilized by many species of animals, birds, and insects as well as the human race.

18. One species, for example a flock of gulls, will sometimes wage wholesale war against another species, such as a plague of locusts. A pack of wolves will attack a herd of musk oxen.

19. However, fratricidal wars among the species against its own kind are unknown in Nature, except for some misguided human species.

20. Nowhere in the realm of Nature does a stronger, superior species hold back its own advancement and expansion in deference to weaker, inferior species. There is no compassion between one species and another, only life and death competition.

21. Species themselves are continuously changing and evolving over the millenniums of time. This can even be greatly speeded up by means of deliberate selection, as in the breeding of dogs and horses. Some species die out. New species evolve. None remain static, but all, including the human species, are forever changing and evolving. Evolution is a continuous process.

22. Eternal struggle is the price of survival.

23. Nature has given each creature a strong natural instinct whose basic drive is the perpetuation of its own kind. Ingrained in this instinct is a complete blueprint for its whole life pattern that will propagate its own kind, generation after generation. A species must follow its ingrained instinctive pattern or perish.

24. Last, but not least, Nature clearly indicates that is her plan that each species continuously improve and up-grade itself, or be ruthlessly phased out of existence.[11]

From these assertions, it is evident that The Creativity Movement is devoid of any notion of a "creator." It is ironic, since the name of this cult is "The

11. Klassen, *Nature's Eternal Religion*, PDF p. 15–16.

Church of the Creator." (This inconsistency will be discussed later.) More importantly, these assertions are the presuppositions that color the entirety of this cult. From them, we can deduce these presuppositions as:

1. There is no creator; all that exists is a result of evolutionary process (see number 1 above).

2. Man is no different in his being from any other animal; man is merely a kind in the species of mammals, much like a bass in the species of fish, or fruit flies in the species of insects (see number 4 above).

3. Because mankind is merely a species, he is not a moral agent any more than a squirrel is a moral agent (see number 8 above).

4. Because species do not procreate with other species, neither should kinds procreate with other kinds (see numbers 10 and 11 above).

5. Species are continuously evolving and improving over time (see numbers 21–24 above).

Evolutionary processes, including the survival of the fittest, are at the core of the beliefs of this cult. Nowhere does this cult attribute the origins of creatures to the handiwork of a creator. In fact, *the very notion of a creator is, to this cult, utter nonsense.*[12]

Webster's Dictionary defines the word "creator" as: "one that creates usually by bringing something new or original into being; especially capitalized: god."[13] The very word "creator" presupposes a personage, whether a personal god or an individual who brings something new into being. Ironically, though this religion has the word *creator* in its name, the Church of the Creator attributes nothing of man's existence, the world or the cosmos to a "creator." The equivocation in the use of the word "creator" is undiscernible.

Though The Creativity Movement rejects any notion of a creator God, it does assert that those who are part of this movement are "creators." Ben Klassen

---

12. In speaking of the authors of the Old Testament, Ben Klassen states, "They are rambling about a God as unreal and imaginary as are Zeus, Mars, Jupiter and a thousand others concocted by the imaginary meanderings of the human fantasy," *Nature's Eternal Religion*, PDF p. 100.

13. http://www.merriam-webster.com/dictionary/creator.

wrote in *The White Man's Bible*, "Members of our religion are called CREATORS whether men, women or children, and the religion itself is known as CREATIVITY."[14]

Again, the Church of the Creator rejects any notion of a Creator God while the Christian faith believes in a transcendent God who is Trinitarian in His existence and the Maker/Creator of all things. In the early days of Christianity, assemblies of Christian leaders met in councils and made summary statements of the beliefs of the Christian Church. The summary statements are called creeds and were to be recited in the worship of the Church. At the Council of Nicea in A.D. 325, the Trinitarian God was described. The pertinent part is as follows:

Ben Klassen

> I believe in one God, the Father Almighty, Maker of heaven and earth, and of all things visible and invisible.
>
> And in one Lord Jesus Christ, the only-begotten Son of God, begotten of the Father before all worlds; God of God, Light of Light, very God of very God; begotten, not made, being of one substance with the Father, by whom all things were made.
>
> Who, for us men and for our salvation, came down from heaven, and was incarnate by the Holy Spirit of the virgin Mary, and was made man; and was crucified also for us under Pontius Pilate; He suffered and was buried; and the third day He rose again, according to the Scriptures; and ascended into heaven, and sits on the right hand of the Father; and He shall come again, with glory, to judge the quick and the dead; whose kingdom shall have no end.
>
> And I believe in the Holy Ghost, the Lord and Giver of Life; who proceeds from the Father and the Son; who with the Father and the Son together is worshiped and glorified; who spoke by the prophets.[15]

---

14. Klassen, *The White Man's Bible*, PDF p. 6.
15. http://reformed.org/documents/index.html.

These summary statements are based on statements found in the Bible that affirm the Trinitarian nature of the Maker/Creator God.[16]

In addition to the tripartite nature of the Christian Trinity, it is important to note that Christianity asserts that each of the persons of the Trinity have certain functions relating to creation. This understanding of differing functions by the persons of the Trinity is often referred to as the "economy" of the Trinity by Christian theologians.[17] These functions will be delineated shortly and will become more critical to understanding the difference between The Creativity Movement and Christianity in the section on anthropology.

The three persons of the Trinity — Father, Son, and Holy Spirit — share all things but are also distinct. The Westminster Confession of Faith (1647) gives a helpful description in chapter 2, paragraph 3, wherein we read:

> In the unity of the Godhead there be three Persons of one substance, power, and eternity: God the Father, God the Son, and God the Holy Ghost. The Father is of none, neither begotten nor proceeding; the Son is eternally begotten of the Father; the Holy Ghost eternally proceeding from the Father and the Son.[18]

What then are the differing functions of the three persons of the Trinity that make up the "economy" of the Trinity? First, God the Father, in complete cooperation with God the Son and God the Spirit, authors the decree of God.[19] Jesus, God the Son, in complete cooperation with God the Father and God the Spirit, executes God the Father's decree, particularly the portion that relates to salvation for men.[20] God the Spirit then "applies" the

---

16. Genesis 1:1–2; John 1:1–5; Matthew 28:19; Luke 3:21–22; see also, "God Is Triune," Bodie Hodge, Answers in Genesis, May 20, 2008, https://answersingenesis.org/who-is-god/the-trinity/god-is-triune/.

17. Not to be confused with modalism.

18. http://reformed.org/documents/wcf_with_proofs/index.html.

19. Isaiah 46:8–11 reads: "Remember this, and show yourselves men; recall to mind, O you transgressors. Remember the former things of old, for I am God, and there is no other; I am God, and there is none like Me, declaring the end from the beginning, and from ancient times things that are not yet done, saying, 'My counsel shall stand, and I will do all My pleasure,' calling a bird of prey from the east, the man who executes My counsel, from a far country. Indeed I have spoken it; I will also bring it to pass. I have purposed it; I will also do it."

20. Replete in the gospels of the New Testament is Jesus asserting that He came to do the will of the Father. See Matthew 7:21, 12:50; Luke 22:42; John 5:36, 17:4, 17:8.

salvation provided by Jesus, God the Son in accordance to the will of God the Father, to all who are called unto salvation that have been given to Jesus by God the Father.[21]

In summary, there is a stark difference between the Church of the Creator, which believes in no creator at all (only evolutionary processes in nature), and Christianity that believes in a Triune God who created all that exists, out of nothing, for His own glory.

Anthropology: The Nature of Man and His Purpose in The Creativity Movement

The study of mankind in philosophical and theological realms is known as "anthropology." Creativity has an extensive amount of writing relating to its understanding of anthropology. This is not surprising given the fact that Creativity is a humanistic cult that perceives man (specifically the white race of men) as the highest of all creatures. Ben Klassen wrote in *Nature's Eternal Religion*:

> If there is one thing in this wonderful world of ours that is worth preserving, defending, and promoting, it is the White Race. Nature looked fondly upon the White Race and lavished special loving care in its growth. Of all the millions of creatures who have inhabited the face of this planet over the eons of time, none has ever quite equaled that of the White Race. Nature endowed her Elite with a greater abundance of intelligence and creativity, of energy and productivity than she endowed unto any other creature, now or in the millenniums past. It has been the White Race who has been the world builder, the makers of cities and commerce and continents. It is the White Man who is the sole builder of civilizations. It was he who built the Egyptian civilization, the great unsurpassed Roman civilization, the Greek civilization of beauty and culture, and who, after having been dealt a serious blow by a new Semitic religion, wallowed through the Dark Ages, finally extricated himself, and then built the great European civilization.
>
> What other race can even come close to this remarkable record of creativity, achievement and productivity? The answer is

---

21. See John 6:39, 14:12–18, 15:26–27, 16:5–15, 17:24.

none. None whatsoever. None can even come close. In contrast, the black man of Africa never so much as even invented the wheel.

Yes, it is the White Man, with his inborn and inbred genius, that has given form to every government and a livelihood to every other people, and above all, great ideals to every century. Yes, we are the ones, racial comrades, who were especially endowed by Nature and chosen to be the ruling Elite of the world. Indeed, we were chosen by Nature to be masters of the world by building it ever better and better. We were destined to be fruitful and to multiply and to inhabit the entire hospitable face of this planet. This is our Manifest Destiny as ordained by Nature herself.[22]

In these short paragraphs, the essence of Creativity's anthropology is discerned. The white race is the highest form of all of nature's creatures. Apparently, the white race has evolved to that lofty position. It is unknown whether the "white race" could be supplanted by another race or other creatures (presumably it is possible given the concern expressed by Klassen in *The White Man's Bible* for the decline of the "white race":

But first, the White Race must, like all the other creatures, again learn to recognize its enemies, or it is certain that it will soon be as extinct as the dodo and the dinosaur. Let us again make this clear: our every position is and must be from the White Man's point of view. From the White Man's point of view the Jews, the niggers, and the mud races are his eternal natural enemies. This is as basic and unalterable as the conflict between the pioneering mother and the rattlesnake. . . .

At this crucial stage of world history, either the White Race will survive, or the Jews and their enslaved mud races. It will be one or the other, and this, too, is a grim unalterable fact of life, whether we like it or not. It is the supreme purpose of the CHURCH OF THE CREATOR to see to it that it will be the White Race that shall survive.[23]

In contrast to Creativity's view of anthropology, Christianity has a much different perspective. For the Christian, man is a created being of God, made

---

22. Klassen, *Nature's Eternal Religion*, PDF p. 17–18.
23. Klassen, *The White Man's Bible*, PDF p. 27.

in the image of God.[24] Man is not the product of an "evolutionary process"; he is a created being whose value and purpose are derived from his being created in the "image of God." Unlike all other creatures, mankind was endowed with moral agency, that is, the ability to discern right from wrong, good from evil. All other creatures have no such ability. Yes, creatures can perceive danger, feel emotions, and choose between alternatives (such as carnivores choosing one animal over another to eat), yet, they have no notion of right and wrong. Moral agency only exists in man because man is made in the image of God.[25] Furthermore, morality to the Christian is found in God's revealed Word, the Bible, which defines morality from the attributes of God. These are summarized in the Ten Commandments and the two great commandments of Jesus Christ.[26]

This notion of moral agency is not explained in Creativity. Words like morals, ethics, right, wrong, salvation, and redemption are all words that speak of morality. All of these words are used by the adherents of Creativity in their documents without any discussion of the origins of man's morality or an appeal to where one can find its origin. Only evolutionary processes in nature produce mankind's reality. Unfortunately for Creativity, men interpret their reality differently. Thus, what is morally right for adherents of Creativity is very likely wrong for other men. Even the white race (the highest of all living things in their view) cannot agree that it is the highest living thing. Many of the white race men believe that men are no better than the animals and therefore should never encroach on the habitats of animals. Some go so far as to argue that animals have "rights" that do not differ from the rights of men.

Another difficulty for The Creativity Movement, when considering problems of ethics from the perspective of nature, is that many creatures in nature exhibit behaviors that would presumably be reprehensible to the members of The Creativity Movement. For example, the black widow spider

---

24. Genesis 1:26–28: "Then God said, 'Let Us make man in Our image, according to Our likeness; let them have dominion over the fish of the sea, over the birds of the air, and over the cattle, over all the earth and over every creeping thing that creeps on the earth.' So God created man in His own image; in the image of God He created him; male and female He created them. Then God blessed them, and God said to them, 'Be fruitful and multiply; fill the earth and subdue it; have dominion over the fish of the sea, over the birds of the air, and over every living thing that moves on the earth.' "
25. Ibid.
26. See Exodus 20:1–17; Deuteronomy 5:6–21; Matthew 22:37–40; Mark 12:29–31; Luke 10:27.

kills and devours her mate after mating. Since morality is based on observations in nature, shouldn't "white women" consider such activity as normative? Many species of animals consume their young after birth either to avoid starvation or to allow only a few the opportunity to nurse at the mother. Again, since morality is based on observations in nature, shouldn't "white females" consider such actions for similar reasons?

In summary, Creativity believes mankind's origins are a result of evolutionary processes and that the "white race" of men is the highest of all creatures. This echoes early evolutionists like Charles Darwin and Earnst Haeckel (who popularized Darwinism in Germany and helped pave the way for Nazism). Both held firmly throughout their writings that what they defined as the Caucasian was superior and others were lesser evolved:

> At some future period, not very distant as measured by centuries, the civilized races of man will almost certainly exterminate and replace the savage races throughout the world. At the same time the anthropomorphous apes . . . will no doubt be exterminated. The break between man and his nearest allies will then be wider, for it will intervene between man in a more civilized state, as we may hope, even than the Caucasian, and some ape as low as a baboon, instead of as now between the negro or Australian [Aborigine] and the gorilla.[27]

> At the lowest stage of human mental development are the Australians, some tribes of the Polynesians, and the Bushmen, Hottentots, and some of the Negro tribes. Nothing, however, is perhaps more remarkable in this respect, than that some of the wildest tribes in southern Asia and eastern Africa have no trace whatever of the first foundations of all human civilization, of family life, and marriage. They live together in herds, like apes.[28]

Creativity cannot account for morality except as to what it believes can be observed from activities in nature. By contrast, Christianity believes that man was created by God and in God's image, which includes an understanding of morality. Morality to the Christian is a revelation of God's own attributes and is therefore normative.

27. Charles Darwin, *The Descent of Man* (New York: A.L. Burt, 1874, 2nd ed.), p. 178.
28. E. Haeckel, *The History of Creation*, 1876, p. 363–363.

Teleology: The Hope and Aspirations of The Creativity Movement

Every religion, philosophy, or cult has goals it wants to achieve. Creativity is no different. What is so very striking is the audacity with which they communicate those goals. This boldness may be part of their attractiveness to some. Following is a long quote from *The White Man's Bible* that is a summation of the hopes and aspirations of The Creativity Movement:

> Whether we like it or not (and we CREATORS accept it) a far reaching revolution is now in the making. Whether we like it or not, the impending upheaval is going to turn upside down the immediate affairs of mankind completely and irrevocably. The coming revolution is either going to totally degenerate mankind into a horde of miserable misfits, or could usher in the beautiful Golden Age of the Superman and a brilliant future beyond.
>
> We CREATORS are riding the wave of the future, and by foreseeing and planning that future we are determined to help mold it in such a way that we, our children and future generations can look forward to a Whiter and Brighter World of such magnificence as to stagger the imagination. The Future World we intend to build. Briefly, here are just a few of the broad outlines of the better world we are determined to build.
>
> ### A Brighter World of Beautiful, Healthy People
>
> A world without cancer. A world without heart disease. A world in which there will be much more emphasis placed on building health rather than curing disease, and in which excellent health will be the norm rather than the exception. This we intend to accomplish by a program we call Salubrious Living.[29] We will have several chapters on this subject. We foresee a future world in which the intelligence of the average individual will be significantly raised in each ensuing generation. A world free of insane asylums, idiots, or morons. A clean world in which there will be very little pollution of the environment. A world

---

29. "Salubrious Living" for The Creativity Movement is primarily a form of "clean and healthy living" but is also the name of a book describing how clean and healthy living should take place. To this cult, "Salubrious Living" is indispensable to the movement. The book is found on their website at: http://creativitymovement.net.

virtually free of crime in which any man, woman or child can walk any time of day or night without fear of assault; a world of law and order; a world free of poverty; a world in which every person will be creatively and gainfully employed, in one way or another during their total lifetime, a lifetime that will be prolonged beyond that of the present world. However, let me quickly emphasize we are not nearly as much interested in prolonging life as increasing the individual's health and quality of life as long as it lasts. Longer life is only a secondary benefit as a result of superior well-being.

Racial Problems Solved

The future world as we envision it, will have no racial problems, no language barriers and no fratricidal wars. It will be well fed, but will have no problems of over-population or crowding. Nor will it have scarcities of food, energy supplies or resources. There will be abundance for all. A happy, affluent and well-rounded life will be within easy reach for everyone.

Superstitions Gone

We see a world in which superstition, fear of hell, and "spooks in the skies" will be buried with the superstitions of our barbarian ancestors. No longer will superstition be exploited for profit by con-artists to torment and dominate the minds of the gullible. We look forward to a world where a man and woman can join in raising a family of fine, beautiful, healthy, intelligent children in economic security. They will have the guaranteed prospects of a stable future world in which they can expect that their children, too, can look forward to having that same opportunity when they grow up.

Bringing Dreams to Reality

This is the future world of Creativity that we envision. A tall order, you say?

Fantastic? An impossible Utopia only contemplated by dreamers? Perhaps. But we not only envision it, we are determined to do our best to bring it into being. We are not merely dreamy visionaries, but on the contrary, we have the specific plans, realistic programs and a militant creed to bring it about. You are part of that program, my dear White Racial Comrade. With your help we not only can do it, we must do it and we will do it. It is our religion, our faith, *our reason for being*[30] (emphasis added).

From the above quotation, certain factual statements can be made of Creativity and its ultimate purpose. Creativity exists to promote and advance the "white race" to a utopian kind of civilization: to achieve this goal, a white person must live a salubrious life, exhibit religious devotion to Creativity, and embrace Creativity's "militant creed."[31] This is quite reminiscent of Hitler and the Nazis! Nothing short of this is acceptable to the Church of the Creator.

The teleological aspects of Christianity will be delineated in the following section.

Further Comparisons to Christianity

Creativity: A Religion That Is Not Creative

Throughout history, religious cults have sprung up and tried to mimic other religions. Christianity has been copied by so many artificial imitations that it is difficult to keep count. Some of those imitations endeavor to be subtle in their efforts to copy, while others (like Creativity) make no effort to disguise their efforts to copy Christianity. For example, Creativity has a "Bible" (*The White Man's Bible*),[32] a "Golden Rule,"[33] a form of the "Ten Commandments" (for Creativity, they have 16 Commandments),[34] titles (in the Christian Church, titles are used to delineate leadership in its various branches, e.g. elder, pastor, bishop, pope; in Creativity, the title of "Pontifex Maximus" is the highest leadership position),[35] and lastly, creeds (the Christian Church has creeds that summarize its beliefs, and Creativity has creeds

---

30. Klassen, *The White Man's Bible*, PDF p. 10–11.
31. Ibid.
32. Ibid.
33. Ibid., PDF p. 9. "What is good for the White Race is the highest virtue; what is the bad for the White Race is the ultimate sin."
34. Ibid., PDF p. 426–427.
35. Ibid., PDF p. 5. "From the traditions of Ancient Rome, not the Catholic Church, we have adopted the title of Pontifex Maximus as head of our church."

in the two books *Nature's Eternal Religion* and *The White Man's Bible*).[36] In short, for a religion that claims to be unique in all of history, it has borrowed so much structure from Christianity that it is a feeble, artificial imitation.

Creativity, like Christianity, speaks of "salvation" and "redemption," but in their documents, there is no defining of these terms and there is certainly no favorable reference to the Christian definitions of these concepts.

Salvation and Redemption in Christianity

Salvation and redemption have very important meanings in Christianity. "Salvation" means to be delivered from something and "redemption" means to be delivered unto or into something. Salvation is being delivered from the consequences of sin and death. Redemption is to be delivered unto eternal life and into the Kingdom of God.

To be saved from the consequences of sin and death means that there is a reckoning, or judging, for the actions of one's life. To the Christian, the one who exacts the reckoning or makes the judgment is the one who has created us, the God of the Bible. The Bible very clearly states, "For the wages of sin is death, but the gift of God is eternal life in Jesus Christ our Lord" (Romans 6:23). The Scriptures also state, "For by grace you have been saved through faith, and that not of yourselves; it is the gift of God, not of works, lest anyone should boast" (Ephesians 2:8–9). These verses speak of faith in something. That something is a person, the second person of the Triune God, Jesus Christ. In the Book of Ephesians we also read:

> In Him you also *trusted*, after you heard the word of truth, the gospel of your salvation; in whom also, having believed, you were sealed with the Holy Spirit of promise, who is the guarantee of our inheritance until the redemption of the *purchased posses-sion*, to the praise of His glory (Ephesians 1:13–14, emphasis added).

These two verses are very profound as we consider the concepts of salvation and redemption. Both are mentioned in these verses and they both speak

---

36. Ibid., PDF p. 7. "One thing more. This book is not meant to be a scientific discourse, nor an historical review of the White Race. I make it very clear throughout: this book and NATURE'S ETERNAL RELIGION are conceived as a religious creed and program written for the masses, clearly and simply, so that anyone with an open mind and a modicum of common sense can understand it and grasp its import."

of a "purchased possession." What is the possession that was purchased? For the Christian, his salvation and redemption were purchased by the shed blood of Jesus Christ on the Cross.[37] Furthermore, God being the perfect judge of the universe then makes a declaration regarding our citizenship in the Kingdom of God. When Jesus rose from the dead, the Bible states that He did that for our "justification."[38] Justification is a legal term that means to be "declared just" or "right."

God stands ready to forgive any and all who confess their sins, turn from their sins, and declare Jesus Christ as Lord and Savior. He will declare "right" all who do so. He will also judge all for their sins that do not confess their sins, repent, and submit to the Lordship of Jesus.

This is reality — not a supposed master race of white men and women led by a self-proclaimed "Pontifex Maximus" who believes in a utopian society. I call on all who embrace The Creativity Movement to denounce the heresies of The Church of the Creator and bow their knees to the King of kings and Lord of lords, Jesus Christ.

Summary of Church of the Creator Beliefs

Doctrine	Church of the Creator Teaching
God	Nature is god and determines the laws of the universe
Authority/ Revelation	Truth originates from the laws of nature and can be understood only by those of the "white" race
Man	A creature of nature with no moral agency; the "white" race is superior
Sin	Whatever is bad for the "white" race is sin
Salvation	Largely undefined; a concept of a utopian society of "whites" only
Creation	Completely evolutionary in all aspects

---

37. Without the shedding of blood there is no remission of sin (Hebrews 9:22).
38. "It shall be imputed to us who believe in Him who raised up Jesus our Lord from the dead, who was delivered up because of our offenses, and was raised because of our justification" (Romans 4:24–25).

Chapter 17

Moonies / The Unification Church

Dr. Mark Bird

I stood there on the sidewalk, amazed at what I had just heard. The lady I was interviewing had told me that Rev. Sun Myung Moon married Jesus Christ to a woman from the Unification Church. "How could anyone believe that!" I thought. The pastor's wife explained that Jesus recently got married because that was the only way he (Jesus) could get out of Paradise and into Heaven. According to her church's theology, *anyone* who wants to go to heaven must be married with Rev. Moon's blessing.

The woman I interviewed was herself married to a man introduced to her by Sun Myung Moon, the founder of the Unification Church. She told me that on an appointed day she was waiting in a room with other women anticipating this "matching." Moon suddenly walked into the room with a gentleman, brought the two together, and left. Later, they wed in a ceremony that Moon conducted. Then, after a purification period of 40 days, they consummated their marriage and began having children. The now happily married lady claimed that because of this blessing and purification process, her children were born without sin. Noticing her kids playing nearby, I asked her, "So your children never do anything wrong?" She replied, "Oh, they're not perfect, just sinless!"

Many other members of the Unification Church can testify to a similar experience, since Rev. Moon matched thousands of couples during his lifetime. Why did he match couples, and why are their children said to be sinless? Because Moon was supposedly tasked by Jesus Himself to finish

Christ's mission to establish a pure new kingdom on this earth. Moon and his wife are the True Parents, whom Unification Church members call "Father" and "Mother." Moon started a new "race" of people, and a new movement to save the world.

According to the Unification Church, Jesus spoke to a 16-year-old Sun Myung Moon[1] in a vision while he was praying on a mountain in South Korea.[2] Moon learned that Jesus did not come to the earth to die, but to show people how to live, and to start a new physical kingdom on the earth. That first meeting with Jesus was the beginning of numerous encounters

Rev. Sun Myung Moon speaking in Las Vegas, Nevada, on April 4, 2010

Moon had with those from the spirit world, where he learned many truths that he shared with his followers.[3] A whole theology was developed, much of it contained in the "inspired" *Exposition of the Divine Principle*.[4] Most Unificationists would agree with the following presentation of these teachings.

1. He changed his name from Yong Myung (his birth name) to Sun Myung because Yong means dragon, which could be interpreted as serpent, or the devil.

2. From the introduction to a set of Moon's sermons: "On Easter morning in 1935, Sun Myung Moon was deep in prayer on a Korean Mountainside when Jesus Christ appeared to him and told him that he had an important mission to accomplish in the fulfillment of God's providence. He was then sixteen years old," (http://www.unification.net/nhtt/nhtt_prf.html). Koreans would have considered him to be 16, since in their traditional culture, someone is 1 year old when he is born. Moon was born in January, 1920.

3. Reverend Sun Myung Moon, *Exposition of the Divine Principle* (New York: The Holy Spirit Association for the Unification of World Christianity, 1996). Unificationists believe that some of those spiritual luminaries were Buddha, Mohammed, Confucius, and Moses. Moon would get all the information he needed to bring to light "all the secrets of heaven." "In the fullness of time, God has sent one person to this earth to resolve the fundamental problems of human life and the universe. His name is Sun Myung Moon," p. 12.

4. Ibid., preface, p. xxi. This book was put together by a disciple of Moon. It is based on many notes that Moon had written down. The most widely dispersed version of it (3rd version) was published in 1966 and the first English translation was made in 1973 by Dr. Won Pok Choi.

Unificationist Doctrine

God

God is dualistic — He has both a negative part and a positive part.[5] The positive or male part is God; the negative or female part is the Holy Spirit. This is reflected in the fact that every person is body (-) and soul (+), and the fact that male and female humans come together to become one flesh in marriage.

1st Adam (and Eve)

Adam and Eve were created as a reflection of the nature of God, and more than a reflection. Adam was the embodiment of God; Eve was the embodiment of the Holy Spirit. As such, they were to be the True Parents of Mankind.

The Trinity and the Fall

God intended for Adam and Eve to form a perfect trinity with him, and have perfect children.[6] But Eve was seduced by Satan and committed sexual sin with him. Feeling ashamed, Adam and Eve had sexual intimacy before they were perfected enough as a couple to receive the marriage blessing.[7] Through this sin of fornication, a new trinity (Adam, Eve, and Satan) was started.[8] God's purpose for Adam to physically procreate the kingdom of God on earth was thwarted.

From that time until Moon's own marriage, no marital intimacy was blessed by God. The consequences of the fall were devastating. Sin became commonplace in the human race. All humans were born with sin, and this evil nature spawned all kinds of problems and destruction.

Humankind needed to be redeemed. Prophets like Moses were sent to teach man God's ways, and Jewish obedience to the law brought us closer to God, but it was not enough. A new Adam was needed to reestablish God's kingdom.

---

5. Ibid., p. 16, "Everything in the created universe is a substantial manifestation of some quality of the Creator's invisible, divine nature. . . . Every entity possesses dual characteristics of yang (masculinity) and yin (femininity).

6. Ibid., p. 172, "If Adam and Eve had not fallen, but had formed this trinity with God and become the True Parents who could multiply good children, their descendants would have also become good husbands and wives with God as the center of their lives."

7. Ibid., p. 64, ". . . Eve, who in her immaturity had engaged in the illicit relationship with the Archangel, joined with Adam as husband and wife. Thus, Adam fell when he, too, was still immature. This untimely conjugal relationship in satanic love between Adam and Eve constituted the physical fall."

8. Ibid., p. 172, "When Adam and Eve fell . . . they formed a fallen trinity with Satan.

2nd Adam — Jesus

Fortunately, Zechariah (the priest who was the husband of Elizabeth and father of John the Baptist) impregnated the virgin Mary, and the Messiah was born.[9] With Zechariah of the priestly line, and Mary a descendent of David, they met the conditions for Jesus the Messiah to be born sinless.

Mary had been told, "You will conceive but not with your chosen husband." She cooperated with God's will, and had a child by the person who represented God on the earth. As the father of Jesus, Zechariah should have claimed Mary and protected her and Jesus, but he didn't. This led to problems later.

As the sinless Messiah (and second Adam), Jesus had a special mission to fulfill. He would redeem mankind both spiritually and physically. To redeem mankind physically, Jesus needed to find a perfect Eve, marry her, and start a perfect family. This would be the beginning of the restoration of the human race.

However, Jesus was killed before his time because the Jewish people, including John the Baptist, lost faith in him.[10] Jesus died before he could find his Eve — he should have married a half-sister (John the Baptist's sister) and started his perfect family, but his mother disallowed that.[11] However,

---

9. In Reverend Sun Myung Moon, *True Love and True Family* (New York: Family Federation for World Peace and Unification, 1997), Moon declares that, "Jesus was conceived in the house of Zechariah" (p. 12). Moon also said at a conference in 1995, "Who was the father of Jesus Christ? Zechariah. . . . The relationship between Elizabeth and Mary was just like that between Leah and Rachel. . . . The result of the relationship between Zechariah and Mary was the birth of Jesus Christ." (http://www.unification.net/1995/950207.html. Reverend Sun Myung Moon Speaks at the Leader's Conference, February 7, 1995, Washington, DC. Translator — Hideo Oyamada). Unificationists leave some room for doubt on this subject, but they also do not think there is a viable alternative to Zechariah being the father, since an actual virgin conception would contradict the natural laws that God has set up.

10. In this chapter, the pronouns for Jesus are not capitalized when referring to the Unification Church's false concept of Jesus.

11. According to Moon, "When Jesus Christ was seventeen years old, he told Mary whom he should marry. Jesus Christ spoke strongly about the necessity for this marriage, no matter what sacrifices might need to be made, but Mary could not accept it. . . . If Mary had confessed who her child's father was, there would have been a problem. Thus Jesus and John the Baptist's sister had the same father, but different mothers. They were half-brother/sister. . . . Under these circumstances, for Jesus to marry John the Baptist's younger sister was unacceptable. Although they had different mothers, they were both children of Zechariah. How could people accept such an incestuous relationship (Leviticus 18)?" (http://www.unification.net/1995/950207.html. Reverend Sun Myung Moon Speaks at the Leader's Conference, February 7, 1995, Washington, DC.).

Jesus did redeem mankind spiritually through his death on the cross, even though dying was not his original purpose for coming.[12]

Though Jesus was not God (any more than you and I are),[13] and even though he did not rise bodily from the dead (he rose spiritually instead), he was the only sinless man in history (before Moon), so he was able to redeem us spiritually.[14]

3rd Adam — Second Coming of Christ

Since Jesus left some of his mission unfulfilled, a third Adam was necessary. This third Adam would be the second coming of Christ, and was to be born in Korea soon after World War I.[15] This Messiah would not be Jesus, but someone else who would redeem mankind physically by finding a perfect Eve and starting a perfect family. Others who were blessed in marriage by him would become part of a restored human race, as their families too would be perfected. Children would be born sinless through marriages blessed by this Messiah.[16]

Who was this third Adam? After hinting at it for years, Moon publicly revealed himself to be the Messiah at a mass wedding in 1992.[17] He fit his own description of the Savior, since he was born in Korea in 1920, soon after the war. The pastor's wife I talked to was excited to tell me about this (our discussion took place later in 1992). She had suspected all along that the Messiah was Moon himself, but was thrilled to have had that recently

---

12. This is why in the year 2000 Moon held a campaign intended to get pastors to take crosses down from their churches. Moon thought that having a cross in a church was misleading. The crucifixion was not why Jesus came.

13. "While on earth, Jesus was a man no different than any of us except for the fact that he was without the original sin. . . . If Jesus were God, how could he intercede for us before Himself? . . . We can conclude with finality that Jesus was not God himself from the words he uttered on the cross, 'My God, my God, why hast thou forsaken me?' " (Moon, *Exposition of the Divine Principle*, p. 168).

14. According to Unificationists, the death of Jesus was not necessary. But since the people had lost faith in Jesus when he came the first time, the devil had a claim on them (it put them over on the devil's side), so Jesus gave himself in death for the people to bring them back over so that they could love again. In that sense, mankind is redeemed spiritually.

15. Moon, *Exposition of the Divine Principle,* p. 399, 382–383.

16. This chapter capitalizes Messiah even when referring to the Unification Church's false concept of the Christ, since the term Messiah is a title and the Unification Church capitalizes the term.

17. According to Moon, the Korean people happen to be the descendants of the lost tribes of Israel. They are the new Israel.

confirmed. The person who had matched her with her wonderful husband, and even had stayed in their home, was the Messiah!

Moon didn't keep the messianic honor to himself. At the wedding, he proclaimed that both he and his wife were Mankind's True Parents. He had married Hak Ja Han in 1960, and considered her his "Eve."[18] Moon and his wife eventually had a total of 14 children (one died as a baby), all of whom were considered perfect, since they were born to the True Parents of Mankind.

The 1992 public announcement was consistent with a declaration he had made a few years earlier. In a secret ceremony in 1985, Moon had crowned himself and his wife as Emperor and Empress of the Universe.[19]

In 2002, the *New York Times* reported on an ad that had been submitted by the Unification Church for publication. This full-page ad presented the text of a Christmas Day meeting in the spirit world attended by Jesus, Muhammad, Confucius, Buddha, and Martin Luther.

> According to the ad, which was presented to newspapers around the country this month, these men and hundreds of others in attendance proclaimed their allegiance to the Rev. Sun Myung Moon, the leader of the Unification Church. At the spirit meeting, the ad said, Jesus hailed Mr. Moon as the Messiah, proclaiming, "You are the Second Coming who inaugurated the Completed Testament Age." Muhammad then led everyone in three cheers of victory.
>
> God didn't attend, but sent a letter Dec. 28 seconding Jesus' remarks. Lenin and other leading communists also sent messages. Lenin said that he was in "unimaginable suffering and agony" for his earthly mistakes, and Stalin added, "We live in the bottom of Hell here."[20]

Two years later, Moon was photographed wearing a gold crown and regal robes. He had just declared in a ceremony before U.S. senators and

---

18. This was after a failed marriage to someone else years earlier, and after a child through that marriage.
19. Nansook Hong, *In the Shadow of the Moons: My Life in the Reverend Sun Myung Moon's Family* (Boston, MA: Little, Brown and Company, 1998), p. 148.
20. http://www.nytimes.com/2002/07/22/business/mediatalk-decisions-differ-on-religious-ad.html.

representatives that he was "none other than humanity's savior, messiah, returning lord and true parent."[21]

Moon also said that up until he started performing his marriage blessings, the only persons in history ever born sinless were Jesus and then Moon himself, as the third Adam.[22]

All these audacious claims came with a great benefit for Moon's loyal followers. It is through the True Parents (Rev. and Mrs. Moon) that God can now bless sexual relationships in marriage, and children can be born sinless. But there is a process by which that happens.

Unification Rituals and Salvation

Unification Church members are "born again" through a Holy Wine ceremony. In this event, original sin is forgiven, and now the believer can go to heaven after being blessed in marriage by the Moons. Children of these marriages have a special status. After the blessing and marriage, and a 40-day waiting period for purification, children will be born sinless — they won't need forgiveness.

Here is the process of salvation as described by a Unificationist Handbook:

> True Parents, standing on a historical foundation of victory, have the authority to engraft all humankind into the original lineage of God. The Blessing is the process through which we become God's original sons and daughters. It consists of these steps:
>
> ### A. Holy Wine Ceremony
>
> This ceremony restores the order of God's original love, cleansing us from the original sin. It is performed in precisely the reverse order of the process of the fall. True Parents give the wine to the woman first, who then shares it with her future husband.
>
> ### B. The Blessing Ceremony
>
> The Holy Blessing was traditionally officiated by Father and Mother Moon in their capacity as True Parents, or an officiating

---

21. http://www.washingtonpost.com/world/asia_pacific/sun-myung-moon-dies-at-92-washington-times-owner-led-the-unification-church/2012/09/02/001b747a-f531-11e1-aab7-f199a16396cf_story.html.

22. From interview of Unificationists Michael and Arlene Candelaresi, Feb. 5, 2015.

couple representing them. The officiators and their attendants cleanse the couples by sprinkling them with holy water, signifying their rebirth into God's lineage as a Blessed couple.

C. Chastening or Indemnity Ceremony

This simple ceremony provides an opportunity for each couple to indemnify[23] any personal sexual past and the historical abuse of each gender by the other. Each partner firmly strikes the other three times upon the buttocks, to repent for and resolve the history of sexual immorality and the misuse of our bodies. This ceremony is of course symbolic. Any abuse or violence between the couple whether emotional, verbal or physical, is a violation of the Blessing vows and not acceptable.

D. 40-day Separation Period

In this tradition, abstaining from sexual intimacy during the first 40 days of marriage is meant to separate the newly Blessed Couple from the history of selfishness between men and women. It can also help heal any painful personal sexual past.

E. Three-day Ceremony of Renewal

The couple first cleanses their bodies with the Holy Wine that now links them to God's lineage. Then with a prayer of offering, they invite the Heavenly Parent to enter their most intimate love relationship.[24]

The process of salvation, including everything that takes place after the renewal, takes time and a lot of effort. According to Unificationists, salvation is "95% up to God and 5% up to us, but it takes all we got to do the other 5%."[25] God does most of the work, but we contribute to our salvation through a complete adherence to the process. Unificationist Kwang-Yol

---

23. "What, then, is the meaning of restoration through indemnity? When someone has lost his original position or state, he must make some condition to be restored to it. The making of such conditions of restitution is called indemnity" (Moon, *Exposition of the Divine Principle*, p. 177).

24. Excerpts from an unpublished handbook made available to members online: DRAFT-Unificationist-Handbook_2013–12.

25. October 2014 interview with Michael Candelaresi, member of the Unification Church since 1974. Michael also happens to be a member of Mensa, having passed an intelligence test that only 2% of the general population can pass.

Yoo said that by following the Divine Principle, "man's perfection must be accomplished finally by his own effort without God's help."[26]

History of the Church

Origin and Nomenclature

The great promulgator of all this heretical theology, Sun Myung Moon, started the Unification Church in South Korea in 1954, calling it the Holy Spirit Association for the Unification of World Christianity.[27] Church members called themselves Moonies (and Moon himself used the term) until around 1990, when leaders in the church began to call "Moonies" a derogatory term. Since the Unification Church is a personality cult, "Moonie" still seems appropriate, but this chapter usually uses the term "Unificationists" to refer to the members.

Move to the United States

In the 1970s Moon came to the United States and preached to large stadium crowds. Thousands of young people were recruited in the '70s and '80s. Many parents during this time complained about the church's extreme indoctrination process and manipulation, since the children had been estranged from their families.[28]

In 1982 (the same year that he was convicted of tax evasion and sent to prison for 18 months), Moon founded *The Washington Times*, a conservative alternative to the *Washington Post*. This is probably the most successful enterprise he established, in terms of political influence, though the church has had to subsidize the paper with millions of dollars every year. The Unification Church also acquired the wire service United Press International, and it has had many other more successful business ventures.

Mass Weddings

Rev. Moon is most famous for the mass weddings he and his wife have conducted, beginning in the 1960s. Moon's followers have been told that through these weddings they would produce a new generation of sinless

---

26. Quoted in *Unification Church* by J. Isamu Yamanoto (Grand Rapids, MI: Zondervan, 1995), p. 82. Another Unification teacher (Young Oon Kim) taught, "We atone for our sins through specific acts of penance," Kim Young Oon, *Unification Theology* (New York: The Holy Spirit Association for the Unification of World Christianity, 1980), p. 230.
27. Its official name now is the Family Federation for World Peace and Unification.
28. http://www.4truth.net/fourtruthpbnew.aspx?pageid=8589952680.

Moon holds a mass "blessing ceremony"

children. Many of the participants in the latest mass weddings are these "sinless" children of the original followers.

The first wedding in 1961 had 36 couples; the next wedding doubled to 72, and the numbers kept increasing for more than 30 years. In 1992, the year Moon declared himself and his wife the True Parents, there were at least 30,000 couples married. In 1997, another 30,000 couples were married in Washington, D.C. In 1999, 21,000 couples exchanged vows in the Olympic Stadium in Seoul, South Korea.

These weddings have continued even after Rev. Moon's death in 2012. There were 3,500 couples married by Mrs. Moon in 2013. She blessed another 2,500 couples (from about 50 countries) in 2014.

These numbers do not include those who were part of the ceremonies via satellite. For example, in 2013, the church claims that 24,000 followers from other countries took part in that wedding through video link. For most of the Blessings, many couples had just met in person for the first time when the ceremonies took place, and in some cases, they spoke different languages.[29]

Beginning with the '90s, many of the participants were allowed to be non-Unification members, so that helped increase the numbers. The non-Unificationist participants only have to agree to be faithful to their spouse, to teach their kids abstinence before marriage, and to promote world peace. They don't have to accept Moon and his wife as the True Parents.[30]

29. http://www.dailymail.co.uk/news/article-2119753/Unification-Church-South-Korea-mass-wedding-2-500-marriages.html.

30. http://www.religionfacts.com/unification_church/.

Other changes over the years include having ministers of other faiths serve as co-officiators at the Blessing ceremonies. Also, since 2001, previously blessed couples have been able to help arrange marriages for their own children, without the Moons' direct guidance.[31]

Numbers/Growth of This Group

As of early 2015, the Unification Church claimed to have about 3 million members worldwide. Of these 3 million, 1 million are said to live in Japan[32] and another half a million are said to live in Korea. However, critics of the movement say that there are far fewer members than that; some say as few as 100,000 worldwide. Perhaps a better estimate would be about 1 million, with most of these living in Korea and Japan.[33] Unificationists believe that the church is growing across many of the approximately 100 countries in which it has a presence. Numbers are increasing in South America, Nepal, the South Pacific, and in Africa. Numbers have been shrinking in the United States since the death of Moon and a scandal involving his daughter In Jin, one-time leader of the American church.[34]

In the United States, there are now only around 10,000 Unification families.[35] In Ohio, for example, there are about 100 families, with 8–10 families in the Cincinnati area.

Besides the fragmentation that naturally resulted from Moon's death, another reason that there are fewer Unification members in the United States is that the intense recruiting efforts that took place in the '70s and '80s are no

---

31. http://www.dailymail.co.uk/news/article-2557521/Here-come-brides-2-500-Moonie-couples-met-just-days-wed-mass-stadium-ceremony-South-Korea.html#ixzz3Nz1Dx3rV.

32. http://familyfed.org/news-story/happy-anniversary-to-ffwpu-japan-6696/.

33. According to religionfacts.com, "Today, the church has a presence in more than 100 countries, though exact membership figures are difficult to estimate. The Unification Church says it has 3 million members, but other sources say it is far less, estimating membership at anywhere from 250,000 to just over 1 million." http://www.religionfacts.com/unification_church/#sthash.CA7t9o9k.dpuf.

34. This explanation of the declining numbers from long-time member Michael Candelesari. Interview Jan 29, 2015.

35. The source of these numbers is Michael Candelesari. There may be much fewer members in the U.S. than that. Here's data from an email correspondence in 2003 to adherents.com: "I have been a member since 1974 and it has always been hard to get a good estimate of the total number of members. One thing that did happen is that in February 2003, Rev. Moon asked one person from each church family in the USA to go to Korea for a two-week outreach program. A bit over 2,400 went, which was the goal. Not every family was able to send someone and a few families sent more. . . . So about 2,400 families, maybe 10,000 members in the USA." http://www.adherents.com/Na/Na_638.html.

longer generally practiced. Most Unificationists now live in their own homes, whereas many early Moonies lived in communal centers, attending many seminars, and working long hours to raise money and recruit new members.

Current Leadership

Since Rev. Sun Myung Moon's death in 2012, Mrs. Hak Ja Han Moon has taken charge of the church, as both the spiritual and physical leader. After she took over, she asked all of her children to give up their leadership positions of various branches of the church. In May 2014, Mrs. Moon appointed her fifth daughter, Sun Jin Moon, as the Director-General of Family Federation for World Peace and Unification International.[36]

Sinless Children?

As the True Parents of Mankind, Rev. and Mrs. Moon were to have their own set of pure children. However, the evidence suggests that their children are far from sinless. Their daughter In Jin, who at one time was the leader of the American church, had a child out of wedlock, after a three-year adulterous affair while in a leadership position.[37] Their eldest son Hyo Jin was deeply involved in drug abuse and sexual promiscuity. He physically abused his wife, Nansook Hong, who was afraid of him. She finally escaped the New York compound with their children and wrote a book in 1998 called *In the Shadow of the Moons*, a devastating exposé of what went on in the Moon family over many years.[38] Moon's daughter Un Jin, who also left an abusive relationship, confirmed Nansook's personal credibility and the accuracy of

---

36. On Feb 1, 2015, Sun Jin addressed the Interfaith Peace Festival in the Philippines. In the speech, she advocated the Unification Church concept of tribal messiahship. She said, "We are each called to fulfill the mission of a heavenly tribal messiah. That is, we should raise up other families to form our own heavenly tribe. Fulfilling our mission as heavenly tribal messiahs is the cornerstone for the complete establishment of *Cheonilguk*, God's eternal Kingdom. For this reason, last year True Mother was delighted to hear that two couples, one from Thailand and one from the Philippines, had each completed their tribal messiah mission by raising up 430 couples. Toward the end of October, she invited all those couples to come to Korea, and she held a great celebration for all of them. We celebrate each Blessing and spiritual rebirth with absolute joy! Thank you and congratulations to these tribes. May all 7 billion of Heavenly Parent's children soon be Blessed. We can then have the greatest celebration the world has ever known." http://familyfedihq. org/2015/02/sun-jin-nims-congratulatory-address-at-the-interfaith-peace-blessing-festival-in-the-philippines/.

37. http://www.newrepublic.com/article/115512/unification-church-profile-fall-house-moon.

38. http://www.washingtonpost.com/world/asia_pacific/sun-myung-moon-dies-at-92-washington-times-owner-led-the-unification-church/2012/09/02/001b747a-f531-11e1-aab7-f199a16396cf_story.html.

her book. (One thing Un Jin specifically confirmed in an interview was that Rev. Moon had an illegitimate son, named Sammy.) Another son in a troubled marriage committed suicide.

It is evident that being the Messiah's children did not keep them from the same vices and problems that plague the average human population. In some cases, the behavior has been more egregious. This contradicts a key element in Unification doctrine. Nansook said, "Rev. Moon has been proclaiming that he has established his ideal family, and fulfilled his mission, and when I pinpointed that his family is just as dysfunctional as any other family — or more than most — then I think his theology falls apart."[39] Though Unificationists explain that children born sinless still have the same choice that Adam and Eve had, and thus can still make bad decisions, it does seem ironic that the Messiah's own family has had that much trouble maintaining its purity. It not only contradicts Moon's theology but also fails to inspire confidence that other blessed couples will have children who remain true to their innate sinlessness.

Moon's Infidelity

The Reverend Moon didn't set a very good example for his children. In 1946, Moon abandoned his first wife and three-month-old son. He didn't return for six years. Sometime later came the divorce. His wife differed with him theologically, and unlike Moon, believed that when the Messiah came, He would literally return on the clouds.[40] But the problems were not just ideological; she also claimed that he was unfaithful to her. Other reports seem to confirm his straying tendencies. Nansook said:

> His wife's departure coincided with the first published reports of sexual abuse in the Unification Church. Rumors were rife that the Reverend Moon required female acolytes to have sex with him as a religious initiation rite. Some religious sects at the time did practice ritual nudity and reportedly forced members to have sexual intercourse with a messianic leader in a purification rite known as *p'i kareun*. The Reverend Moon has always denied these reports, claiming they were part of efforts by mainstream religious leaders to discredit the Unification Church. . . .

---

39. "Life with the Moons: A Conversation with Nansook Hong, Former Daughter-in-law of the Rev. Sun Myung Moon," *TIME Magazine*, October 13, 1998.
40. Hong, *In the Shadow of the Moons*, p. 25.

The record of those early days became all the more confused in 1993 when Chung Hwa Pak, the disciple whom the Reverend Moon is reputed to have carried on his back to South Korea in 1951, published a book entitled *The Tragedy of the Six Marias*. In it Pak states that the Reverend Moon did practice *p'i kareun* and contends that the Reverend Moon's first wife left him because of his sexual activities with other women. The Reverend Moon is said by Pak to have impregnated a university student, Myung Hee Kim, in 1953 while he was still married. . . .[41]

Moon apparently was also unfaithful to Hak Ja Han (True Mother). When Hyo Jin Moon told his wife Nansook that if his Father, Sun Myung Moon, could be unfaithful to his wife, then he could too, she took Hyo Jin's claim to Mrs. Moon. Nansook's mother-in-law became both furious and tearful:

> She had hoped that such pain would end with her, that it would not be passed on to the next generation, she told me. No one knows the pain of a straying husband like True Mother, she assured me. I was stunned. We had all heard rumors for years about Sun Myung Moon's affairs and the children he sired out of wedlock, but here was True Mother confirming the truth of those stories. . . .

> Mrs. Moon told Father what Hyo Jin was claiming and the Reverend Moon summoned me to his room. What happened in his past was "providential," Father reiterated. It has nothing to do with Hyo Jin. I was embarrassed to be hearing this admission from him directly. I was also confused. If Hak Ja Han Moon was the True Mother, if he had found the perfect partner on Earth, how could he justify his infidelity theologically?[42]

Moon's Dead Son Is Greater than Jesus

Besides calling himself the Messiah, what Moon said about one of his deceased sons may be his most bizarre claim. Just days after his 17-year-old son Heung Jin died from a car accident, Moon declared that Heung Jin

---

41. Ibid., p. 26–27. Moon later persuaded Pak to rejoin the church, and Pak disavowed his account of the early history of the church, but Nansook has always wondered what the price was of that retraction (p. 27). Support for the view that Moon practiced *p'i kareun* is found in the book *Change of Blood Lineage through Ritual Sex in the Unification Church*, by Kirsti Nevalainen (BookSurge Publishing, 2010).

42. Ibid., p. 196–197.

was already teaching the *Divine Principle* to those in the spirit world, and had actually displaced Jesus. Nansook said,

> Jesus was so impressed by Heung Jin that he had stepped down from his position and proclaimed the son of Sun Myung Moon the King of Heaven. Father explained that Heung Jin's status was that of a regent. He would sit on the throne of Heaven until the arrival of the Messiah, Sun Myung Moon.
>
> I was stunned by the instant deification of this teenage boy. I knew Heung Jin was a True Child, the son of the Lord of the Second Advent, so I was ready to believe that he had a special place in Heaven. But displacing Jesus? The boy I had helped search for a lost

Sun Myung Moon and his wife, Hak Ja Han

> kitten in the attic of the mansion at East Garden, he was the King of Heaven? It was too much, even for a true believer like myself.[43]

A few years later Moon also claimed that the spirit of Heung Jin had returned in the body of a Zimbabwean man who traveled the world giving messages and physically beating church members who misbehaved.[44] This abuse had Rev. Moon's support for a while.[45]

Instructions from the Spirit World

As the spiritual and physical leader of the Unification Church, Mrs. Hak Ja Han Moon claims to be getting instructions from her dead husband while in prayer. On the basis of these alleged messages from the spirit world, she has made quite a number of changes in the church, besides having her children

---

43. Ibid., p. 136–137.
44. Unificationists don't believe in reincarnation but believe we can come back to the world as spirits. They say that some who have died have misunderstood their purpose (they thought they should be reincarnated) and have come back to possess people. This has negatively impacted both the returning spirit and the person he "possessed."
45. http://www.nytimes.com/2012/09/03/world/asia/rev-sun-myung-moon-founder-of-unification-church-dies-at-92.html?pagewanted=all&_r=0.

step down from leadership. For instance, in 2013, Mrs. Moon declared that when church members pray, instead of saying "Heavenly Father" or "Heavenly Parent," the first words they must say are "Heavenly Parents" and then, "Loving True Parents of Heaven, Earth, and Humankind."[46]

Biblical Evaluation of Unification Church Theology

Could Rev. Moon Be the Returning Messiah?

Unificationists' belief that Moon is the second coming of Christ contradicts Jesus' own teaching on the end times. Whereas Christ said that he would return in the clouds (1 Thessalonians 4:17), Moon said just the opposite. He said in *Divine Principle*, "The idea that Christ will return on the clouds [literally] is totally unacceptable to the scientific mind of the modern age."[47] Moon uses a secular view of reality to support his anti-biblical position.

I asked one Unificationist if it bothered him that Jesus was supposed to return in the clouds. He replied, "No, that doesn't bother me; Rev. Moon did come in a cloud. Hebrews 12:1 speaks of a great cloud of witnesses. Korea has been a Christian nation, so it is a cloud (of witnesses).[48] Since Moon was born in Korea, then Christ came back in a cloud."[49] This Unificationist thought he had a way to interpret Scripture that would support Moon as the second coming of Christ.[50] But the angels said that Jesus would return like he left. How did he leave? He physically went up in literal clouds. Acts 1:9–11 says:

> Now when He had spoken these things, while they watched, He was taken up, and a cloud received Him out of their sight. And while they looked steadfastly toward heaven as He went

---

46. The change to praying to "Heavenly Parents" emphasizes that God is both male and female. It is not a reference to a literal, physical god and goddess (something taught or at least implied in Mormon teaching). It is a reference to the Yin/Yang qualities of God — that he has both positive and negative, or masculine and feminine characteristics as a spiritual being.

47. Moon, *Exposition of the Divine Principle*, p. 383.

48. Moon supports this idea in *Divine Principle*, p. 394. However, though South Korea is now about 29 percent Christian, when Moon was born, Korea was only about 5 percent Christian. Even now, it is not the majority. http://www.pewresearch.org/fact-tank/2014/08/12/6-facts-about-christianity-in-south-korea/.

49. "The great cloud of witnesses" is actually a reference to the believing OT saints mentioned in Hebrews 11.

50. My interaction with this Moonie on the return of Christ reminded me how important it is to take Scripture in a natural, plain way, according to how the original author intended it to be interpreted. Cultists are famous for spiritualizing Scripture and ignoring its original, plain reading. In doing so, they can make the Bible teach anything they want it to teach. But their twisted interpretations are still false.

up, behold, two men stood by them in white apparel, who also said, "Men of Galilee, why do you stand gazing up into heaven? This same Jesus, who was taken up from you into heaven, will so come in like manner as you saw Him go into heaven."[51]

There are corroborating passages that confirm his literal return in the clouds.[52] In claiming to be the Messiah, Moon also claims to be the third Adam. But the Bible says that Jesus, the second Adam, is the last Adam.[53] "And so it is written, 'The first man Adam became a living being.' The last Adam became a life-giving spirit" (1 Corinthians 15:45).

Salvation by Works?

The Unification Church teaches that members are "born again" through a Holy Wine ceremony, and can go to heaven after being blessed in marriage by the Moons. According to Unificationism, man's redemption is works oriented; it is not based on a full reliance on Christ's atoning work for the forgiveness of our sins. Salvation is "95% up to God and 5% up to us."[54] This viewpoint seems similar to what the Mormon scriptures say: "We are saved by grace, after all that we can do."[55] But salvation is not part grace and part works, even if just a little by works. The Unificationist view contradicts Ephesians 2:8–9, which says, "For by grace you have been saved through faith, and that not of yourselves, lest anyone should boast." Salvation is completely by grace. We are responsible to accept that grace (through faith), and cooperate with that grace (we must obey God), but we can't take credit for a portion of our salvation. Though we can reject what God has freely offered, salvation is 100 percent from God. Our works are the fruit of our salvation, not the means to become saved.

Who Is Jesus?

According to the Moonies, Jesus is not divine (any more than you and I are). He was not conceived by the Holy Spirit of the virgin Mary. He is not God incarnate. He did not need to die to redeem us, and he did not rise bodily

---

51. Scripture quotations in this chapter are from the New King James Version of the Bible.
52. For example, Rev. 1:7: "Behold, He is coming with clouds, and every eye will see Him." See also Luke 21:27; Daniel 7:13; Matthew 24:30, 26:24.
53. "Last" is translated from the Greek eschatos, which means "final." Eschatos never has the sense of "the latest" like the English "last" could have.
54. Quote from Michael Candelaresi.
55. II Nephi 25:23.

Comparison Chart on Key Doctrines

Doctrine	Unification Church	Biblical Christianity
Revelation	The Bible is revelation, but it is taken metaphorically when it conflicts with Unification theology. *Divine Principle* is a new revelation. Now that Mr. Moon is dead, Mrs. Moon claims to be getting messages/instructions from her husband in the spirit world while she is in prayer.	Only the Old and New Testaments are written revelation. This Scripture is inerrant, and must be interpreted the way the original authors intended it to be understood.
God	God is dualistic. He has a male and female part. God is Yin-Yang; positive, negative. God, in the act of creation, divided his nature into two, one representing God's masculinity, and the other representing God's femininity. There is no Trinity apart from creation. Jesus, as a separate and finite being formed a spiritual trinity with God and the Holy Spirit, but this is not the orthodox understanding of the eternal Trinity.	God is a Trinity. If there is only one God (Deuteronomy 6:4) and there are three distinct persons (Father, Son, and Holy Spirit) who are identified as this one God (Galatians 1:1; John 1:1, 1:14; Acts 5:3–4; and Mark 1:9–11), then the doctrine of the Trinity must be true — there must be one God who has revealed himself in three Persons, Father, Son, and Holy Spirit. See appendix A.

from the grave. Unificationists deny the essential facts of the gospel.[56] But our salvation rests in the fact that God the Son became flesh to be an adequate mediator between us and God.[57] It is only because Jesus is fully divine and fully human that a sufficient sacrifice could be made to atone for our sin against an infinite God.[58] Jesus not only had to die for our sins, but He also needed to conquer death through His bodily Resurrection.[59] It is only

56. I Corinthians 15:1–4.
57. Hebrews 2:14, 9:13–15.
58. Hebrews 9:14–15; John 1:1, 1:29.
59. Romans 6:9–10; Revelation 1:18.

Sin	Since literal serpents can't talk, this is symbolic. The symbol of the serpent represents Lucifer, a fallen angel. The first sin of Adam and Eve was sexual.	The first sin of Adam and Eve was disobedience to a simple command to not eat of the tree of the knowledge of Good and Evil. This was a literal disobedience of a literal command by literal people in a literal garden.
Christ	No virgin birth, no incarnation; Jesus is not the transcendent God. He is no more divine than we are. Though he died for our sins in some way, he did not rise physically from the dead.	Jesus is the transcendent second person of the Godhead who became a human. As the God-man, Jesus provided a full and sufficient sacrifice for the sins of the world, and then destroyed the power of sin and death through His Resurrection.
Salvation	We contribute to our salvation by our efforts. Members are "born again" through a Holy Wine ceremony, and can go to heaven after being blessed in marriage by the Moons. After the blessing and marriage, and a 40-day waiting period for purification, children will be born sinless — they won't need forgiveness.	Salvation is by grace alone through faith alone in Christ alone. Repentance is a necessary condition for faith to be real, but we cannot work our way toward God. Our works are the fruit of our salvation, not the means to become saved.
Last Things	There is an afterlife. Spirits come back to visit us, but there is no literal hell. Ultimately, everyone will be saved because God will keep giving chances until everyone accepts the truth.	Literal heaven; literal hell. Human spirits either go to heaven or hell when they die. They don't come back to visit us. Spirits that torment humans are actually evil spirits, who are fallen angels. There will be a general (physical) resurrection after which everyone will be judged and sent to their final destination, either an eternal lake of fire or an eternal heaven.

through the death and bodily Resurrection of the God-man that we can be saved.[60] Unificationists deny the essential doctrines regarding both the person and the work of Christ.

In response to my pointing out the importance of Christ's atonement for our sin against a holy God, one Unificationist said to me, "Jesus did not 'pay it all,' and he knew he didn't pay it all. That's why he came back [as Rev. Moon]. We did not really need atonement because ultimately God is a parent who disciplines, not a judge who punishes."[61] This response demonstrates an imbalanced view of the attributes and roles of God. It denies what God's Word says about the character of God.[62]

Why Jesus Came

Unificationists say that Jesus did not come to die, but to get married and set up a physical kingdom on the earth. But in Scripture, Jesus never talked about Himself getting married. He did not say that His purpose was to get a wife and have children. He said that His purpose for coming was to die, to lay down His life as a ransom for sinners.[63] Jesus also predicted His own Resurrection, and the Apostles claimed that this death and Resurrection were the fulfillment of Old Testament prophecy.[64] Peter said that Jesus of Nazareth was handed over to the Jews "by God's set purpose and foreknowledge; and you [the Jews] with the help of wicked men, put Him to death by nailing Him to the Cross."[65]

A False Christ

Rev. Moon is an example of the false christs that Jesus warned about in Matthew 24 and Mark 13:

---

60. John 14:6; 1 Corinthians 15:14–17.
61. Personal interview of Michael Candelesari, Jan 26, 2015.
62. God is a judge: Genesis 18:25; Psalm 82:8; Revelation 19:11. Jesus made a full payment for sin: Hebrews 9:15, 9:28.
63. Mark 10:45.
64. Matthew 16:21: From that time Jesus began to show to His disciples that He must go to Jerusalem, and suffer many things from the elders and chief priests and scribes, and be killed, and be raised the third day. Acts 13:32–34: And we declare to you glad tidings— that promise which was made to the fathers. 33 God has fulfilled this for us their children, in that He has raised up Jesus. As it is also written in the second Psalm: 'You are My Son; Today I have begotten You.' 34 And that He raised Him from the dead, no more to return to corruption, He has spoken thus: 'I will give you the sure mercies of David.'
65. Acts 2:23.

Now as He sat on the Mount of Olives, the disciples came to Him privately, saying, "Tell us, when will these things be? And what will be the sign of Your coming, and of the end of the age?" And Jesus answered and said to them: "Take heed that no one deceives you. For many will come in My name, saying, 'I am the Christ,' and will deceive many. . . . "Then if anyone says to you, 'Look, here is the Christ!' or 'There!' do not believe it. For false christs and false prophets will rise and show great signs and wonders to deceive, if possible, even the elect. See, I have told you beforehand. . . .

"Immediately after the tribulation of those days the sun will be darkened, and the moon will not give its light; the stars will fall from heaven, and the powers of the heavens will be shaken. Then the sign of the Son of Man will appear in heaven, and then all the tribes of the earth will mourn, and they will see the Son of Man coming on the clouds of heaven with power and great glory. And He will send His angels with a great sound of a trumpet, and they will gather together His elect from the four winds, from one end of heaven to the other."[66]

Rev. Moon claimed to be the Christ, but he did not appear in the clouds of heaven with power and great glory. There was no great sound of a trumpet and the gathering of the elect. Rev. Sun Myung Moon's claim to be the Messiah is false. He is not the second coming of Christ. He is not the Savior of mankind. He is a false christ, with many deceived followers. Unificationists, many of whom work hard to make a difference for good in our world, think they are on the right path to eternal life. But as the Bible says, "There is a way that seems right to a man, but its end is the way of death" (Proverbs 16:25). It matters what we believe, and the Unificationists have erroneous beliefs on issues that really matter. Moonies, such as the pastor's wife I interviewed, are putting their faith in someone who cannot save them from eternal death. Rev. Moon died, but did not come back to life. The true Savior of the world died and rose again, showing that He was who He claimed to be, and that He had power over sin and death. It is only through our trust in this Savior that we can be saved. Pray that followers of Rev. Moon turn from a false savior to the true Savior, who alone can eternally satisfy their longing for true love and purity.

---

66. Matthew 24:3–31.

Summary of Unification Church Beliefs

Doctrine	Unification Church Teaching
God	God is dualistic with a positive/male side and a negative/female side (Holy Spirit); Jesus is the sinless offspring of Zechariah and Mary; God is not sovereign; Sun Myung Moon was the new messiah (third Adam)
Authority/Revelation	Exposition of the Divine Principle; Reverend Sun Myung Moon's wife receives guidance through prayer to him
Man	Created as a reflection of God's dual nature to be parents of all mankind; Adam embodied God and Eve embodied the Holy Spirit; man must cooperate with God for salvation; children born in a blessed marriage are sinless while all others are sinful
Sin	Primarily focused on sexual sin and abusing others
Salvation	Largely accomplished by God but 5 percent involves man's adherence to the process of the Divine Principle; participation in the Marriage Blessing ritual is necessary; Jesus provided a spiritual atonement on the Cross; no eternal punishment
Creation	Deny naturalistic biological evolution

Appendix 1

The Triune God[1]

There are numerous passages that teach that God the Father, God the Son, and God the Holy Spirit are distinct persons and yet each hold the attributes of deity.

But the Bible also emphatically and unambiguously declares that there is only one God (Isaiah 44:8, 45:18; Deuteronomy 6:4; Malachi 2:10; James 2:19; Mark 12:29). Hence, taking all the Scriptures into account, orthodox Christian theology has always affirmed that the one true God is triune in nature — three co-equal and co-eternal persons in the Godhead.

This triune God (or Trinity) began to allude to this aspect of His nature right in Genesis 1:26–27. There we read that "God said, 'Let us make man in Our image' . . . God created man in His own image." Here God is a plural noun, *said* is in the third-person singular verb form, and we see both the plural pronoun *our* and the singular *His* referring to the same thing (God's image). This is not horribly confused grammar. Rather, we are being taught, in a limited way, that God is a plurality in unity. We can't say from this verse that He is a trinity, but God progressively reveals more about Himself in later Scriptures to bring us to that conclusion.

In Isaiah 48:12–16 we find the speaker in the passage describing himself as the Creator and yet saying that "the Lord GOD and His Spirit have sent Me." This is further hinting at the doctrine of the trinity, which becomes very clear in the New Testament. There are many other Old Testament Scriptures that hint at the same idea.

1. Used with permission from *Inside the Nye-Ham Debate,* by Ken Ham and Bodie Hodge, (Green Forest, AR: Master Books, 2014).

In Matthew 28:18–20 Jesus commanded His disciples to baptize His followers in the name (singular) of the Father, Son, and Holy Spirit. John's Gospel tells us that "the Word" is God who became man in Jesus Christ (John 1:1–3, 14). Jesus was fully man and fully God. Many other verses combine together to teach that God is triune.

The following chart is an accumulation of many of the passages that show the deity of the Father, the Son, and the Holy Spirit.

	God, the Father	God, the Son	God, the Holy Spirit
is the Creator	Genesis 1:1, 2:4, 14:19–22; Deuteronomy 32:6; Psalm 102:25; Isaiah 42:5, 45:18; Mark 13:19; 1 Corinthians 8:6; Ephesians 3:9; Hebrews 2:10; Revelation 4:11	John 1:1–3; Colossians 1:16–17; 1 Corinthians 8:6; Hebrews 1:2, 8–12	Genesis 1:2; Job 33:4; Psalm 104:30
is unchanging and eternal	Psalm 90:2, 102:25–27; Isaiah 43:10; Malachi 3:6	Micah 5:2; Colossians 1:17; Hebrews 1:8–12, 13:8; John 8:58	Hebrews 9:14
has a distinct will	Luke 22:42	Luke 22:42	Acts 13:2; 1 Corinthians 12:11
accepts worship	Too many to list	Matthew 14:33; Hebrews 1:6	—
accepts prayer	Too many to list	John 14:14; Romans 10:9–13; 2 Corinthians 12:8–9	—
is the only savior	Isaiah 43:11, 45:21; Hosea 13:4; 1 Timothy 1:1	John 4:42; Acts 4:12, 13:23; Philippians 3:20; 2 Timothy 1:10; Titus 1:4, 2:13, 3:6; 2 Peter 1:11, 2:20, 3:18; 1 John 4:14	John 3:5; 1 Corinthians 12:3
has the power to resurrect	1 Thessalonians 1:8–10	John 2:19, 10:17	Romans 8:11

is called God	John 1:18, 6:27; Philippians 1:2, 2:11; Ephesians 4:6; 2 Thessalonians 1:2	John 1:1–5, 1:14, 1:18, 20:28; Colossians 2:9; Hebrews 1:8; Titus 2:13	Acts 5:3–4; 2 Corinthians 3:15–17
is called Mighty God	Isaiah 10:21; Luke 22:69	Isaiah 9:6	—
is omnipresent/ everywhere	1 Kings 8:27; Isaiah 46:10	Matthew 28:18–20	Psalm 139:7–10
is omnipotent/ has power and authority	2 Chronicles 20:6, 25:8; Job 12:13; Romans 1:20; 1 Corinthians 6:14; Jude 1:25	John 3:31, 3:35, 14:6, 16:15; Philippians 2:9–11	1 Samuel 11:6; Luke 1:35
is all-knowing	Psalm 139:2; Isaiah 46:10; 1 John 3:20; Acts 15:8	John 16:3, 21:17	1 Corinthians 2:10–11
has the fullness of God in him (not just "a part of God")	N/A	Colossians 2:9	—
gives life	Genesis 1:21, 1:24, 2:7; Psalm 49:15; John 3:16, 5:21; 1 Timothy 6:13	John 5:21, 14:6, 20:31; Romans 5:21	2 Corinthians 3:6; Romans 8:11
loves	John 3:16; Romans 8:39; Ephesians 6:23; 1 John 4:6, 4:16	Mark 10:21; John 15:9; Ephesians 5:25, 6:23	Romans 15:30
has ownership of believers	Psalm 24:1; John 8:47	Romans 7:4, 8:9	—
is distinct	Matthew 3:16–17, 28:19; John 17:1	Matthew 3:16–17, 4:1, 28:19; John 17:1	1 Samuel 19:20; Matthew 3:16–17, 4:1, 28:19
is judge	Genesis 18:25; Psalm 7:11, 50:6, 94:1–2, 96:13, 98:9; John 8:50; Romans 2:16	John 5:21–27; Acts 17:31; 2 Corinthians 5:10; 2 Timothy 4:1	—
forgives sin	Micah 7:18	Luke 7:47–50	—

claimed divinity	Exodus 20:2	Matthew 26:63–64	—
is uncreated, the First and the Last, the Beginning and the End	Isaiah 44:6	Revelation 1:17–18, 22:13	—
lives in the believer	John 14:23; 2 Corinthians 6:16; 1 John 3:24	John 14:20–23; Galatians 2:20; Colossians 1:27	John 14:16–17; Romans 8:11; 1 Peter 1:11
has the godly title "I Am," pointing to the eternality of God	Exodus 3:14	John 8:58	—
is personal and has fellowship with other persons	1 John 1:3	1 Corinthians 1:9; 1 John 1:3	Acts 13:2; 2 Corinthians 13:14; Ephesians 4:30; Philippians 2:1
makes believers holy (sanctifies them)	1 Thessalonians 5:23	Colossians 1:22	1 Peter 1:2
knows the future	Isaiah 46:10; Jeremiah 29:11	Matthew 24:1–51, 26:64; John 16:32, 18:4	1 Samuel 10:10, 19:20; Luke 1:67; 2 Peter 1:21
is called "Lord of Lords"	Deuteronomy 10:17; Psalm 136:3	Revelation 17:14, 19:16	—

Appendix 2

Is Jesus the Creator God?
A Look at John 1:1–3

Bodie Hodge

Is this even an important question? Absolutely! If Jesus is not God, and therefore the Creator, then He is a created being. If Jesus is created, then how could He have been an adequate sacrifice to atone for sins committed against an infinite God? Jesus must have been God to adequately atone for our sins, which bring upon us unlimited guilt and cause us to deserve an eternal hell. Only the infinite God, Jesus Christ, can take the punishment from an infinite God to make salvation possible.

But does it really matter whether or not we believe that Jesus is God? Yes! If one places faith in a false Christ, one that is not described in Scripture (i.e., a created Jesus, Jesus as a sinner, Jesus as merely one of many gods, etc.), then can this false Christ save them? Not at all. Truly, the identity of Christ is of utmost importance. And yet, in today's culture there are people teaching that Jesus was a created being. They are leading people astray.

What sets biblical Christianity apart from cults and other world religions? It is the person of Jesus Christ — who He is. In Islam, Jesus was a messenger of God, but not the Son of God (i.e., a created being). In many cults, the deity of Jesus Christ is negated or changed,[1] and in many world religions and personal views, Jesus is just another wise teacher. But the Bible says that all things were created by Him and for Him:

> For by Him [Jesus] all things were created that are in heaven and that are on earth, visible and invisible, whether thrones or dominions or principalities or powers. All things were created through Him and for Him (Colossians 1:16).[2]

The biblical Book of Hebrews indicates that God calls Jesus, the Son, God:

> But to the Son He says: "Your throne, O God, is forever and ever; a scepter of righteousness is the scepter of Your Kingdom. You have loved righteousness and hated lawlessness; therefore God, Your God, has anointed You with the oil of gladness more than Your companions" (Hebrews 1:8–9).

We should expect Satan, the adversary of God and the Father of lies, to advance many variants of the person of Jesus Christ. Satan would want all the false views to succeed in some measure to lead people away from the true Jesus.

One may recall the temptations of Jesus by Satan in the wilderness (Mark 4:1–11). The great deceiver even (mis)quoted Scripture in his attempt to trick Jesus into sinning (Mark 4:6). The tactic of the serpent in the garden was to deceive the woman by distorting the plain meaning of the Word of God (Genesis 3:1–6).[3] Satan, through the serpent, quoted the words of God and abused their meaning. We must be aware of the devil's devices (1 Corinthians 2:11). Today, Satan misquotes Scripture through the cultist knocking on the doors in your neighborhood.

John 1:1–3 and the Deity of Christ

Jehovah's Witnesses teach that Jesus Christ is not the Creator God but a lesser created angel (Michael[4]) who was termed "a god" by John in the *New*

---

1. Mormonism, for example, changes the deity of Christ in the Bible to be something different. Jesus is merely one of many people who became gods in an infinite regression of gods in this universe/multiverse system.
2. All Scripture in this chapter is from the New King James Version of the Bible unless otherwise noted.
3. See Bodie Hodge, *The Fall of Satan* (Green Forest, AR: Master Books, 2006).
4. "The Truth about Angels," *The Watchtower*, November 1, 1995, Watch Tower Bible and Tract Society of Pennsylvania, http://www.watchtower.org/library/w/1995/11/1/article_02.htm, retrieved 9-18-2007.

World Translation (the Jehovah's Witnesses translation of the Bible). The NWT says:

> In [the] beginning the Word was, and the Word was with God, and the Word was a god. This one was in [the] beginning with God. All things came into existence through him, and apart from him not even one thing came into existence (John 1:1–3 NWT).

According to the Jehovah's Witnesses' theology (and other unitarian systems of belief), Jesus is something that came into existence. But even their own translation says that apart from Jesus not even one thing came into existence (John 1:3). So then, did Jesus create Himself? Of course that is a ridiculous proposition, but you see how Watchtower (Jehovah's Witness) theology contradicts the Bible, even their New World Translation.

Another contradiction surfaces in such a theology: Jehovah's Witnesses are firm that there is only one God.[5] But they also admit that there is at least one other god, though not as powerful as Jehovah. Jehovah's Witness literature states:

> Jesus is spoken of in the Scriptures as "a god," even as "Mighty God" (John 1:1; Isaiah 9:6). But nowhere is he spoken of as being Almighty, as Jehovah is.[6]

So even though Jehovah's Witnesses say they believe in one God, they really can't be called monotheists. If Jesus is not God Himself, then there is a plurality of gods, assuming Jesus is to be considered "a god" in their view.

Now let's compare the New World Translation of John 1:1–3 to more reputable translations:

> In the beginning was the Word, and the Word was with God, and the Word was God. He was in the beginning with God. All things were made through Him, and without Him nothing was made that was made (NKJV).

> In the beginning was the Word, and the Word was with God, and the Word was God. He was with God in the beginning.

---

5. *Reasoning from the Scriptures* (Brooklyn, NY: Watch Tower Bible and Tract Society of Pennsylvania, 1985), p. 150.
6. Ibid., p. 150.

Through him all things were made; without him nothing was made that has been made (NIV).

In the beginning was the Word, and the Word was with God, and the Word was God. The same was in the beginning with God. All things were made by him; and without him was not any thing made that was made (KJV).

In the beginning was the Word, and the Word was with God, and the Word was God. He was in the beginning with God. All things came into being through Him, and apart from Him nothing came into being that has come into being (NASB).

In the beginning was the Word, and the Word was with God, and the Word was God. He was in the beginning with God. All things were made through him, and without him was not any thing made that was made (ESV).

These translations show that the Word was God, not "a god." Why such blatantly different translations and, accordingly, different theologies? One starts with the Bible, the other starts from a false theology and takes that view to the Bible. The original passage was written in Koine Greek. Following is the Westcott and Hort Greek text (1881) for John 1:1–2:

1. εν αρχη ην ο λογος και ο λογος ην προς τον θεον και θεος ην ο λογος

2. ουτος ην εν αρχη προς τον θεον[7]

Elzevir's Textus Receptus (1624) is identical:

1. εν αρχη ην ο λογος και ο λογος ην προς τον θεον και θεος ην ο λογος

2. ουτος ην εν αρχη προς τον θεον[8]

Even non-Greek scholars can use lexicons and other tools to show without much difficulty that an exact English translation is:

---

7. *Westcott and Hort Greek New Testament (1881): With Morphology* (Bellingham, WA: Logos Research Systems, 2002), S. John 1:1–3.

8. Maurice Robinson, *Elzevir Textus Receptus (1624): With Morphology* (Bellingham, WA: Logos Research Systems, Inc., 2002), S. John 1:1–3.

1. In beginning was the Word and the Word was with God and God was the Word

2. He was in beginning with God

The Latin Vulgate of Jerome in the 5th century correctly translates John 1:1–2 into Latin:

1. *in principio erat Verbum et Verbum erat apud Deum et Deus erat Verbum*

2. *hoc erat in principio apud Deum*[9]

Word-for-word translation:

1. *in* (in) *principio* (beginning) *erat* (was) *Verbum* (Word) *et* (And) *Verbum* (Word) *erat* (was) *apud* (with) *Deum* (God) *et* (and) *Deus* (God) *erat* (was) *Verbum* (Word)

2. *hoc* (He) *erat* (was) *in* (in) *principio* (Beginning) *apud* (with) *Deum* (God)

If God was the Word, as John 1:1 is literally translated, then it is no problem for the uncreated Word to have created all things. As God, He created. How could the Word be with God and God be the Word at the same time? The doctrine of the Trinity (One God; three persons) is the solution here.[10] The Word was with God (the Father) and God (the Son) was the Word. This understanding, consistent with the rest of Scripture, eliminates any contradiction of multiple gods. There is only one God, revealed in a plurality of persons. The Jehovah's Witnesses do not have a solution to that alleged contradiction.

The primary reason Jehovah's Witnesses do not want John 1:1 translated accurately is due to influences *outside* the Bible. As the theological descendents of their founder Charles Russell, who began Jehovah's Witnesses in the late 1800s, they arrive at the Bible with the preconceived notion that Jesus the Christ is not God. Therefore, when a passage that clearly contradicts their theology comes up, there are two options: change their belief to coincide with what the Bible teaches or change God's Word to fit with their current theology. Sadly, they have opted to exalt their theology above

---

9. Jerome, *Latin Vulgata*, adapted from Online Bible, 2007.
10. See appendix 1, "The Triune God."

Jehovah's Word. So who is really the Jehovah's Witnesses' final authority? It is no longer a perfect God and His Word, but fallible, sinful men and their errant ideas about God.

Kingdom Interlinear and John 1:1

It is very interesting to see how the Jehovah's Witnesses Greek-English Interlinear translation compares with the NWT and with more accurate translations. One Jehovah's Witness said that their translation comes from an interlinear translation of the Westcott and Hort text and that the NWT is a good translation of it. But let's check into the two primary interlinear translations appealed to by Jehovah's Witnesses, the *Kingdom Interlinear* and the *Emphatic Diaglott*.

The Kingdom Interlinear[11] says:

KATA   IΩANHN
ACCORDING TO JOHN

Look carefully at John 1:1. The Interlinear doesn't translate *Theos* (θεος) as "a god," which is an unjustifiable change in the NWT (to the right of the interlinear above). Strangely, the interlinear does not capitalize "God" the second time it occurs, though it does the first.

One possible reason they tried distinguishing this particular word for God is due to the spellings of *Theos* (God) in this passage (θεον, θεος) is due to variant endings. Another variant ending is commonly "θεου." All three variants for God are in one passage and each translated as God:

---

11. *The Kingdom Interlinear Translation of the Greek Scriptures* (Bellingham, WA: Watch Tower Bible and Tract Society of Pennsylvania and International Bible Students Association, 1985), p. 401.

. . . who opposes and exalts himself above all that is called God (θεον) or that is worshiped, so that he sits as God (θεου) in the temple of God (θεον) , showing himself that he is God (θεος) (2 Thessalonians 2:4).

There is really no obvious reason for the change to "a god" or a lower case "god" by the NWT or *Kingdom Interlinear.*

Emphatic Diaglott and John 1:1–3

The next interlinear to be checked was the Diaglott. It translates John 1:1–3[12] as:

The interlinear this time incorrectly states that *theos* is "a god," but the side translation disagrees and says the *Logos* was God, instead of "a god." So again, there are mismatches that make no sense.

The Context of the Passage

Interestingly, in defending their translation of John 1:1, the Jehovah's Witnesses say:

> Which translation of John 1:1, 2 agrees with the context? John 1:18 says: "No one has ever seen God." Verse 14 clearly says that "the Word became flesh and dwelt among us . . . we have beheld his glory." Also, verses 1, 2 say that in the beginning he

---

12. Benjamin Wilson, translator, *Emphatic Diaglott* (Brooklyn, NY: International Bible Students Association, Watchtower Bible and Tract Society, 1942).

was "with God." Can one be *with* someone and at the same time *be* that person?[13]

Trying to appeal to context, the Jehovah's Witnesses quote part of John 1:18 and John 1:14 while ignoring the teaching of verse 3 which shows Jesus made all things — no exceptions! John 1:3 makes it clear that everything was created by Christ (the Word). This puts Jehovah's Witnesses on the horns of dilemma. If Christ created all things, then Christ created Himself in their theology. But they say God created Christ, but this means that Christ didn't create all things that had been created and so their translation fails. Either way, they have a big theological problem. We have already shown how Jesus can be *with* God and *be* God — it is through the concept of the Trinity, which makes this passage perfectly readable as is.

Regardless, the context of the chapter should not be neglected. John 1:18 is referring to God the Father as the one no one has seen. We can interpret John 1:18 this way: *No one has seen God the Father at any time; the only-begotten God, Jesus — He has revealed the Father. Anytime anyone has ever seen God, he has seen the Logos, the Son, since the Son is the Word — the revealer.*

Expositor Dr John Gill explains the reference to God:

That is, God the Father, whose voice was never heard, nor his shape seen by angels or men; for though Jacob, Moses, the elders of Israel, Manoah, and his wife, are said to see God, and Job expected to see him with his bodily eyes, and the saints will see him as he is, in which will lie their great happiness; yet all seems to be understood of the second person, who frequently appeared to the Old Testament saints, in an human form, and will be seen by the saints in heaven, in his real human nature; or of God in and by him: for the essence of God is invisible, and not to be seen with the eyes of the body; nor indeed with the eyes of the understanding, so as to comprehend it; nor immediately, but through, and by certain means: God is seen in the works of creation and providence, in the promises, and in his ordinances; but above all, in Christ the brightness of his glory, and the express image of his person: this may chiefly intend here,

---

13. *Reasoning from the Scriptures*, p. 416.

man's not knowing any thing of God in a spiritual and saving way, but in and by Christ.[14]

So we understand that Jesus reveals God and exists as God at the same time. There is not a contradiction between John 1:1 and John 1:18. In fact, they are amazingly consistent!

Islamic Appeal to the NWT

Muslims also deny the deity of Christ, so John 1:1–3 is also a problem to Islam if taken as written. Muslim apologists have appealed to the NWT in an effort to reduce the deity of Jesus Christ:

> "The Word" is only described as being "ton theos"(divine/a god) and not as being "ho theos" (*The* Divine/ *The* God). A more faithful and correct translation of this verse would thus read: *"In the beginning was the Word, and the Word was with God, and the Word was divine."* (If you read the New World Translation of the Bible you will find exactly this wording.)[15]

Christian apologists have responded:

> It should first be noted that all of known manuscripts and fragments of John's gospel contains this passage without any variation. It should also be noted that John 1:1 was quoted on several occasions by early Christian theologians and Church Fathers. . . . Clearly, there is no "ton theos," in this text as Al-Kadhi and Deedat claim. Both sentences have the phrase "ton theon." "Ton theon" is used because it is the accusative case (the nominative case is "ho theos" = "the God") In this [instance] we must use the accusative case, since the text uses the preposition "pros" which means "with" in this context.
>
> Al-Kadhi and Deedat should know that the article "ho" (nominative case) and "ton" (accusative case) both translate as "the.. Incidentally, the Greek word for "divine" is "theios, theia, theion," depending on the gender.[16]

---

14. Dr John Gill, Commentary notes on John 1:18, adapted from Online Bible, 2007.

15. Answering Christianity, Al-Kadhi, http://www.answering-christianity.com/john1_1.htm, retrieved 9-20-2007.

16. Answering Islam, http://www.answering-islam.org/Responses/Al-Kadhi/r01.2.2.06.html, retrieved 9-20-2007.

But this lets us know how influential the Jehovah's Witnesses and the NWT are. The NWT is being used in Islam to take people *away* from Jesus Christ. What is the typical Muslim response to the Bible? They claim that that the Bible was changed *after* Muhammad. Why after you might ask?

The reason is simple. Muhammad repeatedly stated the Bible to be true in the Koran (Qur'an). So the Bible, as Muslims agree, was indeed true in Muhammad's day. Muslims are even called to believe in in the Bible (the Books sent down aforetime).

> Surah 4:136: O ye who believe! Believe in God and His Apostle, and the Book which He hath sent down to His Apostle, and the Books which He hath sent down aforetime. Whoever believeth not on God and His Angels and His Books and His apostles, and in the Last Day, he verily hath erred with far-gone error.

The Qur'an declares the Bible to be a true revelation of God and demands faith in the Bible (e.g., Sura 2:40–42, 126, 136, 285; 3:3, 71, 93; 4:47, 136; 5:47–51, 69, 71–72; 6:91; 10:37, 94; 21:7; 29:45, 46; 35:31; 46:11). Furthermore, the Qur'an makes no distinction between God's revelations (Sura 2:136). Because Muhammad believed the Bible to be true, this puts Muslim scholars on the horns of a dilemma too, since the Koran (Qur'an) does not mesh with the previous 66 books of the Bible.

So their response is that the Bible must have been changed after Muhammad. Of course, there are two problems with this. First, the Koran (Qur'an) claims that *no one* can change the Word of God (e.g., Sura 6:34; 10:34). Second, there is no textual support for this at all. In other words, Bibles we have prior to Muhammad (around A.D. 600) and Bibles after Muhammad are virtually identical, both clearly teaching the deity of Jesus Christ.

Jehovah's Witnesses' Defense of the Word Being "a god"

Leading Jehovah's Witness apologist Rolf Furuli write extensively about John 1:1 and how *theos* should be translated in reference to the Word. He argues for the NWT's rendering of the Word being "a god" as opposed to "God." Several of his claims will be discussed here.

Mr. Furuli has a chart comparing the NWT with a couple of lesser-known translations, as well as the Greek text with *his* understanding of the word meanings. It is shown below:[17]

John 1:1 in Three Different Translations

NWT	"In [the] beginning the Word was, and the Word was with God, and the Word was a god."
NRSV	"In the beginning was the Word, and the Word was with God, and the Word was God."
Goodspeed	"In the beginning the Word existed. The Word was with God and the Word was divine."
Greek text	*ēn arkhē* ("in the beginning") *ēn* ("was") *ho logos* ("the word"), *kai* ("and") *ho logos* ("the word") *ēn* ("was") *pros* ("with") *ton theon* ("the god"), *kai* ("and") *theos* ("god" or "a god") *ēn* ("was") *ho logos* ("the word")

Let's evaluate Mr. Furuli's comments concerning the term *theos* (notice above how he defines *theos* as meaning either "god" or "a god"). He says:

> . . . in the Bible the word *theos* is also used for persons other than the creator, and therefore neither "creator" nor "YHWH" could be a part of its semantic meaning. . . . The word *theos* is a count noun, and John uses it in one of two ways: either in a generic sense or as a "singular noun." We might illustrate this point by use of the OT. Here we find that *elohim*, the Hebrew equivalent to *theos*, is used in the generic sense.[18]

Mr. Furuli takes about two pages to compare *theos* to the contextual uses of the Hebrew word *elohim*. But it would have been better to compare the uses of *theos* throughout the Greek New Testament and see how it was used in Greek context.[19]

---

17. Rolf Furuli, *The Role of Theology and Bias in Bible Translation With a Special Look at the New World Translation of Jehovah's Witnesses* (Huntington Beach, CA: Elihu Books, 1999), p. 200.

18. Ibid., p. 204–205.

19. Ibid., p. 211–213, again equating Theos with Elohim to argue against its Greek usage.

Perhaps the reason such was not done is that it would destroy the point Mr. Furuli was trying to make. A search of *theos* in the New Testament shows that *theos* is overwhelming translated as "God" (even when not preceded by an article) unless context warrants otherwise (only about six times). The NT context for John 1:1 overwhelming supports the idea that the Word is God the Creator, as John 1:3 indicates.

Mr. Furuli goes on to say:

> There are 322 examples of *theos* without the article. Because there is no inherent semantic contrast between the articular and the anarthrous *theos*, the question about the meaning of *theos* in some passages is pragmatic, and thus the context becomes essential.[20]

Mr. Furuli argues that John 1:1b can be translated: "And a god was the Word" since there is no article in front of *theos*, and thus the context must determine the meaning of *theos*. In response, we can first appreciate the concession that Furuli is making: the lack of the article in front of *theos* does not mean that the word *theos* is to be translated as an adjective (divine) or with an indefinite article (a god) rather than simply "God." (Even if it should be translated as an adjective, the verse would still teach the same thing — the Word is of the same essence as the Father.) It is obvious that there are many times that *theos* is translated as "God," referring to Jehovah, even when not preceded by an article. Furuli evidently concedes that.

So now it is a matter of context, says Furuli. We agree that context is crucial. But if context is so important, then why not look carefully at John 1:2–18? Furuli mentions only John 1:14, "with God" from John 1:2, and John 1:18. Why did he not refer to the other verses, including verse 3, which makes it clear that the Word made *all* things that have been made?

Furuli then attacked the eternality of the Word, Jesus Christ. In an attempt to downgrade that "in the beginning was the Word," Mr. Furuli tries to show that Jesus was not eternal, thus not God.

> Regarding the expression "in the beginning was the Word," all we can say with reasonable certainty is that at the particular

---

20. Ibid., p. 206.

point in time called "the beginning" the Word existed. This is a far cry from saying "the Word is eternal."[21]

But again, look at the context. If the Word made everything that was made (verse 3), then he must be eternal. If everything that was made (that is, had a beginning) had their beginning through Christ, then it must be the case that the Word never had a beginning; thus He is eternal. Christ, the Word, created time too, indicating His preeminent and eternal nature.

Ignatius (John's Disciple) and the Deity of Christ

Let's go one further step in this study. John, the author of the Gospel, did not simply write the account and disappear. On the contrary, he was the only disciple of Christ to live out his life and die of old age, even though he too endured tribulation for the Word of God (Revelation 1:9). He, like Christ, had disciples of his own, and the two most popular were Polycarp and Ignatius. It makes sense that John would teach his disciples the truth about Jesus Christ and who He was.

Polycarp wrote very little that has survived. Ignatius had quite a bit more. In Ignatius' letter to the Ephesians, it was clear that he viewed Jesus and the Father as the one true God. He said:

> . . . and elected through the true passion by the will of the Father, and Jesus Christ, our God. . . .[22]

> God existing in the flesh[23]

> Our Lord and God, Jesus Christ, the Son of the living God. . . .[24]

> For our God, Jesus Christ, was, according to the appointment of God. . . .[25]

---

21. Ignatius, Epistle of Ignatius to the Ephesians, in *The Writings of the Fathers Down to A.D. 325 Ante-Nicene Fathers*, Eds. A. Roberts and J. Donaldson (Peabody, MA: Hendrickson Publishers), 1:49 (Long version).

22. A. Roberts and J. Donaldson, eds., "Ignatius, Epistle of Ignatius to the Ephesians," in *Ante-Nicene Fathers: The Writings of the Fathers Down to a.d. 325* (Peabody, MA: Hendrickson Publishers), Volume 1, p. 49 (short version).

23. Ibid., p. 52 (short version).

24. Ibid., p. 56 (long version).

25. Ibid., p. 57 (short version).

> . . . God Himself being manifested in human form for the renewal of eternal life.[26]

> . . . God being manifested as man. . . .[27]

> We have also as a Physician the Lord our God, Jesus the Christ, the only-begotten Son and Word, before time began.[28]

After reading the words of a disciple of John who learned extensively from John, there should be no question what John was trying to say. So it is interesting that the founder of Jehovah's Witnesses, Charles Taze Russell, said with regard to John 1:1 and the Word being God:

> . . . except that where the word Theos is used twice in the same clause the Greek *Prepositive Article* is sometimes used, so as to give the effect of *the God* in contrast with *a God*. An illustration of this is found in John 1:1 — "the Word was with *the* God [*ho Theos*] and the Word was *a* God [*Theos*]." But the careful student (freed from Prejudice) will generally have no difficulty in determining the thought of the Apostle. Indeed, the language is so explicit that the wonder is that we were heedless of it so long."[29]

His interpretation of *Theos* as "*a god/a theos*," he claims is so explicit that he wonders why it took so long for people to realize it. Pastor Russell wrote this in 1899 and yet John's own disciple Ignatius allegedly missed it? This makes little sense logically. The reason the early Church knew John was speaking of Jesus being God is not just from the Scriptures that confirm it, but they were taught this by John, who was their pastor for many years.

So really, what Mr. Russell was saying is that John's disciples, the early Church and the Church for about 1,800 years were wrong and that he [Pastor Russell] was right. This should be a red flag to anyone. Adam Clarke sums up the argument regarding John 1:1 with excellent comments:

> Should it be objected that Christ created *officially* or by *delegation*, I answer: This is impossible; for, as creation requires

---

26. Ibid., p. 57 (short version).
27. Ibid., p. 57 (long version).
28. Ibid., p. 52 (long version).
29. Charles Taze Russell, *Studies in the Scriptures*, Vol. 5, *The Atonement Between God and Man* (1899), reprinted in Bible Students Congregation of New Brunswick (Edison, NJ, 2000), p. 70.

absolute and unlimited power, or omnipotence, there can be but *one* Creator; because it is impossible that there can be *two* or *more* Omnipotents, Infinites, or Eternals. It is therefore evident that creation cannot be effected *officially*, or by *delegation*, for this would imply a *Being conferring the office*, and *delegating* such *power*; and that the Being *to* whom it was delegated was a *dependent Being*; consequently not *unoriginated* and *eternal*; but this the nature of creation proves to be absurd. 1. The thing being impossible in itself, because no limited being could produce a work that necessarily requires omnipotence. 2. It is impossible, because, if omnipotence be *delegated*, he to whom it is delegated *had it not before*, and he who delegates it *ceases to have it*, and consequently *ceases to be* GOD; and the other to whom it was delegated *becomes God*, because such attributes as those with which he is supposed to be invested are *essential* to the nature of God. On this supposition *God ceases to exist*, though infinite and eternal, and another not naturally *infinite* and *eternal* becomes such; and thus an *infinite* and *eternal Being* ceases to exist, and another infinite and eternal Being is produced in *time*, and has a *beginning*, which is absurd. Therefore, as *Christ* is the *Creator*, he did not create by *delegation*, or in any *official way*.

Again, if he had created by *delegation* or *officially*, it would have been *for* that *Being who gave him that office*, and delegated to him the requisite power; but the text says that *all things were made* BY *him and* FOR *him*, which is a demonstration that the Apostle understood Jesus Christ to be truly and essentially God.[30]

Conclusion

The reality is that John 1:1–3 clearly reveals the deity of Jesus Christ, the Word, being the Creator God (see also Colossians 1 and Hebrews 1). As such it confirms many other passages in Scripture that teach that Christ is God. Early Church fathers such as Ignatius, who was a disciple of John the Apostle, also recognized Jesus as God.

The significance of this is a matter of salvation. Without the true Jesus, can one really be saved? Only the infinite Son of God can satisfy the wrath of

---

30. Adam Clarke Commentary notes on Colossians 1:16, adapted from Online Bible, 2007.

an infinite God the Father upon sin to pay the debt in full. Any created Jesus could never have been able to endure the punishment that we all deserve for sin. Yes, having the right Christ is *crucial* to salvation being made possible.

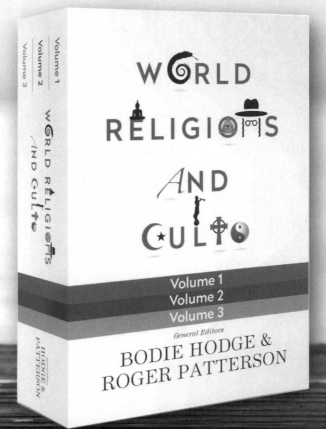

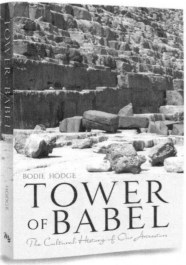